Won't Get
FOOLED
AGAIN

Won't Get
FOOLED
AGAIN

The Who From
Lifehouse To
Quadrophenia

RICHIE UNTERBERGER

Won't Get Fooled Again
The Who From *Lifehouse* To *Quadrophenia*
RICHIE UNTERBERGER

A GENUINE JAWBONE BOOK
First Edition 2011
Published in the UK and the USA by Jawbone Press
2a Union Court,
20–22 Union Road,
London SW4 6JP,
England

www.jawbonepress.com

ISBN 978-1-906002-35-0

DESIGN Paul Cooper Design
EDITOR John Morrish

Printed by Regent Publishing Services Limited, China

1 2 3 4 5   15 14 13 12 11

Contents

Introduction 17

CHAPTER 1 **There Once Was a Note** 21

CHAPTER 2 **The New Revolution** 56

CHAPTER 3 **Teenage Wasteland** 87

CHAPTER 4 **Getting In Tune** 112

CHAPTER 5 **Going Mobile** 143

CHAPTER 6 **Can You See The Real Me?** 167

CHAPTER 7 **The Punk Meets The Godfather** 199

CHAPTER 8 **Drowned** 238

CHAPTER 9 **The Song Is Over** 274

Endnotes 291

Bibliography 297

Index 299

Picture Credits 301

Acknowledgements 302

MAIN PICTURE: **From left to right: Keith Moon, Pete Townshend, and producer Kit Lambert on January 19 1970 at IBC Studios in London during the recording of 'The Seeker.'** RIGHT: **Townshend at work in his home studio in January 1970.** FAR RIGHT: **Townshend became so celebrated for his use of the ARP synthesizer that his picture was used on an ARP owner's manual.**

FOR INSTANT SOUNDS TURN TO PAGE 42

&ARP.
Odyssey Owner's Manual

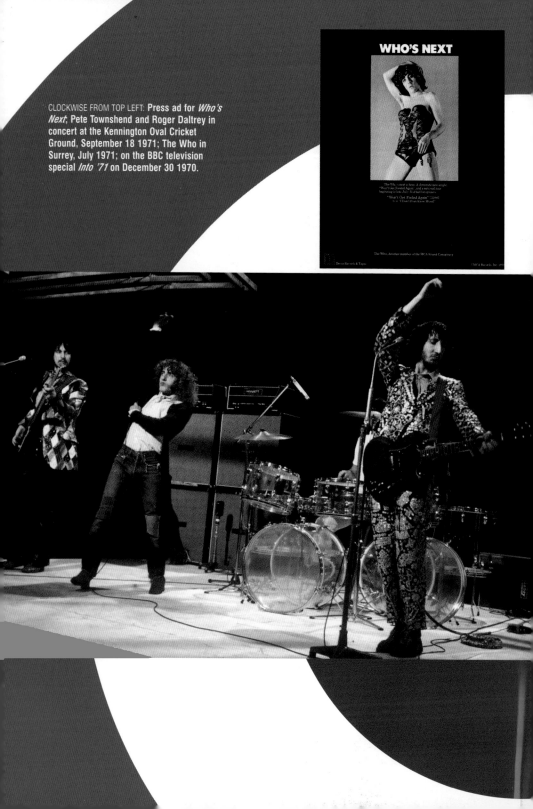

CLOCKWISE FROM TOP LEFT: **Press ad for** *Who's Next*; Pete Townshend and Roger Daltrey in concert at the Kennington Oval Cricket Ground, September 18 1971; The Who in Surrey, July 1971; on the BBC television special *Into '71* on December 30 1970.

WHO'S NEXT

CLOCKWISE FROM TOP RIGHT: **Townshend at his Goring-on-Thames home in April 1973 with Rod Houison, who helped record special effects for** *Quadrophenia*; **a 1971 press ad for various Who and Who-related releases; Townshend backing Eric Clapton at London's Rainbow Theatre, January 13 1973; Townshend and Moon on stage, 1972.**

A MONTH FULL OF WHO

WHO'S NEW

THE WHO
MEATY, BEATY, BIG & BOUNCY

Smash your head against the wall.

John Entwistle.

WHO'S GOLD

WHO'S NEXT

THE WHO
LIVE AT LEEDS

TOMMY
THE WHO

MAIN PICTURE: **The Who touring** *Quadrophenia*, 1973.
ABOVE LEFT: **Press ad for** *Quadrophenia*.

CLOCKWISE FROM LEFT: **Keith Moon, Pete Townshend, Roger Daltrey, and John Entwistle** in the early 70s: four very different personalities that Townshend tried to blend into one character for *Quadrophenia*.

Pete Townshend and his father Cliff taking portable equipment on a field recording expedition on the banks of the River Thames, January 1973.

Introduction

"It just felt like the one that got away. It felt to me like it was such a fantastic idea that just escaped me somehow." Pete Townshend on the failed *Lifehouse* project.[1]

"It's a magnificent piece of work, absolutely magnificent. It's our towering triumph." Pete Townshend on *Quadrophenia*.[2]

In many respects, the two rock operas Pete Townshend wrote for The Who in the early 70s could hardly have been more different. The first, *Lifehouse*, attempted to weave together ideas that still seem futuristic in the 21st century. The second, *Quadrophenia*, was thoroughly down-to-earth, based as it was on The Who's own coming-of-age experiences in mid-60s British mod culture. *Lifehouse*'s concept and storyline were incomprehensible to virtually everyone except its creator; *Quadrophenia*'s tale of a teenage mod was a relatively straightforward narrative.

Most crucially of all, *Lifehouse* was never completed. Despite fitful attempts to revive it in the following decades, in the view of most observers it is still unfinished. *Quadrophenia* was conceived, recorded, and released with relative speed and efficiency. Ironically, though Pete Townshend considered a film vital to the *Lifehouse* project, it was *Quadrophenia* that gave rise to an enduring cinema classic.

The Who, of course, thrived on contradictions in the decade after 1964, when Keith Moon's recruitment turned them from an exciting R&B club band into an unstoppable powerhouse. They were the band with the bloodiest internal fights, sometimes literally, yet the one top British Invasion group to retain the same line-up for nearly 15 years. They were the loudest, most exhibitionist rockers on the planet, but also the band most dedicated to exploring the quirkiest, murkiest, and most philosophical and cerebral corners of the human psyche. For all their mastery of the power pop single, they were the most dedicated practitioners of the rock opera, and the musicians most determined to make rock into a more highbrow art form.

The Who were also the band with the loftiest aspirations for merging the lives of themselves and their audiences into one; Townshend in particular aimed for some sort of transcendent elevation of himself and his followers into a purer plane of existence, with rock music as the vehicle. Such grand ambitions are bound to fail, at least some of the time. Indeed, much of what endears The Who to their audience are those very human failings: the public blow-ups, the celebrated equipment screw-ups, the endless fountain of ideas too impractical to translate into reality. They remind us that, for all their talent and charisma, The Who are flawed beings not so different from their listeners.

Never were both their genius and their flaws so evident as in *Lifehouse*. There have been numerous legendary opuses left unfinished by major artists, including The Beach Boys' *Smile*, The Doors' 'Celebration Of The Lizard' suite, The Beatles' *Get Back*, and whatever Jimi Hendrix's fourth studio album might have been called. But none was as tangled and complex as *Lifehouse*, although *Smile* and *Get Back* might give it a run for its money.

In part that's because no project previously launched by a rock band was as elaborate as *Lifehouse*, a multimedia endeavor before its time. Not only was it a concept album or opera, it was also a film, albeit one that wasn't even properly started, let alone completed. And not only would it be a record and a movie, it would also take shape in real-life concerts, some of which did take place without achieving anything like the results for which Pete Townshend hoped. In hindsight, its failure seems almost inevitable, and to many fans (and even some fellow Who members) a blessing in disguise, because it supplied the material for *Who's Next*, their most popular album besides *Tommy*. In retrospect, *Quadrophenia* could be seen as a scaled-down exercise in relative sanity, even though it was a double album with the kind of extravagant gatefold sleeve and picture booklet never seen these days.

In some ways, however, *Lifehouse* and *Quadrophenia* aren't as different as they may seem. Both were group-executed extensions of Townshend's unmatched abilities as a rock'n'roll auteur, giving vent to his most personal and spiritual fascinations with a power his home demos couldn't hope to achieve. Both used cutting-edge technology, particularly synthesizers. While *Quadrophenia* wasn't nearly as ill-fated as *Lifehouse*, it too would be plagued by reality-checks that kept it from being presented as the group intended, although these were for the most part confined to the stage rather than the studio. And *Lifehouse* and *Quadrophenia* would forever be linked as attempts by The Who to follow up their first rock opera, the 1969 blockbuster *Tommy*, with a concept album of equal resonance. That was an order so tall that some commentators would find it doomed to failure – commercially and culturally, at least – no matter how brilliant the music.

For all the fame of *Who's Next* and *Quadrophenia*, and despite all the interviews The Who (and Townshend in particular) have done in the past four decades, some aspects of the band's peculiar early 70s journey remain murky. In part that's because Townshend's interviews, while a goldmine of information, are in some senses false trails. For Townshend has flip-flopped his opinions on innumerable occasions, not least in his estimation of songs that most regard as masterpieces. Sometimes it seems, for instance, that his regard for 'Won't Get Fooled Again' depends on what day he is asked and what mood he is in, such is his vacillation between pride and embarrassment.

Whatever the creators think of these projects nearly four decades later – and however rocky their road to realization – the quality of most of the music The Who made during this period is undisputed. *Won't Get Fooled Again: The Who From Lifehouse To Quadrophenia* is the story of that era, which saw the band log some of rock's most spectacular failures as well as creating some of its most enduring music.

Richie Unterberger
San Francisco
July 2010

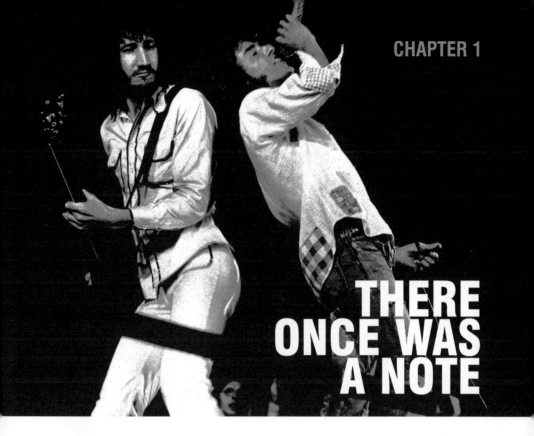

CHAPTER 1

THERE ONCE WAS A NOTE

O n September 19 1970, one of the biggest rock stars on the planet announced an idea so ambitious that it could not be contained by a mere album. He aimed to use music to question and redefine the very foundations of our existence. Pete Townshend made his revelation not to a few lackeys in the midst of an LSD trip but to the world, in the second of his monthly columns in the British music paper *Melody Maker*.

"It's not often that I get this chance, the chance to use an audience, or in this case a readership, to get feedback around an idea," he wrote in 'The Pete Townshend Page.' "I'm not expecting to get letters or reactions or question-timer buzzes or anything like that; I do the talking and I also do the feeding back on your behalf. Kind of assumptive but really the way most things are done today." This was all something of a left turn after Pete had spent the first half of the column discussing The Who's recent Isle of Wight show, but he clearly had something important on his mind.

"Here's the idea," he continued. "There's a note, a musical note, that builds the basis of existence somehow. Mystics would agree, saying that of course it is OM, but I am talking about a MUSICAL note. There is air that we breathe, we swim in it all our lives, we love it with our physical being and we watch it sustain the world around us. We seem adaptable and receptive to almost everything it produces; but most of all, and this has little to do with the essence of survival, most of us enjoy music. I've never been able to quite get to grips with how it all comes about, but artists and writers outside of music have noticed it too."[1]

The "idea" would blossom into 'Pure And Easy,' the song that would be the most cogent statement of the core philosophy of his next rock opera, *Lifehouse*. But the "idea" was so subtle, indeed vague, that few would have suspected it would occupy most of Townshend's time for the next nine months or so, driving him to the edge of a nervous breakdown. By the end of that time, *Lifehouse* would be abandoned, its most commercial songs hacked off for the non-concept album *Who's Next*. And that LP wouldn't even include 'Pure And Easy,' the song that more than any other had put The Who on the road to *Lifehouse* in the first place.

When Pete Townshend expanded on his plans for *Lifehouse*, at London's Young Vic Theatre on January 13 of the following year, the notion of a project mixing live performance, film, and music "designed to reflect people's personalities" and intended to "induce mental and spiritual harmony through the medium of rock music" seemed novel, to say the least. Even if his group had created the first commercially and artistically successful rock opera with 1969's *Tommy*, some feared the guitarist-singer-songwriter had gone off the deep end. But like many of The Who's innovations, it was rooted in a deep-seated desire to stretch pop music's format, which dated back almost to the beginning of the band's recording career.

Who co-manager Kit Lambert, who had taken over the band with Chris Stamp in 1964, would eventually come in for his share of the blame (not least from Townshend) for hindering both *Lifehouse* and *Quadrophenia*. Yet there's no question that he was more responsible than anyone else for getting Townshend to think beyond the conventions of pop-rock songwriting. The son of respected classical composer and conductor Constant Lambert, he was exposing Townshend to classical music as early as 1965. Pete even went so far later as to credit the suspended chords of early Who songs like 'The Kids Are Alright' to the influence of baroque music Lambert had played him, particularly an album of works by 17th century composer Henry Purcell.

"He's a frustrated composer, Townshend," says Richard Barnes, author of the 1982 biography *The Who: Maximum R&B* and co-author with Townshend of 1977's *The Story Of Tommy*. The two have been friends since sharing a flat as Ealing Art College students in the early 60s. "He does the rock star thing semi-reluctantly. It makes him extremely rich. I think he'd much rather be Philip Glass or someone like that."[2]

Just as crucially, Lambert bought Townshend recording equipment so he could compose and make demos at home, well before that became standard for rock musicians. Townshend took to the process almost instantly, and by the time of *Lifehouse* had been honing his songs into shape in home studios for a good half-dozen years, producing demos that were almost as impressive as The Who's versions. Asked by *Rolling Stone* how much the songs changed from their demo incarnations when The Who got to work on them, Keith Moon admitted, "Not a hell of a lot. ... The drum phrases are my phrases, even though it's Pete playing drums. He's playing the way I play. He's playing my flourishes. The same thing for the bass part."[3]

Lambert's greatest influence on his protégé, however, was encouraging him to write songs based around themes that could be expanded into operas. *Tommy* was the first such endeavor to capture international acclaim, but Townshend and The Who had been toying with the concept since at least mid-1966. 'I'm A Boy,' beloved at the time as a quirky British hit single, actually had its genesis as an opera entitled *Quads*, which would have taken place in a future in which parents could determine the sex of their children.

"It was about four kids – a very similar thing to *Tommy*; at least, it would have developed into a similar thing – three of which were girls, and their mother had this obsession to make the little boy a girl," recalled Townshend five years later. "It goes on into later life where the three girls become a singing group, and I had amazing visions of tracks where Keith, John [Entwistle], and I would pretend to be The Beverley Sisters. There was a lot of comedy in it, as there was in the mini-opera, but I think at the same time it was a heavily serious thing as well because it had these flashbacks to childhood, which I was very into at the time."[4]

Quads didn't get far, and could be considered not just The Who's first opera, but their first failed attempt at one. Yet it was an early inkling of Townshend's operatic ambitions and his interest in the futuristic themes that would also inform *Lifehouse*. Later in 1966, several tenuously related Townshend tunes were strung together to form the nine-minute mini-opera 'A Quick One, While He's Away.' More frivolous than any of the other opera-like Who creations, it nonetheless gave both band and composer experience in writing and recording songs linked together by a storyline. If the story is slight and fragmented, so what? Much the same could be said of many classical operas.

More serious in intent was 'Rael,' the glorious five-minute suite that ended the group's third album, *The Who Sell Out*. This may have been the work Townshend referred to when he told *Melody Maker* on April 29 1967 that he was "working on an opera." As beautiful as 'Rael' was, however, few if any listeners at the time suspected its operatic origins, given how disconnected and opaque the lyrics are. "The story was running into about 20 scenes when Kit Lambert reminded me that while I was pretending to be Wagner, The Who needed a new single," Townshend later recalled in *The Story Of Tommy*. "What did I have? I had 'Rael.' Thus 'Rael' was edited down to four minutes." Despite its new brevity, it didn't end up on a single. As Pete also admitted in the same interview, "No one will ever know what it means; it has been squeezed up too tightly to make sense."[5]

In retrospect, 'Rael' contains some of the elements that would later drive the plot, such as it was, of *Lifehouse*. Although it is not clear from first listening (or, for many, from repeated listenings), 'Rael' tells the story of a dystopian future in which overpopulation has run rampant, spurring the narrator's retreat to a fictional homeland. To be exact, it would take place in 1999 and, even more obscurely, announce the emergence of the Red Chinese (the song's "Redchins") as a dominant world power. "The only spiritual note was that the Redchins were regarded as being fairly evil because they were crushing the old established religions as they conquered," said Townshend.[6] Initially written for a full orchestra, 'Rael' was intended to have as its hero the operatically-voiced psychedelic rocker Arthur Brown, the "god of hellfire" who was also managed by Kit Lambert and Chris Stamp. Whether he would have sung on a Who album or on a release of his own is unclear.

The parallels with *Lifehouse* – which would also feature an ominous, almost science fiction setting, with a hero trying to buck the tide of apocalypse – are clear, even if the specifics are quite different. In fact, Townshend felt the track "even resembled the later *Quadrophenia* in some ways. ... In fact both 'Rael' and *Tommy* and the later aborted *Lifehouse* contained various similarities of theme and purpose. They all started as vehicles for the group, so the individual characters in the group all influenced the characters I'd invented very deeply."[7]

It's ironic that Lambert had been instrumental in pulling the plug on the gestation of 'Rael', as Townshend has credited him as perhaps the most crucial force outside the band in guiding *Tommy* to completion. Yet commercial considerations were at work in *Tommy*, too, if not quite in the same way as they'd been when Lambert hoped 'Rael' could be condensed into a single. By 1968, The Who had chalked up a string of hit singles and albums in the UK and made serious inroads into the US market. But they were deeply in debt and in need of a massive hit if they were even to stay together. The Who and Lambert were gambling that *Tommy* would be the international mega-smash they needed both to put themselves on a firm financial footing and break the American market for good.

While the apparently unwritten *Quads* and the truncated 'Rael' had taken place in the future, *Tommy* took place in a murky combination of the post-World War I past and the then-present milieu of late-60s rock. Its plot centered around a young boy made deaf, dumb, and blind by witnessing his father killing his mother's lover, and his subsequent resurrection as a pinball-playing messiah of sorts. In some respects, it was quite a different endeavor from either *Lifehouse*, which would focus on a decimated future and the role of communally experienced music in overcoming fascism, and *Quadrophenia*, which would be built around a non-disabled young mod anti-hero. Yet in other ways, it shared similarities not just with the two subsequent operas but with much of The Who's work dating back to 1965.

In Pete Townshend's writing in particular, The Who had often assumed the roles of misfits in search of identity, torn between a wish to fit in and untamed nonconformity. Their very first records had latched on to the mod subculture as a means of setting both themselves and their listeners apart from mainstream society, even as the mod cult itself was a society of sorts with its own codes of expected behavior. From 'I'm A Boy' onward through 'Happy Jack,' 'Pictures Of Lily,' and 'Tattoo,' they'd explored the shame and violation of being branded as different and undesirable. And going back to 'The Kids Are Alright' and 'My Generation,' they'd celebrated both anarchic rebellion and the joy of joining forces with like-minded souls in one's chosen community. Townshend himself identified such threads in his work early on, describing 'I'm A Boy' as "the kind of thing that society does all the time – refuses to see its problems and tries to twist them. That's how I saw it then. But now, to me, [the song] stands for an assertion of individuality."[8]

The martyr-cum-messiah of *Tommy* might not be the next link in the chain to *Quadrophenia*'s messed-up mod Jimmy. But both protagonists are, in their very different ways, searching to express individuality in a culture that rigidly suppresses it. While the average citizen of *Lifehouse*'s blighted landscape might not be quite as badly off as the sense-deprived Tommy, both have been psychologically and physically scarred by their surroundings. And *Tommy*'s "listening to you" finale makes it clear that messianic performers – Tommy in the rock opera, and The Who in real life – are at their best when they merge with their audience to rise to a level neither can reach on their own. *Lifehouse* can be seen as an attempt to take that concept itself to an unprecedented height, both in its storyline and its ultimately doomed attempt to involve a real-life audience in the creative process.

None of these concepts would have meant much had The Who not coated them with accessible melodies and – in an overlooked nod to the operatic tradition – memorable riffs that were often reprised throughout the song cycle. Released in May 1969, *Tommy* was more effective at doing this than either *Lifehouse* or *Quadrophenia* would be. It had to be; if listeners and radio programmers had listened too closely to the story of a traumatized boy repeatedly abused, they might have been dissuaded from playing the record altogether. Remarkably, it did become the international smash The Who wanted and needed. It would also transform their live act, which would be centered around performance of all but a few songs from *Tommy* in sequence for the next year or so, helping turn them into one of the biggest concert attractions in the world. Their massive equipment debts were paid, and the group could now afford to expand their road crew and get stage lights.

Tommy was The Who's savior, yet very quickly became its albatross. It became so huge that it threatened to erase the group's identity. Reports of new converts who thought the band's name was Tommy and its album called *The Who* might seem apocryphal and exaggerated, although Pete did once claim that "lots of air hostesses on airplanes said, 'I know you all; you're Tommy The Who.'"[9] Yet as Ed Hanel (co-author of *The Who: The Complete Guide to Their Music*) confirms, "I can tell you that Entwistle said essentially the same thing to me in a discussion [in October 1976] at the Edgewater Hotel cocktail lounge in Seattle. I remember the remark because several of my college dorm-mates came by my room in May '69 during exam week to ask if this was the group I had been touting since my freshman year and was the name of the album *Tommy* or The Who, all of which I found rather amusing."[10]

For Townshend, singer Roger Daltrey, drummer Keith Moon, and bassist John Entwistle, the endless replays of *Tommy* to huge concert crowds were becoming more of a chore than a joy after the initial elation had subsided. In the USA in particular, that was what most of those crowds wanted to hear. The Who had enjoyed a small cult following in the USA almost since their inception, and a growing audience since beginning to tour Stateside in 1967, but relatively few of their American listeners were familiar with the band's pre-*Tommy* catalog. And while The Who were no one-trick ponies, they were under pressure to demonstrate that there was more to the group than the rock opera that had vaulted them into cultural prominence beyond the world of pop music.

How to follow up *Tommy*, however, considering that it was not just by far the group's most successful album, but the first widely successful album of its sort by any group? That was the task facing the group as a new decade started. The official dissolution of The Beatles in spring 1970, and the pall cast over The Rolling Stones by events at the Altamont Rock Festival in December 1969, left The Who as the band most respected by rock listeners. But that position could only be sustained by a new LP of equally earth-shattering force.

Tommy had barely become a hit before The Who started being asked about their next project. As *Melody Maker*'s Tony Wilson noted, they'd played excerpts from *Tommy* on stage in advance of its actual release, prompting him to ask their guitarist if they were getting ready to feature something else. "No, we're not really thinking that far ahead," Townshend replied. "We've kept our eye on rock history and we like to learn by others' mistakes, not ours. Any follow-up will be on an intuitive basis."[11]

Such was *Tommy*'s exposure, however, that by January 1970, the same paper's Chris Welch was already referring to its having "been milked to death already." The pressure on Townshend and the band to come with something both similar and different, however, led Welch to ask Pete the inevitable question: would he ever write another opera? "I've got ideas for one," he said. "But a lot of my ideas will be channeled into the film. We'd like to do an album of songs next – other people's songs. Then there are plans for a 'live' album."[12] Four months later, Townshend was still shying away from the challenge: "It would be very very difficult to follow up *Tommy*, and I don't want to do it, and I don't think people really want it anyway."[13]

The "film" Townshend mentioned was a planned translation of *Tommy* into a movie, a notion that had gained momentum almost as soon as the album scaled the charts. As far back as July 1969, Townshend had announced that Universal International would make a *Tommy* film, the band working with a scriptwriter and a $2 million budget. Unlike *Lifehouse*, *Tommy* would yield a film, albeit five years later and very different in nature from the album and the expectations aroused by this premature announcement.

But long before the *Lifehouse* word was uttered, The Who obviously had several irons in the fire, giving vent to ideas that already seemed rather off-the-wall and difficult, if not impossible, to execute simultaneously. Would the *Tommy* film feature new recordings and songs, for instance? Townshend's comments were vaguely inconclusive. Why would they do an entire album of "other people's songs," considering that their songwriting – meaning Townshend's songwriting, although John Entwistle also contributed material of note – was among their most distinguishing attributes?

The live album did appear, however, and wasn't a mere impulse. Who soundman Bob Pridden had been recording concerts for some months. All the shows on their five-week fall 1969 American tour, in fact, were taped, according to Townshend. The album that became *Live At Leeds*, however, was recorded at the University of Leeds on February 14 1970. In an apparent attempt to decisively redefine their image, or at least to emphasize the hardest-rocking and earthiest side of the band, no *Tommy* material (or indeed any new original material) was included – although, as the deluxe CD edition revealed, several decades later, they *did* play most of *Tommy* that night. "It's a side album, something we wanted to do even before *Tommy*," Townshend told *Creem*. "People have always said there's a mile of difference between our recorded sound and what we do live. So we've always wanted to capture a live sound."[14]

For many listeners, such as Richard Barnes, this was the beginning of a period of two or three years "when The Who really peaked." Not having seen the band for a while before watching their set about six months later at the Isle of Wight festival, Barnes – who'd been at many Who shows, starting before they had a record deal – thought they'd "changed totally. I couldn't believe it. They just got such fucking self-confidence, such great sound. It was like looking at the difference between a sort of amateur weekend band and a professional outfit. It was just amazing."[15]

Live At Leeds is often referred to as The Who's successful attempt to put the record straight, proving to the world that there was more to the band than *Tommy*. That might have held true for newcomers to the group, but it also fulfilled the more mundane purpose of buying some time as they prepared new studio releases. The Who had never been as prolific as rivals like The Beatles and The Rolling Stones, and didn't enter the studio for a period of about ten months following the completion of *Tommy* in early 1969, in part because they were so busy playing *Tommy* on the road. January 1970 did find them cutting 'The Seeker,' a rootsy Townshend number that successfully probed some of the themes The Who had been exploring in both *Tommy* and a few of Pete's more introspective late-60s compositions: the futility of asking leaders to supply salvation, youth's restless search for identity, and the absence of easy answers.

For all its merit, however, this first post-*Tommy* release did relatively poorly in the charts, peaking at Number 19 in the UK and Number 44 in the USA. *Tommy*'s mammoth impact, it seemed, would not guarantee big sales for everything The Who put out. While The Who did have moderate-to-sizable hit singles throughout the rest of their career – much more so in their native UK than in the USA – they would never again run off a series of high-charting 45s as they had in Britain in the last half of the 60s. They were now an album band, first and foremost.

The pressure on The Who to deliver a proper *Tommy* follow-up might say more about the hectic pace of pop releases in 1970 than it does about any dearth of inspiration. Townshend, Daltrey (who wrote 'Here For More,' the pleasant folk-countryish B-side of 'The Seeker'), and Entwistle were continuing to write. From March through May, they recorded a few tracks at Townshend's Eel Pie Studios. Comments from both Pete (who doubled as engineer) and John indicated that the cuts were intended for the next proper Who studio LP. Perhaps the decision to record at Pete's was instigated by the group's having produced 'The Seeker' themselves (although Lambert was given the official credit) or Lambert's being out of commission with a broken jaw when the work began. Entwistle, however, indicated in *New Musical Express* that the cheaper cost of working at Townshend's was a factor.[16]

Although they are of reasonable quality, five songs known to have been cut by the group during this period do seem to indicate a lack of direction. Nor would they fit together into a conceptual work, even if some of them might have later been considered for *Lifehouse*. 'Naked Eye,' the best of the new Townshend batch, had evolved out of improvisations during the live performances of *Tommy*'s 'Sparks'; Entwistle's 'Postcard' is a witty sort of tour diary put to record. Pete was still aiming high with 'I Don't Even Know Myself,' one of his most literal quests for self-identity, even if it's musically a bit pedestrian, alternating the usual power-chord driven verses with unexpectedly country-flavored bridges. In his estimation, the song was "kind of blaming the world because you're fucked-up. ... I think the self is an enemy that's got to be kicked out the fucking way so that you can really get down to it. Most of the songs that I'm writing now are a bit like that."[17]

'Water,' with its rather disagreeable motley assortment of policemen, truck drivers, and farmers on the prowl for both water and someone's daughter, has the feel, just about, of something that could fit into an apocalyptic storyline. It was written around the time of Woodstock, in August 1969, as Daltrey said a year later from the stage of the Isle of Wight festival. Townshend seemed pleased enough with it, describing it as "one of the heaviest things The Who have ever done. It's relaxed and fantastically solid."[18] It's a minor item in the Who canon, but does have the mix of spirituality and braggadocio at the heart of much of Pete's early-70s writing, as well as the push-pull between Townshend's and Daltrey's sensibilities. "I used to think he was a bit of a yob, a bit of a thug, and would need to express his manliness," said the songwriter in 2006. "I suppose I felt that I needed to throw that in for him. I was the spiritual one, 'Give me water, give me water,' and him over there would shout, 'Yes, and while you're at it, let's have some birds.'"[19]

'Now I'm A Farmer,' the least impressive of the lot, seems like a failed attempt to fit into the back-to-the-land ethos sweeping the counterculture, albeit with a bit of impish humor suggesting this route certainly wouldn't unlock the secrets of the universe. The Who had actually cut a backing track for the song back in May 1968, Townshend referring to it as having been done for a possible single in an interview with *Rolling Stone* in August of that year.

After it was played to *Rolling Stone* writer Jonathan Cott in demo form, 'I Don't Even Know Myself' was actually reported as a track earmarked for The Who's next studio LP. So was another, 'There's A Fortune In Those Hills' – described by Cott as "a slow wailing country song" – that has never circulated in any guise. Cott also heard the demo of another lost Townshend song from the period apparently not intended for release, the Brian Jones eulogy 'A Normal Day For Brian, A Man Who Died Everyday,' and even printed a verse from the tune. Written immediately after Pete was told that Jones had died, in early July 1969, it remains one of the most intriguing unreleased and unheard Townshend compositions, although he claimed "it really came out very good." [20]

All the while, The Who continued to fit in tour dates around the recording sessions. After they left for a US tour in early June, in fact, the live schedule was heavy enough to make sustained recording sessions difficult if not impossible. Nonetheless, Entwistle's comments to *New Musical Express* on July 4 1970 indicated that the Eel Pie tracks were still intended for a full-length LP. 'Postcard' and one of John's best songs – the nasty proto-metal antireligious screed 'Heaven And Hell,' which had been opening Who concerts since May 1969 and played live as early as August 1968 – were specifically cited as cuts destined for the album.

As it turned out, 'Heaven And Hell' was relegated to the non-LP B-side of 'Summertime Blues,' plucked from *Live At Leeds* for a July 1970 45 release. Townshend later intimated that a better version of 'Heaven And Hell' had been cut for the projected LP, calling the B-side track – an unfinished rough mix recorded April 13 at London's IBC Studios for a BBC radio session – "crappy."[21] As the merest hint of a struggle to come, *NME*'s Richard Green also noted in his piece that "John isn't opposed to recording another epic-like album of *Tommy* proportions, but again he has certain reservations about the length of time it takes to get it to the satisfaction of Pete Townshend, who is something of a perfectionist."[22]

Daltrey told an Isle of Wight Festival audience on August 29 that the group were about halfway through recording the LP, and as late as November 1970, *Creem* was reporting the album as halfway done (when in fact the UK weekly *Disc* had been announced it was being scrapped the previous month). "We aren't pretending that it's possible to make an album of the impact of *Tommy* commercially," Townshend told *Creem*'s Mike Gormley. "But we have said that we wanted it to be good rock. We've kind of experimented in the same way we did with *Live At Leeds*. If it's not good enough we won't put it out."[23]

It must not have been good enough, as they didn't. In spite of entering The Who's live set in time for early shows in their American tour in June, 'I Don't Even Know Myself' and 'Water' would end up buried on non-LP B-sides. This obviously wasn't the original intention. 'Water' was introduced at their show on July 7 at Tanglewood, Massachusetts, as "a brand new song off an album which will be released very shortly"; and Moon announced that 'I Don't Even Know Myself' would be "on our new album that's coming out as soon as we've finished it, recorded in Pete's garage." (A clip of the July 7 'Water' is on the video *Thirty Years Of Maximum R&B Live*, and performances of both 'Water' and 'I Don't Even Know Myself' can be seen on the *Live At The Isle Of Wight Festival 1970* DVD of their August 29 concert; the latter two performances can also be heard on the companion CD, which also features a live version of 'Naked Eye.') 'Now I'm A Farmer,' 'Postcard,' and 'Naked Eye' found a place on the 1974 out-takes collection *Odds & Sods*, where Townshend's track-by-track annotation intimated that those three tracks were actually intended for a maxi-single or EP.

If so, that's an odd strategy for 1970, when EPs, while popular in the UK and Europe through the mid 60s, had almost vanished as a commercial format, even more so in the USA than abroad. Maybe such an EP, even more so than *Live At Leeds*, would have been a placeholder of sorts for The Who in the marketplace as they tried to put together a bigger project. Townshend seems to gently mock the whole period in his *Odds & Sods* liner notes, describing 'Now I'm A Farmer' as a track "from the period when The Who went slightly mad ... we put out at least one [song] about finding 'one's inner self'" – presumably a swipe at his own 'I Don't Even Know Myself.'[24]

An EP to include all the tracks except 'Naked Eye' and 'Heaven And Hell' was indeed announced for Christmas release in late October, at the price usually reserved for standard two-track singles. Townshend told *Melody Maker* it was Daltrey's idea, although as Roger eventually explained, "We didn't release the maxi-single after all, because the tracks were about ten minutes long [a likely exaggeration as the versions eventually released were well under that length], and we couldn't get them all on. We could have cut it down and made it shorter, but it wouldn't have been right. We even tried recording shorter versions, but that wouldn't work either."[25]

When The Who appeared on the BBC television special *Into '71*, on December 30 1970, they took the unusual step of performing two songs from the recent sessions not even available on disc. 'Naked Eye' and 'I Don't Even Know Myself' were both presented with live vocals over pre-recorded backing tracks, possibly in expectation that they would indeed be issued soon. Even as late as January 23, *Melody Maker* reported the EP would probably be released late the following month, but it never did come out. In 1976 Entwistle noted that "the reason that didn't get released was because the record company refused to sell an EP at the same price as a single."[26]

In an interview with Ritchie Yorke in *Jazz & Pop*, Townshend seemed resigned to the inevitability of attempting something of *Tommy*'s caliber, yet without a firm idea of when or how it would be done. "I don't think anyone is going to accept that our next LP isn't a kind of follow-up to *Tommy*," he said. "I think that it has to be done sometime, I think that people want it to be done, and I want to do it. But I don't particularly want to do it in the same way because there's no point."[27]

Clearly there was some indecision, if not some actual confusion, in the Who camp as to what the group should be releasing and recording. This might well not have been a bad thing. In the absence of a worthy successor to *Tommy*, The Who were at least not rushing an ill-advised, hasty jumble of tracks to market. At the same time, they were keeping their chops in shape through touring and sporadic recording. But as vital as Daltrey, Entwistle, and Moon were to the band, the main inspiration for a large-scale project would have to come from Townshend. And even as The Who's recording career languished during much of 1970, influences were coming at Pete from various directions that would shape their next proper experiment.

Since at least the mid 60s, several of pop's leading lights had been intrigued by the possibility of combining rock music with film. Not in the way The Beatles had done in *A Hard Day's Night*, as great as that pseudo-cinema-verité movie had been, and certainly not in the way that rock artists had been used as dressing for B-movie plots since the 50s. Nor even merely as classy concert documentaries, several of which The Who themselves had already graced: *Monterey Pop*, *Woodstock*, and *The Rolling Stones Rock And Roll Circus* (though the last of these, filmed in December 1968, wouldn't be officially issued until 1995).

Instead, what was envisioned was some indefinite combination of music, acting, fiction, and perhaps some live or staged performance footage. The Beatles had toyed with starring in *The Lord Of The Rings* or a script by playwright Joe Orton, and even *Let It Be* had been conceived as a documentary of both an album-in-the-making and the group's return to live performance, although the LP/film/performance ended up being far more compromised than anyone intended. The Rolling Stones had announced plans in 1966 to star in an adaptation of Dave Wallis's novel *Only Lovers Left Alive*, in which teenaged youth pillage a Britain left devastated by a disaster that has killed off the adult population. That production never got off the ground, however, and while Mick Jagger's late-60s role in *Performance* was an interesting study in rock star decadence, music played a relatively minor part. With a line-up featuring two UCLA film students (Jim Morrison and Ray Manzarek), The Doors had tried to mix concert and behind-the-scenes footage with surrealistic imagery in the little-seen *Feast Of Friends*, with generally dismal results. The Who themselves, hard though it may be to imagine, had apparently considered doing a Monkees-like TV series around 1968, *Sound And Picture City*, although it never seems to have reached the serious planning stage.

Almost from the time *Tommy* was released, rumors started to fly about the rock opera being adapted for a 'real' opera, a dramatic production, a ballet, and even a full-length cartoon. Naturally, a film adaptation was also discussed, with Townshend seeming quite keen to get going on it. "The film we are making ... is based on the ideas that went into *Tommy*," he told *Melody Maker*'s Chris Welch in January 1970. "We are very excited about the film and, as you know, our managers Kit Lambert and Chris Stamp originally came out of the film industry; and I've got a lot of friends in the young area of filming. The question is – what is the film going to be about, now that the album has been milked to death already?"[28]

In keeping with the confusion surrounding most Who projects, exactly what this film would have been remains uncertain. So too was the likely source of the money. The Who were now huge record sellers and one of the world's biggest concert draws, but financial organization had never been a strong point of either the band or their managers. Townshend had announced a $2 million budget for a Universal International film in July 1969. Now the prospective backers had changed, with Pete informing *Downbeat*'s readers in May 1970 that "we intend to make a film of it with MGM starting next year. We finally got over a lot of things like contracts and finances, that kind of bullshit. We got the release from Decca [the band's US record label], and now we're getting down to working with directors."

Asked by Derek Van Pelt in the same interview whether The Who would be appearing, Townshend said, "We won't actually be in it. We will be performing musically as a group. We might have narrative roles – a performing narrative; it's still too loose. We don't know. I haven't spoken to any scriptwriters."[29] Actually, Kit Lambert hoped to be involved, as a scriptwriter and perhaps in other capacities. His ambitions to get *Tommy* on screen would soon conflict with some of Townshend's goals, especially when Pete had another combination album-film in mind.

It was true enough that Townshend had some young filmmaker friends, and indeed that his interest in getting involved in some aspect of moviemaking was not solely generated by the opportunity to translate *Tommy* to the cinema. It's still little known that Pete was developing an interest in soundtrack composing, contributing material to several rarely seen films. Considering the laudable cinematic drama he brought to Who instrumentals such as *Tommy*'s 'Underture' and 'Sparks,' it's little surprise that he'd acquired a taste for applying those skills to movie scores. His soundtrack work brought him into contact with a filmmakers' circle, Tattooist International, which remains an overlooked influence on the project soon to blossom into *Lifehouse*.

According to filmmaker Richard Stanley, "Tattooist International was a group of filmmakers who came together while working for Allan King Associates, a documentary film pioneer out of Toronto. We all met at some point or other while working for the Allan King office in Soho [in London]."[30] In the group were Stanley, director Denis Postle, writer and director Mike Myers (not to be confused with the younger comedian of the same name), director Dick Fontaine, cameraman Nic Knowland (who worked on some of John Lennon and Yoko Ono's experimental films), and production manager Judy Marriott.

Townsend's connection with Stanley actually predated their involvement with Tattooist International. It went all the way back to art school, before The Who had taken off. In 1968 Pete had done some music for Stanley's 22-minute graduation film for the Royal College of Art, *Lone Ranger*, and even appeared in it (as the main actor's brother). All of The Who except for Entwistle attended the black-and-white comedy's screening at the Edinburgh Film Festival, indicating some interest in such cinematic projects among the rest of the band as well.

Lone Ranger remains damnably difficult to access for viewing, but soundtrack excerpts that have escaped onto bootleg indicate that Pete might have seen it – as do many pop artists who dabble in soundtracks – as an outlet for ideas too avant-garde to fit comfortably onto his regular commercial releases. While one instrumental composition (entitled 'Lone Ranger Street Reduction') bears some resemblance to the guitar-driven sections of wordless passages from *Tommy*, it also includes flourishes of harsh, swelling distorted notes, bird noises, and rapidly descending organ that would have been too jarring for the most part to make it onto a Who record. The same could be said of the tape effects and buzzing scrapes that are heard on the otherwise jovial, country-inflected harmonica pieces. It's a long way from *Who's Next*, yet the brief circular organ riffs on 'Lone Ranger Street Reduction' foreshadow the repeating patterns put to use on 'Baba O'Riley' and 'Won't Get Fooled Again.'

"The group [Tattooist International] coalesced around a series of 'political manifesto' films made by Denis, Mike, and Dick before its foundation," says Stanley. "The group was intimately connected with musicians in London. Dick was close friends with Jimi Hendrix, I with Townshend and The Kinks; Nic had worked with The Beatles. For a long period we also provided technical services for Lennon and Ono's experimental films, as well as shooting projects for Ringo and George. We had all been connected, also, to the earliest music promotion films before Tattooist was founded. Tattooist worked on a lot of TV documentaries [for our] bread and butter, but music was the link between us."[31]

Although he already knew Stanley, Townshend came into contact with the Tattooist group as a whole via Dick Fontaine's 1970 film *Double Pisces*. Again Pete did original music for the soundtrack, including a demo of 'I Don't Even Know Myself' and a fairly perfunctory instrumental, 'Piledriver,' with Townshend on organ and guitar and Speedy Keene (of the Townshend-produced Thunderclap Newman) on percussion. A few minutes of creepy electronic tape experiments, largely generated by bass guitar and heavy on tape delay that eventually feeds back on itself, have made the bootleg rounds and are also reported to have been done for the movie. These likewise were too far-out to have gone onto Who discs, even as they hinted at some of the territory Townshend would explore in the early 70s.

Even less is currently known about a Denis Postle BBC film about high-energy physics at CERN (aka European Organization For Nuclear Research), originally titled *Oh Dear, What Can the Matter Be?*, for which Townshend also supplied the music. Stanley and Postle established a more direct connection to The Who by making the promo video for 'The Seeker,' a fairly straightforward document of the band miming to the record in a Wardour Street studio. In late summer 1970 they'd work on Murray Lerner's documentary of the Isle of Wight festival, for which The Who's set was filmed.

While Townshend and The Who were definitely thinking about some sort of screen adaptation of *Tommy* by this time, the Tattooist group might well have at least influenced his conception of an entirely different film project. According to Stanley, MGM producer Herb Solow – perhaps best known as vice president of production at Desilu Studios, which had just been responsible for the *Star Trek* TV series – was watching TV in LA and saw a documentary by Fontaine and Postle (likely *Who Is Richard Smith?*, about the British painter of that name). "He liked the style of it so much that he ordered his minions to find out who had made it," Stanley recalls. "That led to his coming to London and meeting Tattooist. He was interested in a 'youth movie.' He had a bunch of money for us to make a pilot or a script. But what, we didn't yet know."[32]

As Postle remembers it, Solow asked him to make something for MGM. Postle and Mike Myers, who had both attended the Royal College of Art in the early 60s, worked up a story of Mike's into *Guitar Farm*. Stanley, then a tenant in Postle's basement, had shot material as a cameraman with Postle. Stanley brought Pete Townshend into the picture. Townshend then wrote a sample track for the *Guitar Farm* project, 'Baba O'Riley,' usually cited as the song that would have been the opening number for *Lifehouse*, and production was agreed for *Guitar Farm*.

Myers actually published the original *Guitar Farm* story sometime in 1969, to his recollection, in the British underground publication *Friends*.

"*Guitar Farm* was on an island where all the missing people went," he recalls. "Glenn Miller was there; so was Amelia Earhart and many other historical figures from the past who went missing. The main occupation on the island was growing musical instruments. On Guitar Farm itself there were acres of guitars sprouting out of the ground. Guitars were picked by guitar player/pickers who would test them for ripeness. In the middle of a field of classical guitars, you would see player/pickers sitting in the typically straight-backed posture of a classical guitarist playing something from the classical repertoire. Nearby someone might be doing scales. Adjacent fields would be sprouting electric guitars, and long-haired Fender pickers and Stratocaster pickers would be putting their crops through their paces, playing licks and riffs from the great rock'n'roll classics. Walking through Guitar Farm was to go on a musical journey encompassing every kind of guitar sound.

"Elsewhere on the island other kinds of musical instruments were being grown or harvested. Deep underground, seams of piano and organ keyboards were being mined. Flutes and piccolos could be found in the shallower fast flowing streams, swaying in the current like aquatic plants. Drums of every kind grew on the surface of the larger lakes, looking like flotillas of different-sized but perfectly round water lilies. Bushes were laden down with ripe plectrums. Every kind of musical instrument grew there and each had its own specialist group of player pickers and harvesters. Moving from one part of the island to the other was to go through a smorgasbord of musical sounds – strains of Chopin wafting up from the piano mine, Hendrix riffs floating over from a field of ripe Stratocasters. There would be encounters with the variety of characters mentioned earlier. Glenn Miller himself could be seen most afternoons walking through a grove of saxophones to strains of 'In The Mood.'"[33]

The links from *Guitar Farm* to what would have become *Lifehouse* might not be too specific. Yet some elements of the story – especially a journey that would enable listeners to experience every sort of sound – may have been reflected in Townshend's quest for every sort of sound in the music he composed in his home studio for his next opus, particularly via his newfound enthusiasm for synthesizers. There were also similarities, albeit in a rather general sense, between *Guitar Farm*'s scenario and the somewhat utopian communal musical experience Townshend hoped to create on stage when *Lifehouse* was presented to real-life audiences. *Lifehouse* would have climaxed with a concert. It wouldn't take place on an island, but it too would be a haven for musical vitality in a circumscribed location, cut off from the vast majority of the world's population.

"There were two main factors that led to the commissioning of the script," Myers says today. "One was Postle's film about Richard Smith that came to the attention of Herb Solow. It was a highly unusual and original piece of filmmaking, as were all of Denis's films at that time. It was bursting with graphic energy and groundbreaking invention; he had a knack of turning conventional filmmaking on its head, and so came up with a new kind of visual language. Perhaps Solow thought we could apply the same techniques to a Hollywood movie and produce something really out of the ordinary. The fact that we were unknown filmmakers with no track record in features, who worked out of scruffy offices in Soho, added spice to what was always a quixotic project.

"The other factor of course, was the marquee value of Pete Townshend's name," says Myers. He doesn't remember Pete contributing much on the creative side, however, "apart from the piece of music that emerged as 'Baba O'Riley,' which I always thought was inspired at least in part by a line of mine from the original story about Glenn Miller being 'washed ashore on a ripple of applause,' the word 'ripple' giving birth to the musical motif in that piece. I don't want to make extravagant claims for myself, but I thought at the time and still do that the line was charismatic, that it had 'poetic force.' Once heard it sticks, and when quoted by me in response to questions about *Guitar Farm* over the years, it has never failed to bring a smile to the listener."[34] One would guess that had Townshend taken inspiration from *Guitar Farm*, it might have also figured into 'Pure And Easy,' a song central to the plot of *Lifehouse* in its worshipful admiration of a note played free "like a breath rippling by."

What exactly was Pete's role in a story that would have been quite a challenge to translate onto film, especially given the limits of 1970 technology? "There were not many sessions with Pete," says Myers. "Three or four max, I would say. I don't think he was very interested in the nitty-gritty details of the story of *Guitar Farm*. He was more concerned with controlling the dynamic arc of the drama, organizing the ebb and flow of the 'highs' and 'lows,' to ensure that strategically and emotionally they were in the 'right' place. He had strong views about this, about the linear structure of a musical narrative and how it could be used to manipulate audience response. At the same time he was very mindful of his responsibilities as a performer and composer, and was wary of abusing the hold over audiences this power and skill gave him. But it does account for the success of his great themed albums, and he obviously saw *Guitar Farm* as a vehicle for another one of those."[35]

Herb Solow remembers the genesis of *Guitar Farm* somewhat differently, but agrees that all concerned were eager to work together. "I was Head of Production for MGM and had done several movies with popular singers, examples being Elvis Presley and Frank Sinatra; years later I did a film starring Sting. There was always an excitement to the live entertainer, and I felt that, in most instances, he or she brought that excitement onto the film. Couple that with the fact that there were some very exciting and innovative young filmmakers in London in the early 70s, and there was reason to work with these British filmmakers and popular entertainers. We were also doing several films in Britain [including Ken Russell's *The Boy Friend* and Mike Hodges's *Get Carter*]. So it made sense that I was interested when a bright young man called Denis Postle contacted me with a film idea to be done with Pete Townshend."[36]

Townshend had announced The Who's intentions to make a *Tommy* film with MGM in the May 14 1970 issue of *Downbeat*, yet the plot Solow and Tattooist were hatching seems to have had an entirely different movie in mind. "I had known Pete for several years already and we were close friends," says Stanley. "We had discussed at length, many times, the intersection between music and movies. We also talked about *Tommy* a lot and Pete first described the project to me in a letter from a Stateside tour when it was still called *Amazing Journey*. I was later present at many recording sessions for the album.

"We had also talked about the as yet unnamed *Lifehouse* project that then centered on a river flowing down to the sea of consciousness (or something like that – you will recall Pete's deep involvement in Meher Baba). I suggested to Pete that perhaps this concept could be used for the MGM script. Pete, Denis, Mike, Ron Geesin, and I went away for a weekend to a hotel to try and pull together the ideas."[37]

That's corroborated by Geesin, an experimental composer with whom Townshend had recently become friendly. In fact, Geesin was introduced to Townshend, he believes, by Stanley himself. Although he has done a great deal of other work and remains active, Ron will always be most famous for collaborating with Pink Floyd on the composition of the 1970 opus 'Atom Heart Mother' and the Floyd's Roger Waters on the 1970 soundtrack LP *Music From The Body*.

"The thing about the Tattooist lot was that they had got some development money to do a giant work," he says. "You know how when you're in your twenties you think you're going to do a Wagner *Ring Cycle*, or something like that. [Indeed, Geesin remembers Townshend owning a *Ring Cycle* boxed set, as further confirmation of the guitarist's operatic enthusiasms.] Pete and I were going to be the sound persons. They booked this hotel in the West Country, and we all went for a weekend to this big fancy hotel way in the country to brainstorm this giant idea. But nobody knew how to start!" he laughs.

"So we had this meeting, and went off into various bushes and around corners, found little seats in the grounds of this big hotel – either singly or in twos or something like that – to try and get the great idea. Nothing happened. Absolutely nothing happened. I suppose it was a time when it was maximum ego flow, and everyone wanted to do their idea. So it never came to anything. It burned all the development money, that weekend."[38]

Yet according to Stanley, who remains friends with Geesin, it wasn't all that unproductive. "The outline that we came up with was about a mythical island where all the people who had gone missing without trace lived," he says, which aligns with Myers's summary of *Guitar Farm*'s plot. "So there was Hitler, Glenn Miller, Amelia Earhart, etc. Everything on the island made musical sounds when it was touched. Into this is thrown a protagonist, Jack, who has also 'gone missing' from reality. It was fuzzy at that stage – but enough for Herb Solow to put up some real MGM money for story development. Mike worked on the script feverishly and Pete was also in on development."[39]

Although this was not exactly *Lifehouse* as Townshend would eventually outline it, Stanley's recollections clearly indicate that Pete, whether he'd be providing the soundtrack on his own or with The Who, was working toward something quite different from *Tommy*. Elements with at least ballpark similarities to what would become *Lifehouse* were being discussed, including the displacement of at least some of the population to an isolated territory; a sort of collective consciousness, inspired at least in part by Townshend's faith in spiritual leader Meher Baba; and the role of music as an almost supernatural force. It's probably never going to be possible to establish an exact timeline for these Tattooist discussions, but that West Country weekend summit probably took place before Townshend mentioned *Lifehouse* in his September 19 1970 *Melody Maker* column. A surviving Geesin diary does mention a "possible meeting" with Townshend, Stanley, and Postle on May 5 1970, at which some such brainstorming may have occurred, although it couldn't have been the exact date of the West Country hotel gathering, as May 5 didn't fall on a weekend.

Townshend also seemed to have a non-*Tommy* film in mind in his interview for the May 14 1970 issue of *Rolling Stone*, in which he told Jonathan Cott he saw a movie as "the ideal thing" for the group's next step. At first he indicated that it might be something like the staged rockumentary of sorts that had been attempted with *The Rolling Stones Rock And Roll Circus*, before adding, "There are people, and I am one of them, who have got a lot of ideas in that direction, for a rock film which is not a documentary and not a story and not a comedy either but a fucking Rock Film. A film which is the equivalent of a rock song, only lasting an hour or longer."[40]

The Tattooist group never did get to work on a Who film, although work continued with Myers, Stanley, Postle, and Solow. In the meantime, other forces were helping to shape Townshend's vision for an entirely different film whose premise and purpose would be far more specific.

For quite some time before *Lifehouse* was launched, Pete Townshend had publicly proclaimed his openness to spiritual matters off the beaten path of Western convention by embracing the teachings of Indian avatar Meher Baba. He had first heard about Baba in autumn 1967 from his friend Mike McInnerney, art editor of the London underground paper *International Times*. Disillusioned with drugs after a horrific acid trip he'd taken on a plane back from the Monterey Pop Festival, Townshend found in Baba some of the meaning and peace of mind so many hippies were trying to find in illicit substances. By 1968 he had become a devoted Baba follower, though for some time this was known to relatively few Who fans; the biggest clue was Meher Baba's credit as "Avatar" on the back of the McInnerney-designed *Tommy* sleeve.

Born in India in 1894, Meher Baba (the name means "Compassionate

Father") began to attract followers in the early 20s, visiting the West and gathering devotees there on numerous occasions from the early 30s onward. If he's known for two things among the general public, it's as the originator of the saying "Don't worry, be happy," and for observing a self-imposed vow of silence from July 10 1925 until his death on January 31 1969. A third well-known fact is that Pete Townshend became a Baba follower, although Baba's precise philosophy remained hard to penetrate even after Townshend made his devotion clear by penning a three-page article for *Rolling Stone*'s November 26 1970 issue, entitled 'In Love with Meher Baba.'

One hesitates to summarize Baba's philosophy in a sentence or two, especially as the second sentence of his Universal Message states, "Understand therefore that I lay down no precepts." As with several major religions, it involves deeds of generosity, love, and charity, with love of Baba acting as a path for his followers to do his work. When Baba stopped speaking, as Townshend wrote in *Rolling Stone*, it was with the declaration, "You have had enough of my words, now is the time to live by them."

What is clear is that Townshend took Baba seriously. "Any focused attempt to get more out of life, more results from events and emotional chapters, whether it be by following Baba or doing what comes naturally, will start to bring visible results in life," he wrote in *Rolling Stone*. "When you are getting things done, you can't help but enjoy life more. When you begin to realize that your own suffering has a purpose, you can bear it with dignity and poise, admit defeat, or that you were wrong, without feeling that your life is worthless."[41] It also gave a more serious, spiritual direction to his songwriting – often blatantly humorous or satirical in The Who's earlier days – on *Tommy*, *Lifehouse* (most obviously on 'Baba O'Riley,' named in part after his avatar), his early-70s solo recordings (where the Baba influence sometimes verged on the blatant), and even certain passages of *Quadrophenia*.

It also made him receptive to an even more unlikely source of inspiration from Eastern philosophy. It's not known when Pete Townshend read *The Mysticism Of Sound And Music: The Sufi Teaching Of Hazrat Inayat Khan*, but it had almost certainly made an impression on him by 1970. Certainly he was the only member of The Who likely to read such a cerebral investigation into the relationship between music and life itself, and indeed one of the few rock musicians anywhere apt to pick up such a book.

While Khan's writings weren't entirely religious in nature, they delved into philosophical musings so pious it might seem they'd have little appeal for a rock musician as loud and earthy as Townshend. By the time Pete read *The Mysticism Of Sound And Music*, Khan had been dead for more than 40 years. He'd given up his life as a composer, singer, and vina player, he explained in his prologue, "because I had received from it all I had to receive. To serve God one must sacrifice the dearest thing, and I sacrificed my music, the dearest thing to me ... Now, if I do anything, it is to tune souls instead of instruments, to harmonize people instead of notes."[42]

Perhaps that appealed to the idealistic martyr in Townshend, but he wasn't about to lay down his guitar. What did connect deeply with him was the idea of using music as a way to spiritually heal and elevate both himself and The Who's audience. Several of the book's passages unmistakably mirror *Lifehouse*'s quest for a hidden note of sorts that could transform the world, or at least the individual, if only it could be found.

In Khan's view, "each person has his peculiar note in which he speaks, and that particular note is expressive of his life's evolution, expressive of his soul, of the condition of his feelings and of his thoughts."[43] It's not such a large leap from there to Townshend's *Melody Maker* proclamation: "There's a note, a musical note, that builds the basis of existence somehow. Mystics would agree, saying that of course it is OM, but I am talking about a MUSICAL note."[44]

According to Khan, such a note can not only express the essence of the individual, but could unite the entire community: "All races, nations, classes, and people are like a strain of music based upon one chord, when the key-note, the common interest, holds so many personalities in a single bond of harmony."[45] Townshend could have had this in mind when he said, near the end of his *Melody Maker* column, that "the key to this unexciting adventure that I'm leading you on is that everybody hears it. Moreover I think everybody hears the same note or noise. It's an amazing thing to think of any common ground between all men that isn't directly a reflection of spiritual awareness.

"The note it's there," he said, "gently breathing and saying annoyingly that it was there all along undisturbed. Being whole again, however, you don't mind listening and enjoying. It's a note, it's notes, it's music – the most beautiful there is to hear."[46]

Where did Townshend fit into all of this? Perhaps he found inspiration from this passage in *The Mysticism Of Sound And Music*: "All the trouble in the world and all the disastrous results arising out of it – all come from lack of harmony. This shows that the world today needs harmony more than ever before. So if the musician understands this, his customer will be the whole world."[47]

Unlike Khan, Townshend really did have a means of reaching the whole world – or at least the Western world and much of the rest – not only through chart-topping albums, but also concerts, radio, and, if it could somehow be managed, film. And unlike Khan, he had the technological means of trying to capture the essence of someone's personality in a note, or a series of notes – or so he hoped. He revealed in a 1983 *Penthouse* interview that he had been at that time working with an avant-garde composer at Cambridge University, possibly Tim Souster, who introduced him to composer Karlheinz Stockhausen and members of the BBC Radiophonic Workshop.

"What we did," said Townshend, "was ask some individuals a lot of questions about themselves and then subject them to the sort of test a GP [General Practitioner] might undertake. We measured their heartbeat and the alpha and beta rhythms of the brain; we even took down astrological details and other kinds of shit. Then we took all the data we'd collected on paper or charts and converted them into music, and the end result was sometimes quite amazing. In fact, one of the pulse-modulated frequencies we generated was eventually used as the background beat to 'Won't Get Fooled Again.' Later I used another one of the pulse-modulated frequencies as the foundation for 'Baba O'Riley.'"[48]

These weren't the easiest sorts of portraits to capture on a guitar, Townshend's usual instrument of choice, or on piano or organ, which he also occasionally played. For the above two songs in particular, it would be necessary to use something entirely different – or, at least, to use a familiar instrument in an entirely different way. By running a 1968 Lowrey Berkshire Deluxe TBO-1 organ into an EMS VCS3 mk1 synth, he created a sound and texture previously unheard in rock music. If rudimentary in comparison with later synthesizer technology, it could still produce those "pulse-modulated frequencies" (in which rhythms derived from heartbeats and brain rhythms were used to modify sounds from the organ) in a manner not quite possible on other instruments currently available.

Although Hazrat Inayat Khan had been writing long before electric guitars were on the market, let alone synthesizers, his writings are nonetheless credited by Townshend as an inspiration to immerse himself in the new technology. "What created the huge prospect of creative potential with synthesizers for me related to a spiritual link which I picked up from reading the Sufi message of Inayat Khan," he said in a 1996 BBC radio special on *Lifehouse*. "When somebody came along and said, 'Here is this device. It is a scientific device. It uses vibrations and oscillations and rhythms and blah, blah, blah, blah, blah, and it is also a musical instrument,' I thought, 'Well heigh-ho! Here is a link.' And what it actually allowed me to do is that it allowed me to contemplate whether or not I could reflect exactly and precisely and scientifically the emotional, spiritual, disturbed state of a human being."[49]

'Baba O'Riley' and 'Won't Get Fooled Again' loom large in the *Lifehouse* legend, and their unusual pulsing intros are often assumed to have been created solely by synthesizers. Yet the organ was vital to creating those now instantly recognizable riffs, if that's the right way to describe sounds that seem so electronic and mechanical in some respects. "One of the really big advantages to using an organ being played through the synthesizer is that home organs were fully polyphonic," says vintage keyboard restorer Matt Cunitz of Berkeley, California, who would replicate those riffs on stage when the band Mushroom performed a re-creation of *Lifehouse* in concert in 2009. "You could hold the chord down, and it [would] play all the notes in the chord at the same time." In contrast, the synthesizers available at the time were monophonic or duophonic, meaning you could only hold down one or two notes at a time. Even though oscillators could be set up so that they were tuned to different notes and played a chord, "you could only hold one key to trigger the oscillators."

In order to do the parts on 'Won't Get Fooled Again,' continues Cunitz, "he's holding down multiple keys on the organ. The TBO-1 [organ] was then plugged into his synthesizer, which modified the basic chords he was playing on the Lowrey in two ways. One part of the synth was given the job of turning the sound on and off in quick repetition and another circuit swept the filter up and down, letting certain harmonics through at different times. Synthesizers weren't generating any tones. The organ was generating the tones, and the synthesizer is modifying or modulating them. He's not playing every note. He's holding the chords down, and between the circuits in the organ, and the modulation that's happening in the synthesizer, it's creating that gurgling Terry Riley-like soundscape.

"The way the organ and synth were used for 'Baba O'Riley' was a bit different, however. Here, he again used the Lowrey organ, but contrary to the long-held belief of many, the famous keyboard sound bouncing through this song has not been sculpted by the ARP [synthesizer]. The Lowrey organs, including Pete's model TBO-1, had a function that is somewhat unique among instruments of its type. A tab labeled 'marimba repeat,' when activated, would play the notes held down on the keyboard in chopped up repetition. Other organs had similar functions, but what is unique here is that half the notes you might be holding down would not make a sound until the others shut off! So as a result there is a sense of randomness as some notes trigger on the beat, and others on the off-beat."[50]

To generate other synthetic effects, Townshend became one of the first owners of the ARP 2500, a modular machine of monstrous size in comparison to more commonplace modern synths. In fact, he was one of the only owners of the ARP 2500, as only about 100-200 were sold. He was also one of the few rock musicians who could have afforded one, as it sold for £5,400 (about $10,000) in 1972. So much did Pete become identified with the ARP that his photo would be prominently displayed on the ARP Odyssey Owner's Manual soon afterward. His use of the instrument on *Who's Next* would even be highlighted on a flexi-disc promoting and demonstrating ARP synths, although the passage from 'Baba O'Riley' excerpted for that disc actually did not use an ARP.

That disc was narrated by Roger Powell, a musician who worked at ARP in the early 70s and personally demonstrated the instrument to Townshend in New York (possibly when The Who came to the city to do some recording at the Record Plant in March 1971, although Powell is unsure of the exact date). "Originally it was considered an educational instrument that taught you about electronics and the physics of sound," says Powell, who by the mid 70s would be playing keyboards and synthesizer with Todd Rundgren in Utopia. "That market was certainly not as big as the vast market available for actual musicians who were playing and recording. My job at that time for ARP was basically to demonstrate the synthesizers – kind of [an] ambassador, if you will, for the company." Among the other top musicians he showed the system were Grateful Dead bassist Phil Lesh, Jim Messina, Weather Report keyboardist Joe Zawinul, and, when the ex-Beatle was on his way to performing at the Concert For Bangladesh, George Harrison.

"ARP was being pretty aggressive at that point about trying to get celebrities and famous endorsers, romancing the popular artists of the day," continues Powell. "ARP was trying to do outdo Moog at that time. ARP's thing was, 'We've got to go after the rock and the jazz guys who are out there already sort of pushing the envelope.' I was getting pretty good at teaching and explaining this, having traveled all around. I remember demonstrating the 2500 to [Townshend], and he was off and patching it pretty quickly. He really got it. Most guitarists had enough challenge getting the cable plugged in from the guitar to the amp, and getting those controls set correctly. That sounds a bit harsh, but I mean, most of them weren't really interested in doing anything other than just plugging in and playing. So there was a marketing challenge right there.

"But of course someone like Pete – and the fellow that I worked with, Todd Rundgren – he was heavy into technology as well, and of course a guitarist. So there was this small handful of very forward-looking guitarists, and of course you would probably not limit Pete Townshend to the simple term 'guitarist.' I would say multi-instrumentalist, composer, producer, technologist. In many ways, a lot like Todd; I hate to use the term Renaissance man, but that sort of applied at that time. Probably the reason that he stuck with ARP is ARP was very willing to work with him, and to attempt to develop some new devices."[51]

Townshend's embrace of synthesizer technology remains an underappreciated cornerstone in the evolution of The Who's early-70s music. It was bold enough for a guitar hero to master an entirely different instrument from the one with which he was identified not just musically, but visually. His gymnastic windmill strums and spectacular guitar smash-ups had become perhaps *the* visual Who trademarks, and the band never would get a grip on incorporating the synthesizer into their stage act, at least at the time. Synthesizers as a whole were only just starting to be used in rock recordings, and when major bands used them they were often inserted as futuristic frosting, as The Beatles had recently done on a few *Abbey Road* tracks.

Townshend, by contrast, was making synthesizers integral to both the melody and rhythm of some of the key new songs he was writing, such as

'Won't Get Fooled Again' and 'Baba O'Riley.' Of course he was one of the few rock musicians who could afford to buy an ARP for his home and tinker with what was then often viewed as a Frankensteinian creation. But unlike many musicians from the pop world, Townshend would use the instrument with taste and subtlety. "Townshend is the only musician I've met before or since who really knows how to work one," said *Who's Next* associate producer Glyn Johns in *The Record Producers*. "He's really got it down. I know keyboard players now who are really into it, but still not to the same extent Pete is. ... And it wasn't a matter of trial and error, he really knows what he's doing with those things and how they work."[52]

"A lot of people tried to use a synth just to duplicate," says Roger Powell. "Everyone thought, 'OK, it's a synthesizer. It synthesizes real sounds. It's used to replace real sounds.' I think that that kind of prejudiced people into a corner, where they didn't actually see the thing as an instrument on its own right. A lot of bands that adopted the early synthesizer were happy with one or two patches, sort of signature patches, and really didn't approach it as sort of an orchestral palette." In contrast, feels Powell, Townshend "approached it more openly and in a more exploratory manner. He has a tremendous ear for production, and wanted to do things differently. Here was a new tool that just gave him so many new colors. He had a more intelligent and open-minded approach to it, which clearly was exemplified in the music."[53]

"Townsend struck me as a much more serious composer and arranger than most rockers," adds ARP co-founder David Friend, who met with Townshend in the early 70s both in Pete's home studio and when The Who passed through Boston in early August 1971. "He really thought about the orchestration and The Who's unique sound. His use of synthesizers was more textural than melodic. While many other synthesizer players, particularly Stevie Wonder, were using the synthesizer as a melodic instrument, Townsend used the synthesizer more like a percussion instrument to create a 'sound' that set off the group's guitar work. I was always blown away with how inventive Pete was in this regard. These were textures that nobody had ever heard before."[54]

Movies, Sufi mysticism, Meher Baba, and synthesizers – all were wielding their influence on Pete as he began to formulate a conceptual work that, in some ways, was considerably more ambitious even than *Tommy*. Townshend, however, was not one to incubate in total isolation. The confused tone of the era's radical politics and the counterculture would also inform his new material, especially 'Won't Get Fooled Again.' The guitar feedback specialist also valued actual audience feedback more than any of rock's leading lights. In the final few months of 1970, he would begin to lay out, explain, and refine what he had in mind in numerous media interviews and articles he'd written himself.

From today's vantage point – when journalists often have a hard time reaching a star's PR department, let alone the stars themselves – the sheer number of interviews Townshend undertook in 1970 and 1971 is astounding. Everyone in The Who had been quite accessible to reporters since the group's first hits, although the garrulous Keith Moon was more so than Roger Daltrey or the relatively retiring John Entwistle. Yet for someone who didn't need an onslaught of publicity to raise his profile or record sales, Townshend not only allowed media access, he courted it.

There were literally dozens of interviews, especially in the five principal British music weeklies of the time: *Melody Maker, NME, Record Mirror, Disc & Music Echo*, and *Sounds*. He also found time to sit for substantial pieces in US magazines like *Rolling Stone, Downbeat, Jazz & Pop, Creem, Circus*, and *Crawdaddy*. Outside the music papers, he managed to get coverage in both the biggest of the big (the *New York Times*) and the underground press (a mammoth four-part interview for the *Los Angeles Free Press*). And amid this blitzkrieg, he somehow wrote quite a few articles under his own byline, including nine monthly *Melody Maker* columns (titled 'The Pete Townshend Page') starting in August 1970; a three-page article about Meher Baba and his devotion to the man in *Rolling Stone*; and, most extraordinarily (and entertainingly) of all, a lengthy *Rolling Stone* review of The Who's own greatest hits collection, *Meaty Beaty Big And Bouncy*.

What's more, Townshend and The Who often treated journalists as mates and even confidantes, not just promotional vehicles who had to be tolerated. Again, it's a relic of a simpler age when rock stars were generally more approachable than they would be in the decades to come. Even by the standards of the era, however, The Who were exceptional.

"The Who were much more open to journalists than any other band of their stature," says Chris Charlesworth, who wrote about the group often as a young *Melody Maker* writer in the early 70s. "I got to know them originally through Keith [Altham], who was the PR man for the band, who was really friendly toward journalists. I wrote something nice about them, and he rang me up on *Melody Maker* and said, 'Hey, that was great. Thanks very much for writing that about us.' I was staggered, absolutely bowled over, that he'd take the trouble to do that. He didn't need me at that point; this was 1970, for Christ's sake. Then I met him in a bar somewhere in central London, and he invited me to a show, invited me backstage, and introduced me to the other three."

In those times before fax and email, it was Charlesworth's duty to retrieve Townshend's *Melody Maker* column by hand, and here again The Who showed personal hospitality that seems unimaginable from this distance. "I had to go down and pick it up from his house in Twickenham, down by the river by Eel Pie Island, where he lived," he says. "And sometimes I'd go in and have a cup of tea with him and his wife, Karen, and see his kids. This was really unusual for a rock star of his stature to have press going to his house, and not to interview him necessarily – just to have a cup of tea, pick up this piece of paper, and go back to the office with it.

"It is extraordinary. I went to all four of their houses, and I was welcomed. And not just me, other journalists as well. But I never went to any of Led Zeppelin's houses, for example, let alone The Rolling Stones' or The Beatles'. The Who were really open to the press, and they were prepared to discuss their failures, too. They were much more thick-skinned than any other group. They didn't seem to have the ego problems that other bands had. They were really honest and open. You can read [in] Townshend's interviews, the self-analysis he went through. Roger didn't hold back if he had something to say; he said it, even if he offended people. Keith was just completely out of his brain, and didn't care what he did or what he said, really."[55]

Veteran rock journalist Keith Altham was in the unique position of both writing about The Who in the early 1970s and, starting at around the same time, doing PR for the band. "It was a great deal more cozy, the relationships between journalists and artists, in those days," he says. "There was much more trust in those days, particularly on the music side. [In] America, you could take *Rolling Stone* and [the New York weekly] *Village Voice* into that category as well. It was only when you got to the kind of *National Enquirer*, the *Sun*, *News Of The World* [tabloids] that you started to get into intrusive areas that they didn't want much to do with. The PR didn't need to be as suffocatingly protective as they have to do, seem to finally need to do, today." Indeed, for a time Altham was both working The Who's PR and continuing to write about them in the music press, which would be considered an unacceptable conflict of interest today but seemed no great problem to anyone at the time.

"Pete, in certain respects, was a frustrated journalist," says Altham. "He started out, I think, with the idea of becoming a journalist at one stage of his life. Subsequently at one period [in the 80s] he became heavily involved with publishing, both as an editor and a sub-editor. So he was obviously very interested in that side of things. He's a very loquacious and articulate man. He likes talking; he likes to find people that are in some ways intellectually stimulating for him to talk to. And consequently, he would make himself available for that purpose as much as anything else, I think."[56] Nor would he limit himself to The Who or even rock music, using 'The Pete Townshend Page' to spout off at length about, among other things, the artificiality of miming to records on TV; the question (asked then as now) "Is Rock Dead?"; whether it was really possible to change the world through pop music; and the differences between the US and UK music scenes.

Townshend obviously wouldn't have gone to such trouble with the media if he wasn't getting something out of it above and beyond mere publicity, a good chat, and a chance to blow his horn. It was also an opportunity to work out some of his ideas in conversation and in print, and not just for the benefit of readers. Part of the extensive interview he'd done with *Rolling Stone* editor Jann Wenner in August 1968 had afforded him the opportunity to launch into a ten-paragraph exposition of a rock opera he'd been considering, then called *Deaf, Dumb And Blind Boy*. Those comments would be the blueprint for *Tommy*, so much so that Townshend would later refer to it as the opera's "original book."[57] When Pete started to write and discuss his next opera, or at least Big Idea, in the press in late 1970, that might have also been the equivalent of taking down notes that could serve as its foundation.

"I'm sure it helped him crystallize things," says Altham. "It's very therapeutic, in a way, if you can talk to a sympathetic journalist. If you're talking to somebody you know likes your work and the band, you can open up a little bit more than you might to someone else. Consequently, sometimes you get feedback in that way, and that's one of the aspects that he used."[58]

"What I do is force myself to do it by announcing things up front," Townshend admitted in an interview for the 1975 book *In Their Own Words*. "*Tommy*, for example, I talked about at incredible length to Jann Wenner in a long, long article in *Rolling Stone* before I'd even finished writing it. I said so much that it just *had* to be finished – I had to get it done! I did the same thing with *Quadrophenia*. I announced it to everybody a long way ahead, so people started to build up to it. It's really good to do it that way, give somebody an idea. You can gauge your own enthusiasm. I mean it could be real genuine enthusiasm and involvement, or it could be an infatuation with an idea. So you can work it out by seeing how well you sell it to somebody else. And if you sell it really well you know that you're behind it. If you sell it to 50 people and you're still really up about it, then you know you're onto one that's going to get done."[59]

If Townshend had hinted at what he had up his sleeve with "a musical note that builds the basis of existence" in his September 1970 *Melody Maker* column, his interview with Roy Shipton in *Disc* the following month was far more specific. First off, Shipton announced, the album for which they'd done some recording in 1970 had been scrapped, as had the *Tommy* film. Instead, he reported, Pete had "the idea for an album that, when it is thrust on the ears of the record buying public, will be considered the successor to *Tommy*. But he isn't just trying to find a follow-up; he wants a follow-through, a development, to go a step further." Furthermore, this epic would also be a possible film.

As the story refers to Townshend already having written three songs "similar in potential" and, a few paragraphs down, an "LP of music," it's not entirely clear what and how much Pete had written at this point. He did make it clear, however, that the album for which 'Water,' 'I Don't Even Know Myself,' 'Postcard,' 'Now I'm A Farmer,' 'Heaven And Hell,' and 'Naked Eye' had been recorded had been abandoned for more promising ideas. He explained that since work had started on that doomed project, Kit Lambert had "come up with the idea for an album with a film. I've got an LP of music but I don't know if the structure is strong enough to hold a film. We won't get that together until next year, but there's definitely an album there."

Already the genesis of the film-album combination was getting muddled. Townshend ascribed the idea to Lambert, but it seems likely he'd discussed something of the sort with his Tattooist International friends. The rights to a

Tommy movie, according to Pete, had somehow passed to Warner Bros, who "can make a film whenever they want, with whoever they want" – another permutation of *Tommy* into cinema that never came to pass (though *Variety* had reported in June that a *Tommy* film backed by producer Ray Stark would be distributed by Warners or MGM). But Townshend seemed certain that some kind of film was in the works, as "Kit and Chris are really keen to get some sort of musical film together for The Who. Really, it's the only step we can take to keep us moving forward."

Turning his attention to the actual music that would serve as the film's base, Pete was already exhibiting the combination of fascinating elements and vague specifics that would frustrate The Who, their managers, and others as the project evolved. "I've got a kind of pivot idea, basically based on physics, closely linked with the things mystics have been saying for a long time about vibrations in music," he said. "Basically, it's about someone trying to discover the note that is everything, the essence, if you like, a musical sort of infinity. But, as we are not capable of finding it, he doesn't find it. It's a cyclic idea, a bit lame at the moment."[60]

At least he did have three songs that could fit into the embryonic concept: 'The Note' (to be retitled 'Pure And Easy'), 'We're Moving' (probably 'Going Mobile'), and 'The Two Of Us' (the ultimate fate of which remains unknown). It seems likely that 'Pure And Easy' was the "pivot idea" to which he was referring, as he'd later write in *Sounds* that it was "originally intended as the pivot piece for a film script I wrote called LIFE HOUSE."[61] His nod to mystics might well have been at least partially inspired by *The Mysticism Of Sound And Music: The Sufi Teaching Of Hazrat Inayat Khan.*

But the more he detailed the plot, the more Pete seemed to be losing the plot. "It's about a set of musicians, a group, who look like The Who, and behave remarkably like The Who, and they have a roadie who is desperately interested in ideals for humanity," he told *Disc*. "It's basically a science fiction fantasy idea. This roadie is wrapped up in electronics and synthesizers. He's fanatically serious about finding 'The Note' and spends all his time converting Egyptian charts and musical mysticisms into electronic circuitry – and discovers all these wonderful and weird oscillations. He's fantastically serious, but the group isn't.

"Anyway, this group find a note which, basically, creates complete devastation," Townshend continued. "And when everything is destroyed, only the real note, the true note that they have been looking for, is left. Of course, there is no one left to hear it; except the audience, of course, who are in a rather privileged position."

Perhaps over-optimistically, considering how things eventually turned out, he also said, "So far it's gained much better reaction within the group than *Tommy* ever did." And perhaps with an eye to how madman Keith Moon might fit into all this, he noted there would be more comedy this time around, with Moon already working on that end of things with the other great loon of the period's British pop scene, Viv Stanshall (whose own group, The Bonzo Dog Band, had broken up just half a year ago). "There is obviously scope for a fantasy film," Pete said. "But it's got to be a serious piece with a humor thing interwoven with it. I think that's the secret of doing anything successful. You have to take what you are doing seriously but you mustn't necessarily be serious about it yourself, all the time."

Townshend did, however, set a high benchmark for whatever he had in mind. "What I want to do," he said, "is attempt a follow-through and achieve something which will have as big an impact as *Tommy* did."[62]

CHAPTER 2

THE NEW REVOLUTION

When Pete Townshend announced his plans for an album-cum-film to the press in October 1970, The Who had recorded so few studio tracks since the completion of *Tommy* that it appeared as though he was suffering from writer's block. Just eight songs seem to have been finished: the half dozen for the abandoned LP or unissued EP, and the two for the single release of 'The Seeker.' Three of those weren't written by Townshend.

In fact, Pete had been composing and recording at home all along. But most of the general public wasn't aware of this, even when some of the songs were issued on a limited-edition LP (variously reported to have been pressed in quantities of 1,000 to 2,500 copies) to celebrate what would have been the 76th birthday of Meher Baba, who had died on January 31 1969.

As that birthday would have been February 25 1970, the album, entitled *Happy Birthday*, ended up marking the first anniversary of Baba's death. It was not a Pete Townshend solo album, as The Who's main man shared space with musical contributions by his experimental composer pal Ron Geesin and The Faces' Ronnie Lane, spoken word pieces by Allan Cohen, and poetry by Mike Da Costa. But Townshend's contributions were the ones that attracted most attention outside of Meher Baba's following. Even so, the LP largely escaped the radar even of Who fanatics, as it was available only by mail order from the Universal Spiritual League in London and the Meher Baba Information office in Berkeley, California.

Happy Birthday didn't wholly escape the mainstream media's attention, however. A small box on the final page of Townshend's 'In Love With Meher Baba' essay in the November 26 1970 issue of *Rolling Stone* gave the LP a complimentary review, as well as supplying readers with the information they needed to buy it by mail. Baba's US reps also engaged in a little direct marketing; one rock fan, Jodi Mitchell, remembers being handed a simple flyer advertising the record's mail-order availability (along with some other Meher Baba literature) on Telegraph Avenue near the campus of Berkeley's University of California branch. It wouldn't be long before the record was bootlegged, spurring the release of Townshend's first official solo LP, although the counterfeits wouldn't be deemed irritating enough to demand a corrective measure for a couple of years yet.

Happy Birthday occupies a curious place in The Who's early-70s timeline. There is no way of knowing exactly when Townshend's five tracks were recorded, but it was most likely shortly before the album's release, especially as one of them is a demo of 'The Seeker.' Other than 'The Seeker,' they don't bear especially strong links to the material he was penning for The Who on either side of *Happy Birthday*'s release. One, 'Content,' is actually a poem by fellow Baba devotee Maud Kennedy that Pete set to music. Yet more off the wall was a quite pleasant and moving rendition of the Cole Porter classic 'Begin The Beguine,' included because it was one of Baba's favorite songs. 'Mary Jane' is a nice drumless country-rock tune, and 'Love Man' a bittersweet romantic ditty with underlying vulnerability subverting the surface machismo. Most reflective of Baba's influence, and the standout other than 'The Seeker,' is the melancholy 'Day Of Silence,' as befitting an album dedicated to a man who spent his last 44 years without uttering a word. This was written on piano on July 10 (most likely in the year 1969), the day Baba followers choose to spend in actual silence while communicating by pen and paper. Townshend took the dictum seriously enough that he didn't pen the lyrics until the day afterward, so as not to break the 'silence.'

What these recordings – and Townshend's prolific home recordings in general – provided was space to make music that was ('The Seeker' aside) not only highly dissimilar to The Who's, but unlikely to find a comfortable place on any Who release. Their rustic folkiness and introspective, philosophical tone, if not wholly absent from The Who's quieter tracks, was certainly unlike the power chord-driven crunch of much of their output. 'Content' and 'Day Of Silence' in particular gave Pete the chance to express a more spiritual, gentler side than the public was accustomed to from his work. The pensive gloom of 'Day Of Silence' wobble off the grooves like a dying autumn day; 'Content,' while lighter in mood, has a similar stately sobriety. These might have been too reflective of Townshend's particular affinities with Baba for the rest of The Who to be comfortable with; and it's impossible to see the group tackling 'Begin The Beguine' in any way, shape, or form, even in jest.

In addition, their placement on an obscure compilation album, unavailable in stores, gave Townshend a low-pressure means of airing some of his more whimsical creations. By and large, the media would not scrutinize his efforts, nor the slightly lo-fi home-recording technique that gave rise to the odd wobble of 'Day Of Silence' and made his solo 'The Seeker' come off as rather lumpy and rudimentary in comparison to The Who's version. There would be no expectations for the album to perform well commercially, no worry about it affecting sales of proper Who product, and little if any speculation that Townshend's solo efforts indicated a loosening commitment to The Who, or even a desire to leave the band for his own career. His Who records could remain both of a piece with their past work and characteristic of the band as a whole, something he'd need to ensure as he settled into the task of writing enough material for the project he'd brazenly outlined. That project, however, would also be heavily dependent on home demos for its ignition, with much more at stake this time around.

While it's impossible to establish precisely when Pete Townshend began writing material specifically for the still-unnamed *Lifehouse*, it's likely a good deal of it was done in late 1970. It's almost certain that he'd penned 'Pure And Easy' and 'Going Mobile' by late October 1970, when he revealed what were probably provisional titles for the songs (entitled 'The Note' and 'We're Moving' respectively) in *Disc*. It's probable that a good number of other songs were done by the end of the year, as The Who held the first of a series of public rehearsals at London's Young Vic Theatre on January 4 1971. Those rehearsals were planned and presented with *Lifehouse* in mind, so presumably Townshend had more than a couple of tunes to present to the band, and probably a good few more than that.

The songs would be worked up at Townshend's home studio, which had evolved quite a bit since he'd used two Vortexion mono tape machines and one microphone at his parents' home in Ealing in 1964. If his liner notes to his official *Scoop* collection of demos are accurate, by late 1970 he was on his sixth home studio, now in Twickenham. With two small adjacent rooms and a separate control room, as well as a Bösendorfer grand piano, this is where The Who had recorded the half-dozen tracks from their half-complete, half-hearted attempt at a full-length album earlier in 1970.

"The demos I made to accompany the *Lifehouse* film script I wrote in '71 are among the best I have ever produced," he wrote. "I had come fully to grips with working multi-track rather than bounce from machine to machine a la Phil Spector. I had managed to get a good tight drum sound in a room only ten feet by fifteen that was crammed with synthesizers, organs and a seven-foot grand piano."[1]

One recording professional who got an inside look at the setup Townshend used for his demos was John Alcock, who subsequently helped construct The Who's Ramport Studios (as well as producing much of John Entwistle's early-70s solo material). "I was one of the founders of an English company named Unitrack," he says. "The goal of the company was to develop multi-track tape machines to compete with companies such as Studer, Ampex, 3M, and Scully. During this time, I started thinking about project studios for artists and small production companies. During my travels around major studios and meeting with some musicians, I was persuading people to offer design feedback and to subsequently test prototype machines." It was in the course of those activities that he met Pete.

"Most musicians in those days either booked studios or had really simple, low-quality gear to record demos," Alcock says. "Pete was one of the very rare musicians who wanted to extend this idea to studio-quality work for later inclusion in, or to form the basis of, tracks in final album recordings. He was way ahead of his time, very knowledgeable, and had developed a keen interest in, and understanding of, hardware synths, together with building and running his studio for his songwriting purposes with the expectation that he could later use elements of this work in final recordings."

Townshend was also ahead of his time, incidentally, in seeing both a need for better home studios for rock musicians and a market for such studios. "He already had amassed substantial knowledge about recording, and we had many common interests," Alcock says. "He liked the idea of developing project studios and thought that this could be a viable business. With the benefit of hindsight it seems we were a couple of decades before our time!" Townshend even invested in and helped Alcock start "a new company, Trackplan, with a view to putting packages of recording equipment together for artists: some standard items, others purpose-built and designed components such as the main recording console, with an innovative design so that they could be (fairly) easily operated by musicians without the need for a recording engineer."[2]

Although Pete played everything, his demos were very much crafted with The Who's sound in mind. "We all know each other so well now that Pete can go and make a demo and he'll play bass just like John, and he'll sing just like I sing," Roger Daltrey said in a January 1971 interview for Gary Herman's book *The Who*. "So it's got to the stage where he knows exactly what it's going to sound like when we first play it. But even then it still changes a hell of a lot in the studio, the arrangements and things; it's a group thing."[3]

Which songs would have been included on *Lifehouse*, and in what running order, are questions that seem doomed to vex rock scholars for eternity. Certainly, about 20 numbers were in consideration at some time or another; indeed, that's the exact number of "new songs" reported by *Melody Maker* as earmarked for the film in a 1971 story.[4] Trying to determine the contents and the order, however, leads to as many different mockups as attempts to reconstruct the running order of The Beach Boys' *Smile*. Townshend's subsequent attempts to reconstruct it, on disc and in concert, are imperfect as well. The two CDs of demos on the 2000 *Lifehouse Chronicles* boxed set clearly include some songs that couldn't have been completed until years after 1971, even if seeds had been planted in the early 70s.

To muddy the waters more, his concert DVD *Music From Lifehouse* (assembled from concerts on February 25–26 2000), while apparently a reconstruction of the song cycle for live performance, has a slightly different selection of tunes and sequence. This suggests that Townshend himself never quite determined what would have gone where. There's also no way to ascertain whether the songs were written in line with a preset storyline or whether *Lifehouse*'s plot, such as it was, was dictated by the songs after they'd been written. More likely, the compositions and story may have been jumbled together in a haphazard fashion as the project progressed.

To guess which of these songs would have found their way onto *Lifehouse* and how they would have formed even the semblance of a story, it's necessary to lay out the basics of the plot. That's hard to boil into a few paragraphs, but Townshend made a game effort in the February 7 1971 *New York Times*, the first occasion on which he tried to explain the story in reasonable detail. He probably felt particularly comfortable doing so to this particular reporter, Nik Cohn, who'd recently published one of the first rock histories, *Awopbopaloobop Alopbamboom* (entitled *Rock From The Beginning* in the USA). The young British critic had been a fervent Who fan for years and even served as partial inspiration for 'Pinball Wizard,' both he and Townshend being avid pinball players.

Pete told Cohn that the still-untitled film's protagonist would be "Bobby." The story would take place about 20 years in the future, "when everyone has been boarded up inside their houses and put in special garments called experience suits, through which the government feeds them programs to keep them entertained."[5] Bobby's role was as an "electronic wizard" – not a pinball one – who would take over a rock theater that had fallen into disuse and rename it the Lifehouse to counter the government regime. His role, too, would be fluid in Townshend's retellings, as even by the end of 1971, he was describing Bobby in *Crawdaddy* as "an old rock and roll musician," talking "a lot about his memories of the old days, which is basically just me, rapping."[6]

"Next he chooses a basic audience of about 300 people and prepares a chart for each of them, based on astrology and their personalities and other data," he told the *New York Times*. "From their charts he arrives at a sound for each of them – a single note or a series, a cycle or something electronic – anything that best expresses each individual." This was an obvious outgrowth of both his reading of *The Mysticism Of Sound And Music: The Sufi Teaching Of Hazrat Inayat Khan* and his conversion of personal data into "pulse-modulated frequencies" at Cambridge.

Bobby's experiments build an audience that attains "a state of harmony, then a state of enlightenment." The Who – and a possible filmed concert – fit into the scheme of things on the Lifehouse stage, commenting on the sounds and celebrating them. "But they aren't the heroes, and neither is Bobby," Townshend said. "The real center is the equipment itself, the amps and tapes and synthesizers, all the machines, because they transmit the sounds. The hardware is the hero."

As the sounds get more intense, Bobby "takes over the government programs and replaces them with the new sounds, so that everyone wearing the experience suits gets plugged into them and shares them, and it goes on – the sounds keep developing, the audience keeps attaining higher states and, in the end, all the sounds merge into one, like a massive insane square dance," Pete said. "And everyone starts bouncing up and down together, faster and faster, wilder and wilder, closer and closer and closer. And finally it gets too much, the energy, and they actually leave their bodies. They disappear." There were, Townshend said, "multiple subplots and refinements," some of which he wouldn't fully elaborate in print until years later. But that, he announced, was "the essence."[7]

It really wouldn't be until his liner notes for the 2000 *Lifehouse Chronicles* boxed set that some of those "subplots and refinements" were enumerated in a more or less comprehensible fashion. These notes name the characters Ray and Sally, parents in a farming family in remote Scotland, traveling to London in search of their runaway daughter, Mary. Mary has gone to London to see a concert that hopes to subvert the very foundations of a British society that's had to don space suits of sorts to survive, so polluted has the environment become. The suits are connected by a huge grid that delivers both survival essentials and entertainment, led by a dictator named Jumbo. With the focus having narrowed – in a possible echo of François Truffaut's 1966 film *Fahrenheit 451* – to easily digested stories, this mass-delivered entertainment is now devoid of music.

That's where Bobby comes in with his concert festival, a possible echo of the rock festivals becoming all the rage in the late 60s, The Who having played at several of the most famous in Monterey, Woodstock, and the Isle of Wight. In a crucial detail not noted back in early 1971, the suits are no longer necessary for survival, and Bobby hopes the music will so energize the audience that they'll throw them off. In the *Lifehouse* world, that's the ultimate anti-fascist statement, so military forces try to stop the concert (where, in some continuity with the story's outset, the entire Scottish family is in attendance). But it's too late to stop Bobby's experiment from taking effect, with the concert audience disappearing in a dance of ecstasy – as do lots of other listeners, listening at home through their suits.[8]

Even as a sketch, it took a lot of faith for many people to swallow, as Townshend would find out when he tried to explain and implement *Lifehouse* over the next few months. "Pete was thinking that somewhere along the line some amazing supernatural thing would happen during the performance, where people would evolve into a higher state of consciousness," says Richard Barnes, who would remain a friend and occasional sounding-board to Townshend throughout the 60s and 70s. "I thought that's where most people left him. I took a lot more LSD than Pete did, but even I felt, 'Hold on a minute, Pete.'"[9]

Filming such a fantasy would be an enormous challenge, especially with 1971 film technology. Writing a score that was integral to the story would have seemed scarcely more plausible.

At the very least, it's known that eight of the nine songs that ended up on the 1971 LP *Who's Next* were demoed by Pete at home and intended for *Lifehouse*. (The exception was John Entwistle's 'My Wife.') But, as the existence of so many more demos proves, there probably would have been enough songs to make *Lifehouse* a double album.

A group of these demos was actually been bootlegged around 1972 on the infamous Trade Mark Of Quality label as *The Genius Of Pete Townshend*. The eight tracks included demos of five songs to make the cut for *Who's Next* ('Behind Blue Eyes,' 'Going Mobile,' 'Love Ain't For Keeping,' 'Won't Get Fooled Again,' 'The Song Is Over') and, more enticingly for early-70s customers, three songs yet to be issued by The Who at that point ('Pure And Easy,' 'Mary,' and 'Time Is Passing'). According to Clinton Heylin's *Bootleg*, the album's appearance generated "rumors of theft from Townshend himself, from Track [Records'] vault and even from a radio station that Townshend had entrusted with an acetate."[10]

The inclusion of a 'Bargain' demo on *Scoop* (which also included the 'Behind The Blue Eyes' and 'Mary' demos) further whetted fans' appetites for *Lifehouse* prototypes. These were finally sated by the official – albeit low-profile – release of all this and more on two CDs of demos included in Townshend's 2000 *Lifehouse Chronicles* boxed set. Beyond the pleasant shock of being able to hear the material in a format blessed by the artist himself, rather than on furtive underground releases, the discs offer scholars an in-depth look into the creative process seldom granted for public consumption by major songwriters.

Yet these demos – still unknown to the average Who listener, especially as they were part of a six-CD boxed set sold only through Townshend's website and already out of print – are more than mere historical relics. Yes, the percussion is boxy; yes, Pete is unable to match Roger Daltrey's range and lungpower; and yes, there's a sketchy and unfinished feel to virtually everything. But demos often get closer to the naked heart of songs than the official end results, and while these versions have a tentative vulnerability missing from the more polished group productions, that's part of their attraction. While Townshend's vocals were thin and tremulous, they possessed a tender everyman quality missing from Daltrey's, and one that seemed more in tune with the complex intellectual and philosophical impulses that had sparked the creation of the compositions in the first place. The songs that didn't make the cut for *Who's Next* – or, in some cases, never found a place on standard Who or solo Townshend releases – also supply valuable pieces of the missing *Lifehouse* puzzle.

Whatever song sequence is mooted for *Lifehouse*, all agree that it would have opened with 'Baba O'Riley.' Its survey of a "teenage wasteland" – perhaps a nod, if only subconscious, to the unfilmed Rolling Stones vehicle *Only Lovers Left Alive* – and desolate landscape set the scene for *Lifehouse*'s grim world of the future; its bombastic riffs are also suitable for a grandstanding curtain-raiser. A nearly ten-minute instrumental demo – first included on another limited-edition Meher Baba-affiliated release, the early 1972 compilation LP *I Am*, and itself edited down from a tape lasting around a half hour – contains the bed of the song, before the addition of lyrics. This features the original pattern Townshend devised for the tune, based on the personal data on himself that he tried to translate into synthesizer-manipulated organ notes and beats, although the song's core hard-rock riff is present on both piano and guitar.

A passing comment to *Melody Maker* in July 1971 (in Pete's track-by-track description of *Who's Next*) indicates that Townshend intended the synthesizer to play a prominent role in *Lifehouse*'s material. "This is the way we expected most of the music in the film to sound," he said, "because we have a pre-recorded tape of the synthesizer in the background."[11] The instrumental version sticks to the structure of the familiar Who recording for the most part, but without the melody line delivered by the vocal. But the bridge in particular veers into a foggier, more extended netherland, introducing disquieting minor-flavored clusters not heard in the official version. And the extended double-time coda, made into a jig of sorts by Dave Arbus's violin on *Who's Next*, runs for a good three minutes. As the organ is subjected to tape delay and the beat doubled, the synthesized notes multiply and collapse upon themselves in a fashion that takes it close to avant-garde territory.

Townshend's vocal demo of 'Baba O'Riley,' in addition to the crucial addition of lyrics, is primarily an exercising in editing, pruning the length by a couple of minutes. That vocal is an illustration of how Pete, for all his increasing facility as a one-man band in the home studio, really did need The Who to put some of the material over. While Daltrey's full-throated wail and cocky roar is ideally suited to delivery of the verse, Townshend is in comparison strained and forced, although he'd retain his lead vocal role for the more delicate and wistful bridge. Other minor variations are a swelling 15-second tone at the beginning and a descending fanfare at the end of the bridge, both of which would be axed when the arrangement was cut down yet again for the five-minute *Who's Next* track.

More than any other *Lifehouse* song, 'Baba O'Riley' reflects the underrated influence of contemporary experimental composers on Townshend's work during this period. One in particular was saluted in the title, a great enigma upon *Who's Next*'s original release. Now it's pretty widely known that 'Baba' is Meher Baba, and somewhat less commonly understood that 'O'Riley' is a homage to Terry Riley. Riley had recently made deeper inroads into the rock audience than any such composer with his late-60s album *A Rainbow In Curved Air*. The looping, overlapping, and stuttering single-note electric piano riffs on the 18-minute piece of the same name, which occupies the whole of side one, bear clear similarities to the synthesizer patterns used by Townshend on *Lifehouse*. Indeed, they are reflected in much of his synthesizer work inside and outside The Who in the early 70s, even as far as the soundtrack for the 1975 *Tommy* movie.

"I used to stay with The Who's lighting man when I was in London in the early 70s, and he told me that he and Pete took psychedelics and listened to *A Rainbow In Curved Air* for hours," says Riley. "So I was aware that he knew about my 60s albums on CBS. I called him a few times in the 70s and we discussed music things, and he expressed being deeply affected by my music. It was mutual. In a phone conversation once with Pete, he mentioned to me that he owned something like 30 copies of *A Rainbow In Curved Air*. We finally met about five years ago when he invited me to a show The Who did near Sacramento."

It is also likely that Townshend knew another of Riley's most famous works, the 1964 composition *In C*, in which musicians are asked to play 53 phrases, but starting at different times. "The kinetic repetitive bright major mode opening of 'Baba O'Riley,'" says Riley, "is reminiscent of *In C* and is one of the most brilliant intros in pop music. It would be a good candidate for one of its sources of inspiration. Clearly 'Baba O'Riley' is inspired on many levels, and seems a brilliant fusion of the rivers of thought flowing through classical and pop music at the time. Pete made it clear from the beginning that it was a kind of homage to his guru Meher Baba and my humble self. I still have kids come up to me after my concerts asking me if I am *the* Baba O'Riley. ... Now that I am in my mid-seventies, I guess I am."[12]

The repetitive electronic instrumental patterns heard in the music of composers such as Riley weren't used in nearly as avant-garde a form by Townshend and The Who. Nonetheless, Pete's enthusiasm for such music wasn't mere dilettantism. Riley was probably not the only such composer Townshend appreciated, as Pete was friendly with Ron Geesin, a quite different example. In fact, Geesin would open a couple of shows for The Who in 1971, and Townshend is thanked "for encouragement and financial backing to make the presentation of the LP possible" on the back of Ron's 1973 album *As He Stands*.

Although he stresses that they didn't talk about composers like Riley when his and Townshend's families got together to socialize, Geesin does see Riley's influence in songs like 'Baba O'Riley.' "That tape delay technique is kind of like an electronic Terry Riley, because whatever you put into the system, it repeats," he says. "But you can put in things that are slightly off the beat, and get complex patterns. So you still get a kind of repeating, but it's like a moiré pattern. When you look through a gauze at another gauze, you get almost like a separating of light, and a kind of rainbow effect."[13]

Beyond the title, Meher Baba's influence on 'Baba O'Riley' seems more musical than lyrical. "The nearest thing I got to the type of music I thought I would come up with [for *Lifehouse*] was 'Baba O'Riley,'" Townshend told

Cameron Crowe in *Penthouse*. "It was a theme that I put together in reaction to Meher Baba himself. That was his theme. That was the sound I thought represented the power and, at the same time, the ease of his personality."[14]

The lyrics might have come into the picture after the base of 'Baba O'Riley' took shape as an instrumental but they are hardly incidental to either the song or the storyline. The famous opening line about fighting for meals out in the fields came right from the *Lifehouse* film script. As Pete explained to *Circus* in late 1971, the lyrics as a whole are specifically "about the farmer, out in the fields, a 50-year-old man, whose kids have run away. He's saying that the whole of youth is wasted. Wherever he looks, all he sees is wasted teenagers."[15] In the *Lifehouse* scheme of things, that would probably mean the farmer who serves as the narrator of 'Baba O'Riley' is the father in pursuit of the runaway named 'Mary,' with both father and daughter figuring in a few other *Lifehouse* songs. The scenario of a farmer and fields being at the center of the action also fits in with Denis Postle's recollection of the song having been written as a sample track for the unfilmed *Guitar Farm* project.

'Baba O'Riley' occupies a relatively understandable place in the *Lifehouse* scheme of things, as do a couple of numbers that obviously would have been placed at or near the finale, 'Won't Get Fooled Again' and 'The Song Is Over.' The role and order of the other five Townshend songs first heard on *Who's Next* isn't as clear. At a casual hearing, 'Going Mobile' seems to be one of the more likely candidates for smooth integration into the *Lifehouse* plot. This celebration of life on the road – as well as evasion of authority figures, as personified by a policeman and a taxman – would seem to fit in well with a chase scene of sorts in which rogue rebels hit the highway as both an expression of freedom and an up-yours to Big Brother.

Townshend made a convincing case for its role in *Lifehouse* on a 1996 BBC radio special on the project. "What formed in my head was not just the song 'Going Mobile,' but the idea that I was in a capsule and it had two air conditioners and an extraordinary kind of filtering system," he said. "What I kind of got addicted to with it was that you didn't get any fumes, basically, and I realized that there's something about air-conditioned, recycled air in cars, which is that you don't get pollution. I figured people in the future that had the ability to clean their own air would have an advantage over everybody else. And so this became part of the story of this world. Who would survive out there in the world who wasn't attached to an experience suit, being fed pure air and pure food? Who would survive who didn't elect to put the suit on? It would either be people who lived at the extremes of society, up in Scotland where the water was clean or something, or alternatively, people who had managed to get hold of air-conditioned cars. The song was about freedom."[16] As Townshend later made clear, it would be the parents chasing their runaway daughter who would be "going mobile" in such a science fiction-type setting, although the tune has an uplifting joy rather at odds with what you'd expect a worried couple to be feeling as they hit the motorway.

In reality its inspiration may have been far more mundane. According to Townshend's *Melody Maker* song-by-song *Who's Next* rundown, the song is "about me riding around in the mobile caravan I've bought."[17] Pete's home demo is pretty close to The Who's arrangement but gives more prominence to acoustic guitars and misses the futuristic wah-wah effects that would be added a few months down the line. It was also a better fit for Townshend's voice (always far better at the upper wispy range than the lower bluesier one) than 'Baba O'Riley,' and would end up being the only *Who's Next* cut to feature him on lead vocals for the entire song.

'Getting In Tune' could easily pass for a reasonably straightforward declaration of good vibes with a hint of romance. But knowing what we do about both *Lifehouse* and what Townshend was reading, it's hard to deny a likely influence from *The Mysticism Of Sound And Music: The Sufi Teaching Of Hazrat Inayat Khan*. Lyrical declarations of singing a well-fitting note, finding harmonies in a loved one's eyes, hearing a symphony in the heart, getting in tune "to the straight and narrow" (one pure note), all could be in line with, or made to fit, a story driven by a quest for the ultimate musical note, and colored by the spiritual connection between music and emotion. The song was "a straight pinch from Inayat Khan's discourse on mysticism of sound," Pete told *ZigZag*, "where he just says music is one way of individuals getting in tune with one another, and I just picked up on that."[18] The most piano-based of the tunes on *Who's Next*, it is close, in its demo version, to the arrangement on the LP, although the early prototype also uses organ.

'Behind Blue Eyes,' perhaps *Who's Next*'s most famous song besides 'Won't Get Fooled Again' and 'Baba O'Riley,' can (like most of the *Lifehouse* songs) stand on its own without any obvious association to what we know of *Lifehouse*'s storyline. But judging by Townshend's extensive comments on the composition in his now-rare 1977 book *A Decade Of The Who: An Authorized*

History In Music, Paintings, Words And Photographs, it would have been a vital inclusion, as it's "about a character called 'BRICK,' who was one of the principals in the 'Life House' story."[19] Most epics need a villain, and apparently Brick would fit the bill, as Townshend writes in his *Scoop* liner notes that 'Behind Blue Eyes' is "about the villain in the story feeling he is forced into playing a two-faced role."[20] Yet the mysterious Brick is not mentioned by name elsewhere in *Lifehouse* literature, including Townshend's summary of the story in the liner notes to *Lifehouse Chronicles* and his *Lifehouse* radio play of the late 90s.

Inevitably, 'Behind Blue Eyes' has come to be seen as a self-portrait of the blue-eyed composer. "As I wrote it, there are, I suppose, a few aspects of my own character revealed in it," he said in *A Decade Of The Who*. "I do tend to lie my way out of things more often than I should – but I'm not as sad and bitter as I seem as the composer of this. I tried to feel like the character would feel when he was betrayed by his workmates. Whatever, people think it's personal so I suppose it's personal – the customer is <u>always right</u>," Pete wrote, underlining the final two words for emphasis.[21] The key line in the bridge about cracking open a clenched fist had its roots in both Meher Baba and real-life experience, Townshend first writing the phrase as a prayer to Baba after losing his temper with a groupie in Denver (probably when The Who played there on June 9 and June 10 of 1970).

Of the *Lifehouse* demos later reworked for *Who's Next*, 'Behind Blue Eyes' is one of the most different from the familiar version, in perhaps the most interesting way. (Pete's then-wife Karen apparently thought so, telling Townshend she liked it from the kitchen underneath after he'd finished the harmony vocals.) Where The Who alternate between haunting acoustic verses and an extended, more typically power-chord-driven bridge that rocked hard, Pete's home recording is gently folky the whole way through.

The bridge especially is in marked contrast to The Who's version, with lonesome plucked chords the only backing for Townshend's vocal. On *Who's Next*, Daltrey snarls that bridge like a man out for bloodthirsty vengeance, Keith Moon doubling the sentiment with his bat-out-of-hell drumming. Townshend sings it with an entirely different restrained menace, although in this context the request to have fingers put down his throat if he swallows anything evil sounds a bit callow. In this incarnation of the song, Townshend sounds at his folkiest, and indeed the arching line near the end of the verses about empty dreams bears a strong melodic resemblance to a line in the traditional folk standard 'The Wayfaring Stranger.' A couple of slightly different demo-sounding versions have circulated unofficially, one of which can be easily differentiated from the cut on *Lifehouse Chronicles* as it starts with chunky chords rather than delicate picking.

The most conventional song on *Who's Next*, and the most obscure (as much as any track on one of the most oft-played LPs of all time can be considered obscure), is 'Love Ain't For Keeping,' a straight-ahead mid-tempo ode to lust. Listeners could be forgiven for thinking this wasn't intended for *Lifehouse*, and was perhaps added to *Who's Next* to make the album sound more conventional as a whole. Yet as Townshend's introduction to the song on the *Music From Lifehouse* DVD makes clear, it too is key to the story, although certainly in a lighter vein than 'Behind Blue Eyes,' 'Won't Get Fooled Again,' and 'Baba O'Riley.'

"In the story, there are a couple of love affairs," he explained to the Sadler's Wells audience in London. "There's a lost love affair between the man who comes to London to chase his daughter, who's run away from home. And there's that lost love affair between him and his wife. And there's a new love affair growing between a young man who's involved in the concert which is happening down in London and the daughter. And this song ['Love Ain't For Keeping'] is actually about the lost love of the older couple, the mother and the father." Perhaps he, The Who, and Kit Lambert were thinking any film had to have an element of romance to have any chance of broad commercial appeal. Townshend's demo is quite short, lasting a little more than a minute and a half, and distinguished from The Who's arrangement not just by Pete's airy high vocal and backup harmonies but by some light synthesizer burbles that didn't make it onto *Who's Next*. And some of the lyrics do carry *Lifehouse*-ish foreboding that could easily be missed from the tune's easygoing surface, with the air fouled by black foundry ash and burning firewood.

A popular hard-rocker, 'Bargain' might not seem to have an obvious place in the *Lifehouse* opus. Nor would it seem inspired by Meher Baba, but according to Pete's hand-scribbled note at the top of its sheet music in *A Decade Of The Who*, that's precisely the case. "This song is simply about 'losing' one's ego," he proclaimed. "As a devotee of Meher Baba I constantly try to lose myself, and find him. I'm not very successful I'm afraid, but this song expresses how much of a bargain it would be even to lose everything in order to be at one with God."[22] He was vaguer when introducing the number at a December 13 1971 concert in San Francisco, describing it as "a song about what you get from being here. If you're alive – whether you're rich or you're poor, whether you're up or you're down – if you're alive you're getting a bargain."

While Meher Baba had been an influence on much of Townshend's writing since 1967, this and 'Baba O'Riley' are the only apparent instances in which it strongly informed a *Lifehouse* composition, albeit so subtly that most listeners never suspected its presence. Townshend's demo is taken at a slower, chunkier (and less effective) pace than the breezy and speedy Who version, complete with handclaps. It too uses synthesizer, but to create gliding, swooping riffs rather than the kind of pulses that form the bedrock of 'Baba O'Riley' and 'Won't Get Fooled Again.'

"Joe Walsh [then guitarist in The James Gang, with whom Townshend had become friendly while touring the USA] had just presented me with an old Gretsch Chet Atkins guitar and it more or less played me on this track," Pete wrote in his notes to the 'Bargain' demo on *Scoop*. "At this time I was still coming to grips with the incredibly rich harmonics that my ARP 2500 synthesizer produced, even with a single voice, and here one part seemed enough."[23]

That leaves two songs with the aura of a hard-to-follow finale, and as it happens each of them ended different LP sides of *Who's Next*, although probably not with the effect that Townshend intended them to have as *Lifehouse* showpieces. In his cut-by-cut *Who's Next* narrative, Townshend told *Melody Maker* that 'The Song Is Over' "was going to be the last number in the film."[24] Far more improbably, he informed the paper's readers that it would probably be recorded by Petula Clark, a curiosity which perhaps fortunately never came to pass. Almost as improbably, he'd later hint that it would have been played in the film by The Bonzo Dog Band, an inappropriately comic choice for a song he aptly described in the same article as "like a mixture of being sad and wistful, but at the same time there's a high point."[25]

Although it is an elegiac ballad to a failed quest in its verses, in its chorus 'The Song Is Over' becomes a triumphantly upbeat ode to the power of music and the determination of the singer to spread it. Perhaps The Who didn't want to leave theatergoers on too downbeat a note had *Lifehouse* ended in tragedy, leaving some room for a ray of hope. Townshend's home demo is one of the more interesting variants from *Who's Next*, with a cheesy but rather endearing organ (almost certainly played on a 1968 Lowrey Berkshire Deluxe TBO-1 model) taking the place of Nicky Hopkins's familiar piano on the opening verse, asserting itself at other points as well. Daltrey would take the harder-rocking choruses on *Who's Next*, but here Pete takes the vocal all the way, adding some ebullient, high background harmonies here and there. The demo version also shares a brief coda with The Who arrangement, in which the first line of 'Pure And Easy' is reprised, here with a more martial drum roll.

'Won't Get Fooled Again' probably would have been the penultimate number in *Lifehouse*, but after its use as the final track on *Who's Next*, it's difficult for the average fan to think of it as anything but the last word on The Who's 1971 output. Although some of *Lifehouse*'s plot, and some of Townshend's lyrics, could be seen as implicitly political in their anti-authoritarian nature, here politics came to the front and center. And not the politics of some safely distant future, but the nature of political power and revolution in all eras, including the one Pete and his audience were living through in the early 70s.

Here Townshend goes beyond the usual rebellious call-to-arms to take a stance that wouldn't automatically be welcomed by a large part of The Who's audience. Revolutionary change, the song wryly observes, might be exciting and necessary, but the differences between the revolutionaries and the despots they toppled weren't as big as either side might have you believe. The very nature of power, he suggested, corrupts and makes the prospect of real, significant change dubious, if not hopeless. Had this been used in a successful *Lifehouse* film, the scene would no doubt have been thrilling, the lyrics including a built-in role for Townshend himself as the guitarist praying not to get duped once more.

This wouldn't have meant much, naturally, if not for some of hard rock's most memorable guitar riffs; a synthesizer pulse even more hypnotic than the 'Baba O'Riley' intro; and, more than any other *Lifehouse* song, enough hooks for a hit single (which it would become in due time). Townshend's demo again testifies to how fully worked-out most of his arrangements were before he passed them on to The Who. Yet it does sound a bit anemic compared to the famous, anthemic Who recording, taken at a clunky slower pace (at times kept by handclaps) with less confidently etched guitar-lines. And there was no way Townshend would match the cathartic, blood-curdling Daltrey scream that led into the *Who's Next* coda.

Although it succeeds as a universal statement about the nature of revolution and authority in general, 'Won't Get Fooled Again' also had a specific role to play in the *Lifehouse* plot. "At one point in the story there's an offer made to the wild ones, the gypsies," Townshend told BBC Radio One's Roger Scott in 1989. "They're offered a kind of amnesty if they accept the status quo. In other words, 'You come into the system, you be part of the system, you become systemized, you come onto the grid with us, instead of running wild concerts and living this wild life, causing a threat to the way that we want to run society, come in with us and we'll give you power in return.' And the hero of the piece warns, 'Don't be fooled, don't get taken in. If you become a leader or I become a leader, we'll just be as bad as everybody else.'"[26]

If the sociopolitical side of 'Won't Get Fooled Again' hit closer to home in early 70s culture than the rest of *Lifehouse*, that might be because part of its inspiration – or, at least, its jaded view of revolutionaries – may have been literally close to Townshend's home. At the time, Pete was living near the Eel Pie Hotel on Eel Pie Island in the River Thames. The hotel's dance hall had seen its share of notable jazz, R&B, and rock shows in the 60s, and among the bands to play gigs on the island were The Rolling Stones, Pink Floyd, The Yardbirds, and The Who themselves. By the late 60s, however, the hotel had been occupied by anarchists and turned into a commune.

As one-time member Chris Faiers writes in his online memoir *Eel Pie Dharma*, a fellow commune resident had befriended Townshend, who even lent him a 16-track tape recorder that appeared in one of the hotel's rooms. "Townshend's house was on the embankment at the foot of the Eel Pie bridge," Faiers writes. "The story went that [commune resident] Mark had taken to visiting Townshend on his nocturnal wanderings, and Townshend initially found Mark interesting, possibly as some sort of acid savant. Their friendship didn't last long, though, the story going that Mark had made a pass at Townshend's wife, and the volatile Townshend had chased Mark back across the bridge with an axe!"[27]

According to commune founder-member, Gavin Kilty, "He would visit the commune regularly, clearly with a view to participating in and becoming involved in the general counterculture movement that to him we represented. (Of course, looking back with a great deal of hindsight, I cannot say, hand on heart, that we were not just there to have a good time, but that is another story.) He often donated equipment to us because we told him we wanted to start a band. He was not a hippie by any stretch of the imagination, but he was interested."

Townshend's interest even extended to some hospitality that – even more than his inviting *Melody Maker* reporters inside his home for tea with the family – seems unfathomable for a rock superstar. "I and Peter Crisp would go over to his lovely house across the river in Richmond and he would allow us to play his guitars," says Kilty. "I fancied myself as a drummer and would often bash away on his kit upstairs, much to his musical disgust, as Peter later told me. We were clearly pestering him because one day we came over in 'high' spirits and he refused to let us in. And that was that."[28]

That would soon be that for the commune as well, with *Rolling Stone* reporting on February 4 1971 – more than four months prior to the release of 'Won't Get Fooled Again' – that it had dwindled to about 30 squatters in "a rotting hulk of a condemned building waiting for the wreckers." In the early autumn of the previous year, the article stated, "things began to go downhill rapidly. The Hell's Angels and skinheads discovered that the commune was weak and untogether and moved in on it. ... Violence became a regular thing, and stealing was so common that locks were put on all the sleeping rooms."[29]

Forty years later, some former Eel Pie commune dwellers think Townshend used 'Won't Get Fooled Again' to vent his disillusionment with his neighbors in particular, and the counterculture in general. "We did not impress him with our counterculture credentials," says Kilty. "And I do not blame him. However, to use the experience of a couple of naive hippies to dismiss the counterculture and to not 'get fooled again' is a bit rich. In the underground culture of London, The Who were never really included. Not psychedelic enough, and slightly aggressive. Still, all water under the bridge now."[30]

The disillusionment was mutual, as Faiers adds when asked to elaborate on Pete's interactions with the commune. "Townshend had a pocketful of marbles, which he said someone had shoved through his mail slot, and Townshend interpreted this gesture as threatening," he recalls. "His demeanor was taunting and vaguely aggressive. At the time I felt he wanted us to beg for a marble from the great musician, and no longer being into worshiping 'rock gods' after having met a few, including George Harrison, I wandered off – maybe a tad more disillusioned, as it seems Townshend must have also eventually become with the denizens of the hotel."[31] (For good measure, Faiers also speculates Pete might have gotten the idea for the "finger down my throat" line of 'Behind Blue Eyes' after hearing about an accidental poisoning at the commune.)

In *NME* in 1971, Townshend confirmed that 'Won't Get Fooled Again' was written "at a time when I was getting barraged by people at the Eel Pie commune. They live opposite me, and there was like a love affair going on between me and them. ... At one point there was an amazing scene where the commune was really working, but then the acid started flowing and I got on the end of some psychotic conversations and I just thought 'Oh fuck it!' I don't really want to be talking to people about things flying around in space."[32]

More than 30 years later, in the *Amazing Journey* documentary, Pete said the song was "exacerbated a bit" by the Eel Pie crowd. "They used to come and knock on the door," Pete recalled, "and say, 'Give us food.' And I'd say, OK and I'd give them some food, and the next day they'd come: 'Give us more food!' And I'd say OK, and the next day they'd come, 'Give us more food!' And I'd say, 'We've run out of food.' And they went, 'What? ... But ... we want more food!' ... And 'give us a car! We want to liberate your car.'" When they came to liberate his baby, Townshend was driven to his limits: "They were wackos. And that was the kind of climate in which I wrote 'Won't Get Fooled Again.'"[33] Perhaps exaggerating for effect, he even told Roy Carr (in a mid-70s interview on a CD included with Carr's book *A Talk On The Wild Side*) that he threatened to call the police on a particularly persistent intruder; when the warning was ignored, "I just grabbed the nearest thing, which was a hammer, and I hit him on the head with it, and nearly killed the fucker."[34]

Whatever the inspiration for 'Won't Get Fooled Again,' it has become not only one of The Who's most defining anthems, but also perhaps the song on which Townshend has flip-flopped his opinion more than any other. In part that might reflect how he's flip-flopped between reveling in and withdrawing from his role as generational spokesman. In *The Who ... Through The Eyes Of Pete Townshend*, he described it as "a song, quite simply, about the family man who is drafted. It's a song about a person with imposed responsibilities, imposed by causes that he has nothing to do with. In other words, it's not that I no longer feel angry, or no longer feel frustrated, or suddenly feel that society is perfect when all along I've been screaming that it isn't – it's that I'm no longer going to be the voice of the people who influenced me in a superficial way."[35]

In a *Rolling Stone* interview in late 1987, he subjected the classic to extraordinarily self-flagellant revisionism. "It's the dumbest song I've ever written," he said. "It was dumb to deny the political role of the individual, the political responsibility of the individual. Burning our draft card is a political act. Throwing your vote away is an apolitical act. And 'Won't Get Fooled Again' was an apolitical song. Luckily, most people didn't listen to the verses. They just listened to the catch. It was an irresponsible song. It was quite clear during that period that rock musicians had the ear of the people. And people were saying to me then, 'Pete, you've got to use The Who. You've got to get this message across.'"[36]

His assessment more than a decade later, in the *Classic Albums* documentary on *Who's Next*, was far more level-headed, indicating he was once again proud to lay claim to its authorship. "'Won't Get Fooled Again' was not a defined statement," he said. "It was a plea – please don't end this story, please don't feel that because you've come to this concert, you've come to this place, that you've got an answer. Please don't make me on the stage the new boss. Because I'm just the same as the guy who was up here before. You know, *you're* in charge. Some of the statements contained in *Lifehouse*, [like] 'Meet the new boss, same as the old boss' ... these were not ironic statements. They were statements that I will stand by."[37]

All of the Townshend compositions on *Who's Next* were made as home demos prior to the official Who recordings of the same numbers, and it's likely all would have been part of *Lifehouse*. They wouldn't have constituted *Lifehouse*, however. For that still leaves about a dozen other songs that have, at some time or another, been indicated or rumored as at least possible candidates. Four of these, at the least, would have been certain inclusions, and on their own they would have pushed the album over the length a single LP could accommodate.

The most obvious is 'Pure And Easy,' cited (under the title 'The Note') as one of the three songs already in the works for the album in the October 24 1970 *Disc*, and described by Townshend himself in a mid 1972 *Sounds* article as *Lifehouse*'s "pivot piece."[38] More than a quarter of a century later, his opinion remained unchanged. "'There once was a note pure and easy, playing so free like a breath rippling by," he said in the *Classic Albums* documentary on *Who's Next*, quoting the first line of the song, "That was where the story of *Lifehouse* was told."[39] What's more, there were two attempts to record it at the *Lifehouse/Who's Next* sessions, and it was one of the songs performed at the April 26 1971 concert at the Young Vic Theatre in London, which was at least partly intended as a live rehearsal of sorts for *Lifehouse* material. The second of these studio versions would appear on *Odds & Sods*, in whose liner notes Townshend mused, "It's strange, really, that this never appeared on *Who's Next*, because in the context of stuff like 'Song Is Over,' 'Getting In Tune,' and 'Baba O'Riley' it explains more about the general concept behind the *Lifehouse* idea than any amount of rap."[40]

That's certainly true of 'Pure And Easy''s lyrics. More than any other *Lifehouse* song, it puts the lessons of Hazrat Inayat Khan's *The Mysticism Of Sound And Music* into practice, extolling the virtues of a note so pure and eternal it can traverse mountains and get millions to cheer. Musically, however, it's also a reflection of Khan's ideal, the melody of its verses suffused with the very sort of uplifting serenity the "note" seemed to promise – and, perhaps, that Townshend was trying to find in his own life, via Meher Baba and other spiritual paths. A more ominous bridge, however, strongly hints at the storm clouds necessary for *Lifehouse*'s narrative tension: a civilization on the verge of extinction, a world in which the "chords of life" (Pete again blurring musical and spiritual boundaries) are losing their joy.

As to precisely where 'Pure And Easy' would fit into *Lifehouse*'s plot, Townshend told *Disc* that the "Bobby" character would find "a musical note which basically creates complete devastation. And when everything is destroyed, only the real note, the true note that they have been looking for, is left."[41] That doesn't make it crystal clear whether the note Bobby finds and the note that's left are the same thing, but it does at least give the protagonist a mission.

Townshend's eight-and-a-half-minute demo is about three minutes longer than both The Who's version and the one that would open his 1972 solo album *Who Came First*, and has a stark, stripped-down feel with more emphasis on the elegiac organ. Despite the longer length, however, the lyrics remain mostly the same. The main differences are a much longer fadeout that was wisely edited for the more widely known versions; a considerably lengthier (and considerably more jagged) guitar solo; and a final verse (about the all-conquering power of sound) dropped from both studio recordings of the song by The Who that have been released. For what it's worth, the "note" – judging from the organ note on which Pete lingers for about five seconds after the lyric "except for one note" – is a C, if slightly sharp.

Townshend also confirmed 'Time Is Passing' as a *Lifehouse* song in his 1972 *Sounds* rundown of *Who Came First* (on which the song was first officially released). If any *Lifehouse* composition could be considered filler or something screenwriters might call 'exposition,' it could be this relatively slight, sunny tune. Displaying Pete's occasional proclivity for pastoral country moods, its arrangement was dominated by more of those oddly unsteady, otherworldly, squirrelly keyboard sounds, possibly generated by a Selmer Clavioline or a Jennings Univox (both of which were early portable tube-synthesizers sold as piano attachments). Also featuring plucked strings and pedal steel, the song was perhaps the least suited of the known *Lifehouse* batch for full-group Who treatment. The Who did try this out in the studio in March 1971, and on stage at the Young Vic. But as Townshend mentioned in both the *Sounds* article and *Who Came First*'s liner notes, he played it to Meher Baba followers on a trip to India in early 1972; maybe it's something he and the band ultimately felt was too Meher Baba-oriented (in feel if not actual lyric) for The Who.

The one known *Lifehouse* song to escape inclusion on any official Who or Townshend release of the 70s is 'Mary.' A demo version appeared on the 1983 *Scoop* compilation. Townshend wrote in his notes to the album that it was "intended to bring some romance into the sci-fi plot."[42] Mary would have been the runaway daughter who has an affair with a young man involved in setting up *Lifehouse*'s showpiece concert in London, as Pete told the audience when he performed *Music From Lifehouse* in 2000. Regardless of how it forced its way into *Lifehouse*'s story, it's a bittersweet folk-rock gem that could have stood on its own as a straightforward song on a non-concept Who or solo Townshend release. Pete's singing on the demo is as confident and relaxed as it gets on those preparatory recordings, and the track is also the best showcase for his underrated folky acoustic guitar skills, especially on the transition from the verse to bridge.

Assuming the material bootlegged as *The Genius Of Pete Townshend* might have come from an acetate given to The Who or others associated with the group to introduce them to the *Lifehouse* songs, it's yet more certain that

'Pure And Easy,' 'Time Is Passing,' and 'Mary' would have been featured, since all of those songs appear on that unauthorized LP. A final certain inclusion that wasn't selected for *Who's Next* is 'Let's See Action,' described by Townshend in the *Sounds* article as follows: "Written about a section of the LIFE HOUSE film, it's about the people who act in a revolution, and the people that sit back. I thought it also said a lot about the way we forget our souls most of the time."[43]

'Let's See Action' would be released in late 1971, as The Who's first single after *Who's Next*. Townshend put a solo version – identical to the home demo featured on *Lifehouse Chronicles* – on the following year's *Who Came First*. Along with 'Won't Get Fooled Again,' it's the only material on *Lifehouse* that is both overtly political and grounded in the countercultural milieu of the early 1970s. It's considerably more upbeat, less cynical, less histrionic, and more spiritual (with Meher Baba all but namechecked in the reference to a feet-warming avatar) than 'Won't Get Fooled Again.' It's also far less exciting and memorable. What's more, unusually among the core *Lifehouse* dozen, it is considerably more effective as sung by Townshend than Daltrey, with Pete's good-natured, easygoing delivery a better fit than Roger's more overwrought interpretation. Townshend's demo is about two-and-a-half minutes longer than The Who's single, the main difference being a longer fadeout of the "nothing is everything" chant – suggesting, as several of the lengthy demo versions do, that one of the subtler benefits The Who bestowed upon Pete's compositions was editing them into more effectively concise (and commercial) statements.

Even with these 12 songs accounted for, that leaves no fewer than ten others included in *Lifehouse Chronicles'* two discs of *Lifehouse* demos, four of which also appear on *Music From Lifehouse* (as does yet another composition). A couple more then-unissued Townshend tunes were performed at the April 26 1971 Young Vic show. The unwary could easily have the impression that there were more than enough songs to fill a double album, if not more. Closer inspection, however, dismisses some of them as likely candidates, though at least a few were probably under serious consideration.

Starting with the strongest contenders, 'Too Much Of Anything' was demoed by Pete, recorded by The Who in April 1971, and performed live at the Young Vic. He would tell BBC Radio One's Roger Scott in 1989 that it was written for the film, though Townshend – one of rock's most conscientious LP annotators – stops a bit short of stating it was a *Lifehouse* song in his notes for *Odds & Sods*, where the number first officially surfaced. The song's warning against the dangers of overindulgence was a bit rich coming from these exponents of rock'n'roll excess, although the tug between the carnal and the spiritual triggered much of Townshend's best writing. As Pete himself acknowledged in those liner notes, "realizing at the last minute how totally hypocritical it would be for a load of face-stuffing drug-addicted alcoholics like this to put this out, we didn't."[44]

More problematic in terms of its inclusion on *Lifehouse* was its relatively middling quality (in the company of much of what Pete had written, at least) and the question of where exactly it would have fitted into the story. For all that, it's not a bad low-key rumination. Once again The Who acted as editors and cut a little more than a minute from the song's length, losing the demo's cool instrumental break where the fluttering synthesizer dovetails nicely with Pete's wordless vocal, as it also does in the graceful coda.

While 'I Don't Even Know Myself' was also demoed by Townshend and performed at the Young Vic, its place in *Lifehouse* seems questionable. There's no obvious spot for it in the plot, although the line about a policeman looking for the singer "and no one else" might have been worked into a scene where the authorities try to smoke out rebels against the fascist regime. Inspired by The Rolling Stones and written on tour in Amsterdam in September 1969, it had already been recorded by The Who in early 1970, with one of its riffs even appearing near the end of the *Live At Leeds* version of 'Magic Bus.' It had also already been shelved as part of the EP that never appeared; but as comments from the time indicate it was subsequently re-recorded, The Who might have reconsidered putting it out in some form.

'I Don't Even Know Myself' and 'Water' were performed at the Young Vic. 'Water' itself might have been at least vaguely under consideration, as it hints at authorities on the rampage, although the *Lifehouse* script would have had to include both policemen and truck drivers to be faithful to the lyric. But 'Water,' like 'I Don't Even Know Myself,' would eventually be consigned to a B-side. The serviceable hard rocker 'Naked Eye' is another EP leftover that could have been in the running, as it was performed at the Young Vic, but Townshend's failure to mark it as a *Lifehouse* out-take in his fastidious *Odds & Sods* comments seems to eliminate that possibility; his notes also explained that it wasn't released as the band were hoping to "get a good live version one day."[45] Perhaps these three songs were included in the Young Vic show merely because they'd been a part of The Who's live set for almost a year and thus easy to work up, rather than due to any intention to integrate them into *Lifehouse*.

'Greyhound Girl' is indeed a 1971 Townshend demo, and even sneaked into official release in 1980 as the non-LP B-side of his solo single 'Let My Love Open The Door.' One imagines it could have just about fitted into the *Lifehouse* scenario as a depiction of two lovers (perhaps Mary and her boyfriend) finding refuge amidst the chaos, particularly as it's placed right before 'Mary' on the *Music From Lifehouse* DVD. Much more so even than 'Too Much Of Anything,' however, it's not a standout in this crowd; indeed the song, delivered as a sort of power ballad on the demo, is about the most ordinary and unmemorable tune of the bunch. With no known Who recording in existence, it must be considered a longshot to make the cut, other than for the very real possibility of extending the album to double-LP length.

Three songs recorded by The Who in spring 1972 are included on *Lifehouse Chronicles* in demo form, but there doesn't seem to be any evidence that they were ever in line for *Lifehouse*, if they were even written prior to that year. 'Put The Money Down' was a June 1972 out-take that surfaced a couple of years later on *Odds & Sods*, while both 'Relay' and 'Join Together' were recorded in May 1972 and released as singles that year. The gurgling synthesizer bed of 'Relay' certainly fits well with *Lifehouse* sonically, and 'Join Together' could have served well as a song of communal music-audience celebration, although *Lifehouse* arguably already had too many of those. It's certainly possible that Townshend considered adding these to the pool of available songs when he toyed with reviving *Lifehouse* later in the 70s. But as 'Relay' and, especially, 'Join Together' were stronger than some of the songs known to have been rehearsed and recorded by The Who in 1971 when *Lifehouse* was on the horizon, the absence of 1971 studio versions probably means they weren't yet written. Pete does perform both songs near the end of his *Music From Lifehouse* DVD, but one wonders if they were included more as a homage to his work from that era in general than because they were set-in-stone pieces of the *Lifehouse* project as originally conceived.

The otherwise comprehensive liner notes for *Lifehouse Chronicles* yield no clues as to why demos of those songs were included. Most likely they date from a post-1971 attempt to revive *Lifehouse* in some form, and weren't intended for its original incarnation. The same goes for demos of compositions The Who wouldn't record until the mid to late 70s that are also included, among them 'Slip Kid' (from their 1975 album *The Who By Numbers*) and, at even more of a stretch, 'Who Are You,' 'Music Must Change,' and 'Sister Disco' (all from 1978's *Who Are You*).

It was ultimately revealed that 'Who Are You' was built around a riff devised by Townshend on the ARP 2600 synthesizer in 1971, but completed much later. Perhaps ideas or riffs later to find their way into the other three compositions date from the early 70s as well, but it's extremely doubtful that the demos on *Lifehouse Chronicles* were done that early. As much as hardcore Who fans welcome their presence in any form, their inclusion, minus full explanations, has generated uncertainty as to their true origins at best, and misclassification as actual original *Lifehouse* songs at worst. Finally, 'Can You Help The One You Really Love,' included as a demo (but not within the two discs identified as *Lifehouse* demos) on *Lifehouse Chronicles*, was written shortly before its 2000 performance on the *Music from Lifehouse* DVD, not when *Lifehouse* was first envisioned.

An educated guess puts the amount of material Townshend had completed for *Lifehouse* by the end of 1970 as somewhere between one and two LPs. Even after *Lifehouse* was abandoned, it would become a matter of some contention as to whether The Who record to feature the songs should be a single or double album. A far bigger hurdle for Townshend as 1971 approached, however, was getting the rest of The Who and their managers on the same page as work began on *Lifehouse* in earnest.

As difficult as it is to gauge which songs were written for *Lifehouse*'s initial incarnation, it's harder still to suss just what sort of film would have accompanied it, who would have directed it, and which studio would have funded and released it. Even at the time, press articles and band interviews gave multiple – and at times contradictory – accounts of the film's pre-production. Subsequent recollections have mostly added to the confusion, and again, only educated guesses can be made as to how *Lifehouse* was intended to reach the screen – which might partly explain why it never did reach the cinemas.

Tommy had already been reported as being in the works from several studios, and the possibility that it could still be made into a movie would impede Townshend's hopes of making an entirely different cinematic vehicle for *Lifehouse*. But even before his October 1970 *Disc* interview first outlined *Lifehouse*, Townshend had been talking up such a film in the press, telling *Jazz & Pop* that The Who were "talking in terms of a film effort – not of *Tommy* but of a similar idea."[46]

A front-page article in the December 19 1970 *Billboard* seemed to clarify that The Who were now working on two separate film projects. One would be *Tommy*, optioned to producer Jerry Gershwin and financed by Universal Pictures; Gershwin had at least a bit of experience with rock film scores, having produced the film *Tam Lin*, which included some music by British folk-rockers Pentangle. The other movie, also part of the Universal deal, would be produced by Track Music – a company run by Who managers Kit Lambert and Chris Stamp, along with Peter Kameron – "developed from an original idea by Townshend," with a score by Pete, starring The Who.[47] Puzzlingly, the working titles were given as *Your Turn In The Barrel* (possibly a facetious suggestion, given that the phrase is the punchline to a timeworn dirty joke) and *Barrel One, Barrel Two*, making it unlikely that the far more appropriate *Lifehouse* term had been dreamed up. Also noted was that a director and scriptwriter had yet to be enlisted, although Townshend has stated that he wrote the *Lifehouse* script. In short, the movie seemed pretty half-baked, even for something still in pre-production.

What, however, of the movie that Pete's Tattooist International friends were hoping to work on, and for which they'd already gotten some funding from MGM? "At the point the first draft of the script was complete," says Richard Stanley, "Denis [Postle] and I were called into a meeting with Track Records' US lawyer and threatened with all manner of terrible things if we went ahead. It became clear later that Kit Lambert and Chris Stamp, ex-feature movie industry people themselves, were jealous of this project (now called *Guitar Farm*) as they were putting together another film deal. Pete was put in an impossible position and, with the band to think of, chose to remove himself from *Guitar Farm*, with great regrets. I also think (but don't know) that this put in sequence the events that led eventually to the split with Lambert and Stamp, and the elevation of Bill Curbishley [to Who manager]. MGM wrote our project off, and [Herb] Solow had already put his energies into the [1970 Robert Altman] movie *Brewster McCloud* that was quite similar in concept."[48] As *Brewster McCloud* was a rather black surreal comedy starring *Harold And Maude*'s Bud Cort as a youngster under the delusion he could learn to fly (crashing to death when he tries to take flight in Houston's Astrodome), it's not clear how The Who could have fitted into such a concept.

"After meeting with Denis and I believe Mike [Myers]," says Herb Solow, "we made a deal to develop *Guitar Farm* as a musical film with Pete Townshend and The Who for MGM. I met with Pete, Denis, and Mike at Pete's house, as well as for dinner at a restaurant in London. The result of the development was a film story written by Denis and Mike. It was the basis for the film and a good beginning. However, with MGM having been sold, once again, and new top (cost-conscious) management in place, the ability to continue developing films became more and more frustrating, the result being that I resigned my position and went into independent production and on to other studios. To my knowledge that was the end of *Guitar Farm*."[49] Solow also clarifies that *Guitar Farm* was definitely not ever known as *Lifehouse*, and was not the same film as the one Townshend would develop for Universal.

Postle confirms that work had been done for a script, and even budgeting and searching for locations, before the project fell victim to the MGM sale. "In 1967, MGM was sold to the Canadian investor Edgar Bronfman Sr, whose son, Edgar Jr, would later buy Universal Studios," he says. "Two years later, an increasingly unprofitable MGM was bought (some say raided) by Nevada millionaire Kirk Kerkorian. What appealed to Kerkorian was MGM's Culver City real estate, and the value of 45 years' worth of glamour associated with the name, which he attached to a Las Vegas hotel and casino. As for filmmaking, that part of the company was quickly and severely downsized under the supervision of James T. Aubrey Jr. Aubrey, known from his days as head of programming at CBS as 'the smiling cobra,' sold off the studio's accumulation of props, furnishings, and historical memorabilia, including Dorothy's red slippers from *The Wizard Of Oz*. Put up for sale was the venerable Lot 3, 10 acres of back-lot property, which became an upscale real estate project. The London MGM studios [were] sold and became an industrial cold store." Postle also notes that "something emerged that we could have done with discovering sooner: Pete Townshend was not contractually free to work independently of the rest of The Who."[50]

Although the exact dates have been lost in the memories of the principals, it seems most likely that sometime in the last half of 1970, the

Tattooist production that might have developed into a *Guitar Farm* film was abandoned in favor of the package with Universal. *Guitar Farm* might not have been a workable Who vehicle at any rate, in part because it would have been so difficult to film the fields of instruments grown almost as crops that were so integral to Myers's original story.

In any case, Mike Myers feels other considerations had entered the picture and taken *Guitar Farm* away from what he had originally intended. "The disparity between Pete's status as living rock'n'roll icon and ours as 'experimental' film-makers was one of several ten-ton gorillas in the room," he says. "Another was the current vogue for transcendental meditation and interest in Eastern religions. In the style of the times Pete and Denis were very much into that stuff. I was not. Those interests insinuated themselves into the script, in what I think now – and probably thought then, but didn't articulate – was a fatal mistake. Because of it *Guitar Farm* was made to carry more freight than it could bear. It was shaped to serve ends other than its own internal dynamics as a story, so it began to look like a piece of work that was disconnected from its own content. No wonder it didn't work! It eventually became a rag bag full of naff symbolism - Captain Sunshine, The Ivory Tower, etc – and everything in it was a metaphor for something else. What started out in my mind as a simple and charming musical fable got twisted into some kind of grim morality tale about the meaning of life.

"I'm not absolving myself from blame," says Myers. "I suppose I could have spoken up but didn't. Also, and this was no excuse, we were inexperienced in the art of making dramas. As filmmakers we were opportunists working the margins, visually sophisticated scavengers of material that more conventional eyes and slower minds missed. We lived off our visual wits. We believed that a new visual language would by definition lead to new streams of content. We thought those skills would get us by and we didn't need to be conventional 'screenwriters' to make it work."

This, incidentally, might have been something else Townshend took from *Guitar Farm* into the *Lifehouse* project – belief that he could be the creative force behind a film without writing a conventional screenplay, and that his sky-high ambitions could work out by virtue of sheer spontaneous inspiration. Myers still feels that might have happened had Postle and Townshend not veered the project into different directions. "Leading up to *Guitar Farm*, Denis and I had a rich collaborative period which resulted in the founding of Tattooist, and we made a few strange and wonderfully original films together," he says. "The engine that drove the project was the assumption that the creative synergy between us would continue and power *Guitar Farm*. Left to our own devices and without the distraction of Pete Townshend and Denis's preoccupation with Eastern religions we might have done just that. But the bottom line is that without Pete's involvement, I doubt the script would have received a dime's worth of funding from MGM."[51]

It's important to note that, judging from Townshend's own spoken and written recollections, *Guitar Farm* might not have been what he was plotting for *Lifehouse* or even have supplied specific ideas that were adapted or altered. He doesn't mention *Guitar Farm* in his detailed history of *Lifehouse* in his liner notes for *Lifehouse Chronicles*. By the time of the *Billboard* announcement in December, he seems to have already been working on something different of his own, and possibly shopping it on his own too. In the *Classic Albums* documentary on *Who's Next*, he remembers writing a treatment and bringing it to Ned Tanen of Universal in Los Angeles, who "loved it, and he offered to fund the whole thing."[52] This could refer to the film script he remembers writing for Universal in the second paragraph of his *Lifehouse Chronicles* notes, or at least a script that grew out of the treatment.

Record company politics might also have played a part in Universal's involvement. Before moving into film production at Universal, Tanen had helped form the UNI label, home to both Neil Diamond and Elton John in the early 70s. Perhaps not coincidentally, UNI was a subsidiary of MCA – as was Decca, The Who's American label. Universal Films – again, perhaps not by coincidence – was also part of MCA. Universal's ownership of the rights to *Lifehouse* would keep the rights to The Who's records, films, and any soundtracks the movies would spawn within the same corporation. Pete confirmed in *The Story Of Tommy* that The Who "had to offer it first to Universal, who were tied up with our recording company in America, MCA."[53]

Whatever the maneuvering behind the scenes, Townshend did have funding, and apparently encouragement, from a major studio to develop *Lifehouse* as the new year approached. Explaining what he had mind to The Who and everyone else, however, wouldn't be so pure and easy.

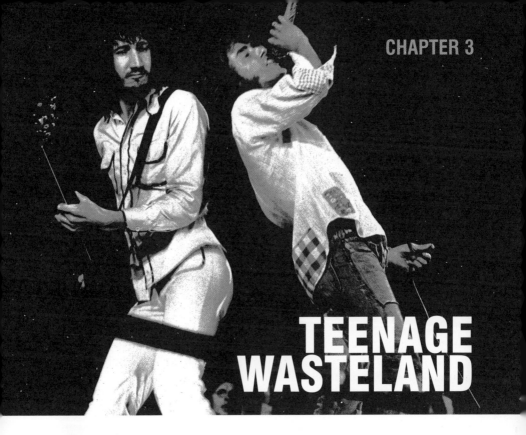

CHAPTER 3

TEENAGE WASTELAND

Pete Townshend had been talking about what he had in mind for *Lifehouse* since September 1970, starting with hints and then gradually supplying more detail. Then, on January 13 1971, he made a formal announcement. At a press conference at London's Young Vic Theatre, accompanied by the Vic's director, Frank Dunlop, he informed the media of The Who's intentions to make a movie filmed largely at the theater itself.

"We shall not be giving the usual kind of Who rock show," Townshend explained. "The audience will be completely involved in the music, which is designed to reflect people's personalities. We shall try to induce mental and spiritual harmony through the medium of rock music." Elaboration of specific details and plot points was not as forthcoming as more high-minded philosophizing. "Rock's real power as a liberational force is completely untapped," he said, "so a new type of theater, a new type of performance has to be devised to present it. If a film of this is made, it will be the first real rock film ... because it will reflect a reality."

Judging by an extensive interview with Penny Valentine that had appeared in *Sounds* on January 2, the project was evolving so rapidly that the plans were changing almost day by day – or, quite possibly, the plans weren't all that organized. Townshend did confirm that filming would start on February 1, and commence before the album, with both the boldness of a man going where no man had gone before and a politician cloaking a lack of policy particulars with sweeping rhetoric. "The only step we can take now with our music is just to take a visual step," he said. "We're not going to be acting. We're not going to be doing anything extraordinary in that area, but we are still wanting to produce the finest music that rock is capable of and, if possible, to kind of act as efficient catalysts, as it were – moving rock out of the rut that everyone thinks it's in and everyone really knows it's in."

Pressed for the movie's basic idea and plot, Townshend flew off in so many directions at once that readers were more likely to be confused than comprehending – a problem he'd have over and over during the next few months. The film, he said, was a "double-barreled idea," which perhaps accounts for why the working titles had been given as *Your Turn In The Barrel* and *Barrel One, Barrel Two* in *Billboard* the previous month. "One barrel is fiction, in the way *Tommy* was fiction. It has music, a story, adventures in it. On the other side is the story about man's search for harmony, and the way he does it is through music. Through going into this theater and setting up certain experiments.

"It would take 60 conversations on from here to make this start to make sense," he said, in a classic understatement, "but the general thing is that I'm attempting to do what a lot of people have tried to do before ... to mirror with rock music the creative process. ... So I've been working on a piece of music that goes from the first single note – oneness – then it divides into twoness and threeness, then it's rock music. Then it wasn't to be oneness again. From there we go to people. We're the notes, we're the divisions, we're the spearheads – the highest form of intelligence – and we're the people that have got the problem."

This was metaphysical territory even for Townshend, but he did get a bit more vivid by adding, "The whole thing is set in the future and yet it could be now, the way we're going. Society's completely overpopulated, it's polluted, it's on the brink." A key to the project's success, he revealed, would be an element that no one could predict or control – the reaction of a real-life audience: "If these people in this theater can find themselves and balance in the midst of all this chaos then through very futuristic media things –

experience suits, holograms and things – everyone else can, they can get above it and lose the illusion all around them ... they don't walk into that theater wondering what's happening. They go in knowing what they're there for and why. Knowing they can't just sit back and leave it to The Who – that it's as much up to them as everyone else and there is going to be some day in the distant future when THEIR piece of music – which I assume I'll be composing – will be played and people will react to it."[1] The film would be started before the album, presumably partly in hope that some genuinely new songs would arise from the band-audience interaction.

"They had this plan that The Who were going to be on stage, and they'd be replaced at the end by holograms of themselves, still playing instruments. Great ambitious thinking," laughs Richard Barnes. "That's Pete's *Lifehouse* thinking, a kind of over-the-top thinking. It swallowed up a fucking lot of money, I know, that hologram stuff."[2]

Besides the holograms and experience suits, Townshend threw quadraphonic and 3-D experiments into the hoped-for mix, confirming that he'd written "a lot of songs about what I think is going to happen, what I'd like to happen."[3] He didn't seem to have a standard script, however, although a rough storyline had been done. At worst, he noted somewhat ominously, it would come out something like the Beatles' *Let It Be* film, which had tried to combine a documentary of an album-in-the-making with a live concert, and not quite ended up with a proper album, a proper concert, or a proper movie.

While it was not mentioned in the *Sounds* interview, the concerts and filming would take place in the Young Vic Theatre, recently founded by Dunlop to develop works for young audiences and provide a venue receptive to experiments by authors and actors. The unlikely alliance had, like so much of what The Who were doing, its seeds in *Tommy*; Dunlop had wanted a theatrical version of the rock opera to be the Young Vic's first production when it opened on September 10 1970. While that project didn't take off, Townshend did get to know Dunlop when he saw *Waiting For Godot* at the Young Vic, bringing the rest of The Who as well.

"Pete said he was trying to work on a musical which would be kind of revolutionary and preach the way to go for everybody, especially the youth of the country," Dunlop remembered in the *Classic Albums* documentary on *Who's Next*. "And I said, 'Well, come on, use the Young Vic free, and do a series of attempts at working on this musical.'"[4] In an unpublished 2004 interview with Phil Sutcliffe, he added, "Pete asked me if we could clear it for some Sunday shows. We didn't want to charge the audience – the ordinary price was the same as you would pay for a local cinema ticket, that was the idea. So we didn't announce it, we just let the word get around."[5]

As haphazard as *Lifehouse*'s pre-production had been, much of what was needed to pull it off was now in place. There were songs – 20 of them, according to a *Melody Maker* item on January 23, although that might well have been an exaggeration – a venue for filming, at least a rough outline of whatever story would take place, and backing from Universal Studios. Now Pete Townshend had to try to explain the still-untitled *Lifehouse* to The Who, whose enthusiasm for, and comprehension of, the project would be necessary to make a success of both the album and the film.

At times, The Who have been considered something of a mouthpiece for the songs and worldview of 'auteur' Pete Townshend. Considering Townshend's facility at playing and overdubbing everything himself at his home studio, some might figure that, had he sung like Roger Daltrey, there would have been no need for him to use a band at all. But The Who were not regarded as a necessary evil by Townshend, who knew that he needed the group to bring his music to its fullest life. Daltrey had the vocal power Pete lacked, particularly in the harder-rocking songs, but he also had an underestimated knack for interpreting Townshend's softer and more melodic tunes with appropriate sensitivity. John Entwistle was one of the best bass players in rock; Keith Moon the best, most inventive, and by a wide streak most manic drummer.

Even beyond purely musical considerations, a charismatic, flesh-and-blood group would be vital to the success of the film, especially as concert footage was now going to be an important part of the movie, and perhaps even its focal point. Townshend's own athletic guitar-playing was itself a major part of their stage act and public image, but so were Daltrey's mic-twirling and sex symbol strutting, Moon's unmatchable flashy drumwork and onstage clowning, and, in an underappreciated fashion, Entwistle's motionless, expressionless persona as "The Ox." And as distinctive as they were as individuals, more than any other band save The Beatles, their separate identities added up to more than the sum of their parts when they worked together, spurring each other to collective heights they couldn't reach on their own.

That collective identity might even have been something Townshend had in mind, if only subconsciously, in his wish for an audience-performer bond in *Lifehouse* that would lift everyone to a state of communal ecstasy unachievable in isolation from each other. "There is a harmony in The Who," he told *Record Mirror*, "which has come from our music. When we give performances there is this elation, which is completely free of any drug stimulus, and it's from the fact that the music is good, and the event is good and the reactions are real. Theater people will know that a really good performance will last in the audience's minds for months afterward. We want to get this going in a permanent way."[6]

Pete had talked about the group's dynamic to *Sounds'* Penny Valentine. "Roger would be the only one to say that the group probably relies on me, thinking it to be true when in fact it isn't. Roger feels that perhaps he's unsuccessful when it comes to creative things. It's got a lot to do with enjoying painting and writing compositions in school. I don't think Roger was ever like that and I don't think today, because he's in a rock band and probably expected to come up with the odd song, that he's automatically going to be able to write. I mean, his talents are elsewhere. And it's not just standing holding a mic, it's in firing The Who, and he does it in a way nobody would understand. ... I don't think I've got control over The Who. I do feel I have a certain amount of responsibility but at the same time the group would well overreact if I said I had control, and I think rightly so. ... Keith has as much control, because where would any of us be without him?"[7]

If Townshend needed the rest of The Who, the others needed Townshend even more. John Entwistle wrote a few Who songs a year that provided a refreshing, balancing contrast to Pete's compositions in their black humor. Daltrey and Moon had penned the odd tune, but with far less frequency even than Entwistle. But none of them were prepared to carry a Who-quality album on their own. That point was made clearer a bit later as each (along with Townshend) started issuing solo side projects, led by Entwistle, who had by January 23 been reported to have completed his debut solo LP. The Who had played numerous concerts in 1970, as well as doing some recording for the unrealized pre-*Who's Next* album, but were probably as anxious as Townshend to sink their teeth into a new *Tommy*-scale project.

But while The Who, and Kit Lambert, had been extremely supportive of *Tommy* and appreciative of the new level of success it brought them, *Lifehouse* was in some ways going to be a harder sell. Although *Tommy*'s plot had been fractured and sketchy, it didn't spin off into anything like the kaleidoscope of ideas and possibilities Townshend was already mapping out in the press. *Tommy* had generated buzz about movie, drama, and ballet adaptations almost from the month it was released; but when it was recorded, the group only had to think about how it would take shape as an LP, not how it might be translated into film and performance. And while *Tommy* and much else that Townshend had written over the past few years had drawn upon cerebral spirituality, none of the other Who members, or their managers, shared Pete's almost religious interest in transcendence into different planes. Their concerns were far more down-to-earth, and not just in matters of sex, drugs, and rock'n'roll, but in the practicalities of maintaining what had become an incredibly successful performing and recording career.

None of them was more down-to-earth and practical than Roger Daltrey, the former sheet-metal worker for whom The Who had been an escape from a life of working-class drudgery. As he put it flatly in the *Amazing Journey* documentary: "The trouble is with *Lifehouse*, no one I've ever met, apart from Pete, ever understood it."[8] And similarly, in the *Classic Albums* documentary on *Who's Next*: "Pete came up with a kind of basic script, which was like a film script. Which didn't make any sense. None of us could grasp it." Yet he tempered his frustration in the same interview, adding, "But it had some good ideas in it. From what I can remember, the one idea that I picked up on was the fact that if we ever do find the meaning of life, it will be a musical note. And I thought, yeah, that in itself is a great idea for some kind of musical story."[9] At least, then, Roger and Pete were on the same page in seeing 'Pure And Easy' as the keynote of sorts for whatever *Lifehouse* might become.

"I guess we kind of looked at each other with blank faces," Entwistle admitted, while describing his first reaction to *Lifehouse* to Redbeard for an *In The Studio* radio documentary on *Live At Leeds*. "We were always very wary of doing concept pieces, because they took so long to write and so long to record. Which meant that we were off of the road and not earning any money."[10]

As Who PR man Keith Altham sees it, Daltrey's participation was needed not merely to sing the lyrics as effectively as he could, but to act as Townshend's reality check. "The whole creative aspect of the band was really largely Pete's bag, I guess, because he was the writer and came up with all the ideas," he says. "But I pretty soon learned a lot of that stuff really only was rationalized by Daltrey, and that his role in the band was much more important than I thought it was on the first impression. Pete would come up with these amazing cosmic, universal concepts, and would say, 'I've got an idea, we'll conquer the universe with this.' And Roger would say, 'Well, let's start with Shepherd's Bush' [the modest West London neighborhood where The Who had formed and built their following].

"And it would get done; it would get turned into something that could actually be utilized by the media and put into practice. Because if it had been just left to Pete, I think a lot of these things may not have actually made it into everyday use. Pete had amazing ideas, all the creative intellectual capacity in the world, but very little common sense. Roger had all the common sense, and the practicality. That's why they were so good for each other, and why they were so often at war with each other. Because there's nothing a creative person hates worse than somebody saying, 'Well, look, you can't do it that way. You got to do it this way. You know, at least we can do a bit of it.' But I saw why they needed each other, and I still do. It's exactly that friction and that kind of editing that goes on between them that has made The Who what they are."[11]

Whatever the rest of The Who thought, plans were laid for the group to play low-key engagements at the Young Vic throughout the winter. Whether these were for rehearsing, filming, composing, or playing concerts, no one could really say – a similarity, as it happened, with whatever The Beatles had been doing throughout January 1969, when *Let It Be* was filmed. By late January 1971, shows for three consecutive Mondays starting February 15 had been announced. "We are writing a story and we aim to perform it on the first day we start work in this theater," Townshend told *Melody Maker*. "About 400 people will be involved with us and we aim to play music which represents them."[12] A comment in the same paper about six months later indicated the audience would have shaped the story too, as "characters would emerge from them and eventually the group would play a very minor role."[13]

However, another Townshend statement in the January 23 *Melody Maker* indicated that, even with the cameras apparently on the verge of rolling, some confusion about the format lingered, as the group were "intending to produce a fiction, or a play or an opera." The project was described by the anonymous reporter as "an audience-participation rock film," the shows incorporating quadraphonic sound and – in what would be a first for The

Who, and an enormous source of irritation nearly three years down the line – backing tapes.[14]

How exactly would footage from the Young Vic fit into this vision? "I had planned to conduct rather simple experiments during these concerts producing pieces of music for some loyal audience members," Pete later wrote in his liner notes for *Lifehouse Chronicles*. "In order to get The Who into the film, I figured I would make them look as though they were really making the musical part of the experiment work: documentary film of our concerts would later be incorporated into the fiction of the film, so the concert (the one at which Bobby's audience disappears) would be a genuine one, not a lash-up by some megalomaniacal film director."[15] Nearly a decade after the Young Vic shows, he even stated in *NME* that at one point he was "imagining a ten-week concert, not just with The Who but with lots of other musicians as well," although using outside musicians doesn't seem to have been an idea that came close to implementation.[16]

As Townshend told Nik Cohn for the February 7 *New York Times* piece, he hoped to see how far the shows could take audience-performer interaction. The Young Vic was the venue, he explained, as "it attracts a completely mixed-up crowd, part theatrical hangers-on, part freaks, part Who fans." The shows would take place every Monday at first, stepping up to two or three or even four nights a week if things went well. "Whatever is necessary," Townshend said. "By the end of six months, anything might happen."[17] But unsurprisingly, as Pete had recently written in 'Naked Eye,' it wouldn't "really happen that way at all."

The first Young Vic show had already taken place before this flurry of mid-winter media coverage. On January 4, The Who had rehearsed to get a feel for the theater's acoustics, deciding to, as Dunlop told *Record Mirror*, throw "the doors open and let anyone come who wanted to. Even the police came and wanted to dance to the music. We don't want it to be just an ordinary musical, but something which will involve the audience, make them contribute to it."[18]

Although the comments implied that Dunlop was an enthusiastic participant in the project, he was in fact about as much in the dark as anybody else. "I didn't actually know what the thing was called," he admitted in 2004. "I don't think Pete mentioned the name *Lifehouse* to me in all our conversations. I did get a handle on it, but I thought, 'How the hell is he going to do it? He's going out on a limb, we have to go with him!' The group thought, 'What's he on about?' I think Roger was wondering, 'Where am I in all this?' ... it was running ahead so fast."

Nor was Frank an actual director on the project, his function limited to moral support and allowing The Who use of the space. "I couldn't help [Townshend] as a freelance director would have," Dunlop said. "I do regret I couldn't go off and just do it. I always felt I wasn't useful or helpful enough to him. *Lifehouse* was a gigantic thing to try. I could tell him, 'I trust you.' I went [to the January 13 press conference] and all I could say was, 'I love The Who and I want this to happen.' But the others were nervous that what was being neglected was the career of The Who. I could see that."[19]

Those others might have included not only some of the musicians, but also co-managers Kit Lambert and Chris Stamp. In subsequent years, Townshend often charged the group's management with sabotaging *Lifehouse* in hopes of reviving the prospects for *Tommy* spin-offs. In a 1996 BBC radio special on *Lifehouse* he said that "they put me together with Frank and told him that we were working on *Tommy*."[20] Furthermore, in his liner notes to *Lifehouse Chronicles*, he writes that Lambert told Dunlop that *Lifehouse* was "unworkable," even though the plan at one point had been for Kit, Pete, and Frank to develop the script. Dunlop, according to Townshend, was advised to merely "go through the motions."[21] That could let *Lifehouse* fail and the focus return to a *Tommy* film, which Lambert – who had only stumbled upon The Who in the first place in 1964 because he was looking to make a film about a pop group with Stamp – hoped to direct, although he had never made a feature film.

In the BBC radio special, Stamp intimated that they did harbor some reservations. "We were still having trouble getting finance to make [*Tommy*] as a movie," he said. "And that is when suddenly we were dealing with *Lifehouse*. Now it's not as if we were that concerned about *Tommy* not being made as a film, but we only sort of finished two-thirds of the *Tommy* project, if you get my drift. And so we are now into the midst of creating another sort of big concept."[22] Dunlop's assessment was more ambivalent. "Kit was pushing *Tommy* and *Lifehouse* all the time," he told Phil Sutcliffe. "He did want the *Lifehouse* to move ahead, and I think the [January 13] press conference was his way of pushing it ahead."[23]

Amid these trepidations, the three announced *Lifehouse* concerts – on February 15, February 22, and March 1 – proceeded as planned. A preview of sorts was added for Sunday February 14, attended by a 200-strong audience specially invited from local youth clubs. Despite strong intimations that at least something would be filmed at these gigs, no footage has surfaced. Nor have any recordings, so some mystery remains as to what The Who played, how the audience reacted, and what if anything proved of use for the *Lifehouse* film and album. All accounts seem in agreement, however, that the shows were a big letdown for the band, and possibly to the spectators and everyone else.

It's some measure of The Who's uncertainty over how things might go that this most media-friendly of bands didn't want the press at the preview. At least Townshend didn't, according to Chris Charlesworth, then a *Melody Maker* staffer. "I didn't really know exactly what he was working on until I went to the Young Vic," he remembers. "And I wasn't supposed to be there, either. Keith had told me, 'By the way, we're rehearsing in the Young Vic on Sunday, do you want to come round and see us?' So I turned up and wandered in, and Pete was a bit rude to me and told me to sod off. He said, 'You're not allowed to write anything about this, because it's not for the press.' And I said 'OK, I promise I won't.' I just felt myself privileged to be watching them rehearse. They'd just start a song and go, 'well ... ' and stop it for a while, and have a chat, and start again. They didn't play anything that I was familiar with; I don't think they did, anyway. They might have warmed up on 'Pinball Wizard' for fun or something, but actually they were rehearsing."[24]

In one of Phil Sutcliffe's unpublished interviews with Young Vic staff, chief electrician Derek Brown remembered Townshend "trying to work out why certain pieces of music were popular or not, and he put it down to astrology. At a number of their concerts they put out questionnaires and checked star signs and so on, and as a result of that he wrote tunes for them." Sadly, no such questionnaires have surfaced, nor documentation of what tunes they might have inspired. In an interesting foreshadowing of a prominent feature of what was to be The Who's *next* opera (that is, the one after *Lifehouse*), Brown also noted that "it was the first time quadraphonic sound had been used in a live concert. So you had to have the sound desk in the middle of the theater."[25]

At least one other member of the band had matters far more earthly than astrology on his mind. As production manager Richard Mangan told Sutcliffe, "I remember queues of young women after the show around the Winnebagos the band had outside. Keith was saying 'you, you and you,' and asked me if I'd like to join in. But I was just married, and I couldn't see my wife understanding."[26]

That aside, The Who were hoping to take the shows seriously. Mangan remembered Townshend even sending a roadie to New York so he could, within 24 hours, obtain a certain kind of foot pedal unavailable in London. Almost certainly exaggerating, Pete later told *Sounds* he wrote about four different scripts, 40 tunes, and four hours of experimental tapes. He also claimed to have spent thousands on synthesizers, lighting, a quadraphonic PA system, "special cartridge type playback machines with very specific logic controls so that as you're playing you can hit a button and get an instant piece of music to play along with you at a given tempo," and "machines that can alter the tempo of music but without altering the pitch so that the music could play along with us at our tempo rather than the other way around."[27]

But the chemistry to ignite the audience involvement and resultant mental and spiritual harmony Townshend had outlined in the January 13 press conference was distinctly lacking. As he lamented in the BBC radio *Lifehouse* special, "Frank Dunlop had a mandate from the Young Vic to allow us in there as long as we were doing something that was manifestly for the public. So he just started to invite people in off the street and all they did was just to get in the way, basically. We got nervous and we started to play 'My Generation' and smash guitars and stuff."[28] In *Penthouse* a few years later, he admitted to second thoughts about the strategy of playing unannounced gigs to whomever might walk in the door, as "all we got were freaks and 13-year-old skinhead kids. If we had advertised the thing as a Who concert, we could have packed the fucking place for a year."[29]

At the time, Townshend had looked forward to a motley crowd of ragtags in the *New York Times*, and a spokesman for The Who's company, Track, had told *Melody Maker* just a couple days before the first proper show that "we specifically want an audience who are not rock orientated. As far as we are concerned we hope the audience has never heard of The Who before."[30] But the group's enthusiasm might have been dimmed right from the get-go. "The first day about 50 skinheads came in and did a dance which I promptly copied," Townshend told *Hit Parader*. "Which is where two boys dance together and they bop one another's shoulders, you lean forward and the two shoulders bop, I thought that was really amazing. Followed closely by a maniac who ran up to the front of the stage, like a hippie, like some drug crazed hippie, and started to yell 'Capitalist pigs! Bastards! Get off the stage!' So I lifted him up onto the stage and beat what shit there was left in him out of him. Whereupon he promptly got up again and got on the drums and said, 'I've always wanted to be in a group!' And then off again and then came back and started to scream. And I suddenly realized the whole thing about it is you almost need the ritual of starting and finishing."[31]

Just how much *Lifehouse* material was actually played remains uncertain in the absence of circulating tapes. But Townshend's *Lifehouse Chronicles* notes leave the impression that it was quickly de-emphasized: "Within a few weeks our 'experiments' had dwindled into trips to the local pub and over-loud short concerts of our early hits for anyone who showed up at the Young Vic."[32]

In *The Who ... Through The Eyes Of Pete Townshend*, the guitarist gave another explanation for the safe repertoire that willingly took some share of the blame for the failure of the Young Vic experiment. "It wasn't because the audience couldn't do their bit, but because the group failed," he said. "*We* were the ones with the preconceptions, and we worried about the audience too much. The audience was told at the door that it was an experiment – someone actually said to them, 'You know it's cheap because it's an experiment, and I can't even guarantee The Who will come on.' So the audience came in and sat down very casually, and a lot people chatted. We came on, and we'd get halfway through doing a few things and we'd look at one another bleakly and go, 'I can't stand it – let's play "Summertime Blues."' And the audience would leap about and we'd look at one another and say, 'Well, *that's* obviously where it's at.'"[33]

John Entwistle had a drier perspective. "From what I understand," he recalled in the *Classic Albums* documentary on *Who's Next*, "we were supposed to take up the Young Vic, and the audience were supposed to be there and live with us. I didn't quite actually get it. And in practice it didn't work, because you brought in a bunch of people from the street that had to go home for their tea."[34] In the recent past, The Who had warned in song of the dangers of the audience expecting too much from entertainers and messiahs, especially in the finale to *Tommy*. At the Young Vic, ironically, they seemed to have fallen victim to the reverse, expecting too much from their audience.

Another comment from the BBC radio interview leaves the impression Townshend was almost too preoccupied by technical matters and routining the songs to pay much attention to spontaneous ideas generated by the audience or anyone else. "I didn't regard the Young Vic performances as a dramatic workshop," he said. "I suppose I was waiting for that to start, I was waiting for that to happen. I'd done my bit, I'd written the script and the other stuff I was fussing with was technical stuff, really, trying to help the band play some of the songs that I had written, help [soundman] Bobby [Pridden] with some of his technical stuff. And what we were doing at the Young Vic which was dicey was that we were working with a quadraphonic sound system which had been pioneered by [Pink] Floyd, it wasn't brand new ... the desk that we were delivered may have worked, but Bobby couldn't seem to get it to work. That was one of the problems."[35]

If the audience wasn't sparking fresh content, the drama not getting workshopped, and the equipment not cooperating, were The Who at least getting some usable concert or crowd reaction footage for the *Lifehouse* film? Apparently not. A crew from TVX, the video arm of the London arts organization the Arts Lab, did shoot some footage. But this only amounted to "a lot of wide shots with the audience in the foreground for about 20 minutes until the tape ran out," as crew member Cliff Evans told Sutcliffe.[36] "Although Pete had written the screenplay, we hadn't begun to conceive how this would look on film, how this would be shot, or any of those things, or how it would be staged," Stamp confessed in the BBC radio program. "None of this had been worked out. It didn't gel. The process of it becoming a concept and it becoming something didn't happen."[37]

The Young Vic concerts wouldn't even last six weeks, let alone the six months that Townshend had optimistically envisioned in the *New York Times*. Soon the plug was pulled on this part of the grand experiment. "I remember the early aspects that I was involved in with *Lifehouse* as being much more allied to the live performances at the Young Vic," says Keith Altham. "Whatever it was that was going to come from those live performances would in some way crystallize the whole concept of the thing in Pete's mind for him. And then they gave up on it. Because Roger related to the kids and the audience and everything else, but he couldn't see what else Pete was driving at, or going to get from what they were doing. It was all kind of too loose for him to actually see an end."[38]

As in many things Who and *Lifehouse*, there was a more unexpected pressure from the everyday world that could have been a factor as well. "There were complaints from the neighbors because we weren't all that far from residential housing," Richard Mangan told Sutcliffe. "[There was] a Peabody [rented housing] estate behind us and flats across the road, and The Who really made the building rattle. They caused a few reactions. I think that might be why we only did three shows."[39]

The Who might also have been thinking of modifying the scope of their extravaganza before it became a folly. Rising expectations made embarrassment and public disappointment definite prospects even before the first concert, with the press buildup reaching fever pitch just days beforehand. The *Lifehouse* story had been first semi-coherently outlined (and first named as such) on February 7 in the *New York Times*. Townshend himself wrote about "Life House" by name in his February 13 *Melody Maker* column, as well as again naming its protagonist, Bobby. He also talked up the upcoming Young Vic shows in some of his most highfalutin language to date: "The Young Vic becomes the 'Life House,' The Who become musicians and the audience become part of a fantasy. ... There is a story connected with each person that will walk into the Life House, but for now we have made one up for them, until we know the real one. We have music that will stimulate them to stay with us through lengthy marathon concerts, and perhaps even boring filming. We have sounds ready that will push us a lot further than we have ever gone before, but what the results will be is still unknown."[40]

It made for good copy, but the press weren't quite sure what *Lifehouse* was supposed to be about either. "I sat for days with the media and The Who doing interviews at the Young Vic," remembers Altham. "Pete was trying to rationalize it in some way, and the only way he knew how, I think, was to try and play it and get it out there with a live audience. Roger understood 'live'; he didn't understand what the hell else he was on about. And I have to say, I struggled with it too, even though I sat through a number of interviews that Pete did with very bright journalists. And I'm not sure anybody really got a handle on it. Because I'm not sure *Pete* had a handle on it, really. Michael Wale did a very good interview with Pete on *Lifehouse* [for the London *Times*]; he was the only one that I thought seemed to be grasping the subject. I was sitting through his interview and thinking, 'Yeah, somebody's finally got actually some idea of what he's talking about.' I'm not sure *I* did, but he seemed to.

100

"It was a kind of really abstract idea. I mean, there were elements in it which had been talked about before. In some ways, he was foretelling the use of the Internet, [the experience suits] that went into everybody's home, and people wouldn't have to move. But in those days of course there was no Facebook, no Twitter, no blogs, no computers. And to good old practical Roger, it meant wiring up everybody's house. That was Roger's famous quote – 'there's not enough wire.'"[41]

In about 30 or 40 years, there *would* be enough wire, or wireless technology, but Townshend's ideas were ahead of what was possible with 70s equipment. "I was somewhat surprised to find out that in addition to all this stuff with this big band called The Who, that he was so interested and fascinated [by], and was beginning to have a command of, the technology of the day," says Roger Powell, who demonstrated the ARP 2500 synthesizer to Townshend around this time. "Pete was already thinking about using computers for composing. He could see into the future of what was going to happen, and the importance of this, way back then. He always seemed to have a big theatrical vision, but sort of based on new technologies that didn't exist. It's only in the new millennium that we have anything approaching what people thought they might be able to do back then."[42]

Confronted with all these obstacles, was *Lifehouse*, or at least the plan to make a magnificent combination film/album/concert from the concept, abandoned by March 1, when the last of these Young Vic events took place? It's hard to say how The Who felt at the time, but in retrospect, Townshend dates the disillusionment as setting in even earlier. In his *Lifehouse Chronicles* liner notes, he describes the January 13 press conference as "the beginning of the end."[43]

His sensitivity to what he remembers as poor or skeptical reactions to that conference might seem odd coming from someone who spouted off in the press more than any rock musician. But there was a difference between being interviewed and writing for print and trying to explain to a crowd of strangers a mission statement that even those closest to him weren't absorbing. "I think Pete wasn't a good speechmaker in those days," mused Dunlop to Sutcliffe. "He wasn't so articulate, he learnt that later. It was all inside him then."[44] He was also dejected by the mysterious lack of creative input from Lambert, and, to his recollection, the lack of money from the $2 million he thought he'd been promised by Universal.

The Young Vic concerts had given The Who an opportunity to get to grips with at least some of the *Lifehouse* songs, but otherwise they didn't seem to have given *Lifehouse* much if anything. If they weren't exactly an all-out failure, they'd certainly failed to deliver what was expected. The same would be true of the next step in the *Lifehouse* process, in which the group would attempt to capture the material on record, far from either the Young Vic or the London studios The Who usually used.

The Who had done a bit of recording in the USA in 1967 and 1968, working on some singles and tracks for *The Who Sell Out* in New York, Nashville, and Los Angeles. These, however, had been pit-stops in the group's manic American tour schedules. When they flew to New York in mid-March 1971, it marked the first occasion on which they were traveling across the Atlantic with the intention of recording much or even all of a complete album. This was Lambert's idea, as he was co-producing an album at New York's Record Plant for LaBelle with Vicki Wickham (most famous for managing Dusty Springfield and producing the mid-60s UK TV show *Ready Steady Go!*, on which The Who had frequently featured). The sessions were intended to last two weeks, but in the event would barely stagger through a few days.

Although Lambert's role in The Who's recordings had diminished since *Tommy*, Townshend was eager to resume collaboration, partly in the hope that Kit could be as much help in bringing *Lifehouse* to fruition as he had been with *Tommy*. Perhaps some dissatisfaction with the tracks cut at Townshend's home studio for the aborted 1970 LP also played a part. As he told *Sounds* early in January 1971, "Recently we've been recording at my own studios; there I really did have control. I mean I was recording the group, producing, writing and everything. When we finished it didn't sound like The Who at all. It sounded like me, like one of my demos. So we had to throw it in my demo tray and go back into the studios we normally use."[45]

If The Who hoped to get a superior sound than they'd been able to achieve at Pete's home studio, or perhaps even than they could get anywhere in the UK, the Record Plant was a good choice. While it had only been open for a couple of years, Jimi Hendrix had given it instant credibility by recording much of 1968's *Electric Ladyland* there. The Velvet Underground had done many sessions there in 1969; John Lennon would record some of his 1971 album *Imagine* there as well. According to Townshend's liner notes for the deluxe CD reissue of *Who's Next*, The Who would be the first band to use its new Studio One, with engineer Jack Adams co-producing with Kit Lambert. (Pete also wrote that he'd worked with Adams in New York before, but it's not clear when that would have taken place; possibly it happened during the New York sessions for *The Who Sell Out*.)[46] According to a Townshend *ZigZag* interview, Lambert even told him they'd record in quadraphonic sound – something they would attempt with more diligence a couple of years later.[47]

It's something of a miracle we're even able to hear some Record Plant tracks on authorized CDs, although some first showed up on the 1990 bootleg *From Lifehouse To Leeds*. According to Chris Charlesworth, who helped assemble the 1995 *Who's Next* reissue on which some Record Plant cuts were first heard, "We actually retrieved the master tape from which that bootleg was made ... [at the time of the recording], it was brought back to England and left at Olympic Studios; I guess The Who played it once and just left it there. It stayed at Olympic until there was a clear-out sometime in the early 80s, and it was thrown in the rubbish. It was rescued from the garbage and ended up being sold to the bootlegger, we don't quite know how.

"Late [in 1994], Pete asked me to try and retrieve it, implying that he'd be willing to buy it back for a reasonable sum, with no questions asked. I put the word out, and although it was a bit of cloak and dagger, I got a call four months later from someone saying he knew where it was, and all I had to do was send a messenger to this address, and I'd get it back. So I got it back, and gave it back to The Who. The bootleggers didn't even charge us."[48]

Although Townshend described the Record Plant sessions in the notes to the *Who's Next* CD deluxe edition as "great fun," they weren't greatly productive, major problems becoming immediately evident. If Pete could take some cold comfort in these not being directly related to *Lifehouse* and his inability to fully articulate its premise, they were if anything even more detrimental to work on the band's next album, and even to the long-term health of The Who themselves. First, Lambert was using heroin, impeding his ability to supervise the sessions. In addition, as Townshend frankly admitted in the same notes, Keith Moon was using hard drugs as well. Typically, Pete didn't exempt himself from his share of blame either, remembering drinking bottle after bottle of brandy.[49]

Partying inside and outside the studio hadn't stopped The Who or indeed other acts who had used the Record Plant, such as Hendrix, from laying down some classic tracks. In March 1971, however, the chaos was apparently spilling over to the control room. "Jack Adams was one of the top engineers at the Record Plant," remembers Jimmy Robinson, who'd taken a job as a second engineer at the studio after playing tenor sax with Buddy Miles's band. "He had done a lot of big records, and he worked with LaBelle a lot. I worked with Jack a few times. I used to call him Merlin, because he would like disappear a lot during sessions. He would not come back for like an hour, maybe two hours. A lot of times Jack would look over at me and say, 'Uh, I've got to go out. I'll be right back,' or something like that. 'And you've got to take over.' One night that happened, I ended up like finishing LaBelle for him, and we became really good friends."

In his days at the Record Plant, continues Robinson, Adams would "take a bottle of scotch and just go and sit in a bathroom stall and drink half of it. He would literally say 'Jimmy, take the board,' and then he would disappear. Somebody would start to get pissed off, and go 'Where's Jack?' and they'd have to go find him. He'd be like in the broom closet or in the fucking bathroom stall, the door locked, passed out."[50]

Another young engineer at the Record Plant was Jack Douglas, later to work on Lennon's *Imagine* and, almost a decade later, as a producer on John Lennon and Yoko Ono's *Double Fantasy* LP. "Up till then, I had only done some jingle dates and one record session with Patti LaBelle during which I had set the console on fire by knocking someone's beer into the transformers," he said in the June 1995 issue of *Guitar Shop*.[51] In an interview with Don Zulaica of LiveDaily.com, he remembered his work on The Who's Record Plant sessions as his first engineering gig, while also intimating that Adams might not have been that into doing Who sessions in the first place. "It was Jack Adams and myself," he said. "Jack was an R&B engineer and I was his assistant. Jack was not into doing The Who. He was into Aretha, just: 'God, let me out of here! Take over PLEASE.' And the first thing they did was 'Won't Get Fooled Again' and my hair was standing straight on end."[52]

"Kit Lambert was technically listed as the producer," Douglas told *Guitar Shop*, "but it was clear that Pete was in charge of the production. He could drive the band nuts with his directions, but also really got them ripping when they tracked. He would especially concentrate on whipping up Keith, because he realized that the band actually took its energy cues from Keith. The energy level was always so up there that many of the solos on the record were done in one pass during the tracking sessions. It really kept the trio sound together."[53]

Although it's been reported that sessions started on March 15, perhaps no proper or at least complete takes were done that day, as the seven tracks that were eventually released were all done between Tuesday March 16 and Thursday March 18. 'Won't Get Fooled Again' may well have been the first song they did, as Douglas remembers, since the version issued as a bonus track on the deluxe edition of *Who's Next* was cut on March 16. While this shows the band getting close indeed to the arrangement used on *Who's Next*, there are important differences that mark this as distinctly inferior. The guitar work is busier and a bit histrionic in its occasional squeals; Daltrey's lead singing isn't supported by backup vocals; a synthesizer-and-drum-dominated instrumental passage follows the "meet the new boss, same as the old boss" declamation, disrupting the momentum; and Roger's famous scream that precedes the line is absent. The transitions between the verses, choruses, and instrumental breaks are at times clumsy, as are some of Daltrey's improvised-sounding vocal interjections. And the recording didn't use the synthesizer track from Townshend's demo, a credible but ultimately not quite as penetrating facsimile being created by playing an organ through a VCS3 live – an experiment initiated, interestingly, by Roger rather than Pete.

The other song from March 16 to eventually emerge was in a couple of respects the oddest Who recording from the *Who's Next/Lifehouse* sessions. The Motown oldie 'Baby Don't You Do It,' a 1964 hit for Marvin Gaye, had been inserted into The Who's repertoire almost immediately after its release, as the discovery of their acetate demo from the period of the song (released on the CD version of *Odds & Sods*) proves. Why would they be revisiting that of all songs at a time when they were ostensibly working on a concept album to take place 20 years in the future?

Townshend would reveal how it could have fitted into *Lifehouse* in his *Lifehouse Chronicles* notes, where he explains how the parents "going mobile" in search of their runaway daughter would furtively listen to old rock records as they toodled in their motor caravan. (In his 1989 Radio One interview with Roger Scott, he described much the same scenario, although curiously it was "two rock'n'roll guys" doing the driving and listening, not a married couple.)[54] What better oldie to revive for such a scene than 'Baby Don't You Do It,' which The Who featured constantly in their mid-60s live shows? (It's also worth bearing in mind that *Tommy* had actually included an oldie of sorts in the band's adaptation of Mose Allison's arrangement of bluesman Sonny Boy Williamson's 'Eyesight To The Blind'; an Allison song, 'Young Man Blues,' was considered for *Tommy* as well, as was a version of another blues song Allison covered, Mercy Dee Walton's 'One Room Country Shack.')

Even odder was the recruitment of a guest session-musician for the track, not to add keyboards, as had happened off and on since 1965, but lead guitar. Nor was the guitarist, Leslie West, a musician the average Who fan would expect to be called to fulfill the role. But West, who'd recently become a star as part of the US hard-rock band Mountain, had encountered The Who as far back as November 1967, when his band The Vagrants opened for a Who concert at New York's Village Theater. Both The Who and Mountain played Woodstock a couple years later, and West met Townshend and Moon in less hectic surroundings at the Speakeasy club in London. Pete also admitted to pinching some of West's licks "for the stage" in *ZigZag*.[55]

"When Mountain finally went over there, Track Records [The Who's UK label] were our agents, and they did pretty good to get us started in England," says West. "Kit Lambert had called my manager, and then they called me and [asked] do I want to play guitar with The Who on this album that they were doing. I don't even know if they had the title yet. I said, 'Well, they have a guitar player.' They said, 'Well, Pete didn't want to overdub, he wanted to do it straight away.' And I said, 'Sure.'"

The very notion of The Who enlisting another guitarist seems absurd. This, after all, was a band that featured one of the greatest rock guitarists, and which had not only functioned as a one-guitar power trio-with-vocalist throughout their entire recording career, but made it one of their trademarks. But as West says, it seemed to fit in with The Who's apparent desire, at these Record Plant sessions at least, to record as quickly and in as "live" a manner as possible. "From what I understood," West recalls, "he wanted to play rhythm, and he wanted me to play lead, so they didn't have to overdub. We were right in the same room, doing it without overdubbing. Roger was singing at the same time in a little room; we had headphones on." West had never even heard the original Marvin Gaye version.

The rendition by The Who on this date, however, was quite different from both Gaye's and the demo they'd cut back in the mid 60s, extending its length to more than eight minutes. West "just went out there, listened to it, and started playing it. The way the recording came out was great."[56] They did give Leslie quite a bit of space for extended blues-rock soloing, and Roger quite a bit of space for vocal extemporizing during the lengthy, semi-jamming passages. But the track wasn't used until it appeared as a bonus cut on the 1995 *Who's Next* CD reissue, although a live December 1971 Who performance of the number in San Francisco would be used as a non-LP B-side the following year.

As both 'Won't Get Fooled Again' and 'Baby Don't You Do It' were recorded in Studio Two rather than Studio One, it's possible both tracks were intended more as warm-ups – as Townshend states in his notes to the deluxe edition – than serious stabs at cuts for an official release. That impression is reinforced by the group's decision to cut without overdubbing, with Douglas confirming in his interview with Don Zulaica that all the vocals were live as well. Although it would have been a disastrously unsuitable A-side in 1971, Pete later told reissue producer Jon Astley, while assembling the CD edition of *Who's Next* nearly 25 years later, that 'Baby Don't You Do It' "could easily be a single."[57]

Much confusion lingers as to what else was recorded at the Record Plant, and who played on the tracks that have surfaced. West is only credited as a guitar player on 'Baby Don't You Do It' of the Record Plant recordings that have gained official release, but remembers being played demos of 'Won't Get Fooled Again' and 'Behind Blue Eyes,' as well as working on 'Behind Blue Eyes' and possibly 'Baba O'Riley' (no Record Plant version of which has ever circulated). It has been reported that Mountain bassist Felix Pappalardi, who was also renowned for his work with Cream, produced the March 16 recordings, but West says Pappalardi wasn't involved. (Townshend, however, did recall Pappalardi producing 'Won't Get Fooled Again' in a December 1971 *ZigZag* interview.)

According to West, Pappalardi *was* approached to participate, with Lambert asking West if Pappalardi played organ. The ensuing confusion, however, reflected the disorganization of the group's Record Plant sessions in general, as West also remembers Pappalardi bringing along both his bass amps and the expectation that he would be helping with production. "John Entwistle came in and said, 'What's this?' Felix said, 'My bass amps.'

[Entwistle] says, 'I'm the bass player in the fucking Who.' [Felix says], 'Well, make up your mind, I'm a busy man.' He thought he was going to be in there to produce. It got a little heated, and he left. What happened was that Kit Lambert thought he was Felix Cavaliere from The Rascals, who *did* play organ. So it was embarrassing to him. He didn't play anything."

Whatever amps the Mountain men brought into the Record Plant, it's hard to imagine a louder in-studio tandem than Townshend and West in early 1971. "I was using a very small Sunn cabinet, with one 12-inch speaker, and a 50-watt Marshall," West told Gibson.com. "Townshend was using his Hi-Watt amps, and he said to me that he wanted to be the loudest. Afterward he came over to me – I guess he was a little embarrassed – and said, 'Can you hear yourself OK?' I told him I could hear myself even if I was in Chicago."[58]

Judging from the annotation on the *Who's Next* deluxe edition, at least three tracks were started on March 17, with work continuing on two of these the following day. 'Love Ain't For Keeping,' whose deluxe-edition version dates entirely from the 17th, is done in a considerably heavier manner than the official *Who's Next* re-recording. Even more notably, Townshend rather than Daltrey handles the lead vocal, without any support from backup harmonies; it's double the length of the version on the *Who's Next* LP, with much more extended guitar soloing, which verges on the tedious on the lengthy rideout; and there's a sweeping synthesizer throughout, but it's largely relegated to the background. For all these reasons, it's markedly inferior to the remake.

The Record Plant version of 'Behind Blue Eyes' is more satisfying, although the opening verse has a fuller arrangement than would the re-recording on *Who's Next*. A celestial organ hovers over the folky guitar riff, and cymbal sweeps and fuzzy hard rock guitar riffs occasionally punctuate the calm. Al Kooper is credited with the organ on the *Who's Next* deluxe edition, and his participation would have made sense, as he'd played organ on some of the New York sessions for *The Who Sell Out* back in 1967. However, according to Kooper, he did not play on this track, nor indeed on any of The Who's Record Plant sessions.

'Pure And Easy,' still considered a core *Lifehouse* song at this point, was also started on March 17, and is executed pretty well, though the drums largely drop out during the bridge. Also, the transitions between the song's sections are less effectively dramatic, and the end hasn't been fully worked out, disjointed handclapping continuing during the concluding organ note. This track too has an organ, and one still wonders who was responsible, especially if it wasn't Kooper

"As far as why New York musicians were used, I think it was just going to be a jam," says Dennis Ferrante, who remembers working as an assistant engineer on 'Behind Blue Eyes' and 'Won't Get Fooled Again.' "They blended just fine with The Who. Jack was cool with the guys, but I felt tension between the band and Kit."[59]

Work on both 'Love Ain't For Keeping' and 'Behind Blue Eyes' continued on March 18, and the *Who's Next* deluxe edition also includes a version of 'Getting In Tune' (then still titled 'I'm In Tune') recorded on that date. Both piano and organ are heard in this arrangement, the piano perhaps contributed by Kenny Ascher, who would later play on several John Lennon albums. (He's noted as a session musician for the Record Plant recordings in Andy Neill and Matt Kent's *Anyway Anyhow Anywhere* Who chronicle, but is not credited in the deluxe-edition liner notes.) This rendition lacks the call-and-response vocals so critical to some of the choruses on the official *Who's Next* LP, and is nearly two minutes longer, the difference being accounted for by a way-too-long instrumental break. Lambert evidently enjoyed it, however, as Townshend's liner notes recall Kit running out holding a sign inscribed DON'T STOP! during a "kicking jam session" at the end of the song. Lambert also changed the color of the studio lighting as songs were recorded, diving across the board during one Daltrey vocal overdub of 'Won't Get Fooled Again' to reach the controls in time for Roger's climactic scream. "He made it," Douglas recalled, "but he wound up with little indentations in his face from the knobs in the monitor section."[60]

Another memory Leslie West has of the sessions indicates he might have been playing on 'Getting In Tune' as well, so similar is it to Townshend's tale. "Kit Lambert was out of his fucking mind, because we were doing one of the tracks, and it was going along great," he recalls. "Kit comes out with a sign that says, 'Great work! Keep it up!' He's putting it in front of our faces as we're playing. Pete stops the session and called Kit a fucking twit for ruining the take. You know, he's running around like a madman with a sign in front of everybody while we're recording. I'd never seen anything like [it]."[61]

There were some lighter moments amid the madness, even if the line between the fun and the madness was getting ever harder to distinguish, particularly when it came to the behavior of The Who's drummer. One evening they were visited by the legendary guitarist Link Wray, whose 1958 hit single 'Rumble' was the first rock recording to effectively use fuzz guitar. As Townshend wrote in 1974, in his liner notes to *The Link Wray Rumble*, "Keith Moon promptly took off all his clothes. He stayed naked until people started to take notice, then when they became bored with his studio streak he dressed as a wasp and buzzed around the studio. This later inspired the [1972] B-side 'Wasp Man,' a tune we hereby dedicate to Link Wray."[62]

"I remember Keith Moon playing on this gigantic Hammond organ between takes," Leslie West recalls with a laugh. "He was out there, and he looked like the Phantom of the Opera. I said to Pete, 'Well, he looks like he's having a good time.' And Pete says, 'No mate, he's being deadly serious.'"[63] Meanwhile, West gave Townshend a Les Paul Jr guitar that he would play on some 1971 Who sessions.

If any more progress was made at the Record Plant that week, however, nothing has emerged from The Who's archives to verify it. Townshend's deluxe-edition liner notes indicate sessions in Studio One lasted for four days starting on March 17, but nothing's emerged from either the 19th or the 20th, although documentation consulted by Jon Astley (who mastered the *Who's Next* deluxe edition) indicates that recording was also done on the 23rd. While a version of 'Time Is Passing' first issued on the 1998 CD edition of *Odds & Sods* is attributed to the Record Plant sessions, this was likely recorded slightly later in 1971 after the group's return to England, especially as *Anyway Anyhow Anywhere* doesn't list the song has having been cut in New York. Possibly work was slowing or grinding to a halt at the Record Plant as the week progressed, and the combination of personal problems and less-than-ideal production wore the band down.

When things came to a head, however, it wouldn't happen at the Record Plant, but in Lambert's room in the Navarro Hotel at Central Park South, where Townshend had called a group meeting. While it was not reported at the time, in hindsight the ensuing confrontation between Lambert and Townshend did not just put another damper on the *Lifehouse* project, it also permanently damaged the relationship between the two men. As Pete walked into Kit's room, he heard his trusted co-manager raging against him to his assistant, Anya Butler: "Townshend has blocked me at every front. I will not allow him to block me this time."[64] So devastated was Pete at hearing himself referred to this way – and not even by his first name, but his last – that at some point during the meeting, he edged toward the open window with thoughts of throwing himself to his death. Butler guessed his intentions, took him by the arm, and dissuaded him. "That," Townshend told *Revolver* in 2000, "is when I gave up on *Lifehouse*."[65]

That's Townshend's version, anyway. It seems uncertain that a hugely successful musician with a growing family – and who had, by his own written admission, just had some "great fun" at the Record Plant – would have been seriously considering suicide.[66] It's also odd that a fellow with such a thick-skinned persona would be so hurt by Lambert referring to him by last name only – a slight he does seem to have carried for decades, mentioning it in his *Lifehouse Chronicles* notes too. It is certain that Pete took personally Kit's diminishing competence, perceived attempts to obstruct the progression of *Lifehouse*, and general turn for the worse. He may have seen it as the abdication of his closest ally outside The Who – and, perhaps, his closest ally of all. "Kit was the only one who could really communicate to Pete what was good and what was bad, and Pete would accept it," Roger Daltrey recalled in the *Classic Albums* documentary on *Who's Next*. "He wouldn't accept anything otherwise."[67]

Whether or not the intention was to record the entirety of the *Who's Next* album at the Record Plant, the sessions had to be considered a failure for the most part. The group had worked on what seemed like at least half an album of songs likely to make the cut for whatever LP resulted, but none of them had yet realized their full potential as studio recordings. Whether or not any elements would be salvaged, at least as tracks upon which overdubs could be done, was questionable. So was whether they'd provide the foundation for anything else to do with *Lifehouse*, whether a film or otherwise. Work would resume on the album soon enough, back in their native London. But this time, unsurprisingly, Kit Lambert wouldn't be in the production seat.

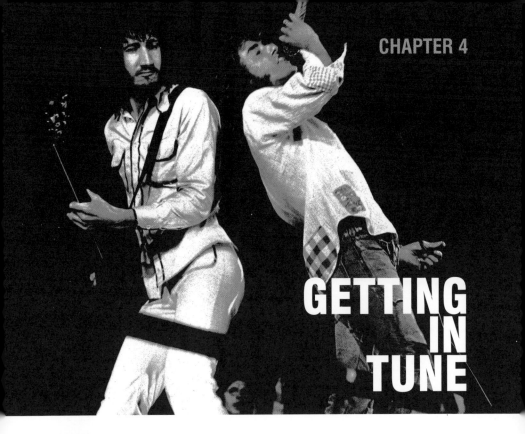

CHAPTER 4

GETTING IN TUNE

When The Who returned to London in late March 1971, it had been less than three months since Pete Townshend had spoken so euphorically to the press about his plans for *Lifehouse* and the Young Vic concerts. To most appearances, however, *Lifehouse* looked dead, or at least on life support. No filming was under way; no funding for the movie seemed forthcoming; and the Record Plant sessions hadn't produced anything resembling the core of any album whatsoever, let alone one that could support the *Lifehouse* concept.

It remains uncertain whether The Who intended to continue pursuing *Lifehouse* in all its multimedia glory. It seems clear they couldn't have filmed without money from Universal Studios, or a script that the rest of The Who and their management could understand and approve. What they could do is what they did best: record and perform live. And even if Townshend's morale had slumped to the brink of suicide, as he has since maintained, such was the group's work ethic that they were immediately ready to do both, with studio work the focus for most of the spring.

As the first order of business, The Who tried to determine whether anything was salvageable from the Record Plant sessions. "We heard the tapes we'd done in the States and they weren't really very good," Townshend admitted in *ZigZag*. "If they'd been mixed in the States when we did them they might have been all right. Tapes done in America can never sound right over here and vice versa." This in turn brought them back into contact with an old colleague they hadn't worked with in about five years: Glyn Johns. He'd end up as the most important figure, besides The Who themselves, in the recording of what would become their next LP.

"Glyn was originally brought in to remix the stuff we had done in New York and do overdubs," Townshend told *ZigZag*. "So he listened to it and said it was great, it was good, but if we started again, he could do it better."[1] In a 1989 interview with Roger Scott of BBC's Radio One, he intimated that Johns had heard the *Lifehouse* demos and expressed interest in getting involved even before the Record Plant sessions.

Buried in an interview that appeared in the *Los Angeles Free Press* at the end of 1971, however, was a remark indicating that the original idea was to have Johns work on live recordings that could be used in the *Lifehouse* movie. "Originally, Glyn Johns was brought in to work on the film," Townshend told Chris Van Ness. "We felt that no one else could handle The Who live as well as he could, plus the fact that he was going to be working on the movie, plus the fact that he designed The Stones' mobile studio, which was what we were going to be working in. I talked to him a few times about it, and he got really excited." Pete might have specifically been looking for an engineer rather than a producer at this point, as, in a typical proclamation that knew no bounds, he noted that he'd "really like to see a good sort of rock movie that's engineered like a rock album."[2]

While virtually unknown to the general public in early 1971, Johns had been one of the most important figures in British rock production for almost a decade. As an engineer at IBC Studios back in March 1963, he'd cut the first truly professional tracks laid down in the studio by The Rolling Stones, hoping to use the demos to get them a record deal and become their producer. Although he didn't become their producer when the Stones got a deal shortly afterward, he often worked with them as an engineer in the second half of the 60s. Considering Townshend's interest in having Johns record The Who live, it's also interesting to note that he had taped the Stones in concert as far back as March 1965, when he made the recordings that appeared on their EP *Got Live If You Want It!* He also engineered numerous other classic 60s British rock records, some with Shel Talmy producing – including some 1965 sessions by The Who that had been instrumental in launching their recording career.

"Glyn was certainly an asset for me because he was such a super-duper engineer," Talmy recalled in 1985. "He certainly helped with the sound, and one of the best things was we had enormous rapport, in that I didn't have to explain to him in any kind of detail what I wanted. By the time we'd worked together for a short time, he knew what I wanted and gave it to me. And don't forget I started out as an engineer, so I did know how to get it myself. So it was a pleasure working with him. It freed me up to concentrate on producing a record and not have to worry about the sound." Talmy, who produced both The Who's 1965 recordings and The Kinks' classic mid-60s records, did note a chink in Johns's armor, at least at that time. He felt Glyn "perhaps produced the best sound records there ever were, but could not pick a hit record if it came and bit him."[3]

Although Talmy and Johns worked on the classic *The Who Sing My Generation* album and the band's three great early hits ('I Can't Explain,' 'Anyway, Anyhow, Anywhere,' and 'My Generation'), acrimony between Talmy and The Who's management would take Johns out of the group's orbit for a good five years. In 1966 Kit Lambert and Chris Stamp broke their contract with Talmy, who, as an independent producer, leased the recordings to Decca Records and its UK Brunswick subsidiary for release. The case was settled out of court, and while The Who were able to resume recording using Kit Lambert as producer, Talmy was awarded a five per cent override on all of the group's recordings over the next five years – which included *Tommy* and the very tracks they were working on in 1971, among them the ones that would eventually coalesce into *Who's Next*.

"Shel Talmy asked me if I'd do an affidavit for him in his defense in court, which I did," Johns recalled in the *Amazing Journey* documentary. "As far as I was concerned, he was in the right. So I did an affidavit saying yes, he was their producer. So they didn't use me for a long time after that. I ran into them maybe a year later at the *NME* awards or something like that, and Daltrey came over to me and said, 'Why on earth did you appear for Shel Talmy in the court case?' I said, 'Well, because he asked me on the one hand, and it seemed to me that you'd broken the contract, so morally he was in the right.' So he said, 'Our main defense, our main attack to Shel's case was that in fact you were doing the production and not him.' Shel did in fact win the case, and the net result of that was Shel continued to be paid a royalty on everything I did, which meant I got a smaller royalty. So it sort of backfired somewhat."[4] Another consequence was that Johns didn't work with The Who between 1966 and 1970, although he continued to build his resume as Britain's greatest rock engineer on records by The Rolling Stones, Traffic, and The Beatles, for whose *Let It Be* he was awarded a co-producer credit.

By spring 1971, evidently enough time had passed for any rancor between Johns and The Who to have dissipated, especially as the group were not inclined to let personality clashes even within the band get in the way of achieving the best sound possible. Five years was also evidently enough time for their collaboration with Kit Lambert as producer to run its course, though he'd for the most part served them well in that capacity since taking the reins in 1966. However, as Johns recalled in the 1982 book *The Record Producers*, "they'd obviously decided they wouldn't work with Kit Lambert any more for some reason."[5]

"Glyn's way of working is much more like a musician, Kit's is more like a film director," Townshend told *Sounds* in July. "I think that's the only way to describe the difference. And I think we're at the point now where we're doing a bit of our own direction, and we need a musician more than a director. ... We knew that [Lambert's] pride was going to be hurt by us producing ourselves, but at the same time we knew that it was the only thing that could be done."[6]

More intriguingly, in an interview with Don Zulaica for LiveDaily.com, Record Plant engineer Jack Douglas said the songs they'd already cut in New York were "re-recorded in London because of a number of problems, one of them being a tax problem – The Who wasn't supposed to be recording in the USA, they were supposed to be touring."[7] That wouldn't have kept them from continuing to work with Lambert in London. But it does hint at a possible reason the New York sessions were halted, although those seem to have been abandoned due to a number of other more important factors.

The first recordings overseen by Johns were done at Mick Jagger's country mansion, Stargroves; this may have been because of Johns's close Rolling Stones connections, or a reluctance to book a more convenient or standard London studio until everyone felt comfortable with the collaboration. Situated in the small town of Newbury in Berkshire, a good 50 miles from London, Stargroves had hosted Stones sessions with a mobile studio since Jagger bought the property in 1970.

The Stones' 16-track mobile would be used for these exploratory Who recordings around early April, possibly as an outgrowth of the hope that Johns could record live music for the not-yet-abandoned film. (In his March *Melody Maker* column, Townshend had indicated as much, stating both that "we hope to record all the sound in our new film using it if it's available," and confirming that Johns "will be working with us on the film when it begins this year."[8]) It's not certain which songs were attempted, or if any recordings were eventually used on the official *Who's Next* LP. But as Johns later remembered, 'Won't Get Fooled Again' was definitely one of the first tracks recorded in some form there, while 'Going Mobile' might have been worked on as well.

"It had been very much a question of seeing how it went," Johns remembered in *The Record Producers*. "I said, 'I'll come and work with you for a week, and we'll see how we get on, and if it doesn't work out, you can have whatever we've done as a prezzy, and we'll call it quits.' But it worked really well, so we carried on."[9] Townshend did recall the Stargroves sessions as "boozy" in his *Who's Next* deluxe-edition liner notes. But presumably the harder stuff was more difficult to acquire in Newbury than in New York, and thus much less of a distraction.

As Pete told the *Los Angeles Free Press*, The Who did a test run of 'Won't Get Fooled Again' that "was fucking incredible, and I thought the whole thing was really going to work. See, in the movie, we were just going to play to the tape and play to the tracks and do the whole thing live, so everything would be live, it would all be the first time, it would all be magic."[10] Here again the implication was that Johns would be working on a live recording, or at least a 'live in the studio' recording.

Despite the scrambled state of Pete Townshend's psyche and Keith Moon's hard drug use, The Who do seem to have assembled quickly and been determined to continue recording after returning to London. After the group and Johns had felt each other out at Stargroves, they continued to work together at Olympic Sound Studios in London, the first session there taking place on April 12 at the latest. Olympic would be far more convenient than Stargroves, and had been used by many major rock artists. Again the Johns-Stones connection might have made Glyn particularly comfortable there, The Rolling Stones having done much of their recording at Olympic since the mid 60s.

As Townshend said in the *Los Angeles Free Press*, "Glyn said, 'If you like it here [in Stargroves], I really wish you'd let me have a try at Olympic; because it would be amazing at Olympic.' This is where he usually works in England. So we went in there for four days – just a casual thing to try out what we wanted to do."[11]

The bulk of what became the *Who's Next* album would be recorded at Olympic in May and June, but it's known that 'Bargain' was first attempted there on April 12 and worked on during at least three subsequent June sessions. More unusually, April 12 also saw the completion of a song that didn't make *Who's Next*, 'Too Much Of Anything,' further confirming that it was a likely contender for *Lifehouse* at this point. The Who gave it a more stately feel than Townshend's demo version, with prominent acoustic guitars and piano. It's hard to say how in tune Roger Daltrey was with the lyric, however, as he re-recorded his vocals in 1974 for the version released on *Odds & Sods*, but it's largely the same track as the one done at Olympic. (Townshend told the *Los Angeles Free Press* that six numbers were done in four days on this first visit to Olympic, but that's likely an exaggeration, at least in terms of completed tracks.)

'Too Much Of Anything' apparently dropped out of serious consideration as better material came to the fore and it was decided to make the record a single album rather than a double. It might have been important in the grand scheme of the LP, however, for reintroducing a musician who'd been absent from Who records for as long as Johns had. Pianist Nicky Hopkins had been a key contributor to The Who's 1965 recordings, playing piano on the *My Generation* album and assorted non-LP cuts, including the hit 'Anyway, Anyhow, Anywhere.' Since then he'd reinforced his credentials as Britain's top rock session pianist on records by The Kinks, Donovan, Jeff Beck, The Beatles, and The Rolling Stones, as well as guesting on Jefferson Airplane's *Volunteers* and even performing with them at Woodstock. Although his contributions to *Who's Next* weren't all that numerous, they'd be essential to two of its songs, 'Getting In Tune' and 'The Song Is Over.'

"They are incredible to work with because they haven't got hang-ups like some people have," Hopkins told *Melody Maker* in late 1971. "Their material is so strong, but it's basically down to me what I play on their records. Pete brings demos in for us to listen to but the piano bits are basically my own. Some of his demos are incredible; they sound better than the finished product."[12] Townshend, for his part, called Nicky "a total genius" in *Rolling Stone*.[13]

The respect was clearly mutual, Hopkins revealing in the same *Melody Maker* article that "earlier this year it came out that I might join The Who. Well, it was suggested by Pete. He told me that if I ever wanted to be in a band permanently they would like me to consider The Who first. I couldn't make my mind up about it and in the end nothing happened."[14] It's an interesting notion to consider, but The Who's image had been one of four such strong and different individuals for so long that it's hard to see how a fifth official member could have been added. Perhaps, if he'd accepted, his role would have not been as a full partner, but limited to playing with them on stage to fill out their sound in concert and on specific studio tracks that called for keyboards, as he was doing for The Rolling Stones in the same period. Or Townshend and Hopkins might have *both* changed their minds. Pete told *Disc* in October 1972 that Hopkins "would really like to tour with us. But we really don't want him. We have a language of our own as a group that has been together for 14 years and it just wouldn't work."[15]

With recording now under way in London for the album that would be called *Who's Next*, and The Who and Townshend no longer talking up *Lifehouse* in the press, retrospective accounts sometimes conclude that *Lifehouse* had fizzled out at this point. Upon close examination, that's not so clear. There are indications that The Who were persisting with the project in its original form, even if the film dimension had stalled. After an absence of almost two months, the band returned to the Young Vic Theatre for two more evening concerts on April 26 and May 5, even recording the first of these. It seems unlikely they'd do more Young Vic concerts if there wasn't some sliver of hope that something of use for *Lifehouse* might emerge from them, or that something unexpectedly positive might happen to reignite their enthusiasm for using it as a workshop of sorts for weeks or months on end.

The purpose of the recording made at the Young Vic on April 26 isn't certain. Jon Astley, later involved in remastering and remixing many Who releases, was at that time Townshend's brother-in-law. "Pete wanted to use it as part of *Who's Next*," he recalls. "His big dream was to actually record live material that could be spliced into *Lifehouse*."[16] That would fit in with Townshend's memory of Glyn Johns being initially brought in to record the band live. Possibly The Who wanted to listen to the songs and how they sounded in concert. It is unlikely they were being considered for a stand-alone record release, especially as *Live At Leeds* was only about a year old at this point. Perhaps they wanted some of the material on tape to act as a reference for themselves and Glyn Johns as they prepared for the most serious phase of recording the album in the studio, although versions already existed of at least a half-dozen songs from the Record Plant sessions.

In his *Who's Next* deluxe-edition liner notes, Pete Townshend dates these Young Vic recordings to winter 1971, between his home demos of much of the material and the Record Plant sessions. With less specific detail, he also does so in his *Lifehouse Chronicles* liner notes. However, this time frame is clearly incorrect, and even contradicted by the prominent dating of the tapes to April 26 in the deluxe-edition annotation itself. Townshend's confusion is understandable, given the rapid crush of events within these several months. But this has helped to create the misleading impression that the Young Vic performances (and possibly the ambition to make *Lifehouse* as originally conceived) were over and done with by the time The Who went to record in New York, which wasn't the case.

The concert was recorded with the same 16-track Rolling Stones mobile studio that the band had used at Stargroves. Overseeing the taping was Andy Johns, younger brother of Glyn, who was already building an impressive career of his own as engineer and producer on albums by the likes of Free, Led Zeppelin, Jethro Tull, and Traffic. Soon, with *Exile on Main Street*, he'd engineer for The Rolling Stones. There was another Stones connection; Ian Stewart (known as 'Stu'), the Stones' roadie, occasional keyboardist, and general handyman, would also be helping out in the mobile truck. Most of the concert was officially issued as disc two of the *Who's Next* deluxe edition in 2003, and while no match for *Live at Leeds*, it is historically invaluable as a document of The Who's progress in that foggy gap between *Lifehouse*'s inception and the sessions that would result in *Who's Next*.

"It might have been Lambert's or Townshend's idea," remembers Andy Johns, who – astonishingly – was unaware that the material had been issued on the deluxe edition when interviewed for this book. "They wanted to see how [the material] parlayed out for an audience, and also to record it so they could see the results and make whatever corrections." Evidently Lambert hadn't been wholly frozen out of The Who's recording process. Andy also recalls him "standing up a couple of times [and shouting] 'Stop! Stop! Stop!' He'd stop them in the middle of a song, stamp around, and do the usual Kit Lambert thing with the big leather coat and the two poodles and the pink gin. They played a full set, but Kit stopped them a couple of times to make various suggestions at the top of his voice. I don't even remember the room being that full; there can't have been more than 200 kids or something like that. It wasn't a very big room."

By Andy's account, there wouldn't have been much recording done if one irate neighborhood resident had managed to get his way. "We were parked out in back," Johns recalls, "and there were these sort of tenement row houses. There's all this racket coming out of the New Vic, and a little bit from the truck, [although] the truck was fairly well soundproofed. And they put on plays at the New Vic, they didn't have rock bands.

"I felt somebody coming into the truck and thought, hello, what's this? I went into the back of the truck, and there's this guy with this double-edged axe, wearing a little sort of undershirt, some braces with a pair of trousers, and big hobnail boots. He said 'Oi, this fucking noise. I can't stand it.' It was only about nine o'clock at night! And he saw the big snake [the cable connecting the studio to the theater] going into the room, he says, 'Oh, I know that's important. I've got this axe. I'm going to chop it in half.' I went 'Stu! There's someone here to see you!' So Stu I think paid him ten quid or something, and off he tottered. But I thought it was some axe murderer. He had this look in his eye; I thought, well, this could be it, then. [But] there wasn't much room to swing an axe in that truck, so it wasn't much good."[17]

Much of the set did feature *Lifehouse* material, including all six of the songs known to have been worked on at the Record Plant, as well as 'Bargain,' 'Time Is Passing,' and 'Too Much Of Anything.' The absence of the key *Who's Next* songs, 'Baba O'Riley,' 'Going Mobile,' and 'The Song Is Over,' does seem curious if the intention was to see how *Lifehouse* material worked live and record it for reference. There are no known Who recordings of these songs prior to this date, so it's an outside chance they hadn't even been written, or at least not yet introduced to the group by Townshend.

The rest of the set suggests that the band might not yet have figured out whether the intention of these concerts was to work on new material, air some oldies for their own pleasure, entertain an audience expecting at least some familiar favorites, or do all of these things at once. The show still included a couple of *Tommy* crowd-pleasers, 'Pinball Wizard' and 'See Me, Feel Me' (still officially unreleased, but available on bootlegs); a few songs on the margin of *Lifehouse* consideration that had been part of their set since mid-1970 ('Naked Eye,' 'Water,' and 'I Don't Even Know Myself'); 'My Generation'; and 'Young Man Blues,' a Mose Allison cover that had been played by the band live since at least 1964, and familiar to Who fans via the version on *Live at Leeds*. There were also three oldies whose only fathomable purpose to *Lifehouse* would have been as the songs the parents played as they went from Scotland to London on the motorway: 'Baby Don't You Do It' (still officially unreleased, although an incomplete performance has been bootlegged), Larry Williams' s 1957 hit 'Bony Maronie' (first issued as a 1988 B-side to a reissue of 'Won't Get Fooled Again'), and Bo Diddley's 'Road Runner.' At a rehearsal from this date that's been bootlegged (and, judging from its sound quality, also recorded from the mobile studio), they also do Rufus Thomas's classic 'Walking The Dog.' Featuring Daltrey singing the lyric with obvious relish, it might have been another oldie under consideration for filling up the live concert or the *Lifehouse* soundtrack.

Generally The Who play well in front of an appreciative audience, but the atmosphere is more tentative and muted than it would be for their post-*Who's Next* concerts. They're clearly getting comfortable with 'Love Ain't For Keeping' and 'Too Much Of Anything' (introduced simply as 'Too Much') as midtempo hard rockers. They seem less settled into 'Bargain,' uneasily speeding and slowing during the verses; unable to mimic the swelling tones that introduce the studio version (if that had even been conceived yet), those notes have to be wordlessly sung. "The new ones are feeling a wee bit lame," offers an uncharacteristically nervous-sounding Townshend in his introduction. "They'll come together."

Of most interest is 'Time Is Passing,' ultimately destined to be a *Who's Next* out-take, but still a strong *Lifehouse* candidate at this point. The wheezing organ and pastoral whimsy of Townshend's demo have vanished, the song having been turned into a typically Who-ish guitar-driven rocker, with Daltrey interjecting some harmonica into the instrumental break. Interestingly, Townshend introduces 'Behind Blue Eyes' as a song that will "probably be released as a single very shortly. It's a bit untypical of the old Who single, but it's one we just feel somehow right about. ... We hope you feel the same way." This is certainly an arrangement they seem to have honed, down to the close harmonies; it and 'Pure And Easy' are by some distance the most refined and confident renditions of new songs in the set. Without Nicky Hopkins, 'Getting In Tune' has to rely on Townshend's alternation of arpeggios and heavy chords to fill the space, which loses delicacy but makes for an interesting contrast to the *Who's Next* version.

The group's tendency to stretch out for too long in concert is apparent in an eight-minute 'Water,' but while 'Won't Get Fooled Again' lasts nearly nine minutes, its length is justified. It is also the first occasion on which The Who used a backing tape on stage. This approach would cause no small headaches later on, but at this show the synthesizer backing was incorporated into the performance fairly smoothly. The rhythm does drag in the instrumental break, but Daltrey's climactic scream is now in place, albeit weedier here than the full-throated roar he'd perfect for the *Who's Next* version. What you don't hear on the *Who's Next* deluxe-edition disc (but can find in unofficial circulation) is a false start, after which the tape is rewound by soundman Bob Pridden as Townshend tunes his guitar.

In a moment of levity, Townshend smoked a cigar in celebration of the recent birth of his second daughter. A heckler then prompts Pete's good-natured response, "I've had more fucks than you've had, mate. Many more! When you catch up, come round." Not so amusing to Daltrey was the sight of youngsters in the crowd making an ex-girlfriend of his uncomfortable; according to Townshend's notes in the *Who's Next* deluxe edition, Roger was on the verge of diving into the audience to rescue her, causing the band's concentration to waver.

"It was a fun evening, and I think we were done by about 10.30 or 11," says Andy Johns. It might have been especially fun for one member of The Who. "When I was setting up for the drums," Johns adds, "Moonie had four floor toms. Two of them were very besmirched. I said to the roadie, 'Why does he need four floor toms?' He said, 'Well, two are for playing. The other two are to put the drinks on.' You could see all these rings from where Moonie had put down various refreshments on the last two floor toms. And we all went, 'That makes sense.' The other funny thing was, he'd use four rototoms, all the same size, tuned more or less the same. So he'd go, duh-

duh-duh, duh-duh-duh, duh-duh-duh, duh-duh-duh, and it would be like hitting one tom. It was really silly."[18]

Whatever The Who thought upon hearing the tapes, the concert was not the end of their idiosyncratic attempts to hone *Lifehouse* material (or perhaps even have the audience hone it) at unannounced concerts. A final Young Vic concert took place on May 5; seven took place at the venue in all. And although the band were recording in the studio during much of May, they played a few barely publicized shows outside of London, distributing posters and leaflets in each town just a day before the concerts, and charging a bargain admission price of 50p (about $1). The songs played at these gigs (in Sunderland on May 7, Birmingham on May 13, and Liverpool University on May 14) were much or entirely the same as the ones featured at the Young Vic on April 26. While Daltrey implied in *Record Mirror* that the group would take second billing to other acts and treat such engagements as rehearsals, as far as is known The Who were the only act on stage at these events.[19]

The indications were that the concerts weren't so much intended to work up *Lifehouse* as to work up a new stage repertoire, as well as seeing how audiences would respond to the use of backing tapes. Taking place before *Who's Next* was in the can, these (and indeed the much-slammed Young Vic shows) might have had an overlooked side benefit as the band got down to finalizing the LP. As Daltrey pointed out in *Record Collector* in 1994, "It was the only album where we played all the stuff extensively on the road before we went in to record it. We played all those songs over and over again. They weren't just Pete's songs, they'd become ours. We were never allowed that freedom after that."[20]

Working with the synthesizer backing tapes could prove to be something of a headache, however. It might have been at one of these shows where, as later reported in *Circus*, "at one of the first performances with the synthesizer, someone forgot to bring the magnetic tape on stage. 'The tape, the tape,' Townshend whispered frantically to a roadie, who disappeared off stage, returned with a roll of wrapping tape, tried to figure out why Townshend looked furious, disappeared off stage again, and came back with a roll of masking tape."[21]

Daltrey chipped in his reservations about using backing tapes in an interview with *Crawdaddy* in August. "It's all right for one number, but ... no more," he shrugged, not realizing that two years later the band would be struggling to play almost a whole album of material with backing tapes.[22] He was more explicit in the *Classic Albums* documentary on *Who's Next*. "I didn't mind the synthesizers and drumming in the back," he said, "but I didn't like it taking over as lead instrument when we had what I consider to be one of the best guitarists in the world in the band. It used to frustrate me a bit."[23] In *Uncut*, he even suggested that "I don't think Pete did much with those sequencing things that he couldn't have done on the guitar anyway."[24]

Forty years later, many listeners might be wondering why the group didn't simply hire a keyboard player to handle at least some of those parts on stage, either in 1971 or when touring *Quadrophenia* in late 1973 and early 1974. Aside from the expense involved and the dilution of the four-strong image so important to The Who (who had never toured with additional musicians, as The Rolling Stones were doing by the early 70s), the limitations of 1971 technology simply made such considerations impractical. "The maintenance fees were going to be ridiculous, and the downtime between songs would have been really long, because you have to reprogram the synthesizer to do each thing," says keyboardist Matt Cunitz.

Even in 2009, simulating *Lifehouse* in concert with his band Mushroom, Cunitz found it challenging to play the parts on stage without unseemly delays and massive banks of equipment. "They would have [needed] like five of these synths onstage, [so] rather than reprogramming them, the player would move from one instrument to the next to change sounds. Which is how you end[ed] up with people like Rick Wakeman surrounded on all sides by multiple mini-Moogs and Mellotrons. Why did he have three of the same instrument onstage? Because he knew he needed a certain sound for this song, a different sound for that one, or even in the course of a song, do quick changes. Older instruments weren't as adept at that."[25]

Another theoretical alternative – Townshend playing the guitar to trigger the synthesizer, which meant he wouldn't have had to abandon his usual position onstage to activate the instrument – was yet more distant from becoming a reality. "The idea that you could accurately control a large synthesizer from a guitar was a pipe dream," says Roger Powell, who by the mid 70s (after leaving ARP, where he'd demonstrated the ARP 2500 to Townshend) was playing synthesizers and keyboards with Todd Rundgren in Utopia. "EMS had a primitive guitar synthesizer, called the Synthi. Todd used that. It was a thing that kind of looked like a toilet seat. It was shiny white plastic. The guitar synthesizer itself back then was extremely limited, and wasn't really designed to control a large system that may have enough stuff in it to be polyphonic [playing more than one note at once]. Now Pat Metheny has the Orchestrion, where it's automatically playing a violin, trumpet, bass drum, and all this, MIDI-generated from a polyphonic guitar pickup. [But] there is a lot of stuff you can do in the studio that is still impossible to pull off live."[26]

The Who seemed to be making the transition from using their concerts as *Lifehouse* workshops to refining the best new songs to see how they'd be recorded and played live, regardless of whether *Lifehouse* came off or not. Nonetheless, for months afterward Townshend continued to regret and rationalize the failure of the Young Vic experiment in the press, and not only because of its technological shortcomings. As he told *Sounds* in a July 24 article, "We originally wanted the Young Vic for six weeks, and this was to be a trial period in which we were going to make the film, but the Young Vic is a government-sponsored bloody organization, and it turned out that we could only have it every Monday, and then everybody started to think that it should be every Monday – I could never see it like that, I always figured it would be something where you woke up and went to bed with it; either that or you came and went every day."[27]

To drag in a *Let It Be* comparison again, The Beatles had found it hard enough to perform in front of cameras in studios nearly every day for a month, let alone in front of impromptu live audiences who'd be hearing freshly minted material and expected to liven it up. Is it a surprise that even The Who, about the hardest-working rock band in the business, couldn't stomach the challenge? "It failed, more I think because we, The Who, couldn't really find the energy to cope with the technical problems, and by the time it came to doing it we couldn't fully identify with the idea," Townshend owned up in *Sounds*. "We proved that it was all possible, but by the time we'd done that, we just didn't have it in us to do it. We'd had so much of it, I mean I was getting slightly ... hallucinogenic I think is the word, and the whole thing eventually just fell apart."[28]

John Entwistle, as was his wont, put things more plainly in the June 10 *Rolling Stone*. "It was supposed to be an experiment," he said. "We'd play a specific song aimed at a particular section of the audience. There was supposed to be feedback or something and the whole thing was to be filmed.

Well, we forgot the film idea because we weren't playing well enough. I never really understood what it was all about. I think it did more bad than good. We weren't well enough prepared. The Who are diabolical at rehearsing."[29]

Where did that leave *Lifehouse*, as either a film or a record? Surprisingly, it was Daltrey, not Townshend, who gave a frank and articulate up-to-the-minute report in the May 8 *Record Mirror*. "It's only since yesterday when we all had a meeting that things have been decided," he said, implying that this probably took place between the two spring Young Vic shows. "We've got enough material recorded for a single album, which would be fantastic, but we'll go on to make it a double, like we did with *Tommy*. It's got a theme because it works best for The Who. It builds where just a series of songs never seems to. It's been really hard for us, not just deciding on the theme, but how to go about it as well. But it will knock *Tommy* away."

Although Townshend recalled not getting the promised money from Universal, according to this article, a contract was in place that "allowed the group considerable freedom." As Daltrey put it, "We aim to have our album finished by mid July. But the stumbling block we are up against is that we can't go out on stage and play a whole new act based on the album. So the best thing is to wait until the album is out and then do the stage act and film it. That will give the audience a chance to know the numbers. We've got a really good film deal, but we had to work hard to get their interest. They don't understand that you can't tie yourself down to a set time with pop, you can't say exactly when the album will be released and when you'll be on stage."

Daltrey also acknowledged the difficulties with the Young Vic shows. "When we went into it we were utterly blind and hoped that it should show us the way," he said. "It's a nice idea which might have worked for us, but it didn't." As for the movie, "All we'll be doing in the film is playing, although that's not the whole point of the album, if you understand."[30] Despite leaving room for the movie to be something along the lines of Townshend's *Lifehouse* script, Daltrey's comments seemed to indicate that it might have been turning into something more like a Who concert documentary, although *Lifehouse* in its purer form would have used such footage as part of a larger plot.

Roger's remarks did at least seem to clarify that around May 1, The Who had decided to do an album, and then a film related in some way to the album, though only after the LP was finished; and it would be a double album based around a theme, not a single LP of unconnected songs. None of this would happen, in part because some tough decisions would be needed for the record to be finished by mid-July, as the group hoped.

The public often perceives the producer as a knob-twiddler, sitting behind a pane of glass in a control room, working magic upon the sounds coming from the artist. In reality his or her role is often non-technical. The producer acts as an editor or arbiter, especially with a band of strong-minded individuals who might have trouble coming to a consensus otherwise. At some point while The Who were recording at Olympic in May or June, the decision must have been made to trim the album from a double to a single, thus abandoning the idea of it being a soundtrack of sorts to a forthcoming *Lifehouse* film. While he wasn't solely responsible, it's likely much of the impetus for the decision came from Glyn Johns.

In the *Classic Albums* documentary on *Who's Next*, Johns recalls a meeting between him, The Who, and their management to discuss where to go with the project. "The general consensus was that the movie script wasn't forthcoming as ... no one really got it," Glyn recalled. "No one quite understood it like Pete did, I don't think. I suggested that we should go in and make a record of the songs, because the songs were just amazing. The fact was it didn't really need the story to carry the songs as individual songs, which obviously Pete couldn't quite see initially. Because he'd written them as part of the story, they illustrated part of the script."[31] Most likely this wasn't the same meeting Daltrey referred to in early May in *Record Mirror*, as that article gave the impression that a film was still on the drawing board.

Johns did give the *Lifehouse* idea a fair hearing, according to an interview Townshend did with Radio One's Roger Scott in 1989. "Glyn took me out to lunch once in Soho and sat me down and said, 'Tell me about this *Lifehouse* story,' so I started to tell him," Pete told Scott. "He let me speak for about an hour and a half, looking quite interested and nodding and going 'Mmmm,' and I got to the end and he said, 'Pete, I don't understand a fucking word you've been saying,' which was roughly what most people were doing. And I was so unbelievably angry, not with him, but with myself, just for being drawn back into it again and being excited by it again."

Townshend, of course, had been getting the same reaction from people for months now. It could be, however, that this was the straw that broke his back – not because of any maliciousness or insensitivity on Johns's part, but because it came from yet another associate, someone whose skills and judgment he very much respected, much further along in the process than when he'd first aired the concept.

As stormy as Pete's relationship with Lambert had become, Kit might have delivered the final verdict. Townshend told Roger Scott that he decided to abandon the *Lifehouse* story "at Kit Lambert's behest. He said, 'Pete, just let it go, it's not going to work – and just take the best songs and put it out as a single album.'" [32] On top of that, there was growing impatience from The Who's frontman to get back to doing what they did best. Townshend told *Crawdaddy* that Daltrey was "ringing me up every day, trying to dissuade me from doing the project, saying what we really needed to do is to work on the road." [33]

Perhaps it was finally hitting home that, as his longtime friend Richard Barnes wittily put it in the DVD *The Who, The Mods, And The Quadrophenia Connection*, "There were two groups: people that understood *Lifehouse*, and people who didn't. The people who understood *Lifehouse* included one, Pete Townshend. The people who didn't was everybody else he ever tried to explain it to, and the whole rest of the human race, which was about four billion at the time." [34]

"Pete kind of tied himself in knots, particularly in *Lifehouse*, with the sort of rigid format that he set for himself," Barnes adds in an interview for this book. "When I was writing my book [the 1982 biography *The Who: Maximum R&B*], I think he gave me a whole load of stuff on *Lifehouse*. I started to read to try and make sense of it, and thought, 'No, I'm going to have a nervous breakdown,' like everybody else." [35]

Townshend hadn't tried to explain it to four billion people, but when it came to finding trusted associates who understood the concept, he was running out of options, and time. "Music-wise it was some of the best songs Pete's ever written," Daltrey acknowledged, almost 25 years later, in an interview with *Record Collector*. "But the narrative wasn't very strong. We would have needed another three years before recording it to make it complete." [36] He was rather more emphatically negative in the January 2003 *Uncut*: "Though there's some incredible music in there and some sparks of theoretical and theological ideas, I think the narrative thread of the story is about as exciting as a fucking whelk race!" [37]

Townshend claimed to have had a nervous breakdown around the time *Lifehouse* collapsed. He and The Who were so busy that, at the risk of sounding flippant, it's hard to figure out when he would have had the time for it. Nonetheless, he explicitly informed *Rolling Stone* in mid 1974, "I had the first nervous breakdown of my life. And I'm just not the sort to have nervous breakdowns. What'd happen is I'd spend a week explaining something to somebody and it'd be all very clear to me, then they'd go, 'Right, that's OK – now can you just explain it again?' There were about 50 people involved and I didn't have the stamina to see it through."[38] As Barnes confirms, "He did have a breakdown, there's no doubt about it, just trying to communicate whatever it was."[39] His withdrawal from lobbying for *Lifehouse*'s completion might have been a matter of self-preservation.

Paring the material down to a single LP, however, probably wasn't a matter of recording as much as possible and cherry-picking the best stuff, as George Martin had infamously suggested to The Beatles when they laid down so many tracks for *The Beatles* (commonly known as *The White Album*) in 1968. To the public's knowledge, only a few songs were attempted at Olympic that didn't make *Who's Next*, including 'Pure And Easy,' 'Time Is Passing,' and a new contender that might have been freshly written, 'Let's See Action.' The rough mix of 'Too Much Of Anything' that had been done at Olympic at April 12 could have been the basis of another track, and three of the 1970 tracks from the discarded EP ('I Don't Even Know Myself,' 'Water,' and 'Naked Eye') could have been salvaged or re-recorded. (The fourth, Entwistle's "Postcard," never seemed to enter into consideration.) 'Mary,' one of the better Townshend demos known to have been targeted for *Lifehouse*, doesn't seem to have ever been recorded by the full band.

That's about an album and a half, with the songs eventually deemed surplus distinctly inferior to those included on *Who's Next*, with the exception of 'Pure And Easy' and possibly 'Mary.' If there were more, it's likely Johns heard them in at least demo form, as Townshend cited Glyn's enthusiasm for his demos as a motivating factor for his getting involved in the production. It's possible that there wouldn't have been enough material to fill four LP sides, at least without diluting the original concept with some Entwistle songs, or even some by Daltrey or Moon.

It might have been more pressing to Johns, and possibly others in The Who, to concentrate on getting the songs into the best recorded shape possible, rather than gathering up enough material for two LPs, finalizing the running order, and worrying about how they'd fit into the *Lifehouse* puzzle. Virtually all of the songs had already been recorded in some form, whether on Townshend's demos, at the Record Plant, or live at the Young Vic. Most of them had not come close to maximizing their potential as vehicles for The Who's group arrangements and commercial radio play.

Yet Johns was very respectful of the demos, and thus the songs as they were first envisioned. "The basic arrangements and sound ideas and whatever else came from Pete's demos always, and the feel pretty much," he said in the *Classic Albums* documentary on *Who's Next*. "So it made my job particularly easy. I was much more of an engineer on their stuff than anything, really. My job was to record it simply and easily and smooth the path as best I could."[40]

"Pete's demos were always fantastic, and were always a challenge," Johns added in *Amazing Journey*. "Very often I'd listen to the song we were about to cut and go, 'Wow, how am I going to compete with that?' Obviously he doesn't play drums like Keith Moon, and he doesn't play bass like John Entwistle. So by the time the band got hold of anything, it became The Who instantly, because of the way those two played. They took his stuff and did their thing to it."

Johns found it a particular challenge "to try and keep what Pete was trying to achieve in the song with Keith and John playing, and Roger singing, which was almost impossible to do some of the time, because he doesn't play like either Keith or John. He doesn't sing like Roger either. I would set them up in a live situation pretty much always, and very often even when we did stuff on *Who's Next*, where Pete had written something on synthesizer, which was [the] rhythm of the basic track, I would play [that] into them on earphones. And they would perform live as a band to that. Not one at a time. Because you couldn't possibly do that. It would be a bit absurd, because they react to each other."[41]

Townshend appreciated Johns's contributions. "Glyn actually brought fresh energy and fresh spirit to the songs," he told Roger Scott, "and he was also at his peak then. He was working at Olympic Studios and it was his place ... he just knew the room backward. So Glyn was able to do what he's so wonderful at. With other artists I think he's probably a tremendous arranger and so on as well, but with us what he was really great at was being a great bouncer of energy, you know, creator of enthusiasm, and getting a fantastic sound."[42]

"He has a strong personality that allowed him to dominate his own process very precisely," Townshend told *Guitar Player* many years later. "The way he sat, dead-center between the speakers – believe it or not he was the first to do this so accurately and it was considered unusual – the equipment he used, the mics he used and where he put them, the reverb he used (always recorded on tape with the source), were all part of a process that he worked with almost intuitively. Many engineers tried to copy him and failed. They simply couldn't hear what he could hear. He built up a sound 'picture' I think. When you went in for a playback you would always be surprised at how solid an image he had created around your playing. Almost like posing for a photo, then seeing yourself in an image that had been Photoshopped. I knew I was gorgeous, but not that gorgeous."[43]

Incidentally, the increased professionalism brought to recording The Who at Olympic did not extend to conscientious preservation of the original tapes over the years. That affects the formats in which *Who's Next* might be issued in the future. "When Virgin bought Olympic studios [in the early 80s], there was a whole rework going on inside the studio," says Jon Astley, who'd worked at Olympic since the early 70s. "They wanted to revamp where each control room was and everything. The basement had Rolling Stones and all sorts of tapes. They just pulled them all out and put them into skips out in the street. One or two people managed to rescue some; I myself got some Hendrix Isle of Wight [tapes] out."

Among the casualties might have been the *Who's Next* multi-track tapes. "The whole thing about multi-tracks, people were reusing them as well in those days," adds Astley. "It was just a method to get to the stereo or the mono mix. So in a lot of people's eyes, the multi-track was done and dusted, and wasn't considered to be of great value, whereas the stereo master would be. The 16-tracks of 'Won't Get Fooled Again' [the only *Who's Next* song done in that format], and the eight-tracks of everything else, were pulled out of the skip. [But] what was recovered – this is not stereo, this is just multi-tracks – was everything except 'Bargain' and 'Getting In Tune.' I think they're the only two; there may be a third. Pete wanted to remix it in 5.1 [surround sound], but he couldn't, because the multi-tracks couldn't be found anywhere. It's rather a sad state of affairs."[44]

Documentation as to the order of the recordings made at Olympic is incomplete and shouldn't be taken as gospel, especially as one of the primary sources (the *Who's Next* deluxe-edition liner notes) contains apparent errors in its citations of guest personnel at the Record Plant sessions. However, if the track-by-track annotation in those notes is to be trusted, at least four tracks were done in May: 'Baba O'Riley,' 'Going Mobile,' 'Love Ain't For Keeping,' and 'The Song Is Over.' The most complex of these was 'Baba O'Riley,' whose structure would change considerably from its Townshend solo demo.

Even for someone known for holding conflicting opinions of his own work, Pete vented an extraordinarily vacillating estimation of 'Baba O'Riley' to the *Los Angeles Free Press*. It almost left the impression he wished he hadn't finished writing the song, let alone had The Who reshape it in the studio. "I think my biggest disappointment with *Who's Next* was 'Baba O'Riley,'" he declared. "It was a long, nine-minute instrumental, and I kept cutting it and cutting it and cutting it; until eventually I cut all the length out of it and turned it into a rock song, shoved some words on it. It's still very, very powerful; it's still my favorite thing on the album – apart from 'Won't Get Fooled Again' – but I think it probably would have been better as an instrumental."[45]

Even assuming Townshend's slightly shorter vocal demo of the song preceded the Olympic sessions, a lot of alteration took place, starting with Daltrey's definitively chest-thumping singing. The length was pruned to five minutes, and although the synthesizer pattern that had started the ball rolling to begin with was still at the song's core, even that would undergo some changes. It's often assumed that the pulse heard on the *Who's Next* recording is a synthesizer, but as noted earlier, it's actually a mixture of synthesizer and organ; the famous opening loop-like pattern is actually played on a Lowrey organ and fed through a synthesizer. It's also sometimes assumed Pete pretty much plugged a pattern into a machine and let it roll, but it was actually the result of some painstaking slicing and dicing.

As Townshend told Redbeard for *In The Studio*'s radio special on *Who's Next*, the process involved "recording random sections of stuff onto tape, cutting tape up, re-recording bits of tape, cutting the tape up again, and getting rhythms from it. I could do it fast. 'Baba O'Riley' has something like two or three thousand edits in it – the master tape goes by, and it's all white. It's just sticking plaster from start to finish. What was very interesting is the stuff that I was cutting out, [which] I was sticking together on a reel to keep it tidy. That piece is very interesting in its own right. But what I then did is, I put a piano over the top, a guitar, a vocal, [to] make it sound a bit more like rock'n'roll."[46]

A wholly unexpected addition to that list was brainstormed not by Townshend, but by Keith Moon, and played by someone not even in The Who. Early British progressive-rock band East Of Eden wouldn't seem to have much common ground with The Who, but as their violinist Dave Arbus remembers, "I had become friendly with Keith Moon before the recording of *Who's Next*. One of our roadies, Chalky White, became Keith Moon's driver and minder and I became friendly with Keith, who took an interest in our band and sometimes used to sit in with us on live gigs. So I got a message from Keith one day asking if I would like to play on one of the tracks of their new album."

Arbus's steadily accelerating violin solo, starting as a sweeping lament and changing into something of a celebratory jig as it keeps pace with the ever-quickening rhythm, would grace the lengthy instrumental coda of 'Baba O'Riley.' "I have no idea why they wanted a violin solo," he says. "Maybe Keith suggested it to them. Anyway, the session was fixed, and I turned up at the studio, listened to the track – which was already complete except for my solo – and after a brief chat (I presume with Glyn Johns), I put down a couple of takes. That was it, very efficient on everyone's part.

"As for the style of my solo, it's sort of the way I played at the time. I thought I was doing something in an oriental vein, so I am interested that you should detect a jig-like quality in it. East Of Eden did in fact invent Celtic Rock, ie, Irish music with a heavy-rock backing, of which 'Jig-A-Jig,' our hit single, was the first example. I am sorry they never asked me to play it live with them. It would have been fun.

"I have to say that I find my solo section somewhat out of context with the number. It seems to be tagged on for no apparent reason. The whole 'Baba O'Riley' episode is quite bizarre – a strange crossing of paths. I am not a fan of The Who's music. It is too loud and aggressive for me. I have only heard them live twice, once when Keith Moon took me to their follow-up gig to *Live At Leeds* at Leeds University, and once when we supported them at a gig [in October 1968] at Eel Pie Island in London."[47] Perhaps the success of 'Jig-A-Jig,' which was probably a hit at the very moment Arbus was asked to the session (having entered the UK chart on April 17 on its way to a peak of

Number Seven), influenced The Who or someone in their circle to get in touch with Dave.

'Going Mobile' incorporates two of the features that would do much to enrich the sonic textures of the songs throughout *Who's Next*: Townshend's underrated acoustic guitar (a much appreciated counterpoint to his more celebrated hard rock riffs) and judicious touches of synthesizer. For 'Going Mobile,' the group played live as a trio. Pete later overdubbed brass synthesizer riffs that acted as tasteful melodic interjections, rather than smothering the song in technology, as numerous British prog-rock bands were doing at the time.

The wah-wah-like guitar solo, incidentally, was produced by patching Pete's electric guitar through an 'envelope follower.' This was a device in his synthesizer which, connected to its filter, would mimic the dynamics of his guitar playing. That piece of ingenuity yielded a much more distinctive sound than his original, more conventionally fuzzy hard-rock tone, which can be heard in a clip of Johns at the mixing board in the *Classic Albums* documentary on *Who's Next*.

'Love Ain't For Keeping' is the closest *Who's Next* gets to a filler track. Again, acoustic guitars are prominent in the mix, serving to distinguish it from the heavier treatment the band had given the song at the Young Vic. If Daltrey had a vote on the final tracklisting, he might have used it for this one, as Townshend told Roger Scott in 1989 that Daltrey "still really loves [it] today, just a short thing which on this record appears like a throwaway, but it's a very good song really. Nice sentiment."[48]

'The Song Is Over' was completed at Olympic on May 11, and benefits from both Nicky Hopkins's piano (which Townshend praised as "amazing" in *Melody Maker*) and some more deft insertions of synthesizer. Oddly, this was never played live, according to the *Who's Next* deluxe-edition notes, "due to its complexity." But if The Who managed to work up a live arrangement for a song like 'Baba O'Riley,' one thinks they could certainly have done so for 'The Song Is Over.' Indeed, it would have been necessary had they done *Lifehouse* in its entirety or near-entirety on stage, as it was intended to be the film's finale. Hopkins was also to the fore on 'Getting In Tune,' completed at Olympic on June 7; there really had to be a prominent part for a pianist here, since part of the lyrics described banging on an old piano.

At least nine takes were done of 'Bargain,' which was first worked on at

Olympic on April 12, although additional recording was done on June 5, 18, and 19, indicating this might have been among the last songs to be put to bed before the release of *Who's Next*. Of all the *Who's Next* songs of which an earlier group recording exists (in this case the live one from the Young Vic), this is the one that improved the most. The revved-up tempo makes the Young Vic version sound sluggish, and while Keith Moon excelled throughout *Who's Next*, there may be no other song on the album (possibly excepting 'Won't Get Fooled Again') on which his drum parts both shine so brightly and are so stylistically suited to the tune's straight-ahead pile-driving rhythm.

On 'Bargain,' Townshend played lead guitar on a vintage Gretsch given to him by his buddy Joe Walsh. But the effects attracting the most attention were the swooping 'portamento' ARP synthesizer riffs in the instrumental breaks, which still had a futuristic quality when first heard in the early 70s, and the swelling guitar notes at the beginning. These were produced by fading in guitar notes with a foot-controlled volume pedal, and have an air-sucking aura due to the notes' lack of attack, producing the same effect as backward tape manipulation. The Who are not thought of as a band that trade vocals, but the manner in which the delicate Townshend-sung bridge offsets the bluster of the Daltrey-delivered verses works wonders to balance the mood (as it also does in 'Baba O'Riley' and, with Pete on verse and bridge and Roger on chorus, 'The Song Is Over').

The recording and completion dates of the two other Pete Townshend compositions on *Who's Next* are unknown, though both were major statements, and both were issued as singles. 'Behind Blue Eyes' was a key *Lifehouse* number, intended for the villain, referred to as 'Brick' by Townshend in *A Decade Of The Who*, but as 'Jumbo' in later interviews and liner notes. "What The Who did was add tremendous edge to it," Pete observed in the *In The Studio* radio special about *Who's Next*. "The thing that I anticipated whenever I wrote a song was that if there was a hint of edge, if there was a hint of power on the demo, the band would take that and amplify it a thousandfold."[49] Much of that edge is supplied by the transition from the acoustic folky verses to the hard-rocking bridge. Daltrey particularly identified with the lyrics, as he'd often used his fists to get his way in The Who's early days.

While 'Won't Get Fooled Again' had definitely been recorded in some form at Stargroves, it's not certain whether any elements of that were used in the final track, or when the version on *Who's Next* was completed. Although much of what was done in the studio was a matter of refining and smoothing elements already present in the versions recorded at the Record Plant and the Young Vic, here The Who used the synthesizer track from Townshend's demo – something they hadn't done at the Record Plant, and couldn't do on stage without technical hiccups.

It's hard to think of 'Won't Get Fooled Again' as avant-garde, now that it's been a hit single and played to death on classic radio, becoming one of the most famous of all rock anthems. But building any rock track – let alone a hit single – so heavily around extended passages of unaccompanied synthesizer was radical in 1971. As Glyn Johns accurately noted in the *Classic Albums* documentary on *Who's Next*, both it and 'Baba O' Riley' "used the synthesizer in a completely different way than anyone had ever used one before, where it actually provides the rhythm. It's not just a sound, but it's the rhythm as well ... nobody I knew anyway knew how to work one. They were really difficult to program and get any kind of sound out of."[50]

At least five other songs are known to have been recorded by The Who at Olympic in spring 1971. Three of these would be deemed surplus as the group whittled the available pool of material down to a single LP; another, John Entwistle's 'When I Was A Boy' (then known as 'Time Waits For No Man'), was probably only intended for release on 45. The fifth was a late entry that would end up as the most surprising inclusion on *Who's Next*.

The song Townshend most regretted sacrificing was 'Pure And Easy.' Although the Olympic version was included on *Odds & Sods*, perhaps Pete was dissatisfied with the remake; in his interview with Roger Scott, he indicated that "it didn't work out well."[51] The group, or Johns, perhaps felt that the use of its chorus in the coda of 'The Song Is Over' would have made including 'Pure And Easy' repetitious, even though riffs and lyrics had been reprised throughout *Tommy*. Nothing seems obviously wrong with the recording, although perhaps the transitions between the song's discrete sections could have been snappier. It seems to have been a victim of worries about being able to fit it into a single-LP running time, or fears that it couldn't be easily positioned in the sequence now that it was no longer part of an overarching story or theme. An intriguing comment in *The Who ... Through The Eyes Of Pete*

Townshend suggests the songwriter saw it as fitting into what *Lifehouse* had become in the process of making the LP. "It really should have been on *Who's Next*," he said, "because *Who's Next*, if nothing else, was a culmination of the frustration of The Who trying to go somewhere."[52]

'Time Is Passing,' eventually issued on the 1998 expanded CD of *Odds & Sods*, was a more obvious candidate for exclusion as one of the less impressive compositions and one that was no longer needed for *Lifehouse*'s exposition. It's interesting, however, that while The Who had worked up a hard-rock version for the Young Vic, at Olympic they restored the oddball vibrato-heavy keyboard sounds heard on Townshend's demo. The band also enhanced the texture with some tasty acoustic guitar and, in the instrumental break, a dab of country guitar and piano.

Sadly, the version on *Odds & Sods* is missing half of a stereo mix. As the CD's notes state, it was remastered from a damaged master tape. "I ended up using just half of the stereo, because about 30 seconds into it, one side of it disappears," explains Jon Astley, who produced and mastered the *Odds & Sods* CD version. "That's the way it was actually recorded [in] the master, the mix. A channel's missing, so I just took the right-hand side and monoed it up. I just think they mixed it and didn't listen to it back" – another possible indication that 'Time Is Passing' never got too far into the running for the *Who's Next* finals.[53] (Note that 'Pure And Easy' is referred to as having been cut at Stargroves, and 'Time Is Passing' at the Record Plant, in the *Odds & Sods* expanded CD liner notes. The 2002 Who chronicle *Anyway Anyhow Anywhere* places these at Olympic, and seems the more reliable source, as it incorporates some information that came to light in the intervening years.)

Nicky Hopkins's boogie piano style is at the forefront on 'Let's See Action,' at this point still entitled 'Nothing Is Everything.' It may have been dropped because it wasn't considered strong enough, or viewed as ill-fitting in light of its position in the *Lifehouse* storyline. But The Who couldn't have thought too badly of the song, because they made it their next UK single later in the year.

If The Who were still considering going for a double LP after all, they did have a couple of alternatives to pursue. One, as previously noted, was to use some of the songs cut for their unfinished 1970 album, and indeed 'Naked Eye' was worked on (possibly only on the mixing end) on June 7. The other was to see what compositions John Entwistle might have available.

That's how 'My Wife' entered the picture. Asked if he had any songs, John came up with that one, and it was recorded in June. He'd later say it was the only number he had left over from his just-issued solo album, an odd statement if true, since it's better than any song on that LP besides his solo version of 'Heaven And Hell.'

It's a bit surprising Entwistle hadn't been approached to contribute songs to *Lifehouse*. *Tommy* was also very much Townshend's baby, but the dour bassist's 'Cousin Kevin' and 'Fiddle About' had been effective songs in that rock opera. With its villainous authority figures, polluted desolate landscapes, and characters tromping around in 'experience suits,' *Lifehouse* could have offered interesting possibilities for Entwistle to exercise his trademark dark humor in song. 'My Wife' was indeed darkly humorous, but could not be heard as slotting into *Lifehouse* in any way – another sign that even a tenuous attempt at thematic linkage between the songs had been abandoned for the forthcoming album.

"I'd just had an argument with my wife, and I put the leads on my two Scottish deer hounds and we [went] onto a huge 3,000-acre park right behind, stormed out of the house," Entwistle told Redbeard for the *In The Studio* radio special on *Who's Next*. "I was walking, and I sort of made up this imaginary wife that was following me that was a lot more violent than my wife. My wife was five-foot two-and-a-half. But by the time I got back, I let the dogs go and rushed upstairs and demoed it, because it was one of those instant songs that you get when you get the words and the music at the same time. I was singing it to myself all the way round the park. The dogs thought it was very peculiar. They kept coming back to me and thought I was calling 'em. It was one of those instant songs.

"I think [it was] maybe because we didn't have anything like it on *Who's Next* that it actually got used. Everybody really liked it."[54] It certainly wasn't like anything else on *Who's Next* or *Lifehouse*. A hard rocker, with ominous beefy horns on both the instrumental break and extended fadeout (laid on by Entwistle himself in just half an hour), it told the tale of a man on the run from a woman done wrong with murder in her eyes. But few *Who's Next* listeners knew the ins and outs of the *Lifehouse* plot, and few would question its position on side one, starting up almost as soon as the last note of 'Love Ain't For Keeping' faded, and incongruously followed by 'The Song Is Over.'

How did Entwistle's wife of the time react? "She always thought it was very funny," he told *Record Collector* in 1995. "She had the ambition to come on and hit me over the head with a rolling pin halfway through when I was singing it on stage."[55]

'My Wife' generally proved very popular with fans and is perhaps Entwistle's most famous Who song other than 'Boris The Spider.' John Swenson went so far as to describe it as "a lot of people's favorite track on the record" in the first edition of *The Rolling Stone Record Guide*.[56] Nonetheless, the decision to include 'My Wife' can be debated on both thematic grounds and its musical merit. Quite atypically for a Johns/Who production, the mix is blurry, and Entwistle's double-tracked vocals are positively hard to make out. Considering much of the song's appeal lies in its comic lyrics, that's a problem, and not one that's been greatly ameliorated by CD reissues.

Still, in the same way that George Harrison's songs acted as nifty contrasts to Lennon & McCartney's on Beatles albums, despite usually not being as good, at least one Entwistle tune could fulfill a similar function on The Who's next album. That might have been a consideration as The Who made their final track selection. This almost certainly took place sometime in June, as handwritten tape boxes of master reels dated June 1971, with all nine songs sequenced and separated into their appropriate LP sides, can be seen as insets in the jewel box packaging for the *Who's Next* deluxe edition. Townshend would later tell the *Los Angeles Free Press* that Johns played the album to them for their final approval the day before the *Who's Next* cover photo was taken on July 4, but he's probably off by a few days, as The Who were playing in Sheffield on July 3.[57]

The Who could have spent more time on the record, had they wanted to make a *Lifehouse* double album, which remained a possibility even as late as mid 1971. The Beatles had taken considerably longer than two or three months from start to finish on *The White Album*. But business and personal pressures, some of them self-imposed, would have made it difficult for them to be granted an extension. Although Townshend's chronology of events can vary between interviews, his chat with the *Los Angeles Free Press* intimated that he'd committed to putting out an LP soon about halfway through the Johns sessions, and found his mental state veering between the hallucinogenic and the schizophrenic. "I just phoned up Chris Stamp, our manager, and said, 'Look, we've got to knock it on the head. Let's just put out an album, otherwise I really will go crazy.' And I would have done; no doubt about it."[58]

The strategy The Beatles had rejected for *The White Album* was referred to, a little disparagingly, in Townshend's explanation to *Crawdaddy* as to why a single LP was issued instead of a double. "We were going to do a whole thing," he said, "then we figured it would be far better, much more solid to just pick the best stuff out and make it a good, hard, rock-solid album. ... We were very, very afraid of doing what The Beatles did, just laying ourselves wide open like they did with their double albums [although The Beatles had made only one] and making it so that it was too much, too many unlinked ideas which to the public would look like untogetherness, despite the fact that it's always there in the background. We decided on a single album because, really, it was the straightest thing to do. Basically every angle, every tangent that we went off on we eventually arrived back, if you like, to where the group used to be. The more times this happened the more times it reinforced Roger's stand, which was that the group was perfectly all right as it was and that basically I shouldn't tamper with it."[59]

Also looming for The Who were a three-week American tour at the end of July and some UK shows in the first half of that month. As they probably burned through money faster than any other band, the group really did need to get on the road to raise some cash. Psychologically, all of The Who – including Townshend, but more so the others – needed the buzz of doing concerts. Daltrey, Moon, and Entwistle, having given *Lifehouse* a good six months of work without an end in sight (and having granted Townshend a good amount of time to start assembling the material before that), might have been running out of patience.

"I've a feeling that the other three just wanted to get on with it," says Chris Charlesworth, who had conducted one of the first major post-Olympic interviews with Townshend that summer. "They'd [have said], 'We can't keep doing this, Pete. We've got to just go out and do a rock concert like everybody else, and it'll be a damned good one, or a rock concert that's better than everybody else. But we're not going to learn another hour and a quarter's worth of songs that are linked together.' I think The Who could have built a fantastic song-sequence, or song-cycle, based around *Lifehouse* with those songs if the other three had been as keen on it as Pete."[60]

Bands have split up under much less pressure than this. Some comments in interviews of the time left the impression The Who were considering that option, although potential bust-ups had been reported so often since 1965 that even the average Who fan had become accustomed to taking such claims with a grain of salt. In the May 8 *Record Mirror* interview, Daltrey claimed "we were never nearer to breaking up than we were three months ago. It's not through lack of interest in the group; it's just a desperation feeling."[61] In the *Los Angeles Free Press*, Townshend confided, "I thought everybody wanted to leave the band." It was when they were in the same room listening to Johns's compilation of the tracks into an album, he added, that "we knew we were going to stay together," but that might be overdramatizing the situation.[62]

But realistically, what were The Who going to do if they didn't stay together? Solo careers, at least on the scale they were enjoying as a band, were out of the question. As proof, in what's now a relative footnote, May 14 had seen the release of John Entwistle's first solo album, *Smash Your Head Against The Wall*. This was the first solo release by a member of The Who, unless you count Townshend's barely distributed contributions to the limited-edition *Happy Birthday* LP on behalf of Meher Baba. Indeed, it was one of the few LP releases by a member of any major group of the time that had been issued without the individual in question having left the band. In decades to come, it would become common for musicians to maintain ongoing solo careers without leaving the band with which they'd risen to fame, as all four of The Who would do within just a few years. In 1971, however, it was unknown.

"The only songs that they have used of mine since my solo albums started have been 'My Wife' and 'When I Was A Boy,'" Entwistle explained in *Rolling Stone* in late 1974. "I started realizing there was no real outlet for my songs because The Who were more or less based on Pete's style of writing, and Roger sang Pete's compositions best. I'd written my music for me to sing, really; I couldn't see Roger singing them. So I realized it was a choice – I was getting so frustrated that it was either leave the band or do a solo album."[63]

If the plan had been to see whether a member of The Who could establish an ongoing solo career while maintaining his position in the group, however, *Smash Your Head Against The Wall* was a mixed success at best. The record didn't chart in the UK, and wasn't even released in the USA (in a remixed version) for another five months, after which it crept up to Number 126. More importantly, the songs weren't even up to the level of what Entwistle wrote for The Who (save 'Heaven And Hell,' which had already been issued in a group recording as a B-side). Some cultists appreciated its morbid comic streak, and it did give John the chance to air material which would never find its way onto a Who record. But it demonstrated that he needed The Who to both be a star and be at his musical best – as was true, to varying extents, of the other three members, should they be thinking of going off on their own.

As summer began, The Who – more than two years after the release of *Tommy*, and after a year trying to create a rock opera which would have an even bigger impact – didn't even have a finished rock opera to show for all the work they, and especially Pete Townshend, had put into *Lifehouse*. They had at least completed their first studio album since *Tommy*, albeit in compromised form. They were also about to embark, for another period of a little more than two years, on the path to their *next* rock opera, which would be as different from *Lifehouse* as *Lifehouse* had been from *Tommy*.

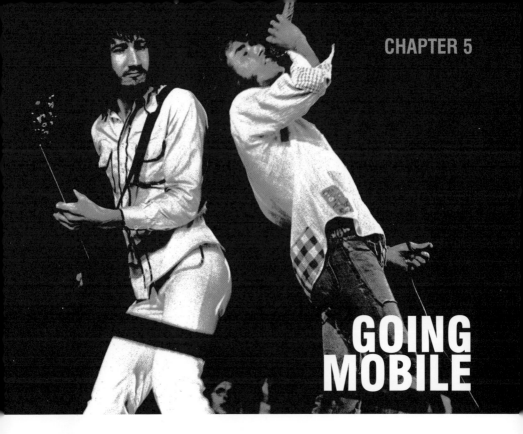

CHAPTER 5

GOING MOBILE

I t's a measure of how eager the record business was for Who product – and, perhaps, how eager The Who were to get new material into the shops, with just three new studio tracks having been released since *Tommy* – that a single from their new LP would be issued two months before the album's UK release. On June 25, 'Won't Get Fooled Again' was issued on 45 in the UK (albeit in a severely edited version that took a good five minutes off the LP cut), possibly even before Glyn Johns had played the group *Who's Next* in its finished form. If the mission was to raise The Who's profile, it was successful, with the single reaching Number Nine in the UK and Number 15 in the USA.

Chris Welch's *Melody Maker* review – the day after the single's release – showed that fans and the press were not just enthusiastic about the record, but ecstatic to have a new song in any form. "An explosion of drums and guitars – The Who blast back!" he trumpeted. "It's so good to hear those Townshend chords flailing again, Roger's drawling vocals, Keith's joyous drums, and the Entwistle bass leap and twist in a welcome burst of energy. Even the sign-off ending has a kind of triumphant 'we did it' effect. Apart from the dramatic intro, it's a straight-ahead tune. No complications, no problems. A hit. And the flip, 'Don't Know Myself,' is equally good."[1] (In the same paper the following month, Townshend referred to the B-side as a new recording of the song originally cut for an EP in 1970, although not all sources agree on this point; he also remembers The Who recording it twice in *A Decade Of The Who*.)

Amid the joy, however, was a reminder of what could have been – and just how late in the game *Lifehouse* might have been considered salvageable. When the single was issued in the US on July 17, the inner label read in part "from the motion picture *Lifehouse*." (Six years previously, Capitol Records had famously jumped the gun in a similar fashion when the inner label on The Beatles' 'Ticket To Ride' single announced it as hailing from the upcoming movie *Eight Arms To Hold You*, although at least that film would be made, as *Help!*)

Even at less than half its true length, and isolated from both the album it closed with a bang and the *Lifehouse* project for which it was originally intended, 'Won't Get Fooled Again' provoked a strong reaction from a prominent segment of The Who's audience. It perhaps wasn't the kind of reaction Townshend was hoping for when the Young Vic shows were arranged, but it certainly showed that some of his listeners were paying close attention and not about to shy away from giving him their feedback.

On July 14, at a housewarming party for Keith Moon's new home in Surrey, with several members of the press in attendance, Pete got talking with a few writers for *International Times*. As London's leading underground paper, *International Times* was a crucial voice for the counterculture, and one of the publications outside of the music press most inclined to give rock intelligent coverage. One of its designers, Mike McInnerney, had played a significant role in Townshend's own life, helping introduce him to the teachings of Meher Baba and designing the cover for *Tommy*. *International Times* was also noted for its coverage of radical politics, and Townshend found himself in the hot seat for his ambivalent attitude toward the revolution.

In a lengthy open letter to Pete in the September 9 issue, Mick Farren, Chris Rowley, and J. Edward Barker laid out "the reasoning behind the feelings of puzzlement and worry that we feel when playing the new single. Whereas the music is still strong, kicking-out aggressive music, the lyric is seemingly defensive and negative, even potentially damaging to the consciousness of kids who still strongly identify with The Who as an extension of their lifestyles. In fact it's calculated to bring down anybody seeking radical change in which [sic] we know you agree is a depressingly corrupt society. So why?"

After some musings on the nature of radical leadership, in the tangled style of the period's underground press, the concluding paragraph got down to business, "Specifically the danger in the new single seems to be that it fails to differentiate between the megalomaniac and the courageous individual who is prepared to stand up and voice the sentiment 'fuck you' to authority. ... Are you expressing a desire to escape the pressures of your situation, to say in effect 'all right I'm a Rock Star and nuthin' else and I can't help you' – because this is essentially a negative approach to things. No one really expects to see you opening a 'problems of youth guidance service' but at the same time we'd be interested to know what use a self-realized man is gonna be to the community and the world in general. ... The Who have become a brand name for change," the trio fairly accurately noted, "and perhaps even a symbol with which kids who are fucked over in the streets can identify with."[2] The writers hoped for a more committed stance from the group and its leader.

Then and now, many artists of Townshend's status would brush off such an open letter without a public acknowledgement, if they even read it. Pete was not the typical rock star, however. Even by his standards, his published response was extraordinary in length and seriousness. While he claimed to have been "amused and invigorated" by their conversation at Moon's, however, he wasn't at his most articulate in print, waffling as much over the value of radical camaraderie as he had in 'Won't Get Fooled Again' itself. He was more effective when focusing tightly on the song at hand. "The Who don't 'return' a positive attitude to youth because it is expected of them or because they get rich from their music. They REFLECT the negative attitude which a lot of kids are taking to the fight for power which is being waged in their name, but not on their terms, not using their ethics. 'Won't Get Fooled' is partly a personal song, but mainly a song which screams defiance at those who feel that any cause is better than no cause, that death in a sick society is better than putting up with it or resigning themselves to wait for change. It mainly screams defiance at those who try to tell Us (The Who) what we have to do to with money that isn't ours, power that belongs not to us but our audiences and lives that long ago were handed to the Rock world on platters."[3]

If it seems presumptuous for underground pressmen to have cornered Townshend at a party and on paper, it should be pointed out that he knew these journalists on a social level, in keeping with The Who's fairly intimate relationship with the media in general. Nor were these any old yobbos with a mimeograph machine; they, and the underground readership they represented, were regarded by Pete with seriousness and respect. Farren had himself been in an underground psychedelic band, The Deviants, and would go on to a lengthy career as a rock critic and author; Rowley became a respected science fiction writer; and Barker was a well known underground cartoonist. Farren had numerous conversations with Townshend at UFO, the legendary London psychedelic rock club where Pink Floyd had made their reputation, and even remembers how "one night we had a long conversation about 'I Can See For Miles' being hailed as the greatest rock'n'roll record of all time, because he really thought it was his masterwork. What he was getting out of *IT* and [fellow British underground paper] *Oz* was a more respectable analysis of his work, which both was useful to him as an artist and flattered his ego, or made him angry. He'd always been within his means pretty damn generous to *IT* and other underground causes. That's the background our reaction to 'Won't Get Fooled Again' was based in.

"We were all at the time taking politics very seriously," Farren continues. "It was really very much a case [of] either you were part of the problem or part of the solution. In retrospect ['Won't Get Fooled Again'] was Pete's reaction to it, and to some degree it was valid. But at the time we were 'What are you, defecting from the revolution? Fuck you Pete!' This was the gist of the conversation at Moon's place, and then it carried on with the correspondence. 'Won't Get Fooled Again' was kind of hinting that if the radical left was in power, there'd be massive confusion. That was not a statement we expected out of Pete Townshend.

"At the time, me and Edward were facing two years in jail for publishing fucking Robert Crumb comics. So we came to get a bit pissed at the kind of suggestion that we'd be busy exterminating people if we were ever allowed to rise to power. The Tories were taking back the government, and Pete decided to go all kind of soul-searching on us. It's all fun in retrospect, and it made a good little flurry. It was a storm in a teacup, but it's the way things were, and I'm glad it happened. It's water under the bridge now."

Asked today if the song's ambivalence might have made more sense and been far less risible had it been couched in the *Lifehouse* storyline, Farren isn't buying it. "Remember it was also a fairly heavy commercial single," he says. "It wasn't just an album track that slipped out. Yeah, it might have made more sense had it been within the context [of *Lifehouse*]. It's all very well saying, 'Well, if it had been in the science fiction story I meant it to be it would have…' Bollocks, you know? It wasn't. It was promoted as a major single at a very crucial time."[4]

The gathering at Keith Moon's house served as a launch party of sorts for the album that was now entitled *Who's Next*. "I think it was Moon deciding to have a party because the record was coming out," remembers Farren. "It was Moon's idea, so it wasn't a Track Records party. I think there was some kind of Magical Mystery Tour set-to, where we all had to turn up at some pub in Central London and a bus turned up. We were told to get on the bus, and we drove the 25 or so miles out to Moon's place getting drunk as skunks before we even got there. It just went on and on from there, with pyrotechnics, sausages, and obscene amounts of alcohol. That too was part of those rather unique times."[5]

It might have been more an excuse for Moon to party hard than a proper vehicle to promote the record, which wouldn't come out for another month. Ten days before the event, however, The Who had taken the final decisive step to preparing it for release, shooting a cover picture that would become one of the most iconic LP sleeves of the era. Taking the photo was American Ethan Russell, who had over the past couple of years shot some of the most famous pictures of The Beatles and The Rolling Stones, including the cover photos for *Let It Be* and the Stones' *Through The Past, Darkly (Big Hits Vol. 2)* compilation. Glyn Johns had called him around mid June to let him know the album was almost finished, suggesting that something could be shot to tie in with the song 'Going Mobile': Townshend had a Land Rover in which he would go "mobile" like the character in the song.

Russell and Who roadie John Wolff (aka Wiggy) drove around the English countryside scouting locations. "I got it into my head that the photograph should be set in something resembling a dry lake bed," Russell recalled in his 1985 memoir *Dear Mr Fantasy*. "It was a look common in American advertising of automobiles. As a dry lake bed was out of the question in England, we looked instead for an unobstructed, treeless hillside."[6] Townshend was nonplussed, however, by the image of a Land Rover on a hillside in sunset with its headlights on.

According to both Townshend and Russell, another quite different cover was under consideration. "*Who's Next* nearly came out with the most revolting pornographic cover you've ever seen," Townshend told *ZigZag*. "In the end, it turned out to be mildly pornographic, but slightly boring at the same time. Dave King [who'd designed the famous cover for *The Who Sell Out* with Roger Law, as well as co-designing the UK cover of Jimi Hendrix's *Electric Ladyland*] was commissioned to do a cover and he came up with one with a huge fat lady with her legs apart, and where the woman's organ was supposed to be would be a head of The Who grinning out from underneath the pubics."[7] Without naming King, in *Dear Mr Fantasy* Russell recalled "a 24-inch-by-12-inch montage of extremely fat naked women" having been delivered to the recording studio, only for it to be rejected "because Jimi Hendrix had already done something almost identical on [*Electric Ladyland*], only the women in that instance were not fat."[8]

While it makes a great story, it should be noted that King told the author of this book that he was not commissioned to work on *Who's Next*, and had nothing to do with this cover. Something of the sort *was* produced by someone, however, as that precise image appears in Richard Barnes's *The Who: Maximum R&B* biography. It looks as if the 24-inch-by-12-inch montage could have been used on an inner gatefold, not on a front cover; had it been the actual cover, it would have taken up both the front and back covers. It was used once, according to *The Who: Maximum R&B*, in an advertisement, although it's hard to imagine it was a very effective one. (Another odd ad for *Who's Next* was taken out by Decca in US trade papers featuring, in the words of *Stereo Review*, "two Amazon hookers with only the album title as copy.")[9]

With something needed immediately as the release date loomed, Russell went on the road with the band on the first weekend of July in the hopes that something would emerge. One idea was to photograph The Who destroying a dressing room, but as logical a notion as that seemed on paper, the group couldn't summon the appropriate enthusiasm. A photo of the band (likely taken backstage on July 4 at Leicester's De Montfort Hall), sitting amid turned-over chairs and disheveled refreshments, ended up on the back cover, and pictures of the group leaning against decrepit brick buildings weren't used at all.

Driving around with Pete on July 4, large cement blocks sticking out of a slag heap caught Russell's attention. The group convened around one of them, the photographer at first thinking they should tentatively absorb its aura, much as the apes had with the famous monolith in Stanley Kubrick's 1968 film *2001: A Space Odyssey*. The Who were never the most reverent of creatures, however, and it wasn't long before Townshend began pissing on it. The aftermath is what's seen on the *Who's Next* cover, though as Russell revealed in his memoir, some water cans had to be splashed on the structure to help out those unable to urinate on demand. "What a pathetic act of rebellion!" Townshend laughed in his 1989 Radio One interview with Roger Scott. "Pissing up against this perfectly innocent concrete block."[10]

In a way, the *Who's Next* cover did look like something the travelers might have passed while "going mobile" in *Lifehouse*. Here was a true desolate wasteland in line with the environmentally devastated landscape that was to be *Lifehouse*'s setting. It would have looked even bleaker had Russell not substituted the sunset from his photograph of the Land Rover for the gray sky in the background. But even for a band renowned for its sense of bawdy humor, it's doubtful a *Lifehouse* cover would have used an image so frivolous. In hindsight, it could have been a final step of Townshend letting go of the *Lifehouse* project as frustrated exhaustion mounted and his original concept turned into an entirely different creation beyond his artistic control, *Who's Next*.

"When Glyn Johns said 'Listen, I don't think it should be a double album, I think it should be a single,' I didn't have it in me to protest," Pete told radio host Redbeard during the *In the Studio* special on *Who's Next*. "When Ethan Russell – Glyn's friend, the godfather of his son – was suggested as the person to take the album cover, I didn't have it in me to protest. And when he suggested that we piss up against an edifice that he'd found in the middle of a slag heap, I didn't have it in me to protest. So I was kind of led by my nose into what has actually become probably the most important album of The Who's career outside of *Tommy*. So sometimes God has his ways of making you behave."[11]

Even before the album was released, Townshend's interviews expressed an ambivalence toward *Who's Next* that continues to haunt him to this day. On the one hand, he was genuinely proud of the music on the LP; on the other, he continued to regret abandoning *Lifehouse*. "I think the new album is a high point musically for the group," he told Chris Charlesworth in the July 17 *Melody Maker*, which marked one of his first major interviews in months. "There is a lot of exciting stuff on it. We were going to put out a double album because we have enough material recorded, but we decided to keep it for the stage act."[12]

Here Pete seemed to be hinting that the surplus songs in strong-to-slight running for the double album would find some use on stage. 'Pure And Easy,' 'Too Much Of Anything,' 'Time Is Passing,' 'Don't Even Know Myself,' 'Water,' and 'Baby Don't You Do It' had already been played as part of their July 3 show in Sheffield, and while 'Time Is Passing' and 'Too Much of Anything' would be dropped from their US summer shows, 'Naked Eye' came back into the set. The group might have even been thinking that they had an entire LP in reserve, as Townshend also told *Crawdaddy* that summer, "We've got two albums, only one of which is being put out. The other's being kept till we need it."[13] Clearly, however, such an album would be notably inferior to the standards The Who were aiming for, unless it was marketed as a special-interest or fan-targeted release of sorts, which star bands rarely authorized in the early 70s. Some *Lifehouse* rejects did come out in 1974 on *Odds & Sods*, but that was hardly a *Who's Next Vol. 2*, as it included out-takes and rarities from other phases of their career.

In *Melody Maker*, Pete also made it clear that the *Lifehouse* film wasn't happening, admitting to some of his failures with painful honesty. "We haven't got a film and won't have one," he said. "We were trying to be a bit too ambitious as far as changing The Who's sound and making technological advances which I thought were needed." He also owned up that it was wrong to choose the Young Vic as the venue to workshop the idea. "It's not going ahead now and, in fact, it's definitely finished. The album is all we have to show for it, apart from the experiments of playing with tapes."

Here also was the first tantalizing announcement of the possibility of the public getting to hear at least some of the demos. "I would like to put out an album of demos which I have done," said Townshend, "but they are very much like the finished product from the group and [would] probably only be of interest to real Who freaks."[14] Demos would in fact leak out, starting the following year with Townshend's first proper solo album (some, in fact, had already appeared on the Meher Baba *Happy Birthday* compilation). But it would be almost another 30 years before the *Lifehouse* demos were released in their entirety.

Another confession of failure suggested that the very mastery of one-man productions that went into those demos might have led to *Lifehouse*'s downfall when Townshend tried to apply the same principle to a different medium. "With songs, I outline the idea to [The Who] and then make a demo," Pete noted in *Crawdaddy*. "That's where this experiment fell down. You can't make a demo of a film. I wrote a script, but I'm not a scriptwriter so that wasn't overly well received. We got very very close to what would have been a revolution in rock and roll, but we didn't really have the fodder to carry it off."[15]

Nearly 20 years later, Townshend's ambivalence toward *Who's Next* had if anything increased. "It has tremendous merit," he told Roger Scott in his 1989 Radio One interview. "It's a wonderful record. It's probably the best *record* that The Who ever made. But I think one of the reasons why it marks The Who's subsequent decline is that it was almost like life was giving me a little ticking off, you know, saying, 'Don't get too big for your boots, little rock'n'roll person, you can make good records, but nothing else,' and I hated to feel that rock was limited. So for me it was a personal disaster, because I really felt I was going for broke with it."[16] Daltrey, in predictably saltier language, eventually acknowledged in *Rolling Stone* that scaling back the opera into a regular album had cost it some respect. "*Who's Next* holds up much better [than *Tommy*]," he said, "but nobody wanted to take it seriously because it was just nine songs and no great thing about a bloody spastic."[17]

The timing of *Who's Next* release was commercially suspect, coming a few weeks into their summer American tour; the usual strategy would have been to start the tour right after its release to maximize sales. (As Daltrey had told *Record Mirror* that the band were fighting to get it out before their July 24 departure for the States, a plan to do so might not have panned out.) Also, in a reversal of the way things had usually worked for British bands, it came out a couple of weeks earlier in the USA, where it was released on August 14. Both the earlier release date and the tour may have reflected a concentration upon the American market, a considerably more lucrative one for The Who than it had been in the pre-*Tommy* days.

The Who had been playing the bulk of the *Who's Next* material in concert for three months before their first US date, not just at the Young Vic, but at subsequent UK gigs as well. In those days, in-concert pre-promotion of material not yet on disc was more common, and could in some ways have worked to the album's benefit by building a buzz, as a few pre-release shows with *Tommy* songs had done. And when it finally came out, the reaction of the press and public to *Who's Next* was decidedly unambivalent. It was an immediate smash, reaching Number Four in the USA and topping the charts at home, garnering rave review after rave review. Although industry statistics are not infallible, it is The Who's best-selling album, according to the Record Industry Association of America's website, having gone triple platinum; by this measure it has even outsold *Tommy*.

While *Who's Next* is considered one of the core "classic rock" albums, its status was not established in retrospect. Quoting from all the ecstatic reviews of the record would fill up a few pages, but as a sampling, longtime Who champion (and future Who biographer) Dave Marsh wrote in *Creem*, "*Who's Next* is to The Who what *The White Album* must've been to The Beatles ... A fine, fine record, one you can shake your ass to and think about both, one that does everything The Who can do in legend."[18] For *Melody Maker*, the group had "come up with a phenomenally good record. For uncomplicated sheer rock, it may well turn out to be The Who's biggest recording triumph yet, for there isn't a duff track."[19] *Rolling Stone* named the LP its Album Of The Year, giving The Who its Rock Band Of The Year award to boot. The *Village Voice*'s esteemed Pazz & Jop poll voted it the best record of the year as well.

More than anything The Who have done, except perhaps *Tommy* and the 'My Generation' and 'I Can See For Miles' singles, *Who's Next* would continue to enjoy almost unabated popularity and airplay over the next four decades. *Rolling Stone* again led the charge when it came to canonization, John Swenson calling it "what may well be the finest rock record ever made" in the first edition of *The Rolling Stone Record Guide* in 1979.[20] Rankings in all-time best-of lists have become routine, some of them including Number 28 in *Rolling Stone*, Number 50 in *NME*'s 2006 best-of list, Number 13 in VH1, and Number Three on *Guitar World*'s Greatest Classic Rock Albums. In one of the earliest such surveys ever done (for the 1979 book *Rock Critics' Choice: The Top 200 Albums*), it rated Number 19, with four prominent critics – Dave Marsh, future film director Cameron Crowe, BBC radio presenter Anne Nightingale, and stalwart UK music journalist and veteran Townshend interviewer Penny

Valentine – placing it in their Top Fives.

Much of the album – especially 'Won't Get Fooled Again' and 'Baba O'Riley,' though 'Behind Blue Eyes,' 'Bargain,' and 'Going Mobile' don't trail far behind – still gets saturation radio exposure in the classic-rock format, particularly in the USA. In recent times, it has been common to hear soundbites at sport stadiums, culminating in The Who themselves (or what was left of them) performing 'Won't Get Fooled Again' and 'Baba O'Riley' at half-time at the 2010 Super Bowl.

Why such massive success, and all without a huge hit single? One reason is that *Who's Next* sounded better, or at least cleaner and deeper ('My Wife' excepted), than any previous Who record. As Swenson wrote in *The Rolling Stone Record Guide*, "for the first time The Who was able to capture the live energy of a concert in the studio, and the result was devastating."[21] In that they had much help from Glyn Johns (credited, incidentally, only as "associate producer" despite his undisputedly crucial contribution). There was also the consistent commercial appeal of almost all of the nine songs the record had been reduced to, 'Love Ain't For Keeping' being perhaps the only track not to get wide exposure. Had a double album of any sort been issued instead, its impact would have been far more diffuse, owing to the alternation of powerhouses with far less immediately accessible and arresting tunes.

It was also a matter of timing. Although FM radio had been key to building the American following of superstars without huge hit singles, including Jimi Hendrix and The Who themselves, by the early 70s it had crossed over from the underground to the mainstream. Most of *Who's Next*'s tracks entered and remained in heavy rotation on FM stations, almost as if they were Top 40 singles finding a home in a different medium.

"For FM radio, the album was incredibly deep," says Michael Tearson, then a young DJ on WMMR – a key outlet for The Who as the most respected FM rock station in Philadelphia, one of the band's biggest US markets. "We could play every single song. Nothing on the LP was second-rate. It had anthems. It rocked. It was one of the first albums that felt arena-sized from the first note. It compromised nothing! It was rebellious, swaggering, young. Just what we DJs wanted to feel we were saying, back in a day when we each programmed our shows all by ourselves, without consultants, without the computer program Selector to give you the preselected show."

Nearly 40 years later, Tearson (who continued on WMMR for many years, and is still very active in radio today as a program host on Sirius/XM and other outlets) can still quote song lyrics from *Who's Next*'s staples off the top of his head. "They were epic anthems," he says. "These songs made grand gestures speaking to a generation freshly tasting the bitter aftertaste of disappointment in the collapse of the euphoria of hippie-era hope. 'Teenage wasteland, it's only teenage wasteland' – every generation has a moment like that. 'Meet the new boss, same as the old boss' – a generation meets the realities of mortgages or rent, family, and adult life. 'No one knows what it's like behind blue eyes' – a generation struggles to find a sense of self, any sense of self. 'The song is over/I'm left with only tears' – every generation inevitably finds its own heartache. I think part of why we really identified with The Who is we instinctively realized that they, just like us kids, were absolute fuck-ups at heart."[22]

As a consequence of its constant airplay on FM radio, however, *Who's Next* sold to quite a few people who weren't specifically Who fans, or particularly aware of the group's legacy. That meant bringing their message to a wider audience than ever before, but in some ways, for a band that valued audience communication as much as The Who did, that was a mixed blessing. Now that audience included sports hooligans, drunken frat boys, and others who couldn't care less about Pete Townshend's spiritual message, let alone bridging the gap between listener and performer to transcend to a new reality.

This was The Who's new or at least wider constituency, vaulting them to the forefront of 70s arena rock. In some ways they embraced their yet higher level of success and superstardom. But for Pete Townshend, at least, there would always be a sense of promise unfulfilled, and he rarely passed up the opportunity to point out what could have been done, even while praising *Who's Next*. "It was a great humiliation that *Lifehouse* didn't come off, because I'd put so much energy into it," he lamented to Roger Scott. "I worked on that for two and a half years and it didn't come off, so it's great for me to listen to the record and not just feel that the songs are good, but to also know that one of the reasons they're good is that they've got their roots, in a sense, in this great fairy story."[23]

Nonetheless, it is *Who's Next*, and not *Lifehouse*, that would have an eternal life, and make a vivid imprint on millions of fans who have yet to hear of *Lifehouse* to this day. "The songs of *Who's Next* have lasted so well so long, [as a] very active part of classic rock's bedrock, because they spoke forcefully to fans," Tearson concludes. "Generation after generation of fans has discovered The Who and how personally those songs address the most personal issues of the listeners. They relate to them. Always have, and I suspect always will. *Who's Next* has attained a universal permanence reserved for very few. Much of The Beatles, some of the Stones, and not much else has that stature."[24]

When The Who wrapped up their American tour and returned home in late August, they could have been forgiven for basking in some glory as *Who's Next* rocketed up the charts on both sides of the ocean. It seemed premature to ask about what might be next after *Who's Next*, or for even the voluble Townshend to discuss such a prospect. But while *Lifehouse* seemed dead for the moment, they were, perhaps as gluttons for punishment, continuing to talk up doing a movie of some kind.

The lurking prospect of turning *Tommy* into a film never seemed far away. Even before the group had gone to the USA, Townshend had told the London *Times* that Joe Strick (director of a 1967 adaptation of *Ulysses* and the Academy Award-winning 1970 documentary short *Interviews With My Lai Veterans*) was interested. "Roger was going to do the lead in it, and we thought that if Roger was going do to a part, we'd all do a part," Pete told the *Los Angeles Free Press* late in the year. "Then I got involved in it, and we suddenly realized that [Strick] was trying to get *us* to make the film. He figured that was the best thing to do, but we realized that we weren't capable of making the film. We didn't have enough interest in it."[25] Universal at one point had even scheduled September 6 for starting shooting on a *Tommy* film, but didn't follow through.

The album's continual failure to translate to the screen particularly grated on Kit Lambert, who'd written an unused script. "He just became obsessed with that," feels Richard Barnes. "Because *Tommy* very much was Kit Lambert's too. I think when he wrote that film script, that's what he thought *Tommy* would be." In a way that would have fulfilled an ambition he'd held before even meeting The Who, when he was interested in film, not management; as Barnes points out, "when he first came along to the Railway Hotel [in 1964] and saw The High Numbers, it was a *film* he was looking to do, not manage a pop band."[26] Yet as Townshend said later in *The Story Of Tommy*, "Universal hated the screenplay, but took two years to say so."[27]

In July 1971, Pete confirmed to *NME* that he still felt The Who should be making a film. "There is so much that the whole Who organization, our whole team, could do in a film," he believed. "I don't think there are very many other groups who have the knowledge of stage rock theatre but at the same time the necessary lack of ego to carry it off. At the moment we are leaning heavily on the fact that we are good experienced musicians and can put on a good stage act. But – and I hate to rub it in – what we really need is a film."[28]

In September, with just a couple of gigs to fulfill (one a charity concert at London's Oval Cricket Ground), the group actually gathered at Roger Daltrey's country home in Sussex to talk about a film project. Details of what The Who were after and what they actually discussed are sketchy, but it seems likely they'd lowered their sights a bit from *Lifehouse* and were hoping to do a documentary film of some sort, perhaps taking what would have been their concert scenes in *Lifehouse* and expanding them into a feature. The proceedings were even filmed by Richard Stanley, who'd been friendly with Townshend as part of the Tattooist International group, and Chris Morphet, the hope being that footage from the meeting might be used in the movie itself. Since neither Stanley nor Morphet can recall any details of the gathering, it's likely no earthshaking possibilities were generated, although Pete reiterated his idea (also expressed in some press interviews at the time) that making a movie was about the only challenge left stimulating enough to keep the group going.

In an interview with Chris Welch for the October 23 edition of *Melody Maker*, Daltrey did announce a film, but in such a confusing manner that it seemed to be at least three projects at once. "We start in January, and Pete is writing the music," he stated. "The film should have been *Tommy* when the LP came out. That's when there should have been a film. In the film we do what we are good at – and that's playing. We'll get more involved as it progresses. It's going to be called *Guitar Farm*, but I don't want to say too much about the story" – a wise move, perhaps, in view of the holes Townshend had dug himself into when talking up *Lifehouse*.[29]

But what would this film have been, assuming Roger wasn't just leading the press on? Was it *Tommy*? Was it an entirely new concept, complete with new Townshend songs? Was it even a revival of *Guitar Farm*, the film idea Townshend had brainstormed with Richard Stanley and the Tattooist International group before *Lifehouse*?

Even more confusingly, *Rolling Stone* had reported on August 5 that Townshend was working on a soundtrack for *Joad*, "a film based on the novel *Guitar Farm*, which is based on the antics of Adolf Hitler and Glenn Miller wheeling around in a Lincoln."[30] The possibility can't even be discounted that the participants' chronological recollections are so off the mark that *Guitar Farm* might not have been conceived until after *Lifehouse* had dissipated, although most indications are that *Guitar Farm* was developed and discarded in 1970, not 1971. (In addition, *Guitar Farm* was never a novel, the *Rolling Stone* piece to the contrary.) But *Guitar Farm* and Tattooist International director Denis Postle's memory of Townshend writing 'Baba O'Riley' as a sample track for the project, and director and writer Mike Myers's speculation that Townshend took part of the inspiration for the same song from a line in the original *Guitar Farm* story, seem to indicate that his involvement with the *Guitar Farm* team predated The Who's attempts to work on *Lifehouse* in 1971.

For good measure, Townshend told *Crawdaddy's* John Swenson at the end of The Who's American summer tour that "we want to make a movie *about* what The Who are going to do – what The Who do." He also announced their intentions to make "a TV special which is going to be a documentary about us preparing to make the movie," as if that hadn't already worked out badly enough when The Beatles tried much the same thing with *Let It Be*.[31] Whatever the case, Daltrey's *Melody Maker* declaration was another false alarm, since The Who would not begin any film project in January 1972.

The group seemed to summon more enthusiasm for the straightforward task of assembling their first proper greatest hits collection, *Meaty Beaty Big And Bouncy*, in September. Although Who compilations had appeared in the UK (with the 1968 Track Records LP *Direct Hits*) and other territories, *Meaty Beaty Big And Bouncy* was the first quality effort along these lines, especially as it managed to include several 1965 tracks produced by Shel Talmy that had been unavailable for previous anthologies. The jacket design (by Daltrey's cousin Graham Hughes) used a photo of the Railway Hotel, where The Who had played a weekly residency for months in 1964, in the inner gatefold. It obviously wasn't a mere cash-in for Townshend, who treated *Rolling*

Stone readers to a 26-paragraph review of the compilation in its December 9 issue (originally written for a friend for publication in the *San Francisco Flyer* before it came to the attention of *Rolling Stone* editor Jann Wenner).

The LP (originally to be titled *The Who Looks Back*) indicated a growing interest within the band in their own history, now that they'd survived and thrived longer than almost any other British Invasion group. "This album is as much for us as for you," Townshend concluded in his *Rolling Stone* review. "It reminds us who we really are, The Who." [32] If only in hindsight, it might have helped ignite interest in exploring their own history in song – a concept that, two years down the line, would expand into a full-blown rock opera. In the review, Pete even mentioned plans to reissue The High Numbers' 1964 single 'I'm The Face' on The Rolling Stones' record label, and while that wouldn't come to pass, some of its lyrics would be quoted in *Quadrophenia*.

Even with *Who's Next* near the top of the charts on both sides of the Atlantic, *Meaty Beaty Big And Bouncy* was released on October 30 in the USA and November 26 in the UK. The days when compilations of archive material were deemed unhealthy competition to a current release were obviously well in the future, and in another surprising move, a Who single of two leftovers from their June studio sessions was issued in mid-October. The release of 'Let's See Action'/'When I Was A Boy' even seemed to take Pete Townshend by surprise. "The tracks were recorded at the tail end of the sessions for the last album," he told *Melody Maker*, "but I didn't realize it was going to be released so soon. We might have a bash at ['Let's See Action'] on stage but we haven't rehearsed it yet. It's a very relaxed number for us." [33]

A review of the 45 in *NME* seemed to confirm that someone had unleashed the disc on impulse. "It was a snap decision to release this new single with virtually no forewarning," the paper enthused, "though I don't think the boys will go far wrong with it! Even though Daltrey works himself up to quite a frenzy in the vocal crescendo, it's a much less berserk and abandoned item than the majority of the group's discs. A rocker with a thoroughly infectious and swinging beat, that's sustained by crashing cymbals and underlying clanking piano, it's tight and controlled with a great feeling of togetherness. ... Seems likely that this could fare better than many of The Who's singles, because the appeal of both performance and material should be wider than the more limited scope of its heavier work." [34] The review's failure even to mention the Entwistle-penned-and-sung B-side could be a reflection of its lack of quality, as it's a plodding nostalgic ballad that's not even up to the standards of most of John's Who songs, let alone Townshend's.

NME's optimism notwithstanding, 'Let's See Action' seems a curious choice for a single, and not a terribly commercial one. *NME* didn't seem to realize that the heavier Who songs were becoming their most popular tunes, not relatively average midtempo exhortations like this one, highlighted by a mantra-like "nothing is everything" refrain that seemed like a refugee from a more introspective Meher Baba-based composition. Townshend certainly knew it was coming out at some point, however, and might have even planned it as a deliberate, more positive contrast or sequel to 'Won't Get Fooled Again.' In his response to critics of that hit in *International Times*, he'd urged them to "listen to our next single. It was recorded at the same session as 'Fooled' and is a planned, predetermined follow-up."[35] Not atypically, Pete had changed his tune just a few months later in the *Los Angeles Free Press*, dismissing 'Let's See Action' as "pretty insipid, actually. It was done at the tail end of the recording session for 'We Won't Get Fooled Again' which is what I suppose I really feel most strongly now."[36]

'Let's See Action' might have been more palatable to the more politically engaged of his listeners, urging as it did the need to get involved and rabble-rouse for freedom. The fact was, however, that it wasn't nearly as exciting as 'Won't Get Fooled Again.' Nor, as much as counterculture agitators might have hated to admit it, was it as lyrically incisive and thought-provoking. Peaking at a mere Number 16 in the UK, it wasn't even issued in the US, Townshend enigmatically telling *Sounds* "it didn't seem right [there]."[37] Instead Decca opted to pluck another tune from *Who's Next* for the American market, 'Behind Blue Eyes,' with 'My Wife' on the flip. At one time it was even scheduled to be a single in the UK before it was (as Townshend said in *NME* in August) rejected as "we thought it was too much out of character."[38] 'Behind Blue Eyes' didn't do too badly in the States; its modest peak at Number 34, however, reinforced the group's status as an album rather than singles band.

'Let's See Action' might have been an olive branch to those who accused The Who of not being on the right side of the revolution, but Townshend's patience with those who questioned the band's politics would be tested by an acerbic exchange in *Melody Maker* early that fall. A reader wrote in to accuse rock musicians in general of hypocrisy for preaching anti-materialism, and

The Who, Pink Floyd, and Yes in particular for charging high prices for concert tickets. Townshend took the bait with a one-page reply entitled "Creators or Capitalists?" "If prices are high, it is only because we are trying to raise our standards, not fill our pockets," he said, adding that The Who would "inevitably use the money they have earned to instigate a change in the direction they think Rock should go. Not to create new leaders or play for free till we (and the roadies) starve, but to do something permanent about the only part of our work we can really control, live performances."[39]

Reader John Rudd wasn't buying it, pointing out that "It seems short-sighted to the point of self-deception to claim that the ideals of peace, equality etc, which refer to what we want society to be can be replaced by the musicians' personal ideal of self-perfection ... he can claim that it's perfectly consistent to charge rip-off prices to pay for his expensive equipment because it's necessary to change 'rock' and achieve the ideals. I'd admire him more if he forgot about ideals completely in that sense."[40]

Whether Rudd's reasonably articulated reply had pushed a particular button or Pete was generally fed up with trying to debate with disgruntled fans, his reply in the November 6 issue was remarkably ill-tempered. "I admit it," he sardonically rejoined. "Not only do we charge too much for entry to our performances but we all made it in the first place by sleeping with record company executives. Of course my ideals aren't really what I PRETEND they are. I'm merely indulging in honest to God lying. Why tell the truth anyway? People don't listen ... Fuck off the lot of you!"[41]

In truth, Townshend had never had much of an affinity for anti-capitalist radicalism, famously booting Abbie Hoffman off the stage when the activist tried to make an announcement in the middle of The Who's Woodstock set. His idealism, and songs like 'Let's See Action' and 'Won't Get Fooled Again,' had led some to think he might participate in some genuine political activism but, like most rock stars, he never would join or lead a cause to overthrow the materialistic society that had made The Who's superstardom possible.

A few disillusioned punters excepted, audiences were generally happy to pay the ticket prices and fill the seats as The Who spent much of the fall touring the UK and USA. For all *Who's Next*'s success, the band's popularity as a concert act remained central to both their appeal to audiences and the esteem in which they were held by rock critics. *Rolling Stone* hailed the symbiosis in the article accompanying their simultaneous Album Of The Year and Band Of The Year awards. "In the hiatus that followed the international success of *Tommy*," it wrote, "many wondered whether The Who could sustain the fantastic creativity that had marked every phase of their history from the early 60s on: 1971 was the year they answered the question. They toured the world, putting on shows filled with a revitalized energy and exhilarating release that not only took us back but also pushed us ahead. They articulated a sensibility strong enough to sustain many people's interest in hard rock, when the very genre was being called into question by the meaningless popularity of so many untalented groups. And finally, they released the best of all hard rock albums in 1971."[42]

Chris Charlesworth of *Melody Maker* reviewed one of the first British shows that autumn, on Entwistle's birthday (October 9), at a gymnasium in Surrey University in Guildford. The hall held only 600, admission was restricted to the university's students and the show was only advertised 24 hours in advance. Charlesworth's review was not untypical of the raves the concerts received in the press. "There isn't a band in the land that couldn't take a lesson or two from The Who," he observed. "They used the best possible combination of songs to whip up the excitement to an awe-inspiring climax as huge searchlights beamed down on delirious fans drunk with ecstasy at the group's new finale. ... 'Behind Blue Eyes,' with its strong vocal lines, showed just how good The Who's new PA system can sound, while the use of pre-recorded tapes during 'Baba O'Riley' and 'Won't Get Fooled Again' brought the audience to their feet on each occasion. Perhaps The Who are getting too good, and that's why they are knocked for being predictable. Perhaps they are, but many an unpredictable band would be unable to generate like The Who. I hope to hell they never change."[43]

Nearly 40 years later, Charlesworth's enthusiasm remains undimmed. "I was stood at the front, the stage was about three-foot high, and I was just blown away," he recalls. "I saw the set [from this period] four or five times – the half-dozen or so numbers from *Who's Next*, selections [from] *Tommy*, coupled with the old hit singles and a bit of improvisation toward the end where anything can happen. Just out of this world, it was. Pete was awfully difficult to please, [but] the other three were more than delighted. Those shows were fantastic."[44]

Without question, the group's concerts in the last half of 1971 showed them playing well and enthusiastically. The limitations of the power trio format made it inevitable that there would be less sonic variation than on their studio recordings, but they did at least, as Charlesworth's review noted, bring along pre-recorded tapes for the two *Who's Next* songs that relied most heavily on synthesizers. Dave Arbus wasn't along to play violin on 'Baba O'Riley,' but Daltrey gamely substituted his underrated, infrequently wielded, raunchy blues harmonica. Roger alluded to the complications of using backing tapes at their December 13 show in San Francisco, when he remarked in his introduction to 'Baba O'Riley': "We use a tape to put a synthesizer sound on the stage because it was a lot easier than getting someone to play it. We'd get all that hang-up we couldn't handle really if we got someone else. Anyway, Pete plays the synthesizer on the tape so it's just like having two Petes." To which Moon waggishly shouted: "Bloody hell, one's enough!"

What the shows didn't offer was much in the way of spontaneity. Most big groups then and now largely stick to the same set in the same order, and The Who did so for months on end, including just five *Who's Next* songs. 'Love Ain't For Keeping,' 'Getting In Tune,' and 'The Song Is Over' might have been judged too slow for the show, although 'Going Mobile' was a curious omission.

The Who weren't searching for an audience-performer combustion that might give rise to new material, as they had in the Young Vic. The size of the venues would have made such interaction impossible in any case. Still, it was another mark of the loss of adventurousness of the *Lifehouse* project, as ambitions were superseded by professional fulfillment of what the audience wanted most – as could be said, to some degree, of the *Who's Next* album itself.

There were a couple of guests who supplied at least a bit in the way of unexpected novelty. One was John Sebastian, who played harmonica at the October 9 Guildford show. Sebastian was known for mild-mannered folk-rock as both The Lovin' Spoonful's leader and a solo singer-songwriter. Maybe he relished the chance to get down'n'dirty, having also lent his harmonica to The Doors' 1970 track 'Roadhouse Blues' (as well as playing with The Doors at a May 1970 show). Another was Townshend's experimental composer friend Ron Geesin, who opened a couple of the shows in early October. "He did two test gigs with us," Pete told *ZigZag*, "and to put it mildly, he wiped the floor with The Who – just him and his bits of paper and his piano playing. He's so far ahead of his time as a performer that people just can't pick up on it. ... He was going to do the tours with us but got weaseled out of it by a bit of politics, unfortunately."[45]

In Geesin's view, the reaction of the audience said something about differences within The Who themselves as to what kind of risks should be taken on stage. "Pete [said], 'It would be good to have something a bit stimulating as an opener,' and he got me to do two gigs," he remembers. "He liked a challenge, because when I went out there, the place was different because of the way I performed. It was confronting the audience, and they didn't know whether it was supposed to be funny or very serious or what. Whereas Pete wanted a challenge, certainly Roger Daltrey wanted mediocrity so that he could go out and shine after it.

"Now when I came off – it was probably [at Reading University at] the first of the two gigs – I got a hell of a good response, because it was a big 2,000-seat hall. I came off to a lot of applause, and Roger Daltrey gave me one fucking hell of a lecture on how not to go down so well before they went on. It was something else; I never forgot that. He explained how somebody had gone on, like a folk guitarist or something, and they managed to not quite last a half hour before they were booed off. He thought this was the way to go. This was what they wanted, you see? In other words, I had gone down far too well, because it made it difficult for him to get the energy up there.

"But Pete thought it was great, because he thought the level of the whole thing had risen. Not only did I provoke the audience, I provoked The Who, or brought things out that were not directly spoken of. It was good fun but of course, they didn't do it again. They did the two gigs, and that was that. They didn't want to make a habit of that," he laughs.[46]

More typical were their final shows of the American tour, at San Francisco's Civic Auditorium on December 12 and 13, where 16-track recordings were made to consider for use on a possible live release. Whether The Who would have issued a live album so soon after *Who's Next* is debatable. It had been less than two years since *Live At Leeds*, and when you throw *Meaty Beaty Big And Bouncy* into the mix, that would have meant that three of the last four Who albums would have been concert LPs or greatest hits collections. It couldn't have been an auspicious omen that Keith Moon

163

was put on the plane to San Francisco in a wheelchair after indulging in barbiturates and brandy, although he rallied to play well enough after a shaky start to the first of the shows.

Much of the material from the December 13 show eventually made it into official release; one of the songs, 'Baby Don't You Do It,' was used quite soon as a 1972 B-side. It and five others appear on the double CD, *View From A Backstage Pass*, available only through The Who's website, while their cover of Freddie King's 'Goin' Down' showed up on the *Two's Missing* rarities compilation. The rest of the set has circulated on bootleg, albeit with sub-standard sound. (A version of 'Behind Blue Eyes,' with the December 12 show listed as the source, appears on the 2010 compilation *Greatest Hits Live*.) Together they provide evidence of the band's strengths as a concert act, but also their weaknesses, at least when the music is listened to cold, away from the excitement of the event. The group go on for too long too often, especially in the numbers lending themselves to lengthy guitar improvisations. When keeping a lid on that tendency – particularly in 'Bargain' (prior to the instrumental coda) and 'Baba O'Riley,' the most refreshing contrast to the official studio recording, due to Daltrey's harmonica – the musicians are more effective.

Even at the end of a tour and year that had seen The Who refine the material over and over, on stage and in the studio, the mood could still vary considerably on consecutive nights. "The first night, Townshend was angry," recalls David Teborek, in the audience for both San Francisco shows. "He was pissed off. He made some comment to the crowd about, 'I don't see you throwing any money to us.' I'll tell you, his playing was exceptional. His leads were real fiery; he was real keyed up. I don't know what he was angry about. I went back the second night, he was much more laidback. But his guitar playing wasn't nearly as exciting as it was the first night, when he was pissed off. It was sort of like he was kind of bipolar: in a manic mood, the first night, and slipped into a less than manic mode the second night. But the first night was much better."[47]

As Joel Selvin's review of the concerts in *Night Times* demonstrated, however, the group's highly visual concert act – something that an archival CD can't capture – remained at a remarkably high level after such a grueling year on stage and off. "Their dramatic stage presentation actually breaches the brink of violence – Townshend kicking his microphone into the audience several times or Roger Daltrey beating two tambourines together until they're demolished," he wrote. "All this balanced with their absurd sense of the comic, infusing the element of good-natured – almost wholesome – fun. The Who have to be one of the great spectacles of the modern rock world. ...

"What their musical prowess lacked was more than compensated for by the intense energy of both the music and the stage act. Spastic Townshend running in figure eights and darting toward the microphone like a crazed orangutan playing the guitar. Daltrey's statuesque poses and whirling microphone were geometric by comparison. The contrast was startling and their interaction almost choreographed. ...

"Before it was over Townshend had tripped and sprawled on the stage a few times, kicked his microphone over two more times. Daltrey was throwing his microphone even beyond his reach now, while Moon flailed furiously and bassist John Entwistle stood stone still and impassive – as he had the entire concert – his legs crossed leaning against his amplifier. They brought it to an end on one final note, staggered to the center of the stage, arms entwined around each others' necks, sweating and grinning and waving goodbye. Townshend and Moon both actually had enough strength left to dance off the stage."[48]

The heavy touring ended in mid December, having helped put off the inevitable question of what The Who could do to follow up *Who's Next*, whether that involved a film, attempting to mount another concept piece, or something else. "Since *Who's Next* came out, we've been working to fill in the time that we wasted on the *Lifehouse* thing," mused Townshend to the *Los Angeles Free Press* in December. "We spent eight months off the road, and since July we've been working pretty much every day."

That giant interview – actually conducted by Chris Van Ness a few days before the tour reached LA, on a December 3 off-day in Denver – was about as close as Pete got to summing up his mindset as 1972 approached. Asked if he had a compulsion to do another album, Townshend's four-word response, coming from one so gifted at spinning multi-paragraph answers to questions from the press, said it all as to his state of exhaustion: "Not at the moment."[49] Yet another unfulfilled film scheme was unveiled when Townshend revealed that rock critic Nik Cohn was working with them on a script. Cohn was actually traveling with The Who for much of the tour. A 1975 article of his for *New York* magazine, 'Tribal Rites Of The New Saturday Night,' would indeed be made into a smash film-with-music several years later when it was developed into *Saturday Night Fever*. Nothing came out of his travels with The Who, however, other than a story for the UK magazine *Cream*.

Pressed by Van Ness as to whether The Who would do another extended work, however, Townshend was more talkative. "I personally am writing extended works all the time," he said. "*Who's Next* was an extended work, but it wasn't finished, if you like. I don't know whether I'll ever be able to do one as complex as *Tommy* without the help of Kit Lambert, because he was as much a producer in the writing as he was in the studio. I suppose the next thing we want is an extended work by The Who and their people, rather than an extended work by me. But beyond that generalization, I don't know. ...

"I think at the moment, all our hopes, if you like, are pinned on a film. But I suppose that, deep down inside, I know that the music's got to come first in anything that we do. And if the music comes first, I want the music to stand on its own, and if it stands on its own, we don't need a film. So at the moment, I'm just waiting for next year when I'll get a wee bit of time, and I'm just going to think very clearly about what needs to be done. I mean, I literally haven't had time to think."[50]

In 1972, The Who would neither launch a film nor complete an extended work. In fact, they'd hardly release anything at all. But the idea would start to form for a rock opera that, unlike *Lifehouse*, would be completed as Townshend had envisioned it, if in far less dramatic fashion than *Lifehouse* had crashed and burned.

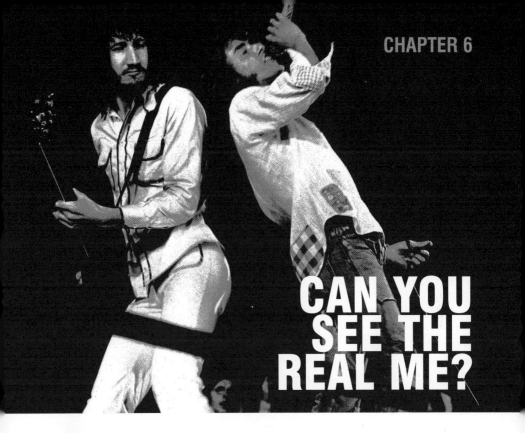

CHAPTER 6

CAN YOU SEE THE REAL ME?

Back in October 1970, before the word *Lifehouse* had even appeared in Who articles, *Disc* asked Pete Townshend "about the idea for a double album showcasing The Who individually with sides by individual members of the group." Townshend replied, "It would be a good expression of solidarity but showing clear-cut musical differences. I could do a good side, and John could, and Keith could make an hilarious one. Roger might require help because he doesn't write much, but we would all be able to use anyone in the group we wanted to. If I did tracks it would be inevitable that I would use Roger's voice here and there."[1]

Here Pete was sketching out an album that, like Pink Floyd's 1969 double-LP *Ummagumma*, would allow each of the four members to record solo tracks on an album billed to the group (although the Floyd had used just one of the LPs to do so, with the other a live disc performed by the full group). There's no evidence that Townshend and the group ever seriously pursued the creation of a double LP with one side for each member. In December 1970, *Creem* suggested "that probably won't happen, as only half the group are hot on the idea and John Entwistle is already preparing an album of his own tunes anyway."[2] Remarkably, however, they would eventually pursue a far more ambitious spin on the idea: to record a double album, as a group, that attempted to explore four different sides of one individual, each represented by one member of The Who.

At the same time, the group were getting interested in a four-dimensional notion of a different sort. A little-noticed innovation of their shows at the Young Vic Theatre in early 1971 was quadraphonic sound, then employed by very few artists, although Pink Floyd had used it in concert as far back as their May 12 1967 performance at London's Queen Elizabeth Hall. By the early 70s, quadraphonic sound was being developed for sound recordings as well as live presentations. The Who were eager to explore the possibility of making a quadraphonic LP.

Just one of those brainstorms would have been more than enough for most bands. Typically, The Who would try to combine both of them into the same project, and not quite succeed in pulling off either. What would make their next rock opera a success would come not from futuristic science fiction tinkering, nor the reflection of split or multiple personalities. Instead it would come from looking back into their past, with help from friends who had known them before they had even performed their own material. And there would be more than a year of fitful stops and starts before the album known as *Quadrophenia* would finally start to take shape.

The first few months of 1972 were as quiet a time professionally as The Who had known for about a decade, since back when they were known as The Detours, with Doug Sandom on drums. For all the noises they'd made even through 1971 about coming to the brink of splitting up, there wasn't much to occupy them as individuals, at least on the artistic side. Entwistle wrote material for his second album at his home studio. Daltrey dabbled in record production, producing The Ellis Group's *Riding On The Crest Of A Slump* at Olympic. The record featured vocalist Steve Ellis, former frontman of Love Affair, who'd had a few late-60s British hits without making a dent in the USA. Daltrey had previously produced a single, 'Accidents,' for a yet more obscure group, Bent Frame. As he enigmatically informed *Melody Maker*, "for political reasons it never came out."[3]

As the least disciplined member of The Who when he wasn't behind the drum kit, Keith Moon was the most at sea when it came to finding professional outlets outside the band. In October 1970, he had produced, and drummed on, 'Suspicion,' a single by former Bonzo Dog Band man Viv Stanshall (with Entwistle on bass and brass). Perhaps only semi-facetiously, he had summarized his production contributions to *Rolling Stone* as supplying the booze. Although there were thoughts of a Moon-produced Stanshall album, that might have been too much to expect from the two looniest characters on the British pop scene. Certainly the public wasn't prepared to take 'Suspicion' too seriously after Stanshall told *NME* he had "recorded it as a laxative to clear the system out."[4]

Keith had also played a part on Stanshall's BBC Radio One series in 1971, and had a small role in the notoriously incomprehensible Frank Zappa movie *200 Motels*, shot during the first week of February that year. Zappa had offered parts to both Moon and Townshend on the spur of the moment at London's Speakeasy Club, the night before shooting. Only Keith turned up, playing a nun, a part originally intended for Mick Jagger. Then, in July 1971, Moon had drummed on The Scaffold's 'Do The Albert,' with Stanshall and fellow Bonzos man Neil Innes also pitching in. All of these projects were more comedy than rock'n'roll, although as he wasn't a songwriter of note, that might actually have been a logical path to pursue.

At this point The Who hardly needed more publicity, but Moon helped keep their profile high in the press. Not only did he do interviews, he even invited journalists such as Chris Charlesworth and *NME*'s Richard Green to hang out and party with him at his estate, Tara. "I think his major contribution was not in a creative role working with Pete," Who PR man Keith Altham muses. "What he did do was take an awful lot of weight off them when they needed it taken off them, in terms of publicity and generating publicity. Not just for publicity's sake, but at the time when perhaps they needed to create a little bit of outrage somewhere and it was encouraged. Also, it was a means of occupying Moon. Because if Moon wasn't occupied, he just went off the rails."[5]

In contrast, Townshend took advantage of the downtime to indulge not in partying with the media but in his innermost and most serious spiritual pursuits. Early in 1972 he went to Arangaon, India, to spend time with Meher Baba's close family and disciples, kneeling at Baba's tomb and kissing the ground before it. "I really felt like a speck of dust," he recalled in the *Daily*

Express. "It was fantastic. Suddenly everything was in proportion. It only lasted three seconds. I yearn to reach that state of excitement and absolute pure peace again."[6] He also participated in a ritual where followers stood around the tomb to sing 'Begin The Beguine,' which, as absurd as it sounds, was considered totally appropriate in this milieu; the Cole Porter standard had been one of Baba's favorite songs (and was covered by Townshend on a home demo on the 1970 *Happy Birthday* Baba tribute LP). "It totally zapped me out when I was there," he told *Disc*. "I stood up after all this and was crying and everything."[7]

Townshend might have appreciated the chance to show his devotion half a world away from The Who; they were never inclined to take such religious matters seriously, and were even known to mock or taunt him if he tried to combine Meher Baba and The Who on the same agenda. Shortly after the start of The Who's fall tour, the previous November, he'd visited the largest Baba center in the world in Myrtle Beach, South Carolina. According to Nik Cohn's *Cream* article, 'On The Road Again,' he had, for the next few days, "locked himself in his hotel room and talked to no one. Onstage he moved and played like a zombie, in dressing rooms he crouched in corners, dead-eyed, drained, and twitched whenever anybody came close or touched him. The rest of the group enjoyed this immensely. Baba has always made them sick and now was their chance of sweet revenge. So they took up the avatar's basic slogan – 'Be Happy Don't Worry' – and rubbed Pete's nose in it. A shattered shambling wreckage, he tried to back off but they pursued him, harried him relentlessly. 'Be Happy,' Keith kept chanting, exultant, flinging it out like a scarlet rag. 'Don't worry, be happy, don't worry, be happy.' Pete made no response. Just sat there and continued to suffer."[8]

But if his bandmates had a hard time taking Townshend's guru seriously, another longtime friend was convinced of both Pete's sincerity and the benefits Baba's organization conferred upon him. "Although I'm an atheist, I kind of got involved with it because he challenged me to," says Richard Barnes. "I couldn't help seeing how wonderful it had been for [Townshend and his wife]. They really were kind of content, interested, honest, and open. They were [at] about the period where they should start being egotistical, aloof, and just about making money and becoming famous. But they weren't, quite the opposite. I was impressed that it seemed to make them much more normal."[9]

Around the anniversary of Baba's death, in February 1972, another tribute LP appeared with contributions from Townshend, although these were a little more modest in scope than the ones he'd done for *Happy Birthday*. Entitled *I Am*, the album included his nearly ten-minute instrumental demo of 'Baba O'Riley,' a piece he may have been determined to release in at least one form, given his stated preference for it over The Who's recording. Yet more unusual was his seven-minute version of 'O Parvardigar,' conceived while he and his wife were on holiday on Osea Island in the Blackwater Estuary in South-east England (and recorded on August 31 1971). It set Baba's 'Universal Prayer' to Pete's music and vocals. A German version was also recorded, using a translation by Austrian Baba follower Hilde Halpern. It was not released until its inclusion on a 2001 EP that also included both the original recording and a live performance with just vocals and acoustic guitar, recorded in India in January 1972.

As Townshend explained in *A Decade Of The Who*, 'O Parvardigar' was written when he tuned his guitar to a chord and picked out a melody in the style of top British folk guitarists Bert Jansch and John Renbourn (then both in the folk-rock group Pentangle). Never having written that way before, he recorded it onto a cassette player and "was so struck with its 'stillness' that I dedicated it to Meher Baba." He'd also been trying to rework the prayer so that it could be set to music, and realized that what he'd just taped would fit the words "with very few minor alterations. At that time I felt almost as if I had had nothing to do with the writing process at all – call it coincidence if you like – but it's one of many!"[10] Some tasty unobtrusive synthesizer flitted across the recording that made its way onto *I Am*, filled out by piano, drums, and harmony vocals, in the manner of most Townshend demos.

Neither track could by any stretch of the imagination have found a place on a Who release, but *I Am* provided an appropriate outlet. Townshend also contributed synthesizer, guitar, drums, and engineering to most of the other material on *I Am*, which included tracks by Billy Nicholls, Dave Hastilow, and poet Mike Da Costa. "I think the American Meher Baba groups had produced an album which we kind of laughed at, because they were the sort of things that a spiritual group would produce, we thought anyway," says Richard Barnes, who silk-screened the covers of the *I Am* LP. "So [Pete] wanted to do something that was not so much that kind of gentle, folksy maudlin sort of thing." Predictably, it wasn't long before the LP came to the attention of hardcore Who fans, providing an incentive for Townshend to make it more widely available, to counteract bootlegging if nothing else.

Less predictably, *I Am* became a favorite of Keith Moon, despite his mockery of Townshend's devotion to Baba. "I was hanging around at Moon's house a lot. He'd just moved into Tara," says Barnes. "Each room used to have these tapes that just repeated and repeated, and he'd have them going day and night. One would have The Beatles, one would have Jan & Dean, and they'd have a jukebox in what he called the study which would play a lot of interesting music, including a lot of real simple pop like The Partridge Family, as well as Chuck Berry and stuff like that. But Moon used to play that second Baba album all the bloody time. It seemed so strange and out of place there. In all that mad rock'n'roll nonsense, mayhem, 24-hour party stuff, you'd be hearing 'O Parvardigar.'"[11]

Although there's no evidence that The Who returned to the studio until May, an April news item in *Circus* reported, with hopeless optimism, that "a new LP is in the works and will probably emerge before the summer begins." Details of the album, it continued, were "being kept secret even from officials at Decca Records" (whose association with The Who would actually end soon). It also claimed that "a Who film is also on its way," and that Nik Cohn had been told to prepare content for "a realistic documentary on The Who's career by following the group's members at every possible moment," although by this time Who fans had learned not to take such items too seriously.[12] The film wouldn't appear, but The Who did enter Olympic with Glyn Johns by May 19 at the latest to start working on new recordings. (Townshend also got some of his cinematic ambitions out of his system by playing on a couple of cuts at Olympic for Ron Wood and Ronnie Lane's soundtrack for *Mahoney's Last Stand* around this time.)

It's not certain whether the band had an album and concept in mind or were just convening to see how things developed. It's been suggested that they still hoped to do something with the material left over from the *Who's Next/Lifehouse* project, whether it was building a new LP around the rejects or even reviving *Lifehouse* itself. Both prospects seem unlikely. An album made up of the surplus songs and out-takes would not match the strength of *Who's Next*. And putting *Lifehouse* together at this date would have meant reusing or re-recording most of the songs on *Who's Next*, which seems impractical from both commercial and artistic standpoints so soon after the LP's 1971 release.

The sessions in late May were productive, however. They yielded the next two Who singles, although neither was destined to be among their biggest-selling or most memorable 45s. The better of the pair was 'Join Together.' Lyrically it was a fairly basic call for listeners to merge together with the musicians, but it was more musically effective than 'Let's See Action.' The catchy chorus helped propel it to the British Top Ten, and it did reasonably well in the USA, making Number 17 near the end of the summer. Musically its most distinctive signature was a combination of Jew's harp twang with harmonica that has often been mistaken for a synthesizer, such was Townshend's stature as the most distinguished and imaginative user of the instrument in rock music.

'Join Together' has been cited as a song originally intended for *Lifehouse*, and, played by The Who in the big concert scene, it would have fitted comfortably into the storyline as a celebration of rock and its audience. The absence of a *Who's Next* out-take or any evidence that the band played it live in 1971, however, makes one wonder if it had actually been written in time. Indeed, in the *Classic Albums* documentary on *Who's Next*, Townshend says it dates from some time after *Who's Next*, when he, with Daltrey's encouragement and help, did a new script for the *Lifehouse* story. "This second version of *Lifehouse* became about a world in which music was banned ... particularly rock music," Pete said. "Only the most trite, empty, lightweight music was allowed. Muzak was allowed. And 'Join Together' was a song written to accompany that."[13] Assuming this script revision took place sometime between mid 1971 and May 22 1972 (when 'Join Together' was recorded), however, it doesn't seem like Townshend and Daltrey got too far with *Lifehouse Mk II* either.

Also sometimes cited as a *Lifehouse* leftover is 'Relay,' which is lyrically sharper yet musically duller. While it doesn't have as obvious an association with *Lifehouse*'s plot, its intimations of duplicitous authoritarian control, revolution, freeway travel, and looking inside one's soul for "the only quiet place" match up with several elements of the basic scenario. The synthesizer gurgles are so rigid they almost anticipate electronic techno-pop, the mechanized beats exercising uncommon restraint on Keith Moon's hell-bent percussive style. Not the most obvious of hit singles, it would be held over for the time being.

So would the most pedestrian of the songs known to have been cut at

Olympic this spring, 'Put The Money Down,' an average mid-tempo rocker with more of the strangled synthesizer textures Townshend seemed to favor around this period. Too vague lyrically, in its mixture of a disoriented protagonist and guys walking on water, to make a strong case for a *Lifehouse* connection (even though it has sometimes been regarded as a possible song for that project), it would later emerge on *Odds & Sods*. Daltrey finished his vocal track in 1974, shortly before that compilation's release. Even that almost didn't happen. "'Put The Money Down' only had a guide vocal," Entwistle told *NME*'s Roy Carr in 1976, "and that held up the release of *Odds & Sods*, but I just couldn't get Daltrey down to the studio to record a new vocal. So I sent him a message asking if it'd be all right if I did the vocal, and almost immediately Daltrey replied that it was OK as long as he could overdub the bass parts. Next morning he was in the studio!"[14]

'Join Together,' 'Relay,' and 'Put The Money Down' are presented in Townshend demo form on *Lifehouse Chronicles*, differing from The Who's versions mostly in their greater length (save for 'Relay') and Pete rather than Roger handling the lead vocals. 'Join Together' rambles on for a good two additional minutes, in fact, again testifying to The Who's strength as editors of the prototype versions. The group's version could have been longer, however, Entwistle telling *NME* of the existence of an unedited take lasting three minutes longer.

A couple of Townshend demos reported as originating from this period don't seem to have been suitable for whatever album The Who were working toward, conceptual or otherwise. 'Riot In A Female Jail' is about just that, with its gauche line "I ran right up to the gates, so that I could be the first one raped." It marks a return to the off-the-wall subject matter of songs more associated with the era of *A Quick One* and *The Who Sell Out* than with *Tommy* or *Lifehouse*. Its slow bluesy rock is a little on the turgid side. 'Can't You See I'm Easy,' featuring a twanging guitar-riff, almost sounded like a cover of a song by an early-70s singer-songwriter or soft folk-rock act – not an area, to put it mildly, that would have been The Who's forte.

'Get Inside,' possibly a very early version of 'Rough Boys' (from Townshend's 1980 solo album *Empty Glass*), has also been reported as a demo from this period, although it hasn't circulated. Pete described another song, 'Ambition,' as having been recorded by The Who in 1972, in a webcast more than 30 years later in which he performed it with just his voice and guitar. It's difficult to tell how the band might have played it from that version, but it sounds like a rather formulaic early-70s Who number that no one would have fought to include on a release.

A Townshend composition recorded on June 5, however, would prove the unlikely seed of The Who's next real album, a conceptual work on which, ironically, the song itself wouldn't appear. Sung mainly by Pete, 'Long Live Rock' was, on the surface, a merely competent song in a genre The Who were starting almost to make their own – the anthemic celebration of rock itself. 'Long Live Rock' could have been called "an anthemic celebration of rock, warts and all," with its snapshots of back-alley scalpers, befuddled promoters, and yawning punters. The proud declaration "we were the first band to vomit in the bar" is black humor worthy of John Entwistle, and the whole song has an air of frivolous self-parody about it. It seems likely it had only recently been written. Townshend's 1987 collection *Another Scoop* includes what he called an "innocent, bouncy little demo" of the song, dated May 2. Yet, as Pete made plain in his liner notes to *Odds & Sods*, this apparent throwaway would have been the title piece for the latest concept LP brewing in his head: "I had an idea once for a new album about the history of The Who, called *Rock Is Dead – Long Live Rock*. That idea later blossomed into *Quadrophenia*."[15]

The idea of doing a history of The Who in song was ingenious. Certainly there'd be plenty of source material, the story being richer in anecdotal detail and unexpected twists and turns than any scriptwriter (including Townshend) could have produced. It's curious, however, that none of the other songs under consideration at Olympic could have been part of such a history, except perhaps 'Join Together.' It has to be assumed that the idea, as intriguing as it was, never got far beyond the 'Long Live Rock' song itself. But a variation on the idea – focusing on a specific and fascinating juncture in The Who's history, starring not The Who themselves, but a fictional character embodying various traits of both the band and their audience – would indeed be Townshend's next grand scheme.

The group might already have been thinking that some of their new material might fit such a story. Two other songs known to have been written around this time would eventually – unlike 'Long Live Rock' – become part of *Quadrophenia*. It's not known exactly when 'Love Reign O'er Me' and 'Is It In My Head?' were recorded, but it seems probable they were at least started at the same spring sessions in Olympic. For one thing, they are the only two

Quadrophenia tracks on which Glyn Johns is credited as engineer and associate producer. For another, they're the only two *Quadrophenia* songs copyrighted in 1972 – not long after the Olympic sessions, on July 12 (along with two other songs cut at Olympic, 'Long Live Rock' and 'Put The Money Down').

Neither was specific to what would eventually be developed as *Quadrophenia*'s story, but both were inserted fairly seamlessly when the time came. 'Is It In My Head?' was an introspective ballad of a man feeling beaten down and helpless, though the line about picking up phones (earphones, perhaps) to "hear my history" is a giveaway that this could just have been a *Long Live Rock* refugee. As in a good share of The Who's early-70s material, delicate verses alternate with harder-charging choruses, a structure that blueprinted both the power ballad (in the diluted form adopted by countless middling hard-rock bands) and the grunge rocker (in an amped-up form influenced by punk rock). Such was also the case, though in a more extreme and memorable way, with 'Love Reign O'er Me.' Outside of *Quadrophenia*'s context, it could have served as an epic of romantic anguish without anyone batting an eye; within *Quadrophenia*, however, it would ultimately serve as the grandstanding finale.

Both were probably already demoed by mid 1972. Pete's home recording of 'Love Reign O'er Me' appears on *Scoop* and is similar to the *Quadrophenia* version in arrangement, but with less grandiose synthesizers. It's also missing the crashing drums, Daltrey scream, and Townshend's climactic dive-bomb scrape of his pick down the strings that would become signatures of its *Quadrophenia* incarnation; in contrast, Townshend's tentatively sung "love," followed by acoustic-guitar strums and a brief descending piano glissando, sounds anemic. A Townshend demo of 'Is It In My Head?' that has circulated unofficially wasn't altered much by The Who, though Daltrey could handle the upper-register vocals at the end of the verses with much more ease than Townshend.

If anything else was even written for *Quadrophenia* at this point, let alone recorded, no evidence has come to light. Sensibly, there seemed to be no rush in making an album out of whatever material had been recorded in the spring, or hastily writing and recording enough material to fill it out into an LP. The Who didn't seem to be in much of a rush to do anything; when asked about the band's future plans in the May issue of *Guitar Player*, Townshend responded, "We have plans for avoiding what we feel is going to be a very political year. No schedule, no gigs."[16] They would tour Europe that summer, but sessions for the album that would turn into *Quadrophenia* would not resume for almost a year.

By mid June, it had been a good nine months since any new Who recordings had hit the market. Within just a few years that would be considered an unremarkable bout of silence from rock superstars, but it was a long gap by 1971-72 standards, finally broken by the release of the 'Join Together' single on June 16. As perhaps the first installment of a plan to eke out *Lifehouse*-era leftovers on post-1971 discs, the B-side featured a propulsive, if somewhat overlong, six-minute cover of Marvin Gaye's 'Baby Don't You Do It' from their December 13 1971 San Francisco concert. If the plan with the flipside was to give the fans something new without raiding the band's hoard of recorded or unrecorded Pete Townshend originals, it was a good one, as 'Baby Don't You Do It' had never been included on a prior Who release.

To promote the single, the band played – sort of – for the first time since December when they filmed a promo clip for 'Join Together' before a studio audience on June 25. It was broadcast on the BBC's *Top Of The Pops* a few weeks later. Toward the end Townshend and Daltrey stepped off the stage into the audience, mingling among the dancers, Roger getting hoisted on some shoulders. It could be interpreted as a small-scale facsimile of the performer-audience fusion envisioned for *Lifehouse*'s concert finale. But this was hardly the first time a major rock band had staged such a scene. The director of the clip, Michael Lindsay-Hogg (who'd filmed The Who in late 1968 for *The Rolling Stones Rock And Roll Circus*, and directed The Beatles' *Let It Be*), had also directed, in September 1968, the promo clip for The Beatles' 'Hey Jude,' in which a large in-studio crowd had similarly engulfed the group.

With The Who not set to begin their European tour until August 11, a couple of members of the band had time to polish off their solo projects. One was John Entwistle's second solo album, *Whistle Rymes*, recorded in the spring at west London's Island Studios at the same time as The Who were doing some sessions at Olympic. The more interesting project was Pete Townshend's first proper solo album, *Who Came First*, which he mixed at Olympic, also in the spring. Ordinarily a solo album by the leader of one of

177

the biggest rock bands on the planet would be big news, especially in an era when such side projects were viewed as harbingers of a possible breakup. *Who Came First* wasn't so much an album, however, as a compilation of home demos, instigated at least as much by commerce as artistic ambition.

Townshend was aware that the *Happy Birthday* Meher Baba tribute album containing some of his demos had been bootlegged for some time. Perhaps exaggerating for effect, he claimed in his *Los Angeles Free Press* interview that some stores had phoned up and asked for 28,000 copies.[17] At the time of that December 1971 interview, he hadn't seemed too bothered about reports that it was getting bootlegged. If a *Melody Maker* report is to be trusted, a US boot entitled *Pete Townshend Meher Baba* was selling for $11-12 – more than twice the retail price of the average LP in those days.[18] By early 1972, with another Baba LP including Townshend material now in circulation, Pete and Decca Records were feeling like they should take some counteractive measures.

"The main reason for instigating the making of this album was partly the bootlegging that went on in the States," Townshend confirmed to *Sounds*. "It wasn't incredibly widespread or anything but the reason I did the two limited editions – private in-joke Baba albums – in the first place was to say something about Baba and write some music for that circle of people. When it got taken out of my hands and it was selling, via bootlegging, I realized that what I'd done for Baba lovers wasn't necessarily what should be done for the outside world. And that I should tackle it afresh and do it as Pete Townshend of The Who, rather than Baba lover 456 who HAPPENS to be Pete Townshend of The Who."[19]

An interview he'd done about Baba on March 27 for the BBC television religious series *How Can You Be Sure?* also played a part in the decision. "A lot of people came up to me and said 'Listen, nobody wants to sit for half an hour listening to you talking about it,'" he told *NME*'s Nick Logan. "'If you've got anything to say about Baba, do it through music. You're a musician – that's why you got on the programme in the first place – so play, sing songs, do what you were bloody born to do.'"[20]

This was an about-face, incidentally (not that such turnabouts were anything new for Pete), from his comments in *Circus* just a few months previously about a far more famous album that had made no secret of its artist's spiritual beliefs: George Harrison's *All Things Must Pass*. "I wouldn't venture to do anything of that sort myself," Townshend said. "Listening to

Harrison's album I felt that he was really allowing us to hear his personal conversations with his master, his conversations with God. He could say better some of the things he has to say if he allowed himself to be interviewed."[21] Having allowed himself to be interviewed many times about Baba and almost everything else under the sun, maybe Townshend thought it was time to allow himself to say such things in song.

Yet *Who Came First*, despite consisting of home demos, was not merely a replication of the Baba albums. In fact, just four of the nine songs had appeared on those LPs. What's more, two of those four tracks (Ronnie Lane's 'Evolution' and Billy Nicholls's 'Forever's No Time At All,' both from *I Am*) were written and sung by other performers, although Pete did play acoustic guitar on the Lane track and engineer the Nicholls song. 'Content' was drawn from *Happy Birthday*, and 'Parvardigar' (retitled from the original 'O Parvardigar') from *I Am*, but the other five tracks were new to disc.

Among the recordings appearing for the first time, some missing *Lifehouse* gaps were filled by his demos of 'Pure And Easy,' 'Let's See Action,' and 'Time Is Passing.' 'Sheraton Gibson,' a nice folkie ode to life on the road, had been written on tour in Cleveland in June 1970; as Townshend would later write that it was the first track on which he used synthesizer, it must have been recorded shortly afterward. The most off-the-wall inclusion, a cover of country star Jim Reeves's ballad 'There's A Heartache Following Me,' had been selected because it was one of Meher Baba's two favorite songs; the other, 'Begin The Beguine,' had already been covered by Townshend on *Happy Birthday*. "He said that the words [of the Reeves song] were very much the words that the Messiah would sing," Pete told *Rolling Stone*.[22]

Issuing a batch of home demos, not all of which were even written and performed by the artist, wasn't a customary approach, even for solo side projects. But Townshend, in addition to cutting off the bootleg trade, deliberately wanted to present music that was unlike The Who's in both sound and content. "I've felt really there's a part of The Who process which comes directly from my demo recordings at my studio at home," he explained to Penny Valentine in *Sounds*. "There would be very little point in putting out a record which consisted of tracks that could have been done by The Who or had been done by The Who."[23]

Yet the three *Lifehouse* rejects had been recorded by The Who, and one, 'Let's See Action,' had even been released by the group on a recent single.

Why its sudden reappearance? For one thing, as Townshend forthrightly informed *NME*, "I think the album version is better than the single, quite honestly. That's one of the reasons I put it on there. I was disappointed with the single. It was too relaxed, not uptight enough."[24] On a deeper level, he told *Sounds*, "I put ['Let's See Action'] on very specifically because I felt it said more about Baba than it did about the revolution. It was written about the revolution but somehow, in retrospect, I felt it was more about the action here (hits the chest) than here (raises fist in the air). And also I felt The Who's version was a bit joggy, a bit casual ... the other stuff, a lot of it was specifically written for Baba albums and for Baba people to listen to."[25]

To drive the point home even more, he'd donate the proceeds from the LP's sales to a trust fund to benefit the spread of Baba's teachings, with Decca (in the USA) and Track (in the UK) giving 15 per cent of the retail sales to the same organization. "I think it's because [the George Harrison-organized concert and triple-LP *The Concert for Bangladesh*] set certain traditions that the industry are very proud of, and rightly so, and they are anxious to perpetuate this," he told *NME*.[26] Ultimately it raised about $150,000 in the USA, most of which was used to make a film about the life of Sufi leader and Baba disciple Murshida Duce. In the rest of the world, nearly $100,000 was raised, most of that going to the Avatar Meher Baba Trust in India.

"He told me, 'I've got a fantastic deal,'" Richard Barnes remembers. "The record company was bending over backward to get it. I think there are times in your life when your sun is shining, and Townshend could do no wrong as far as the record company was concerned at that time. They'd give him anything." Certainly Pete made the most of the opportunity it in turn gave him to help Meher Baba's following, and not just financially. "Townshend's done more in the West for Meher Baba than anyone," declares Barnes. "I don't know if anyone would have heard of it if it wasn't for him."[27]

What's more, an eight-paragraph Townshend essay about his reasons for making the LP, which appeared in a Decca Records ad for the record in US magazines, emphasized the Baba connection. "Meher Baba is an amazing man," he wrote. "He's dead now, three years since, but one still gets the feeling of a NOW presence. No single thing that has ever happened to me has changed the way I see and do things in this world so much. This album is meant to reflect these changes. Allow them to breathe outside of the confines of The WHO, and yet also feed back to The WHO."

Pete also played up the Baba aspect in *Rolling Stone*, describing the album as "bits and pieces of material that I've had knocking about my studio which The Who have never used and which I thought would fit into the general mood of this album, which is basically an album in a way dedicated to Baba, but mainly dedicated to the people who want to know the way I feel about him. I find that when I try to talk about Meher Baba and being in a group, and trying to sort the two things out, I can't put it into words. So I thought maybe I should use my talent – with a small 't' – as a musician and try to put the feeling and the mood across that way, instead of continually talking."

'Parvardigar' was too explicitly devotional for some people, including Chris Stamp, who "tried to get to me to take that track off because he said, 'People aren't going to be able to take it from you,' so I said, 'Well, they are going to have to fucking live with it.' ... Even if you're an atheist you could still dig this, because it's in praise of life."

Townshend also made the distinction between *Who Came First* and the typical side-project solo album. "This record hasn't let me do things musically that I hadn't done before," he told *Rolling Stone*, "because it's music that was already in existence. If I were doing a proper solo album, I would probably show off more – how well I can engineer, or how well I can play the piano. In a way we're using chuck-outs. But then, I do like the idea of people hearing what I do at home."[28]

Maybe it was because the record was so unlike The Who, or maybe because the unconventional reasons for its release (and the diversion of profits elsewhere) limited record company promotion, but *Who Came First* got a surprisingly muted reaction. Originally announced as an early-August release (and even given a track-by-track preview by Townshend in *Sounds* on June 24), but not issued until the beginning of the fall (in part because of complications arising over the gatefold sleeve design), it didn't even chart in the UK. Its peak of Number 69 in the USA was more encouraging, but still a modest commercial reward, especially considering there was no competing fresh LP product from The Who at the time. It also can't be overlooked that an entire album featuring Townshend's lead vocals (save for the two tracks by non-Who musicians), and none of his customary electric guitar pyrotechnics, might have been considered too uncommercial for radio airplay, especially as he'd never been the usual featured singer with The Who.

Rolling Stone's David Silver did give it an all-out rave, however, praising it as "a brilliant and moving album," "an amazing work," and "a godsend."[29] Quoting Townshend's description of the album in the liner notes as a "gynormouse ego trip," *High Fidelity* assured readers that it was "one of the most refreshing ego trips around."[30] Rock critics were generally kind but a bit reserved in their praise, focusing on the record's lack of similarity to The Who and production failings. One was *Melody Maker*'s Chris Charlesworth, who found it sounding "a bit thin here and there compared to the guts of The Who. Pete isn't the best singer in the world, neither is he the best drummer, and it's on these two points that the album loses marks."[31]

"Townshend is giving those who care an intimate peek at what he's really like at home," said John Swenson in *Crawdaddy*. "*Who Came First* lacks the cuteness of *McCartney*, the polish of Stevie Wonder's *Music Of My Mind*, or the bent for electronic experimentation of [Jerry] Garcia's solo, all of which were also one-man shows. Townsend's album is stark; if anything, it sounds a bit like what Eddie Cochran used to do. I can understand Townshend's passion for Baba a little better by supposing that Pete fashions himself as a kind of Eddie Cochran reincarnation. The virtues of *Who Came First* are simplicity and taste, in that order."[32]

Who Came First has qualities above and beyond its usefulness for boosting Baba and airing material unsuitable for The Who, however. As thin and shaky as Pete's vocals were, compared to Roger Daltrey's, they also conveyed a more personal quality that brought the listener close to the heart and mind of the composer. The songs also have a folkish melodicism and fragile vulnerability sometimes lost in his more celebrated Who efforts. In that way they do convey the spiritual succor he'd found in Meher Baba, without preaching or tying it ('Parvardigar' excepted) to a specific faith.

They might also reflect the kind of lower-volume music, and sincerity, of his performances to actual Meher Baba followers. "I did go to a lot of Meher Baba meetings where Pete would play," remembers Richard Barnes, "and I was thinking, 'My god, Who fans would give anything to see this.' Where he put 200 per cent into it, on acoustic guitar to these old ladies and stuff. He wouldn't go necessarily to a Baba gathering and play 'Pinball Wizard.' [It] would definitely be 'The Seeker' and that sort of stuff, [or] 'Parvardigar.'"[33]

While running times for early-70s albums were more limited than they'd be in the CD era, the track selection can be debated, as some highlights of the *Happy Birthday* LP in particular were inexplicably not included, among them 'Day Of Silence,' 'The Love Man,' 'Mary Jane,' 'Begin The Beguine,' and Pete's demo of The Who's 'The Seeker.' Fortunately these were all eventually added to CD reissues of *Who Came First*, along with his three contributions to the 1976 Meher Baba LP *With Love* (and an unimpressive bluesy home demo of indeterminate date, 'I Always Say').

During this period, Townshend also found time to donate another demo, 'Classified,' to the spring 1972 compilation album *Glastonbury Fayre*. A nice if slight ode to browsing the classifieds, with an attractive low-key blend of acoustic guitar, piano, and synthesizer, its existence remains unknown even to many hardcore Who fans, despite its subsequent appearance as a non-LP B-side on Townshend's 1980 solo 45 'Let My Love Open The Door.' 'Classified,' incidentally, was part of a spurt of songs (also including 'Love Ain't For Keeping' and 'Sheraton Gibson') that Pete composed nonstop into his tape player in Cleveland in June 1970. He had been listening to Bob Dylan's *Self-Portrait*, perhaps an underrated influence on the relative simplicity of some of his non-Who songs of the period.

The preparation for *Who Came First* complete, there was one more order of Who-related business to take care of before the group began their European tour. Four days before the first show, the band went to Olympic to cut the B-side of their next single. Of all The Who tracks blessed with official release in the early 70s, none is a more trivial throwaway than 'Wasp Man.' It's also the last of the few Keith Moon compositions to grace a Who record, inspired by his larking around in a wasp costume during Link Wray's visit to their March 1971 Record Plant sessions. The musical inspiration was the theme to 'Batman,' which The Who had cut for a 1966 EP, yet this was even more stripped-down and minimally melodic, if such a thing were possible. With few vocals other than Moon's maniacal "sting!" shouts, and Daltrey buried on harmonica as Townshend cranks out a rote three-chord power riff, this was apparently a sop to Keith – the world's greatest drummer, but not a gifted songwriter.

"It was Keith's turn for the B-side money and he was into wasps that week," Entwistle frankly recalled in his liner notes to the *Two's Missing* compilation of 1987. "Just take a guitar riff with nowhere to go (except home) and a manic drummer's impression of a wasp trapped in a vocal booth and there you have it!"[34] Moon seemed to take it barely any more seriously. "All the band ever says to me when they're in the studio singing is 'Get out!'" he told *NME*'s Richard Green. "Then I act as barman, because they all get terrible dry throats, and I have to keep on pouring out the brandy all the time. Also, if I'm in the studio looning about while they're trying to lay down a vocal track, they can't sing if they're laughing at me dressed up as a wasp. You know, there's nothing worse, when you're trying to be serious, than to have a human wasp flying all over the studio."[35]

Moon's royalties from the 45 weren't abundant, as the A-side, 'Relay,' fell just short of the UK Top 20 after its release just before Christmas, despite being hailed by *NME* as "their best single to date." In the USA, where it had been released a month earlier (oddly retitled 'The Relay'), it barely made the Top 40. That made three singles in a row since *Who's Next* that had failed to set the world on fire (although 'Join Together' hadn't done badly), solidifying the group's position as an album band who couldn't rely on hit 45s to tide them over as the next LP incubated. But while no additional studio work would be undertaken in 1972, The Who's next album was starting to hatch as Townshend got a more definite idea of where to take the 'Long Live Rock' concept.

The Who had been reported to be working on an album at various points in the first half of 1972; *Melody Maker* stated on June 24 that it would be released by the end of the year. The following year, Pete Townshend even told the same paper that a rough assembly of an album had been put together that sounded like a "shadow" of *Who's Next* before falling through in May 1972. Yet the day after the European tour started, a Townshend interview in the August 12 *Sounds* let slip, almost casually, that whatever LP might have emerged from the Olympic sessions was getting superseded by something else he had in mind. "I'm doing this new thing at the moment," he said. "We were halfway through the album and I said 'Look Glyn, I don't think I can stand this another moment longer – I've got to write another opera.' He was really excited about it. I said it was going to take a lot of time which would mean that the album couldn't be out in August but it would have to wait until January. He told me not to worry." Townshend also revealed that he was halfway through the opera, and had already sought Kit Lambert's feedback on the project.

Confusingly, Pete went on to refer to 'Relay' and 'Long Live Rock' – the only new, as-yet-unreleased material The Who were adding to their set for the European tour – as numbers from "the new album we recorded in June." Steered back to the subject of the opera by Penny Valentine, Townshend clarified both that it was a different endeavor from whatever album The Who might have previously been working on that year, and undoubtedly what the world would come to know as *Quadrophenia*. "At the moment I'm pretty excited about it," he declared. "I think musically it's going to be like a film. What I want to do is ... well, it'll be a decade of The Who in January. And to take ten years of a sound and the way I've written, the way John's written, the way the sound's changed and the character of the group's changed. What's happened to the individual members of the group, how they've changed. So I thought a nice way of doing it was to have a hero who, instead of being schizophrenic, has got a split personality four ways and each side of this is represented by a particular theme and a particular type of song."[36] He might have been struck by this idea considerably in advance of his conversation with Valentine, as in a December 1972 *Sounds* column she remembered him "mulling it around when I talked to him about three years ago."[37] (In an interview with *Rock* magazine, he specifically dated the idea for *Quadrophenia* as having come to him in November 1971.[38])

Pete went on to peg himself as the "good part," a boy scout-like figure who gets violated and fails to make good; Roger as "the bad part," "breaking windows in colored people's houses," turning over cars and such; John as the romantic, going with the girl next door until caught by her mother; and Keith, naturally, as the insane practical joker. While it sounded to his ears like old Who material, he'd pile on the synthesizer and "more and more snazzy recording until you get to the point where he finds himself coming together, fitting together like a jigsaw. Going from that period of sort of fucked-up amazing spiritual and social desperation, despair with politics and everything – to come together as one piece of music which is The Who."[39]

In *Clash* magazine in 2009, Townshend would claim that "in a sense it was a sop to the band and their US fans to base Jimmy [as the protagonist was eventually named] on the four members of The Who. It helped us all get inside it. In reality I believe we in the band worked the other way round: each of us in The Who based ourselves on characters (sometimes groups of characters) we had observed in the early days in our audience."[40] If he did have American fans in mind, it's strange that he picked a setting, mid 60s

British mod culture, with which their followers across the Atlantic would be largely unfamiliar.

The already complex process of blending four Who personalities into one could have been yet more tangled. "Originally, it was a very ambitious cooperative project," Pete told John Swenson in *Modern Hi-Fi & Stereo Guide*. "I wanted everybody in the group to write their own songs and stuff. Everybody was supposed to engineer their own image, as it were. ... As always, the band kind of looked at me like I was crazy and walked away. I've explained it to a lot of people and everybody seems to be able to understand it but them. Then John [Entwistle] wrote a song which he wouldn't play for me because he thought it summed up the whole album in one song."[41] The Who had actually tried once before to split the writing chores evenly, in part for publishing reasons, for their second album, 1966's *A Quick One* (Townshend ended up writing about half of it, and Daltrey just one song). Fortunately for the quality and consistency of the ultimate product, this brainstorm never took hold; Pete wrote all the songs that eventually appeared on *Quadrophenia*.

The idea of narrowing the focus to the mid-60s trials of one particular mod doesn't seem to have fully crystallized yet, but his comments in *Sounds* made it evident that several situations and lyrics that would crop up in *Quadrophenia* had already been outlined and even written. There was a song about being kicked out of the house ('Sea And Sand') and an argument with a father about a haircut ('Cut My Hair,' at one early point considered as the opera's title), Pete even quoting a line to Penny Valentine from The Who's first B-side ('Zoot Suit,' from the 45 they released as The High Numbers) that he'd used in the latter song. Another tune would trail a lad "really fucked up with drugs and chicks and his family, not getting on at school, identifying himself with a militant group, tries to help workers' causes and finds that not only is he powerless but they resent it" – incidents that would end up sprawled throughout several of the record's tracks. "Gradually their son is being eroded before their eyes, turning into something they can't relate to any more," he explained. "He gets very desperate and tries to look around for an answer in the shape of religion, jobs, woman, family, something."[42]

Quadrophenia was about a year from completion, but in most respects this is a remarkably accurate preview of the finished product, especially compared to his relatively inarticulate attempts to explain *Lifehouse* in 1970 and 1971. Just so it couldn't be mistaken for a one-off flight of fancy, he briefed *Melody Maker*'s Michael Watts on a similar idea, reported with far less detail, for the paper's August 19 issue. "I'm not only writing something that's less of an opera than *Tommy* ever was, but it's even about adolescence," Pete said with a self-mocking laugh. The songs, Watts reported, sounded like "old Who singles."[43]

As another stop on what seems to have been a deliberate round of interviews with the UK music press, he told readers of the August 19 edition of *NME* that The Who's new rock opera would be about teenage life. According to Pete, the melodies and lyrics of the work-in-progress were reminiscent of 1966-67 songs like 'I'm A Boy,' 'Odorono,' and 'Tattoo.' "I shouldn't call this an opera cos it's even less of an opera than *Tommy* was," he worried. "But what I'm trying to do is get the writing to reflect the changes in The Who's character. So it starts with a sort of 'Can't Explain' '65 feel and progresses like a reflection of The Who's history. ... So that at the end of the action there is an incredible amount of synthesizer."

There *would* be a lot of synthesizer on the finished album, even though the idea Townshend was apparently considering – to have the record re-create various Who styles in chronological order – was abandoned. The four-sided identity conceit was already named at this point, but not yet singled out as the opera's title. "It's a four-barreled thing with one hero in the middle who, instead of suffering schizophrenia, suffers from quadrophenia," he summarized, making perhaps the first reference to the opera's title in print, though it wasn't yet italicized and capitalized.[44] He even went on to describe one song, 'Joker James,' in detail – although, ironically, it would not make the *Quadrophenia* album. (It eventually appeared as a late-70s recording on the film's soundtrack.)

Obviously something had happened to prod Townshend's thinking in a different direction over the past few months, assuming he still had a 'Long Live Rock' concept in mind when The Who were recording at Olympic over the spring. While he certainly absorbed stimuli from numerous sources, a few in particular might have nudged him toward examining The Who's mod roots.

Although the mod movement had died years ago, Pete had been a mod (sort of) and had kept in touch with some of the friends who had been crucial to building the group's mod following nearly a decade earlier. One was Richard Barnes, a classmate and flatmate of Townshend's when the two were attending art school in the early 60s. "He was gonna do an album about The Who called *Rock Is Dead, Long Live Rock*," says Barnes in the DVD *The Who, The Mods, And The Quadrophenia Connection*. "He then got interested in the character in this, and thought 'No, I'll write this thing called *Quadrophenia*' – typical Townshend, very sort of structured thing. I remember he was explaining it to me. He came around, he said, 'What I want to do next, I want to celebrate our mod past ... also, it's going to be a catharsis. By celebrating the mod thing, we're going to free ourselves from our legend, and we can go in new directions,' because he wanted to do other things. He felt constrained, I think, by the demands of the Who fan."[45]

"He said to me that he want[ed] to make a record about the four members of the band," says Barnes today. "He had this great thing weighing down on him, because Roger would keep saying, 'You can't treat us like your backing band,' and stuff like that. I did say to Pete once, 'Why don't you do Who stuff, and then do your solo stuff?' Because he was always torn between what he wanted to do, and what The Who and Who fans wanted. Because the Who fans wouldn't accept a lot of the stuff that he wanted to do solo; they wanted Who-type-sounding heavy rock stuff."

Richard remembers Pete telling him that *Quadrophenia* "was to reflect the four characteristics of the band, but also it was to celebrate the mod thing that was so important for them in the early days. And to get rid of it, so that [they] could move on to become whatever: the next Who with an orchestra behind us, or like Kraftwerk, or whatever they were going to do."[46] That fits in with Townshend's proclamation, to Barnes himself in *The Story Of Tommy*, in which he summarized *Quadrophenia* as "a grand flourish to tie up all the loose ends of The Who's obsessive thing with adolescence and rock."[47] Yet *Quadrophenia* would be operatic and sophisticated enough to fulfill Pete's drive, despite the failure of *Lifehouse*, to continue his quest to do a "serious" work. "It sounds trite, but I think he had this bloody fear that *Tommy* was all he was going to be known for as a 'composer,' rather than a rock star," Barnes notes. "*Tommy* was kind of the beginning."[48]

Hanging out with Barnes might have kindled Townshend's interest in using a mod as the centerpiece of *Quadrophenia*, as might his correspondence with The Who's most fanatical fan bar none, Irish Jack Lyons. "Pete and I started writing to each other just before he had written *Quadrophenia* (I had moved to Ireland). Pete and I were mods together at the Goldhawk Social

Club [in London] in '64. We knew everybody in the Shepherd's Bush area, all the local mods and the faces. We shared a lot of the local mod experience. Having sent him my old Goldhawk Social Club membership card, we exchanged lots of memories about some of the things we did as mods."

Although Lyons is namechecked in 'Long Live Rock' as the guy "in the alley selling tickets made in Hong Kong," he's not definite that 'Long Live Rock' – the song, at least – could have served as the kernel of *Quadrophenia*. "We'll have to take Pete's word for that, but if you listen to 'Long Live Rock' it's got very little to do with the mod ethos," he feels. "It's more a lyrical celebration of a 'boisterous Who' like the way the band were in the '67-'68 period. But it's Townshend's prerogative as a writer to lay claim on any piece of his work as original muse."

What he does believe is that "Pete took my character and placed it in the embodiment of Jimmy Cooper" – the protagonist of *Quadrophenia*, named only "Jimmy" in the album (and then only if you assume he's the Dr Jimmy in the song of the same name), though he's called Jimmy Cooper in the 1979 *Quadrophenia* movie[49]. That was corroborated by Townshend in the May 1974 *Hit Parader*, where he disclosed that "one guy who I used to think about a lot when I was writing *Quadrophenia*, [was] a friend of mine who is a very sort of uneducated guy ... he's Irish actually, but probably because he was Irish was always sort of lyrical and could always explain himself incredibly well."[50] Furthermore, Pete described Irish Jack in the May 26 1979 *NME* as "one of the original mods who I'd left behind and who, I'd discovered, was in pretty bad shape, and so I sat down and wrote about three days in *his* life."[51]

"In a sense, Jimmy Cooper represented what you might call the 'failed' mod," Lyons adds. "He was stuck in a dead-end job. He was a dreamer, a romantic, a helpless dancer. He was always going to upgrade his scooter; he was always going to get that girl with the ravishing blonde hair; he was always going to leave home and get an apartment. In the end, of course, he never accomplished any of these things. And as Pete said in the *Quadrophenia* song 'I'm One,' Jimmy was really no more than one in the crowd. That was very much how I was as a mod, besides being a personal friend of Pete Townshend. I did the exact same job as Jimmy in the post room at the London Electricity Board on Shepherd's Bush Green [note, however, that this is the job Jimmy has in the film, but that it is not referred to on the album]. And my home life wasn't too different from Jimmy's."[52]

189

While Barnes agrees that Irish Jack and mods like him were part of the inspiration, he believes it could have also probably been "about someone like Pete Meaden, who was their manager when they were The High Numbers, who was a top mod. We were very impressed with Pete Meaden, Pete particularly, because Pete was into the mod scene. Early on, we knew nothing about it all. [Townshend] and I used to wander around the West End and we'd meet these mods and were very impressed with it, and discovered Carnaby Street by accident. It was the thing he'd been looking for all his life, really, kind of a movement of young people with ideas on fashion and music. Meaden was really obsessed and spouting about it."

Yet like *Quadrophenia*'s manic mod Jimmy, Pete Meaden, as Barnes observes, "was flawed, and toward the end of his life [which ended in July 1978], he had mental problems. We tried to help him. We didn't try enough, I don't think. And his dream with The Who didn't really happen. The mods were into Tamla/Motown, jazz, and R&B, not British bands, and he wanted them to have something they could focus on over here. They had, say, Georgie Fame, who played R&B and jazz, but he didn't look like a young pop star; they had no kind of rock band. So his thing was quite a brilliant idea – to get The Who [to be that band]. But he had no money, that was the problem. The backer [Helmut Gorden, briefly involved in The Who's management before the arrival of Lambert and Stamp] was saying, 'Well, where's my return on my investment?'"[53]

Meaden did 'write' both sides of The Who's 1964 flop debut single, 'I'm The Face'/'Zoot Suit' (credited to The High Numbers), though both were rewrites of American R&B songs with new lyrics blatantly tailored to the mod experience. 'I'm The Face' was just bluesman Slim Harpo's 'Got Love If You Want It' with new words; Meaden worked the same unsuccessful magic on 'Zoot Suit,' which used the Dynamics' soul single 'Misery' as its prototype. Yet as both are briefly quoted in *Quadrophenia* itself, Meaden had an influence on the record, whether or not Townshend specifically had him in mind as an inspiration. The High Numbers single "was shit, really, it was kind of a mediocre record," Barnes admits. "But Meaden did get them known. He got them dressed as mods. If The Who had stayed with Meaden, I'm sure it would have been very interesting. It would have been equally as interesting as going with Kit Lambert and Chris Stamp."[54]

For what it's worth, when Meaden (then a patient in a mental hospital just outside London) was asked about *Quadrophenia* by Steve Turner in 1975, he responded, "I identified with it entirely. ... He's talking about a mod, well, I am a mod, the mod who made mods out of The Who." Turner quoted from that conversation when he spoke to *NME* in 1979: "He had listened to [*Quadrophenia*] and thought: 'I am Jimmy. Townshend's writing about me!'"[55]

Another intriguing role model for "Jimmy" has been largely overlooked by Who literature. Early in the morning of May 18 1964 – pretty much the era in which *Quadrophenia* is set, although it does just predate The Who's first record – a 17-year-old trainee accountant mod named Barry Prior somehow fell 100 feet to his death off a cliff in Saltdean. It was just five miles east of Brighton, during a weekend that saw some of the fiercest rioting between mods and rockers ever recorded at the seaside town. It's been speculated that Prior might have committed suicide, and that he was another inspiration for Townshend's down-and-out mod. Fred Butler was one of the mod gang camping with Prior at the clifftop. "I don't know what could have happened," he told the Brighton *Evening Argus*. "There was no trouble or fighting. We came out here to get out of the way. Perhaps he got up in the night and went for a walk. No one saw anything and there were no screams."[56]

On this point one should be wary of conflating the *Quadrophenia* film with the album, as Jimmy only drives a scooter off the cliff (and probably jumps off to safety just before the bike hurtles into the sea) in the movie. Still, it's not too far off the final scene of the short story accompanying the double LP, which finds the nameless protagonist stranded on a rock in the sea near Brighton, bleakly contemplating his life as it flashes before his eyes. *Quadrophenia* film director Franc Roddam seems to be under the impression that Prior's death, or something similar, sparked the story. "There's this place called Beachy Head [about 22 miles from Brighton], with these white cliffs," he remarks, in his commentary track to the DVD release. "And some mod drove off there and killed himself. That moved Pete Townshend enough to come up with the original concept. And we took the concept and we then turned it into the film."[57]

Irish Jack Lyons is dubious. "I certainly don't recall ever talking to Pete about Barry Prior," he says. "It was a very sad death but nobody knows for sure what really happened to him. It may not have been suicide. His friends had pitched a tent at the top of Saltdean cliffs to stay clear of the trouble, and when they woke up in the morning suffering from a ferocious comedown after a night of pills, they saw Barry lying at the foot of the cliff. There is no evidence to connect his death to suicide, ushering in a further connection to Jimmy's so-called suicide attempt on the rock. Jimmy Cooper might have thought of suicide, often, but he would never have had the guts to go through with it. He was a bit of a weakling, often feeling sorry for himself."[58]

The Who *had* played at Brighton during mod-rocker riots that spring – not on this precise weekend, but a bit earlier, on March 29. If Townshend didn't know or know about Barry Prior, he certainly might have drawn inspiration from some of the mods he saw in Brighton that Easter. "When we played at Brighton during the riots, Pete and I walked up and down the beach," says Barnes. "It's quite a trip – the stones and the sand and watching the fights and the kids. I think he got a lot of it from there." The importance of those fights might have been overestimated, however – not so much by the *Quadrophenia* album as by the *Quadrophenia* film and some historians. "The fighting wasn't what it was all about," says Barnes. "It was about the fashion, the dances, the hairstyles, and the scooters, not the fighting. The original mods wouldn't want to get their trousers dirty, they wouldn't fight."[59]

For all *Quadrophenia*'s through-and-through Britishness, however, Townshend was drawing not just from the experiences of UK fans and mods, but the experiences of Who fans everywhere. "New York to us is like what the Goldhawk Club is like to us in England," he said in *Melody Maker*. "They find The Who to be a kind of gut release which is what I get from The Who, too. They're people from the dead suburbia of New York who need a release from everyday life. It was conversations with people like that that made me begin work on *Quadrophenia*, not just in America but in England, too. *Quad* was for them pretty directly."[60]

There's also the possibility that *Quadrophenia* is, in some ways, an autobiographical portrait of Townshend himself. Again this might have been fanned by the film a half-dozen years later, where Phil Daniels bore an undeniable (if shorter) resemblance to Townshend, amplified by a scene in which hc slumps against a wall of photos, nearly resting against a picture of Pete himself. Townshend himself owned up to at least a little identification with Jimmy in his introduction to 'I'm One' at a December 4 1973 show at the Spectrum in Philadelphia.

"It's all about the way I felt, because I wrote it," he told the sellout audience of nearly 20,000 listeners. "When I was a nipper I always used to feel that the guitar was all I had. ... I wasn't tough enough to be a member of the gang, not good looking enough to be in with the birds, not clever enough to make it at school, not good enough with the feet to make a good football player. I was a fucking loser. I think everybody feels that way at some point. And somehow being a mod – even though I was too old to be a mod really – I wrote this song with that in mind. Jimmy, the hero of the story, is kind of thinking he hasn't got much going for himself but at least he's one."

Characteristically, he would soon caution against viewing Jimmy as a stand-in for Pete Townshend. "I identify very strongly with Jimmy in several ways, but certainly not all," he told Cameron Crowe in *Penthouse* a year later. "He's a workshop figure. An invention. And while he may seem a lot more real than Tommy, he isn't. *Tommy* was set in fantasy, but there was something very real about its structure. Jimmy, on the surface, looks like a simple kid with straightforward hang-ups, but he's far more surrealistic. I don't fully identify with Jimmy's early experiences ... his romanticism, his neurosis, his craziness. I never went through a tormented childhood."[61] He was yet more emphatic when speaking to Redbeard for the *In the Studio* radio special about *Quadrophenia*. "Jimmy is very much the composite of a bunch of kids that I know by name, that I grew up with in my neighborhood," he said. "That I know, and [are] not me, and are not like me. I am not like Jimmy in the story of *Quadrophenia*. I am very clear about my role here as a writer, as someone that has observed the rite of passage that a group of young people went through."[62]

In truth, Townshend might not have been writing about any mod in particular, or himself, but about all of them – and everyone. As he emphasized in his introduction to 'I'm One' in Philadelphia, "I think everyone feels that way at some point." And as he said when he outlined his idea in *Sounds* back in the summer of 1972, "When you write about somebody that has EVERYTHING happening to them you somehow realize how everything does affect everybody."[63] *Quadrophenia* is not simply the story of Jimmy, The Who, and the mods. The reason it would endure as a classic statement of youthful quest for identity is that it's about all of us.

When Townshend started to discuss the embryonic *Quadrophenia* in the press, his presentation of the idea and the reaction to it were more subdued and cautious than they'd been when *Lifehouse* had been ballyhooed in early 1971. Perhaps The Who had cried wolf too often to the press in the last couple years, especially when all the aborted film projects (*Lifehouse* and otherwise) had also taught their fans and the media not to treat their pronouncements as gospel. Pete might have been feeling burned by having built expectations for *Lifehouse* too high, even if the success of *Who's Next* was some compensation.

Still, he made sure to sketch the state of the opera to Robin Denselow of *Rolling Stone* on September 9, shortly before one of the final shows of the European tour (an open-air concert in Paris, supported by Country Joe McDonald, attended by an audience of 400,000, and sponsored by the French Communist Party). The spring 1972 sessions at Olympic, he confirmed, would not be their next album, while also revealing that the *Quadrophenia* opera was originally planned to fill just one LP side. "We did half an album, all very good, but put together it sounded like shades of *Who's Next*," he said. "So I said, 'Fuck this' ... well, everybody did unanimously. We decided to have one side of the album just good tracks, and the other side a mini-opera. So I went off and started working on that, and really got excited about an idea I had, put about 14 or 15 songs together, and went rushing back and said, 'Listen, I'm not going to play this stuff, but I can tell you that what I've got knocks shit out of what we have already done, so let's shelve all that, put a couple out as singles, and I'll incorporate some others and we could do a new opera.' So that's basically what I'm working on at the moment."

The theme, he added, was now "a mixture of the history of the group and the story of a kid who's going through adolescence, and then becoming very spiritually desperate and then finding the secret to life. When he's a child he doesn't suffer from schizophrenia but from quadrophenia." He went on to note that the album would be in quadraphonic sound, again running through the basics of how the four sides of the hero's personality would each match up to a member of The Who. "The whole thing is hopefully going to be one of the most powerful things that I have ever managed to organize," he concluded, "because I have really got faith in the basic idea."[64]

Another alternative, aired by Townshend in the September 23 *Record Mirror*, would have been to make a double album, one side of which would have been unrelated songs from the spring 1972 sessions. The other three would have been devoted to the mini-opera. It seems unlikely this idea could have gotten far. For The Who to do an opera at all, a double album really needed to be devoted in its entirety to the concept. In addition, for a record to be titled *Quadrophenia*, but with only three rather than four LP sides occupied by the opera, would have been an incongruity that opened the door to endless jokes. Pete's plan did suggest that he didn't yet have enough material for the opera to fill up a double album. In *Record Mirror*, he also said The Who "might put out a super-condensed single called 'Joker James,' which I wrote at the same time as 'I'm A Boy,'" but the not-so-great song would not find release as a single or on *Quadrophenia*.[65]

Still, with 14 or 15 Townshend songs and a concept that seemed much more comprehensible than *Lifehouse* (the integration of the quadrophenia aside), one would think Pete and The Who would be raring to go into the studio upon returning to the UK in mid September. But it would be quite some time before work on *Quadrophenia* proper commenced, in part owing to extenuating circumstances, and in part because each of the four would be engaged in activities of his own.

First off, in late September the group purchased a building in Battersea in south-west London that they could convert into their own recording studio. Overall, that was an innovative and forward-looking strategy, hopefully enabling them to gain control over the recording process to a degree impossible in the various studios where they'd worked in London (and, for that matter, the USA). Few bands had gone this route, in part because few could afford it. But practically speaking, it would be a long time, with much in the way of financial and technical obstacles, before the studio was in working shape – as Jimi Hendrix had found when he committed to building Electric Ladyland studios, completed shortly before his death in 1970.

For his part, Moon was making his acting debut – *200 Motels* didn't really count – in *That'll Be The Day*, playing a drummer in an early-60s rock band fronted by pre-Beatles British rock star Billy Fury. An acceptably hard-boiled look at making the transition from adolescence to adulthood in the late 50s and early 60s (starring David Essex as an aspiring musician), it's also notable for the first official appearance of 'Long Live Rock,' sung by Fury at a holiday camp as part of "Stormy Tempest & The Typhoons." How exactly the song ended up here isn't known; maybe The Who figured their own version would be released long before the film's premiere on April 12 1973. Whatever the case, it's a ghoulishly sluggish version, during which Moon can barely be seen.

Also that fall, Entwistle issued his second LP, *Whistle Rymes*. More pointedly than his debut, *Smash Your Head Against The Wall*, it showed his unfortunate tendency to drift into mediocrity when working on his own. Nor did it do any better than its predecessor, limping to Number 138 in the USA and again missing the UK charts. Already, however, John was working on his third album. If nothing else, he was prolific; when *Rigor Mortis Sets In* was issued in spring 1973, it marked his third album in three years, during which time The Who had only managed to issue one.

"John was quite prolific," says John Alcock, who co-produced *Whistle Rymes, Rigor Mortis Sets In*, and 1975's *Mad Dog* with Entwistle. "He'd get on a roll, and write several bits of songs quite quickly – a riff here, a verse there, a chorus idea. We'd record snippets of ideas in his home studio just to preserve them, returning later to wade through ideas and choose which ones to develop. John knew that there were many song ideas which were entirely unsuitable for The Who, particularly when he started writing his quirky fun stuff, like those songs contained on *Mad Dog* and *Rigor Mortis*. This style of writing was influenced by John's love of rock'n'roll roots styles.

"John just loved playing, both in the studio and live – and, as we know, he was a phenomenal bass player. But he had an ear for orchestral arrangements, and he loved different types of rock. I think he also liked the idea of touring (which he thoroughly enjoyed) and could see that putting together a touring band playing his brand of almost rock-revivalist material could be a lot of fun, and give him an opportunity to play smaller, less serious venues in an almost party atmosphere. He had a great time making these records, and it's just something he wanted to do as a break from The Who when they weren't busy. He wasn't content to relax during times when The Who weren't touring or recording, so he needed an outlet to keep himself engaged."[66]

Townshend, in addition to continuing to write and make home demos for *Quadrophenia*, was also involved in a classically oriented remake of *Tommy*. Produced by Lou Reizner, the LP was recorded by the London Symphony Orchestra and English Chamber Choir, with Townshend as narrator, Daltrey as Tommy (naturally), and Entwistle as Cousin Kevin (ditto), with parts for Stevie Winwood, Richie Havens, Merry Clayton, Rod Stewart, Sandy Denny,

Ringo Starr, Richard Harris, and others. With mostly the same cast (and Moon subbing for Starr in the Uncle Ernie role), it was also performed live for charity at the Rainbow in North London on December 9.

The first of the *Tommy* spin-offs to reach stage or disc, it went to Number Five in the USA in LP form, and also nearly managed to cause a headache for *Quadrophenia* when Reizner asked for extra material. Townshend made 'Love Reign O'er Me' available to Maggie Bell, who played Tommy's mother and, despite being little known in the States, had achieved some recognition as the lead singer of the Scottish R&B-oriented rock band Stone The Crows. He ultimately denied Reizner permission to use it on the album, however, as it would have come out almost a year in advance of The Who's still-unreleased version. If this gift was even considered, it may have indicated that Townshend still didn't quite realize how important a song 'Love Reign O'er Me' would be for the group as the sweeping conclusion to *Quadrophenia*.

Daltrey's plans for his first solo album had been reported at the beginning of the fall, and early the next year he'd record it, with early-60s British rock star Adam Faith as producer. In the December 2 *Sounds*, however, he sounded as gung-ho about The Who's future as ever. "Time off from the normal Who activities has given us a lot more fight," he judged. "We were getting so bloody tired out. It feels now like it did three years ago. We're starting the new album very soon, some concerts here, we're going to concentrate more on singles, get back to that rough and ready Who sound ... we're bloody ready to get cracking again. It'll probably be more like the old Who than *Who's Next*. It's more or less making the group into one person – needless to say I'm the incredibly nasty part! See I don't think *Who's Next* was what people wanted of us. The new album won't be a step backward. It'll be more of the old Who but with obvious differences. We want to go in there as rough and ready as we can."[67]

Later that month, in *Record Mirror*, he upped the stakes by comparing The Who's new album to the one everything they'd done was measured against. "There will definitely be another *Tommy*," he boasted. "We said we never would, but we will, and it will be about one person with quadrophenia, and will probably form one-half of a double album."[68]

Even at this point, the group were still uncertain of how much of that LP the opera would occupy, and it does seem odd that Daltrey thought anything less than a double album could bear comparison to the group's previous

197

masterwork. However, Townshend was also sharing some reservations about whether to make it a double album. "I originally wanted *Quadrophenia* to be one album, because I felt more people would buy it," he later told *Disc*. "Not because I thought we'd sell more copies or make more money, but I thought it would find its way into more people's hands by being a single album and therefore cheaper. I'm not really a double album fan, but we'd put so much effort and time into it that it would have meant cutting two-thirds of the material, and we'd already hacked a third off to get it onto the double album."[69]

If it seems strange in retrospect that The Who waffled so much and so long about *Quadrophenia*'s format, it was entirely consistent with the way they'd run their whole career. "When you look back at The Who's history and it looks like they knew what they were doing, bear in mind that most of those things ... it was chaos, really," says Richard Barnes. "So they might have put it out, changed their mind the next day, and then changed their mind again. Things went from crisis to crisis. It was making money, so it wasn't all that bad, but it was almost like six steps forward and five steps back all the time."[70]

As was common for The Who, they were getting ready to tackle their latest big project with uncertainty surrounding everything from the length of the album to whether their new studio would be ready in time. Roger the realist acknowledged in *Sounds* that "it'll be murder to record [in their new studios] but we need a lot of hassles. We do need that. The Who thrive on fighting."[71] It would indeed be difficult to record in the new studios. There would be plenty of hassles before the album was ready, and one of the most famed punch-ups in Who history, with Roger right in the thick of it.

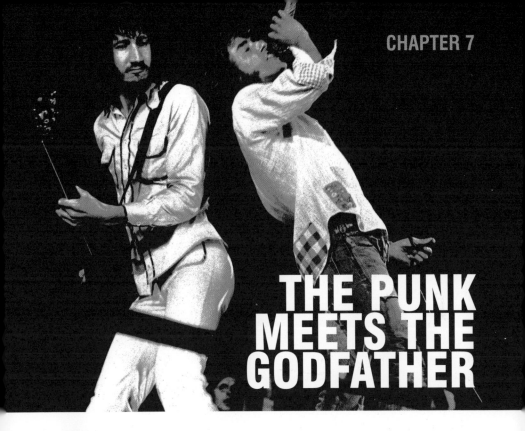

CHAPTER 7

THE PUNK MEETS THE GODFATHER

The first few months of 1973 were quiet for The Who, even considering the expected delays while the band's new Ramport Studio was built in Battersea. In several interviews in late 1972, Pete Townshend had talked enthusiastically about the progress he was making with *Quadrophenia*. But on February 10 1973, a *Melody Maker* piece gave the impression that the project had been abandoned: "His idea last year for a set of songs linked together by plotting down the separate lines of each of The Who has been scrapped now."

Maybe reporter Mark Plummer had caught Townshend in a black mood, or maybe Pete was having difficulty making The Who's four personalities part of an opera whose true core was the story of modmania, not quadrophenia. Townshend seemed almost on the verge of despair, admitting that *Lifehouse* was a failure, and again discussing a plan to revive it in some form – this time, as a book (which, surprise surprise, did not appear). He now thought, *Melody Maker* reported, that *Who's Next* was not "strong enough and should never have been released." He summoned up more enthusiasm for having helped out at a heroin-addicted Eric Clapton's January 13 comeback concert at

London's Rainbow Theatre than he did for any of The Who's projects. He also said that his main priority was coming up with a new stage act for the group. This, of course, depended on generating new material, and he didn't seem optimistic that it would revolve around a story. "I can write in a journalistic way and I can describe a piece of music in words that nearly match the music itself, but I'm finding I can't write a strong plot," he said.[1]

In January, the group went through the motions of promoting 'Relay,' miming to it for Russell Harty's ITV chat show, followed by a notoriously chaotic, uninformative group interview (excerpted for the 1979 documentary *The Kids Are Alright*) in which Keith Moon seemed more intent on disrobing himself and Townshend than answering questions. Maybe there were thoughts of making 'Long Live Rock' a follow-up single; on January 29 they taped a spot for BBC television's *The Old Grey Whistle Test* where they played to pre-recorded backing tracks of both it and 'Relay,' which lasted nearly a minute longer than the record, owing to a longer fadeout/coda. (Oddly, Daltrey sang the vocals to the second verse of 'Long Live Rock,' even though Pete Townshend took the lead on all the verses on the eventual studio version.) Even given that The Who weren't a conventional act, it was extraordinary to use precious BBC airtime to play an original song unavailable on disc. It never did come out in 1973, but it did appear the following year on *Odds & Sods*.

Roger Daltrey took advantage of the downtime to record his solo debut LP, *Daltrey*, with producer Adam Faith. To his credit, it did not attempt to emulate the hard rock of The Who, and sounded even less like the band than had the solo efforts of Townshend and Entwistle. Not having the songwriting chops to carry an album, he instead turned largely to material co-written by a young Leo Sayer and pianist David Courtney (who co-wrote a couple of the others with Faith). The result was a much poppier, almost MOR record than might have been expected, streaked with folk-rock, country, and pop orchestration. Roger eschewed the breast-beating hard-rock singing for which he'd become most known, favoring a gentler touch. It wasn't up to the standards of The Who, however, and while it reached Number 45 in the USA and yielded a British Number Five hit single with 'Giving It All Away,' no one was questioning his allegiance to his main group, least of all Daltrey himself.

"It was just nice to get out of the group environment for a change, and learn more about singing," he explained to *Melody Maker*. "I wanted to sing other people's songs and this gives me, as a singer, a lot more scope and when I get back to singing with The Who, it can only help the group. I definitely wanted it to be different from The Who, and I don't think The Who would touch anything that's on the record, so therefore it doesn't take away from The Who. I couldn't touch any rock and roll on the record because I can't do that any better than I can do it with The Who, or if I could then it should be done with The Who."[2]

If Townshend had indeed scrapped plans for an album linking four different Who personalities together, it was only a brief hiccup of doubt. As with *Lifehouse*, he was almost certainly demoing prospective songs for *Quadrophenia* all along at his home studio. It's known that one ('Sea And Sand'), at least, was done there on November 1 1972; it's likely that two of the others, 'Is It In My Head?' and 'Love Reign O'er Me' (discussed in their demo form in the previous chapter), were also done before they were copyrighted on July 12 1972. Although not all the songs on *Quadrophenia* have come to light in demo form, the demos that have emerged indicate that the compositions and arrangements, if not the overall concept, were well on their way to coming together before The Who could regroup in the studio.

Townshend's demos of most of the songs for *Quadrophenia* have made it into official or unofficial circulation, with some curious omissions. Even assuming that the album's two atmospheric instrumental pieces ('I Am The Sea' and 'The Rock') and its overture of sorts ('Quadrophenia') might not have been demoed, three – 'Helpless Dancer,' '5:15,' and 'Doctor Jimmy' – have never surfaced in demo form. Only 'Love Reign O'er Me' (on *Scoop*) and 'Can You See The Real Me?' and 'Sea And Sand' (on *Scoop 3*) have gained official release. Townshend would later tell *Sounds* upon *Quadrophenia*'s release that he deliberately didn't produce complete demos, just "rough sketches," as "an approach that was designed to allow everybody to breathe."[3] But like Pete's demos for *Tommy* (also mostly unavailable commercially, although some appeared on the 2003 expanded CD edition) and *Lifehouse*, they're instructive and enjoyable for anyone interested in the roots of the group's work.

They are also, in many respects, surprisingly close to the band's final arrangements, again testifying to Townshend's knack for figuring out what he wanted well in advance of routing the material with the group. "He would lay down all the parts himself, get everything just right, show it to the band and say, OK, learn your parts," says Rod Houison, who would build Pete's next home studio in Goring-on-Thames around the time *Quadrophenia*'s songs were being readied for studio treatment (the album's demos themselves were made in his Twickenham home, as the ones for *Lifehouse* had been). "He's such an astounding musician. He wanted a lot of strings on *Quadrophenia*, and he wanted the demos to produce a reasonable cello sound. So he bought himself a cello and sat upstairs for two weeks and learned to play cello, and adequately enough to lay down a small section. He's always astounded me like that. He's just a phenomenal musician." (Townshend had also played a cello back in 1966 on an out-take of 'Happy Jack,' released on CD in 1995.)

In laying down the demos, Houison continues, "He would have a pair of speakers, big Lockwoods, probably six inches apart in this little studio in Twickenham. He would angle his left ear from one to the other, just to make sure he was getting a balance with the sound. Now, that sounds horrendous, but I took these things to a major cutting room, and had to do almost nothing. The cutting engineer just said, 'There's nothing to do,' [and] just cut it flat. His ear was good." That was Pete's *left* ear, Rod laughs, since "as explained by somebody else in the band who shall be nameless, if after every drum solo you've got to turn around, and with your guitar get the drummer back into time, then your right ear is going to suffer. Because you've got how many watts of guitar attacking your right ear."[4]

But while they are essentially similar to the *Quadrophenia* versions, the demos also contain some interesting – if most often small – differences. 'The Real Me,' such a powerhouse of an opener on the double LP, here has a much slower, funkier beat. It also boasts a far more pronounced, rubbery synthesizer base, and some pretty bluesy guitar interjections from the third verse that were dropped in favor of pushing Entwistle's bass to the fore. Even more intriguingly, a final verse in which Townshend fulminates against rock'n'roll and best friends letting him down was dropped entirely. Pete's liner notes to *Scoop 3* reveal that this was meant to be sung by the "godfather" (of 'The Punk Meets The Godfather'), although it's not clear how that would have been integrated into the song or story; he also revealed that the demo was cut in spring 1973, making it a latecomer to the pool of material. 'I'm

One' almost sounds as if it has a channel missing, with Pete singing the first and last verses a cappella, and singing to a gently jogging rhythm track of just bass and drums for the rest of the demo.

Other variations are more minute, but interesting nonetheless. 'The Punk Meets The Godfather,' while already featuring an artificial ghostly simulation of the stutter of 'My Generation,' has a more even beat to the verses and, oddly, has the 'punk' speaking in the first person instead of accusing the godfather. 'I've Had Enough' is drumless, accenting a jagged, nervously staccato bassline, and ends with a grandstanding vocalization of the song's title that's totally missing from the *Quadrophenia* version. 'Drowned' is far more guitar-dominated than the studio arrangement, piano not entering until the coda. Drums go missing again on 'Bell Boy,' and Townshend takes the part of the bellboy on the comic bridge – which, after you've become familiar with Keith Moon's memorable performance of the role on *Quadrophenia*, can't help but sound forced and stilted in comparison.

While Townshend and The Who have not seen fit to issue many *Quadrophenia* demos, the inclusion of 'Sea And Sand' on *Scoop 3* suggests Pete felt proud enough of it to let it stand as a performance that could be appreciated on its own merits. The stately keyboard part, played on a newly acquired Bösendorfer grand piano, and the lack of drums put this a little closer to early-70s singer-songwriter territory than other Townshend or Who recordings of the era. As Pete acknowledged in *Scoop 3*'s liner notes, "This demo demonstrates how well my songs for the story work (harmonically speaking) without any of the frills I started to add when we recorded the songs with The Who."

In other ways, however, the demos illustrate how even some of the more idiosyncratic features of the arrangements were worked out beforehand. 'Cut My Hair' has the beeping synthesizer part; 'The Dirty Jobs' has Pete playing the cello, or at least a cello-like part, in line with Rod Houison's memories of Townshend mastering the cello at short notice to use on demos; 'I've Had Enough' has the galloping chorus that uses a banjo; and 'Bell Boy' has the peculiar squelched synthesizer sound, almost as if the notes are being squeezed out through a toothpaste tube, that did much to give the *Quadrophenia* track a rousing, symphonic aura. 'Bell Boy' is a real highlight of the batch that deserves official release. The bellboy part aside, Townshend's voice sounds more at ease than it does on most of the tracks, and the drama of the opening verse is amplified when a clanging guitar asserts itself after the first few lines.

Even more importantly, the demos prove that the restatement and recycling of lyrical and instrumental themes throughout *Quadrophenia* were already present to some degree, and not inserted as the group worked on the album in the studio. 'Sea And Sand' and 'I've Had Enough' both have a verse in which the hero brags about his scooter and jacket; 'I've Had Enough' briefly quotes the chorus of 'Love Reign O'er Me'; and the instrumental break of 'Drowned' shares a riff with '5:15.' The reuse of motifs was crucial for this to be classified as a "rock opera," as it had been in *Tommy*, and indicates that Townshend was definitely working on these songs with an opera or song cycle in mind, not simply as a batch of discrete numbers that might somehow coalesce into a concept album. In addition, the demos often quote from some of The Who's own early songs: the 'My Generation' stutter in 'The Punk Meets The Godfather,' the 1964 High Numbers single 'I'm The Face' in the coda to 'Sea And Sand,' and the line from that single's B-side 'Zoot Suit' in 'Cut My Hair,' which also throws in a line from 'I Can't Explain.' This shows that Pete was inserting references to the group's own past, as a vestige of The Who history-cum-opera he'd first envisioned.

He was also recording some purely instrumental tracks for use as possible introductory or linking themes, as he had for *Tommy*. One such unfinished theme, which at one point uses the melody from the chorus of 'Cut My Hair,' appears on *Scoop*, unimaginatively titled 'Unused Piano: "Quadrophenia."' "This theme was never finished," Townshend confirmed in the liner notes, "yet somehow it still captures the atmosphere of triumph and futility attempting to coexist in the heart of the hero I created."[5]

With much of the material in demo form, and The Who off the road save for a one-off concert in Holland on March 10 (parts of which were televised six days later), the group seemed ready to tackle *Quadrophenia* in the studio as spring approached. (A US West Coast tour in February, and a possible trip to Japan, were tentatively announced but not undertaken.) Apparently jumping the gun, the April issue of *Circus* even reported that they'd started recording a new album in London on January 15. A few bugs in the system would delay this for a few months yet, and by the time work had started for real, an entirely new production team would be in place.

One reason for the delay was that Ramport wasn't finished quite as soon as The Who had hoped. "Clearly they wanted their own studio for creative reasons, so they weren't constricted by studio time and costs," says John Alcock, who helped with Ramport's construction. "I imagine that they also considered renting it out when they didn't need it, thus recouping some costs. I vaguely recall being asked to come down to look at the building soon after they acquired it. It was an old church hall, I think, and was ideal for a studio location. Brick built, very solid old construction, high ceilings, great location, and private, off the beaten track. I think the project team was led by John 'Wiggy' Wolff, and the idea was it should be constructed and be ready for the scheduled recording of *Quadrophenia*. My initial role was to translate some of the ideas into some plans; things like vocal and piano booths, [a] large (for that time) raised control room, equipment rack access, storage, treatment etc, and to help spec and source some of the equipment."

As usual for The Who, things didn't go quite as smoothly as planned, although Alcock says the delays weren't all that uncommon or lengthy as such things go. "As usual in such projects – even today! – the time projections for this construction were way too optimistic," he says. "The plans were made, and construction started. There were some mistakes – some of the drawings were wrong (embarrassingly) and had to be fixed on the fly, and some of the designs weren't entirely right when I look back, knowing now much more about refined techniques. I think the control room window had some issues, as the isolation wasn't working right, and I remember an issue with the framing of the elevated control room, but again these were fixed without too much delay. My memory isn't that great, but my sense is that any construction delays may have been a couple of weeks, not months.

"It's worth remembering that studio design in those days was much more 'suck it and see.' Although there were some accepted acoustic treatment concepts, the underlying science wasn't nearly as developed as it is today: the idea was to get it 'about right' and tweak it later, by some construction modifications and making final minor room voicing adjustments using monitoring graphic EQs. There were almost no acoustic consultants or designers in business at that time. Having said that, the construction delays I don't think were that serious; solutions were figured out along the way, and building out the rooms was completed."

Although the group did come to the newly constructed Ramport Studio (aka "The Kitchen") on March 3 to rehearse, the 16-track console was found to be inadequate. "I believe that more serious delays were to do with equipment," Alcock continues. "Consoles, in particular, were custom designed in those days, and the process was neither quick nor inexpensive. I recall spending time with Dick Swettenham at Helios [Electronics] (who I already knew well as he'd been a potential customer for the Rolling Stones mobile from my Unitrack days) discussing The Who console [later replaced by a Neve]. I think this was the main delay, although I do have a vague recollection that the bones of the Helios Ramport wrap-around quadraphonic console started life as a canceled order from another studio, which cut down on some time. Tape machines also had fairly long delivery schedules, and I think that there was some other equipment which was also delayed. So ultimately, the decision was made to record using Ronnie Lane's mobile studio, built in an Airstream trailer (which was mostly a recent Trackplan project) parked outside Ramport."[6]

Before that plan was figured out, The Who, perhaps impatient to get rolling in some fashion, did some work at another studio. In May, Kit Lambert set up preproduction sessions at Stargroves, Mick Jagger's country mansion, where some tryouts for *Who's Next* had been recorded. And now, even though he'd already worked on two 1972 tracks that would appear on *Quadrophenia*, Glyn Johns was no longer on board.

While Townshend would in later years be quite complimentary about Johns's engineering and production work on *Who's Next*, there were apparently simmering dissatisfactions with both Glyn and Olympic Studios. Equally surprisingly, considering the debacle at the Record Plant in March 1971, Pete was missing The Who's previous producer. As he put it to Penny Valentine in *Sounds*, "For the first time The Who were being recorded by someone who was more interested in the SOUND than in the image of the group. Glyn's not particularly interested in Who image, whereas when Kit was producing us that was all he cared about. I don't think Glyn produced. I think he engineered.

"This is why in the end, when it came to the crunch about what to put on the little label, we put 'co-produced.' Because Glyn had done something that was different to what Kit did but Kit definitely PRODUCED The Who. He would produce material out of a band that had nothing to offer. Glyn couldn't do that. If we go into the studio and I haven't written anything there's no way he can produce. A producer is somebody that produces something out of thin air."[7] Townshend wasn't the only one to express reservations about Johns's influence. "*Who's Next* was a bit airy-fairy for The Who," Daltrey told *Record Mirror* in late 1972. "I think we left too much up to Glyn Johns and Pete and got a bit lost."[8]

The very skills that made Johns the ideal man to act as an editor of sorts in trimming *Lifehouse* down to *Who's Next* might have worked against him as another rock opera mushroomed. Townshend was looking for the sort of unpredictable big-picture imagination Lambert had brought to *Tommy*, not the more technological and disciplined assets Johns brought to the table. "The way I create things is that I blind myself and I go behind for a year, come up with something at the end and then I explain it to people the following year, despite the fact that I didn't know what I was doing or how I came about it," is how Pete put it in *ZigZag*. "Glyn's much more considered. He would say, 'What have you got *now*?' I'll answer, 'Well, nothing; but I never do at this time of the day,' and he'd say, 'Well, unless you've got anything now I think the best thing to do would be to put the album together this way.' Of course, halfway through *Tommy* if he'd asked me the same question, I'd have had to say nothing because we had nothing – a lot of disconnected songs about a deaf, dumb, and blind boy.

"Glyn was very adamant that from his point of view as an observer he couldn't see any concept," Townshend continued, talking again about *Who's Next*. "And I think maybe he could have been wrong. I don't really know. I think that as a producer, he perhaps stands a little too much away from the ethereal concepts that a group gets involved in because it's active. It's working, and it's exciting and [he] tends to just to listen to what comes out of the speakers and take it at its face value without realizing, of course, that a whole lot of people who are interested in The Who are very deeply into everything that we're doing, all of the time."[9] It might also be that the collaboration had run its natural course. "We'd put in a fantastic amount of work together," Townshend told *Melody Maker*, "and it was pretty much an exhausted relationship at that time."[10]

"We've done a bit of recording in the past year but we weren't getting the sort of thing we were after," Daltrey told Chris Charlesworth in the April 7 *Melody Maker*. "That's why we built our own studio. We weren't really happy in most of the studios we've worked in in London. Hopefully our own will work; we'll have to make it work because it's our last chance. I think, maybe we're a bit choosy, but that's Pete for you. I don't give a toss where we work but I'm sure we'd be happier in our own place. We were getting an 'Olympic' sound with using their studios before, and I think for The Who to have an 'Olympic' sound is a bad thing to happen."[11]

Quadrophenia engineer Ron Nevison offers another possible cause for the break. "I think I found out in later years that the reason they didn't go back to Glyn Johns was because Roger was pissed off at him for getting distortion on one of his vocals," he recalls. "An absurd reason."[12]

Johns was sanguine about the turn of events. "Because *Tommy* had been so successful, which had been done with Kit Lambert, I think Pete felt that he needed to work with Kit again on *Quadrophenia*, because that was a concept thing as well," he speculated in *The Record Producers*. "It was all very amicable – there was no problem about me not doing the whole album or anything like that, because I can remember Pete ringing up and telling me he needed Kit, and I understood. Kit and I never got on either, as it happens."[13]

Richard Barnes confirms that Glyn and Kit didn't get along, and sees Lambert's strengths as a sounding board who could give shape and coherence to Townshend's sometimes unwieldy raw creations. "*Tommy* very much was Kit Lambert's too, to give him his due," he says (and he should know, having talked with Townshend in depth about the process for their 1977 book *The Story Of Tommy*). "The thing was a random, all-over-the-place mess until he sat down, wrote a sort of short film script of it, gave it a plot, and dropped a lot of stuff. Pete does tend to meander and wander all over the place. Plotting is not his forte."[14]

Be that as it may, it's strange that Lambert decided to bring Jack Adams, who'd engineered at the Record Plant sessions, over from America to engineer at Stargroves. "He was invited to come to England to work with The Who by Kit Lambert," says fellow Record Plant engineer Jimmy Robinson, who was Adams's roommate for a time in the early 70s. "He was gone for a long time; maybe a month and a half or something, it seemed like. He took a guy named Doug Graves with him, who was an engineer and keyboard player. Something went wrong over there, I don't know what. But he came back abruptly, and I remember he was calling Kit Lambert names. Jack went into a big drinking period after that, like serious depression. And that, maybe three or four months later, was the last time I ever saw him."[15] Another reason the Stargroves sessions didn't work out, according to *Rolling Stone*, was that the best acoustics were in the mansion's entrance hall, which was too inconvenient a recording location.

Whatever went wrong at Stargroves, it provided an opportunity for another American, Ron Nevison, to enter the picture on the engineering side. "There was an engineer that I think was all set to do the *Quadrophenia* album, an American," he remembers. "I don't remember who it was, to tell you the truth. It was determined that he was too inebriated to do the sessions. He was pretty fucked up, in other words. Suffice to say that they had a guy lined up that, for good reasons, didn't get the job."

After touring as a sound mixer with Traffic, Nevison had moved from the USA to England a few years previously to work at Island Studios for Chris Blackwell. He'd built studios for members of The Faces, including the mobile facility for Townshend's buddy Ronnie Lane that was being used at Stargroves. "I went out with Ronnie's mobile, wherever it went, whether I was the engineer or not," he says. He took it out to Stargroves "and over the course of a week or so, I got to know all the Who guys really well, especially Keith Moon, who kind of took me under his wing. I then got a call that they wanted me to bring Ronnie Lane's mobile down to Ramport, because they had to start working on this album, and the control room wasn't together. I guess they figured that if I built the fucking studio, that [they] could give me a shot at recording it. I was really not hired to do the *Quadrophenia* album. I was hired to run Ronnie's mobile, and get the tracks cut."[16]

The Who finally began their *Quadrophenia* sessions at Ramport on May 21, about nine months after Townshend had first discussed the opera in the press. Work was certainly serious by June 3, when they transferred material from eight-track to 16-track. Although Daltrey had said in the April 26 *Rolling Stone* that they would have a new LP out by June, that was now an impossibility. The recording console still wasn't ready; the producer would pretty much fade out of the project; and they were using an engineer with whom they'd never before worked. Yet within only a couple of months or so, they had the basis of a classic double album.

As much as The Who yearned to work in their own state-of-the-art studio, when they assembled at Ramport, they weren't even able to do 16-track recording without some jiggling. They'd enlisted Ronnie Lane's mobile, according to Nevison, as "the studio part [for Ramport] was together, but I don't think all the modules were there on the console. They were at least a month away from getting that board ready; it was enormous. At that point, [the mobile] was only eight-track. Ronnie didn't pay for 16, and I had a lot of problems going 16, because [the Airstream trailer with the mobile was] like a tube. In those days, the tape machines were enormous. There wasn't room enough, without putting the tape machines right in the middle of the room, to go up to 16 tracks. Each track required a set of electronics, so we had to put eight modules down at the bottom [of the tape deck], and eight modules up top. Because of the curvature of the Airstream, we had to put these modules next to the capstan motor; I got into all sorts of problems with hum. We finally got it all sorted out. In fact, it was the very first eight-up, eight-down Studer A80 [a two-inch, 16-track tape deck configured so that eight modules were above the deck and eight below it] in history.

"We cut the first half-dozen *Quadrophenia* tracks – maybe just four, I don't remember – with the eight tracks. The very first backing track we cut was 'I've Had Enough,' I remember that. I don't believe he had a demo; I think he just showed them the song, and they rehearsed it a bit and found parts, Pete suggested things or whatever. Then, over the course of a weekend, I converted it to 16, and we recorded the rest of *Quadrophenia*'s backing tracks on 16-track. And I did eight-to-16 copies on the first few backing tracks, so it ended up being 16-track. But I was only hired to actually record the initial [sessions], and they liked what I did. So when we were finished with the backing tracks and the studio was ready, I was on board as the guy; they kept me on. I was just in the right place at the right time."[17]

Despite the delay in getting fully up and running, Ramport did prove up to snuff, something overlooked by accounts emphasizing the construction snags and the storm that flooded the studio during one particularly crucial track (more of which later). "Ultimately, I think Ramport was a huge success," says John Alcock. "It had a great feel, sounded good, and I later produced several albums there, including both Thin Lizzy albums with which I was involved. It was one of the 'hot' studios in London for a while, and I was sad to hear it was eventually sold. As with many good studios in the 70s, the success was based more on serendipity than technical specifications – it just felt and sounded like a great place to record rock bands."[18]

As the engineer for most of *Quadrophenia*'s tracks, Nevison got a close-up view of how songs were changed from Townshend's home recordings. "They weren't demos," he remarks. "These were masters. The demo aspect about them was the fact that he played drums and bass. The arrangements were set. The tempos were set. He'd be very careful to just do basic bass and drum parts. But he was very careful not to do what Keith or John would do. Because he didn't want them to follow what he wanted them to do. He wanted Keith and John to do their own thing. He'd leave enough room for Keith to do his thing, and John to do his thing. Pete was very precise; he had it ready to go. And, you know, it went very easily. It was very surprising. It was very smooth. He knows exactly what he wants." As Daltrey now had a studio of his own, he was able to work on his vocals there before recording with the group, which was a big help in devising some of his acrobatic phrasing.

Quadrophenia, even more so than *Who's Next*, made heavy use of Townshend's synthesizer. However, as Nevison points out, his synth parts were not recorded in the studio. "The ARP 2500, which he used exclusively during the *Quadrophenia* sessions, was a modular synthesizer," he explains. "He never brought that down to the studio. He kept that at home. You couldn't move that around. You couldn't keep sounds on it. You'd spend an hour getting a sound, then you'd play it, and then you'd have to take out all these patch cords and patch up for a different sound. You'd never get the sound exactly the same; you couldn't click a button and keep it. It used to go out of tune all the time, so you'd have to tune up all the oscillators. It was an enormous pain in the ass.

"So Pete would work at night feverishly recording these things on his 16-track. There was no way that we could spend as much time as he needed for the synthesizer parts, so on these synthesizer tracks, Keith would play to a click [track], and we'd record the drums and bass and guitar. Three of them would play – well, four of 'em, you know, Roger would sing. And we'd just keep going over it until we got it right. That was mainly because Pete wanted to use the hours and hours and hours of synthesizer stuff that he'd put in on these demos. The straight-on rock'n'roll ones, like '5:15,' we just cut without a click."[19] (This possibly accounts for why no demo of '5:15' has ever emerged.)

Townshend may have been very much the auteur of *Quadrophenia* – in fact, it is the only Who album on which he wrote all the material – but the tracks did leave a lot of room for the rhythm section to shine as instrumentalists. Entwistle in particular played not only some of the best bass of his career, but some of the best electric bass by anyone, his nimble and pungent runs combining grace and throbbing power. The songs, and perhaps the production, lent themselves far more to Moon's unpredictable torrent than had *Who's Next*, especially on the more uptempo numbers, such as 'Bell Boy' and 'I've Had Enough.'

"Keith had so many drums, I couldn't get microphones everywhere," says Nevison. "He had two hi-hats, he had like eight tom-toms, he had I don't know how many cymbals, and a gong. And two kick drums, and oh my god ... so that was a challenge. The rest of it was very easy. Recording John's bass, I used mostly the amp. His amp sounded great. He had a great feel and a great sound. And Pete, same thing with the guitars. They weren't real, real picky about their sounds either. I mean, they were picky, but they weren't like up your ass about it."

While Entwistle had played horns on Who records since 1966, his brass had been relatively under-utilized on the group's early-70s recordings, despite having been key ingredients of hits such as 'I'm A Boy' and 'Pictures Of Lily,' as well as *Tommy*'s 'Overture.' He reasserts himself in this department on several *Quadrophenia* tracks, with tasteful versatility, whether it's the forlorn windblown call of 'I've Had Enough' or the chunky, almost jazzy riffs on '5:15.' The interplay of his horns with Townshend's synthesizers remains an underrated asset to the diversity and depth of *Quadrophenia*'s sonic textures.

"When you think of *Quadrophenia*, you don't think of synthesizers so much," says Nevison. "You think of strings and you think of horns. [Townshend] used synth horns, and of course, Entwistle used his real horns. All the different themes that Pete had for *Quadrophenia* were perfect for that. It was a nice blend." The horn parts (50 in all, Pete told *NME*) were, like Townshend's synthesizer contributions, not recorded at Ramport. "I never recorded any of the Entwistle horns," Nevison says. "He did them in his studio. He would take the tapes home at night, and Pete would take the tapes home at night; they'd all record stuff at their own studios. John had his own studio in his house, and he had his own engineer."[20] (John Alcock confirms that at the time he met Entwistle, the bassist "had a simple studio setup in his house," and thinks it was assembled for him by Who soundman Bobby Pridden and Who roadie Cy Langston.[21])

The Who also got a little outside help from Chris Stainton, who played piano on 'The Dirty Jobs,' '5:15,' and 'Drowned.' Ordinarily Nicky Hopkins would have been the first keyboardist they'd call. But Hopkins was unavailable, and Stainton had gotten to know the band while playing with Joe Cocker, who supported The Who on a few shows in Chicago in May 1969. "Pete had watched the Joe Cocker set and seemed to be very impressed by the piano riffs I was playing in 'Hitchcock Railway,' which I lifted from Jose Feliciano's version," says Stainton. "He never forgot it, and years later asked me to play in that style on the *Quadrophenia* album."[22]

Townshend happily owned up to the influence in public. "We were just doing 'Drowned,' which was using a Chris Stainton riff that I pinched from 'Hitchcock Railway,' and we met a friend of his," he told *Sounds*. "I said it would be really nice if he [Stainton] came down, and the next day he came down and we did that number, and he enjoyed himself so much that we used him on a couple of other pieces."[23]

If Townshend was hoping for the same kind of input from Lambert as Kit had given to *Tommy*, however, he would be disappointed. In Nevison's estimation, "Kit had very little to do with *Quadrophenia*. He was there at some point, but he was just there as the manager. Pete really ran the show. Everything started when Pete got there, and everything finished when Pete left."[24] According to Richard Barnes in *The Who, The Mods, And The Quadrophenia Connection*, "Pete would say [Lambert's] contribution seemed to be to turn up with some flash chef and food while we were recording, and expensive champagne."[25] Although Lambert is credited for pre-production and (with Chris Stamp and Track Records co-founder Pete Kameron) as a co-executive producer on *Quadrophenia*, The Who were pretty much on their own at Ramport, despite what Townshend might have hoped for at the outset of the recording.

As for Lambert, says Barnes, "unfortunately he was no longer that kind of support that Pete needed." Barnes does feel Lambert could have been of use, however, had he been in the right frame of mind. "The thing about *Quadrophenia*, it doesn't have a great plot," he adds. "It's a bit thin. It's about a mod who sort of thinks, 'Oh fuck, it wasn't what I thought.' It's a bit subtle, really, for rock. There's no one stabbed, no murders, no love. And – this you can't emphasize more than anything – he didn't have Kit Lambert to come in and say, 'Oh, what about introducing …' To come in and sort of say, 'Well, it's getting a bit lost here, Pete. Why don't you reprise this bit?' or whatever. Because Kit Lambert's got a great understanding of film scripts, plotting, film structure, opera structure, because his dad was in opera. I think it's flawed, *Quadrophenia*, as a work, because of that. Because it gets lost in the middle. It's all muddy, and the songs all sound the same.

"They were in many ways trying to edge out Lambert, but I do think Pete missed [having] someone to help him with plotting. Like if you're going to introduce a character and he does something, you've got to have a resolution later on. Pete says one of the first things that turned *Tommy* from being some kind of rambling rock opera was Lambert insisting on reprising things. It was Lambert that came up with this sort of structure. It changes the whole story. This is where someone like the pre-*Tommy*, [pre-]out-of-his-head Kit Lambert would have pulled it together in the middle and said 'No no no, it's getting a bit heavy here, put in a ballad or something,' or whatever. Because it gets very turgid. The middle five tracks all sound a bit similar, with manic Moon drumming and that."[26]

Even more seriously, Daltrey had become dissatisfied with Lambert and Stamp's handling of the band's finances. When a check from Lambert to cover some of Ramport Studio's construction expenses was invalidated, and Townshend found that much of his publishing money was unaccounted for, a break became inevitable. Bill Curbishley and Peter Rudge began to assume more of the band's management, which itself led to some confusion.

"Whenever there's four managers, there's always going to be a little push and shove, and the guys that were on the road with the show are the ones that end up with the best loyalties to the band," says Donald K. Donald, promoter of the notorious 1973 Montreal show that found The Who thrown in jail after celebrating too hard at the after-gig hotel party. "There was probably no need for a band to have four managers. I think it probably caused some complications, because there were always little issues back and forth. You'd get a comment from one manager about the other manager and whatnot."[27]

"Kit was getting less and less reliable," Keith Altham adds, "and less and less likely to be there when he was needed. He was having his problem with drink and drugs, and it kind of did what it's done to dozens of people in the music business – removes them from reality. Although he loved the band and he loved Pete, he just didn't have a grip on what his job was, or what it had been. Pete couldn't rely on him any more, and the band couldn't rely on him any more. I think that it was inevitable that somebody would step into the breach and handle the day-to-day running of the band, because it wasn't being picked up."[28]

○

The excellence of the musicianship, and the imagination and complexity of the production of *Quadrophenia* are unquestioned. The best equipment, playing, and engineering in the world, however, wouldn't have meant anything without both good songs and an overriding concept that made them more moving and resonant in this particular combination. These are the heart of *Quadrophenia*, and the ingredients upon which the record's longevity ultimately rests.

American unfamiliarity with the history of the mid-60s British mod movement would cause some initial confusion about the record's concept and message in the USA, which by 1973 had become The Who's biggest market. *Quadrophenia* itself would become the primary vehicle through which many Americans educated themselves about the mods, a decade (and, subsequently, decades) after the movement's heyday. The mod ethos, however, was absolutely crucial to an understanding of both the record and The Who as a band.

The mods' emphasis on flashy clothes, scooters, amphetamines, and brawls with "rockers" who favored older fashions and earlier rock'n'roll music might seem frivolous from this distance (although the early American soul music and R&B the mods favored, as well as the British Invasion bands they adopted, proved timeless). Yet mod was vital to forming a rebellious, creative identity for both The Who and many British youths – which, given the group's preoccupation with rebellion and identity, made it ideal grist for their mill.

And as The Who weren't really mods, but had been adopted by the mods as their band and spokesmen, they were in a sense outsiders in the movement they championed and to some degree capitalized upon. That in turn made them well positioned to identify with the story of a kid who desperately wanted to be a mod, but couldn't quite fit in, either with other mods or society at large. It was a story they had, to at least some extent, experienced firsthand, in real life – which made it easier to relate to than *Lifehouse*.

It was also a movement whose historical significance Pete Townshend had reflected upon well before *Quadrophenia*. Although his August 1968 interview with *Rolling Stone* is most renowned for containing the seeds of *Tommy*, Townshend spent almost as much time discussing mod. "One of the things which has impressed me most in life was the mod movement in England, which was an incredible youthful thing," he told Jann Wenner, just three years after the Who-mod connection was at its peak. "It was a movement of young people, much bigger than the hippie thing, the underground and all these things. It was an army, a powerful, aggressive army of teenagers with transport. ... We used to make sure that if there was a riot, a mod-rocker riot, we would be playing in [Brighton]." He even went as far as to state that "most mods were lower-class garbagemen," foreshadowing the picture of Jimmy hauling trash in the *Quadrophenia* booklet.[29]

A comment by Townshend in a small item in the June 1973 *Circus* made the mod dimension in his new work clear, as well as letting slip that the opus now had a name, although *Quadrophenia* had already been cited as its tentative title by *Rock* magazine on April 9. "It's a rock opera, and the working title is *Quadrophenia*," he announced. "I'm constructing a central figure, a kind of archetypal mod, incorporating each member of The Who into a facet of his character. It's as if his story is the biography of The Who. I seem to be doing a sort of musical *Clockwork Orange*. Yet *A Clockwork Orange* was a comedy, whereas this is more of a tragedy. It encompasses so many tragic things that happened to the mods."[30]

Perhaps unwilling to provoke lazy *Tommy* comparisons, Pete didn't reveal the similar name of *Quadrophenia*'s protagonist, who even on the album is mentioned by name in just one song, 'Doctor Jimmy,' and not in the most distinct of fashions. Yet as Townshend confirmed in *Rolling Stone* on January 3 1974, the hero *is* Jimmy. "The name is a little joke," he said. "I'm thinking of calling my next hero Bobby." (He'd already used up that name for *Lifehouse*.) Turning serious, he laid out the story and character as precisely as he ever did to Charles Perry and Andrew Bailey in the same article.

"Jimmy has made a sort of mistake in labeling, you see," he began. "He feels a failure because he thinks these Ace Faces, these mods he admired who were the best dancers and fighters, [who] had the bike, the birds, the most up-to-the-minute clothes, were really demi-gods because they had the things he wished he had. The exact kind of bike a fashionable mod had to have, for instance, cost £300 and it took a working-class kid a hell of a long time to scrape that lot together. But actually the people he was admiring weren't guys who were his own age who were better than him, they were a few years older and more experienced.

"He's a little late in the game. In a sense he's a failed mod, because he's made the ultimate mod mistake, bad timing. This is 1965 and the mod scene is already falling apart – and what does he do but go to Brighton *just to remember*. The crazy days when 300,000 mod kids from London descended on that little beach were only three weeks ago, but already he's living on his past. And he meets an old Ace Face who's now a bellhop, at the very hotel the mods tore up. And he looks on Jimmy with a mixture of pity and contempt, really, and tells him, in effect, 'Look, my job is shit and my life is a tragedy. But you – look at you, you're dead' ...

"All he knows is that things aren't right in the world and he blames everything else. And it's getting in a boat, going out to sea and sitting on a rock waiting for the waves to knock him off that makes him review himself. He ends up with the sum total of frustrated toughness, romanticism, religion, daredevil desperation, but a starting point for anybody. He goes through a suicide crisis. He surrenders to the inevitable, and you know, you *know*, when it's over and he goes back to town he'll be going through the same shit, being in the same terrible family situation and so on, but he's moved up a level. He's weak still, but there's a strength in that weakness. He's in danger of maturing."[31]

But at the same time, *Quadrophenia* is not just the story of one mod, or even just of mods and The Who. It's the story of a whole generation – of what Townshend might have considered 'My Generation,' to reference his most famous song. "It has come out looking more like the story of mods per se than it really is," he told *Melody Maker*'s Chris Welch when the album was released. "It's the story of a kid, and as you said, it could really be the story of anybody. I hate to say 'study' but it's a series of songs about the frustrations that come with growing up and those most commonly associated with rock, and the morality of the rock audience. At one moment they can go on a Ban The Bomb march and the next moment they are pouring LSD into their heads."[32]

This could account for the references to menial laborers, gays, discrimination against black workers, psychiatrists, a starving country, and even "karma" that have confused those who thought *Quadrophenia* (especially the more concentrated movie version) was supposed to be the story of a mod caught between adolescence and adulthood. It's not only the story of Jimmy, but the story of his society, invested with self-conscious intellectual reflection that Townshend brought to the project as a man in his late twenties, even if mods like Jimmy (and Pete himself) largely lacked that quality in the mid 60s.

The Who added another layer of complexity in not consciously trying to replicate their actual mid 60s music, even though *Melody Maker* had reported back in August 1972 that the songs sounded like old Who singles. *Quadrophenia* instead used the music of its time, the early 70s, to comment on an era almost a decade old. The abundance of synthesizers itself placed the record close to progressive rock, as did the intricate production. In his interview with Redbeard for the *In the Studio* program on *Quadrophenia*, Townshend himself even called the early-70s Who sound an "extraordinary kind of mixture of grandiose rock'n'roll, somewhere between Electric Light Orchestra, Emerson Lake & Palmer, and Godzilla The Hun."[33] But no other progressive rock had the emotional punch of The Who's power chords, thrashing drums, and blood'n'guts vocals.

While retro oldies covers albums were right around the corner from the likes of David Bowie, The Band, Bryan Ferry, and John Lennon, that direction was never considered (although Daltrey himself had thought about making an album of rock and soul covers for his debut solo LP). Neither was the option of telling the story with original songs written and performed in the style of the early mod Who.

"It could have been stated a lot more simply, obviously," Townshend told *Modern Hi-Fi & Stereo Guide*. "It could have been stated in a simple song, like 'My Generation,' if I could still write a song like 'My Generation' in 1973, but I can't, and the audience wouldn't dig it. ... The whole thing has to be put in terms of something not just to do with today's rock record buying audience, but also in style with The Who's status."[34]

"The album would have been a disaster if any other music idiom, say like covers or typical 60s music, had been used," says Irish Jack Lyons, one of the mod Who fans who inspired *Quadrophenia*. "People forget that the whole point of *Quadrophenia*, written in '71 and '72, is that it's a look back, a retrospective. And to arrive at where you were at, you need a vehicle. Pete Townshend's choice of music to journey in that vehicle was spectacular."[35]

◉

Even after coming to grips with all this context beforehand, a song-by-song plow through *Quadrophenia* does not necessarily yield an easy-to-follow, conventional storyline. (*Tommy* hadn't either, and *Lifehouse* probably wouldn't have, no matter what form it eventually took.) It does allow an appreciation of how The Who unfolded Townshend's themes to maximum effect, but the sky-high ambition of the project inevitably meant that some listeners' expectations would be unfulfilled. In case anyone doubted it was a rock opera, however, they'd be put straight by the opening track, 'I Am The Sea,' in which snatches of all four of the songs to be assigned as themes to separate Who members are nearly buried underneath the roar of sea waves.

A Roger Daltrey growl leads into the LP's first proper song, 'The Real Me,' which kicks into gear with the explosiveness of a mod firing up his scooter. Although this wasn't the song assigned to Roger as his "theme," it could well have been, with its barely controlled rage against family, psychiatrist, preacher, and a girl's cold rejection. There's also a hint of madness in the mother's admission that craziness runs in the family. But what it's ultimately about, more than virtually any other Who song in a catalog full of such things, is a quest for identity, compounded by the failure of others to see our real selves.

Musically, it's The Who at their power-chord-driven best – no synthesizers yet – and arguably John Entwistle's finest hour as a bassist, especially when the guitar drops out to put the focus on a call-and-response of sorts between his penetrating zaps and Daltrey's snarl. "I played some of the best bass I've ever played on the [album], so I was really happy with it," he said in the *In the Studio* special on *Quadrophenia*. "But 'The Real Me' was like take number one, and I was taking the mickey out of the song, I was just playing whatever I wanted to play. We did a few more takes, we kept coming back to it, and it ended up as a bass solo with vocals."[36] Feeling he was in a rut, Entwistle changed to a Gibson Thunderbird bass for the *Quadrophenia* sessions, which affected both the sound (cutting out all the treble, in his estimation) and his way of playing, adding another element that distinguishes the record from previous Who albums.

As Townshend pointed out to *Q* magazine in 1994, "You have the big, big, big bass of John Entwistle, the big, big drums of Keith Moon, the power chords, the huge voice of Roger Daltrey, and what they're actually saying is 'I'm a pathetic little wimp.' I was able to offer essentially frail material to this incredibly powerful elemental machine and I had to allow for that in my writing. I had to know that however delicately I wrote, however poignantly I put the thing together, however direct, however right, however honest and true it was, I then had to hand it to this fucking war machine and it would be churned out like Wall's pork sausages. Every single track on *Quadrophenia* sounds like a bunch of Rwandans trying to terrorize the natives, doesn't it?"[37]

'The Real Me' might have made a better single to preview the album than the track that was chosen, '5:15.' It did get issued on 45 in the USA in early 1974 (inching into the chart at Number 92), with an extended instrumental ending that fades out. There's no fadeout on the album, however, where Daltrey's eerily echoing and overlapping repetitions of "me" telegraph Jimmy's multiple personalities before giving way to the instrumental simply entitled 'Quadrophenia.' In what is almost a companion piece to 'I Am The Sea,' the four themes for each member of The Who are, in the words of the LP's lyric sheet, "heard tarted up a bit."

While little discussed, the instrumentals 'Quadrophenia' and 'The Rock' were taken quite seriously by Townshend as pieces crucial to establishing the opera's mood and themes. "Stuff like 'Quadrophenia' and the 'The Rock' were fuckin' incredibly difficult for me to get together without feeling that I was on a Keith Emerson trip," he told *NME*'s Charles Shaar-Murray. "I wanted the music to be solid and really relate, and be emotive without creating a sort of 'Big Country' drama. It was very tricky. It hasn't really come off, but it's really great to hear it. It's amazing to hear a song like 'Can You See The Real Me' followed by 'Quadrophenia.'"[38]

'Cut My Hair' then fills in the physical and psychological scenery in earnest, down to the fried egg that makes our hero sick first thing in the morning, letting us know Jimmy is being thrown out of his house for sins like pill-popping (here coded in a reference to "a box of blues," which probably went over the heads of many listeners, especially in the USA). But this is the more introspective, melancholy side of mod, not the angry young man of 'The Real Me.' Jimmy admits he has to work himself to death just to fit in – as concise a statement of his dilemma as any in the opera. The mundane reality of his depressing life, sung compassionately by Townshend in the piano-dominated verses, alternates with the zoot-suited brawling mod he becomes outside the house in the chorus. The shift in mood between verse and chorus had been a feature of Who songs for a while, especially when Daltrey and Townshend traded lead vocals. Used in a few *Quadrophenia* songs, it's a device of underrated effectiveness in conveying the contradictory impulses bouncing around Jimmy's psyche.

'The Punk Meets The Godfather' occupies an odd place in *Quadrophenia*. The lyric sheet describes it as "a mini opera with real characters and plot," but there aren't any overt references to Jimmy or mods. It could almost belong to an entirely different story, with its exchange between a "punk" (this a good three years before "punk rock" became a common term) – representing, it seems, the audience, or at a stretch, apprentice mods looking up to cooler older ones -- and a "godfather," apparently a stand-in for the kind of rock stars The Who had become. The audience-rock performer interchange is a disillusioned one. The punk nastily reminds the godfather he wouldn't be anything without his followers; the godfather replies that he's a punk in the gutter too, who's never tried to preach or teach. That was obviously a point Pete had been rolling over in his mind for some time, as he'd told WMMS-FM in Cleveland on August 12 1971 that "one of the reasons The Who have been so long-lasting is because of the fact that we've been careful not to preach and careful not to teach."

Here Townshend might be trying to work in The Who's own history as a subplot, a reexamination of the group's legacy having been a goal of the opera, although it was eventually superseded by Jimmy's story. In his intro to the song at one of the group's first shows after the album was released (in London on November 12), he stated that "that song was all about when the hero goes to a rock concert," only to be insulted by someone in the band when he lines up to see them at the backstage door. The song features *Quadrophenia*'s most memorably anthemic power chords. When the godfather declares he's the "punk with the stutter," a creepy strangled, squiggled voice sardonically mimics the stutter of The Who's own 'My Generation,' almost as if to mock the futility of the younger generation's (and the younger Who's) rebellion. The effect is sometimes thought to have been produced by a synthesizer or vocoder-like device, but according to Nevison, an Eventide flanger was probably used.

'I'm One' – enigmatically titled 'I'm One (At Least)' on the lyric sheet – might be the closest Townshend comes to weaving explicitly autobiographical elements into *Quadrophenia*. It is the only song on which he takes sole lead vocal, and the last verse could well be a description of his own guitar playing and singing, or at least his estimation of it in his early days: "fingers clumsy, voice too loud." True, the short story in *Quadrophenia*'s gatefold jacket doesn't mention Jimmy being a guitar player, let alone playing a Gibson model, as the singer of 'I'm One' does. But *Quadrophenia* isn't necessarily one long interior monologue, and some of the songs could be sung by characters other than Jimmy, as the godfather did in part of the preceding track. Jimmy *is* a Who fan (although his enthusiasm for the group seems muted in the short story), and 'I'm One' – yet another Who song alternating pretty folkie verses with hard rocking anthemic choruses – could be The Who's cameo in the libretto, or at least Townshend's.

'I'm One' led off the double LP's second side, the remainder of which features *Quadrophenia*'s most introspective and least mod-oriented compositions. 'The Dirty Jobs' is an almost-political sketch of the oppression of the working classes, although it's a reminder that many mods had to take menial dead-end jobs to afford their scooters and zoot suits. Here Townshend's gift for symphonic strokes of the synthesizer reaches its zenith, giving way to the lonesome horn and piano rumble that opens the most blatantly operatic piece of the song cycle, 'Helpless Dancer.' This drumless track could almost be an excerpt from a stage musical, so dramatically does Daltrey declaim his mounting frustration with all manner of modern ills. It's designed as Roger's "theme," but it's not a perfect fit with his contemporary image as the combative earthy Who frontman: Daltrey admitted in *Rolling Stone* that it was based on the Roger of 1965. It's doubtful Roger had much truck with the song's vaguely anti-establishment sentiments either. At a November 12 1973 concert he introduced it as being about "when you do something that stinks," a reference to Jimmy's brief stint as a garbage collector in 'The Dirty Jobs.' "There's always a lot of other stinky things around. And [Jimmy] gets mixed up with the most stinky thing of all – politics!"

'Is It In My Head?' may originally have been intended to stand on its own outside *Quadrophenia*, as it dates from 1972 sessions with Glyn Johns. It is among the album's most low-key numbers, the tension getting ratcheted up again on side two's closer, 'I've Had Enough.' Here the mod setting comes back strongly, Jimmy clearly becoming fed up with ... well, everything, but certainly the dancehalls, pills, fashions, and street fights indulged in by mods in search of the ultimate sensational kick. In a neat trick, Townshend previews one of the record's key numbers when Daltrey sings the chorus of 'Love Reign O'er Me.' But that's a brief respite from the angst, the song ending side two with the kind of blood-curdling scream Roger was making a stock-in-trade in the wake of 'Won't Get Fooled Again.'

On a record where much of the appeal lays with the continuity and overlap of mood, '5:15,' which starts the second half of the program with a bang, stands out as one of the most accessible tracks. Written by Townshend on London's Oxford Street and Carnaby Street while he was killing time between appointments, this is The Who at their brassiest, Entwistle letting loose with some almost mischievously playful horn riffs. The lyrics are on the risqué side for 1973, what with the 15-year-old "sexually knowing" girls, "pretty girls digging prettier women," and men in drag in a glittering ballroom.

The more assertive part of this chunky rocker reinforces the lyrical message: Jimmy the mod is starting to implode, getting out of his brain as a defense against the world, and especially the mod ideal, collapsing around him. It wouldn't be half as poignant, however, without the plaintive Townshend-sung reprise of a line from 'Cut My Hair' ("Why should I care?") in the intro and outro, backed only by piano, or the meditative interlude where Jimmy pleads to be left alone as forces wear him down from the inside and outside. In a rarely mentioned contribution of considerable wit, Moon briefly slows the drums near the end to mimic the clatter of a train slowing to a halt at its final destination, a trick he'd draw out at far greater length when the song was performed in concert.

The image of the pilled-up mod shooting off to Brighton on the 5:15 train is one of *Quadrophenia*'s most durable, in part due to the memorable photo of him doing so in the accompanying booklet and the comparable scene in the *Quadrophenia* film. Yet it can't be emphasized enough that part of what makes *Quadrophenia* as a whole so durable is the inclusion of more sensitive musical and lyrical moments. 'Sea And Sand' is a highlight in that regard, projecting Jimmy's loneliness, isolation, and regret, as he wanders the beach near Brighton. The reprise of a boastful verse about scooters and flash mod threads from 'I've Had Enough' here operates almost as a flashback to better times, or at least times in which he thought he was feeling better. While some critics have opined that mod was never about sex or romance so much as the more laddish pleasures of pills, music, biking, and fighting, a couple of verses here make it obvious that this mod has an eye on a certain girl. His hopes are characteristically dashed by bitterness toward more well-heeled peers and the opposite sex. When the coda (with Townshend on vocals) reprises the chorus of The High Numbers' 1964 single 'I'm The Face,' it's almost as if the mod movement in which he's put so much faith has become a Greek chorus to mock his cluelessness.

None of *Quadrophenia*'s songs are exactly good-time tunes in the manner of, say, 'Going Mobile,' but 'Drowned' comes close musically in its near-boogie. The resemblance between Chris Stainton's rollicking piano part and the one he played on Joe Cocker's 'Hitchcock Railway' (on the 1969 album LP *Joe Cocker!*) is not coincidental. Asked if he and The Who were conscious of the similarity, Stainton replies, "Very much so. As I mentioned before, Pete loved that style of playing and wanted to use it."

'Drowned' also occasioned one of the most colorful stories of the *Quadrophenia* sessions. As the song was being recorded, according to Stainton, "there was a violent rainstorm going on outside. The roof of the studio was leaking, and by the end of the recording there were several inches of water on the floor of the piano booth."[39] As Ron Nevison recalls, "The night we cut 'Drowned,' we were cutting a live track, which meant that acoustic piano was in an isolation booth. As we're cutting the track, I started seeing emergency lights, because an Airstream has windows. I open the door – it was pouring rain – and it was the fire department. The roof [had] caved in from water and [the water] went right down into the vocal booth, where Chris Stainton was playing, and flooded his booth. I think Chris just kept playing," he laughs.[40] ("When the take was finished," Townshend later recalled in *A Decade Of The Who*, "he opened the door and about 500 gallons gushed out.")

On a more serious note, while *Quadrophenia* is not thought of as a work influenced by Meher Baba, the heavy presence of beaches and, especially, water in the second half of the opera bears his mark. "['Drowned'] is a love song, God's love being the Ocean, and our 'selves' being the drops of water that make it up," Pete says in *A Decade Of The Who*. "Meher Baba said, 'I am the Ocean of Love.' I want to drown in that ocean, the 'drop' will then be an ocean itself."[41] In *Rock* magazine, Pete told Bruce Pollock that the song had actually been written shortly after *Tommy* "as a kind of tribute to something Meher Baba had said ... like God is like the ocean and that individuals are like drops of water. They think they're separate, but once they're in the ocean, they know they're an ocean – but so long as they're a drop of water, they think they're a drop of water. And that's what 'Drowned' was about ... being a tear or whatever." [42]

Townshend first used water as that metaphor, incidentally, in a relatively ignored song never considered for *Quadrophenia*: 'Water,' the 1970 out-take that would end up as a 1973 B-side. "That was probably my first experiment in that area of trying to take the idea of love being like liquid," he revealed to filmmaker Murray Lerner. "Like love to the aspirant being as important as water to somebody that was parched in the desert." [43]

It might not show up on greatest hits collections, but 'Bell Boy' is one of *Quadrophenia*'s high-water marks, and the song whose characters and action have the most cinematic vividness. This was Keith Moon's "theme" and appropriately he sings the part of the bellboy himself – or, for the most part, speaks it, in what Pete called "good old Lionel Bart fashion." [44] Moon's comic persona is a good fit for the role, reveling in the absurdity of Jimmy's discovery that the leader of the mods is actually working as a bellboy at a Brighton hotel.

Townshend had written about things being much different than they appeared to be since 'Substitute,' and it cuts two ways in 'Bell Boy.' Any illusions Jimmy held about the nobility of the leader of the gang are shattered; it's "the last straw for him," Pete said in his explanation of *Quadrophenia* in *Zoo World*. [45] But as Keith's part makes evident, the bellboy is feeling as much of a disconnect between the great days at the beach and the bleakness of his everyday life as Jimmy is, letting us know that it's not only the blatant losers who feel that pain.

Moon, of course, attacks his part with relish, playing the Cockney-accented clown as he's ordered around at work, yet shifting to a far more sensitive gear in the tremulously sung passage about sleeping on the beach and remembering better days. The band also reach their heights as an ensemble. The track features some of Moon's most high-energy drumming (especially in the opening roll); synthesizers that groove and squiggle with exuberance; Moon's voice trailing off as it mutates into a siren-like note of guitar feedback at the end; emphatic, responsive backing vocals and bittersweet vocal harmonies; and even some crunchy power chords. The breezy Daltrey-sung verses – the confident strut on the beach changing to ominous terror when he spots his former idol in a bellboy's uniform – and the morning-after comedown of the bellboy's sadness switch between blissful daydreams and too-true reality. While seldom trumpeted as such, it remains one of Townshend's greatest lyrical triumphs.

'Bell Boy' brings the most consistent of the original *Quadrophenia* LP's sides to an end, and some of side four has the feel of moving the story along to a worthwhile finale. 'Doctor Jimmy' is the most anxious of the record's songs, detouring briefly to quote John Entwistle's theme, 'Is It Me?' (not a song in its own right, although its refrain is briefly heard prior to 'Doctor Jimmy' as a link between 'Helpless Dancer' and 'Is It In My Head?'). Jimmy is on the edge of a nervous breakdown here, boasting about his willingness to take on anybody, which gives Entwistle a chance to blow some of his grandest horn fanfares. The references to rape and deflowering a virgin – not coded, using the actual words "rape" and "virgin" – and the blustering exclamation "fucking will he" were bold for 1973, ensuring there was little airplay of this particular track. (The offending word was indeed crudely edited out of a syndicated radio broadcast of The Who's December 4 concert in Philadelphia.)

"'Doctor Jimmy' was meant to be a song which somehow gets across the explosive, abandoned wildness side of his character," Townshend told *Rolling Stone*. "Like a bull run amok in a china shop. He's damaging himself so badly so that he can get to the point where he's so desperate that he'll take a closer look at himself."[46] While he called the song the "archetype" of Jimmy's character, he also acknowledged the actual lyric was "much narrower though, we just see the bragging lout, none of the self-doubt or remoteness."[47] Although it might be assumed Jimmy's mood here is most akin to the aggressive "Roger" side of his personality, that's not quite true. Townshend pointed out to *Hit Parader* that the lines about taking and raping whatever comes along were "really the way I see Keith Moon in his most bravado sort of states of mind."[48]

The arrangement, Townshend later noted in *In Their Own Words*, was the most classical he'd ever attempted, making for a good segue into the record's final instrumental piece, 'The Rock.' While this is primarily a link track to mirror Jimmy's anguish when he gets stranded and contemplates suicide, Townshend maintained in the same book that the rock symbolized The Who, "something you could swim out from but you had to come back to it." More

Meher Baba "Ocean of Love" influence comes into play here. "The ocean is like … everything," Pete added. "I mean universal in a mystical sense."[49]

'The Rock' may be one of the least likely tracks to be played on its own at home or on the radio, but it has special significance to the songwriter. "I feel closest to Jimmy when he's reached the stage, late in the album, of being stuck on the Rock," Pete told *Penthouse*. "He's surrendered himself to the inevitable, whatever that is, and has put all his problems behind him. Jimmy's not become any kind of saint or sage, he hasn't found *anything*, much less himself. Basically, he isn't going to be any different. He's just reached the point in his life where he's seriously contemplated suicide – as we all have – and the fact that he chose not to kill himself has left him with a fantastic emptiness. A need to be filled."[50] It could be that Townshend had in mind his own recent brush with suicidal thoughts, when he'd contemplated jumping out of a New York window in March 1971 in the midst of a dispute with Kit Lambert over *Lifehouse*. In his *Zoo World* summation of *Quadrophenia*, Pete went as far as to call 'The Rock' "one of the finest tracks that I've ever been involved in, in any music … there's the four themes representing each facet joined into one, and this really the symbolic sort of thing where the boy's quadrophenia is, if you like, resolved, because he suddenly realizes a kind of a point to life, and symbolically the four pieces of music all join together into one theme."[51]

'Love Reign O'er Me,' Pete's "theme," might be the ultimate over-the-top Who ballad, and thus makes an appropriate end to the record, with some of Townshend's most classical synth strokes and some of Daltrey's most effectively overwrought singing and screaming. Although the track was mostly recorded in 1972 with Glyn Johns, Keith Moon's throw-in-the-kitchen-sink percussion at the end was added at Ramport, where Daltrey taped his vocal on July 17. As Richard Barnes remembers in *The Who, The Mods, And The Quadrophenia Connection*, "They bought Moon all these percussion toys – tubular bells and huge gongs and everything – and they said, 'At the end of it, hit everything you've got. Go mad.' And he did. Nevison was saying, 'I hope we got that. Because you could never do it again.' Because he broke so much of the stuff for this last sort of chord."[52] Nevison confirms the story: "Keith trashed the whole thing."[53]

But for all the orgiastic violence that goes into that final thrash, scream, and magnificent climactic chord, 'Love Reign O'er Me' has a spiritual dimension that might escape most listeners. "It refers to Meher Baba's one-time comment that rain was a blessing from God," Pete wrote in *A Decade Of The Who*. "That thunder was God's voice." Like 'Drowned,' "it's another plea to drown, only this time in the rain."[54] So while the seaside settings and sound effects of *Quadrophenia* were a natural consequence of much of the story being set in or near Brighton, they were also a link to at least one aspect of Townshend's spiritual beliefs.

There was no real "ending" to Jimmy's story, and while it wasn't the sort of work to spur speculation about what happened to the hero at the end of side four, Townshend confirmed its ambiguity in his explanation of *Quadrophenia* to Michael Wale in *Zoo World*. "I don't really know how I imagine that the boy walks away from the rock or whether he jumps in the sea, or whether he drowns or whether he wins or loses or whatever," he said. "I haven't really made up my mind about what happens; maybe I'll leave that to you."[55]

But while Jimmy might be stranded on a rock, as opposed to Tommy being elevated to messiah, both come to a sort of self-realization and redefining of their identity by the end of their respective operas. "What I tried to demonstrate in *Quadrophenia* is that despite the fact that this boy is trying to lose himself in the mass of people that surround him, he can't do it," Townshend declared during the *In The Studio* radio special on *Quadrophenia*. "He can't lose himself. Everywhere he turns, he finds himself. And in the end, he has to accept himself. There begins another story, which is the story of Jimmy as a spiritual being."[56]

Pete did in fact write at least a little material that didn't get included on *Quadrophenia*. His claim to *NME* on November 3 1973 to have culled the best songs from a pool of about 50 seems like a wild exaggeration, but was backed up at least a bit by his assertion that "I originally had a much, much longer story. We could have made it a quadruple album. There's still a fantastic amount of material which is potentially quite good stuff, but what I really wanted to do was to make the album something that invited you to forget The Who a little bit and make you think about other things."[57]

Townshend's liner notes to *Scoop* confirm that several pieces he wrote for the opera were left off the album, one of them being the unused piano theme previously discussed. It's possible other instrumental or thematic pieces were discarded as well. According to documentation consulted by Jon Astley, on July 2 they recorded four "overtures" – 'I Am The Sea,' 'Finale,' 'Wizardry,' and 'Two Fills' – none of which made the album (except 'I Am The Sea') unless they were ultimately given other titles. A three-minute instrumental entitled 'Wizardry' has circulated unofficially, but it's a rather perfunctory synth-dominated piece with a feel far more jovial, and far less grandiose, than the wordless overture-like tracks featured on the final album.

"There were three or four strands which were meant to be interconnecting themes," Townshend told Redbeard for the *In The Studio* radio special on *Quadrophenia*. "There were kind of interludes to lighten the piece. In the end, they weren't included because of lack of time on the record. And a couple of them were developed as complete songs for the album which accompanied the movie later on as, as it were, bonus tracks. But those songs were not completed as songs at the time that the original record was made."[58] These were 'Four Faces' and 'Get Out And Stay Out,' both included on the *Quadrophenia* soundtrack album in 1979, and both far below the standard of any of the songs included on the original LP.

Another such number was 'We Close Tonight,' which was, as Pete told Bruce Pollock for *In Their Own Words*, "about this romance, this girl at school, and how I blew the relationship because I lied a lot."[59] Although The Who did record it on June 20, it wasn't released until it appeared on the 1998 expanded CD version of *Odds & Sods*. Sung by Entwistle with a cameo by Moon, it's far lighter and poppier in tone than anything on *Quadrophenia*. It would have been ill-suited for the opera, not least because of its fairly mediocre quality. It could well have been one of the tunes Townshend referred to when he told *Modern Hi-Fi & Stereo Guide*, "I had to scrap a lot of songs that were very light because they just didn't fit in."[60] Maybe Pete threw it into the hat to give John and Keith some vocal duties. If Moon's jokey accent for his part gave The Who the idea to have him play a similar role on 'Bell Boy,' that alone would have made it a worthwhile exercise.

Another *Quadrophenia* reject was written back in the mid 60s. 'Joker James,' as Townshend had enthusiastically recounted in *NME* back in August 1972, was "about this kid who loses all his girlfriends because he plays tricks on them. He's going out with one little girl and, just at the tense romantic moment when they sit down on the couch, a whoopee cushion goes off and

229

it's all over. There's a line that goes 'Mary Anne's so glum since Joker James gave Mary Anne some onion-flavored gum.'" Furthermore, Pete had 'Joker James' targeted as Moon's "theme," since "it's a bit of natural typecasting that Moon is Joker James. Moon's is the irresponsible daredevil part and of course he's a terrible practical joke player in real life. You'll open your hotel room and a bucket of water will fall on your head." [61] Fortunately the song, too mediocre and juvenile for *Quadrophenia*, didn't make the cut, and Moon was awarded the vastly superior 'Bell Boy' as his "theme." That line about Mary Anne's gum, incidentally, does not appear on the late-70s version of 'Joker James' on the *Quadrophenia* film soundtrack, and no one seems to have missed it.

Quadrophenia was undoubtedly a success as a set of good-to-great songs and an investigation into the life and near-death of a mid 60s mod, whose trials held universal lessons for anyone searching for meaning and self-realization. Townshend was less successful, however, in incorporating the secondary concept of Jimmy's "quadrophenia," with four sides of his personality represented by a different member of the band. For one thing, the "themes" assigned to each of The Who didn't exactly match up with their respective images, at least as the public perceived them. Moon was a natural choice to portray the loony bellboy, but Daltrey's role as the "helpless dancer" didn't entirely square with either his street-fighting man pose or the sensitivity he'd displayed on thoughtful Townshend compositions dating back to 1967's 'Tattoo.' While Pete had given himself the role of "a beggar, a hypocrite" (according to the accompanying short story in the gatefold LP), 'Love Reign O'er Me' seemed more akin to the sensibility of a romantic.

Yet the role of the "romantic" went to John Entwistle – a label wholly at odds with his image as a black-humored, motionless ox. There was plenty of room in Jimmy's meltdown for some gallows humor, and maybe John could have written a song along those lines that would have been a better theme for himself. But using Entwistle compositions of any sort was not considered. "I wrote the thing on paper before we went in," Pete recalled, "and there was just no room for anything else." [62] More obscurely, as Entwistle revealed in April 1975, "Until recently, I've never been able to write for Roger's voice. I could now, I've learned to write a song to order." [63]

Townshend did at least clear up why Entwistle had been awarded his unlikely *Quadrophenia* role in a September 26 1974 interview with Melvyn

Bragg for BBC television, in which he called John "a great secret romantic. And I thought this would be nice to let the world know what a romantic he was. And he's the romantic side ... the Hollywood-type, dream-laden-type thing that there is a girl somewhere, the perfect girl, the perfect life, the perfect sitting room where the television is good all day long."[64]

Pete was perhaps better at delineating the quadrophenic concept to journalists than in song. His explanation of his own fourth of the character – to Michael Wale in a *Zoo World* piece entitled 'Townshend explains *Quadrophenia*' – rang truer than his "a beggar, a hypocrite" soundbite. "It's the life I'm most into at the moment, and this facet is that the boy has a slight feeling deep inside that things aren't quite right, and that there must be another answer, and that he feels a certain sort of falseness to the way he's living his life, and perhaps a certain falseness to all the values that he holds most high," he explained. "In other words, he's becoming interested in certain abstract things, even as a type of Shepherd's Bush mod that he's portrayed as, he still has these feelings of, I suppose, spiritual insecurity, verging on spiritual desperation, and in a way the whole album is a study of spiritual desperation on the adolescent."[65]

Numerous critics at the time and since *Quadrophenia*'s release have singled out the flawed realization of the "quadrophenic" concept as the opera's chief weakness. Townshend was perhaps biting off more than he could chew in his attempt to blend it into Jimmy's storyline. The packaging of *Quadrophenia* makes it impossible to ignore that attempt, as it's both outlined in the short story and graphically reflected on the cover. Ultimately, however, it doesn't really matter to the success of the opera. Jimmy's confusion and conflicting aspirations are detailed and enacted well enough that the overriding message of a youngster being torn apart in different directions comes through on its own. Had The Who not telegraphed the "quadrophenia" with the packaging and the assignment of four different themes, its presence, and hence its failure to be integrated into the work, might never have been noticed.

In the end, a key to the majesty of *Quadrophenia* was the splitting of roles within The Who themselves – not something they'd devised for *Quadrophenia*, but something they'd been living for nearly a decade. In particular, it would fall to Daltrey to sing most of the intensely personal songs that Townshend had composed. For those who view *Quadrophenia* as the work of an auteur, that might seem a dilution of the purity of Pete's vision. But it was Roger who brought out the emotion that Pete carried in his head but lacked the vocal ability to fully bring into reality. How could Daltrey do this with a fictional character, and remain true to what Townshend had in mind?

The explanation, as stated many years later by Roger in the *Amazing Journey* documentary, was worthy of Pete's best interview soundbites. "I think it's true to say that I've lived every one of those songs that's Pete's written," he said. "If not in the physical [sense], I know damned well that in the emotional, and the psychological, I've lived every one of them."[66]

As good as The Who's performances for *Quadrophenia* were, there was more to be done than simply blending their tracks when it came time to mix the album at Pete's new home studio in Goring-on-Thames. More than any other rock album, perhaps (although Pink Floyd's *Dark Side Of The Moon*, also released in 1973, gave it a run for its money), *Quadrophenia* made innovative and purposeful use of sound effects to set its mood and accentuate various aspects of the lyrics and story. Most of these were not lifted off other recordings, but taped in the field specifically for the LP.

These are not mere novelties or gimmicks. They are essential to the overall impact of the opera, almost as if they're part of the non-musical soundtrack to a movie on record. Beach noises and wave crashes are a big part of this, but so are the grim newscast report of a mod vs rocker riot as a kettle comes to a boil; the roar of a stadium crowd near the end of 'The Punk Meets The Godfather'; the rush of a passing train at the end of 'I've Had Enough'; the chanting striking workers in 'The Dirty Jobs'; the bleat of a train whistle near the start of '5:15' (recorded at Waterloo Station after the engineer had been bribed £5 to blow it as his train pulled out, in violation of regulations); and, most wittily of all, the distant sound of the first few lines of The Who's own classic record 'The Kids Are Alright' after 'Helpless Dancer,' simulating the sound of hearing a band in the dancehall. It reminds us that the group were a part of Jimmy's life too, if somewhere off in the background.

"It's not a story, more a series of impressions of memories," Townshend explained to *NME* when the album was released. "The real action in this is that you see a kid on a rock in the middle of the sea and this whole thing explains how he got there. That's why I used sound effects: to establish atmosphere. Some of the sound effects, I've tried to manipulate impressionistically. It's something that's new to me and I'm not particularly good at it, but I'm glad I did it."[67]

"I recorded most of them myself," says Ron Nevison. "The biggest project was the sea. I took Ronnie [Lane]'s truck down by myself on a weekend down to Cornwall, only because I had vacationed there previously. I knew where I wanted to go, I had a perfect spot, and it was a great day. I put four microphones out, and recorded quadraphonic sea sound (of course, I only got to use stereo). So I set up four [Neumann] U 87s, two on the rocks and two in the back, waited for the tide to come in, spent about three, four, five, six hours, I don't remember. When the tide went out, I recorded a bunch of sea noise. That's the sea that you hear throughout the album, especially at the beginning.

"I recorded the rain in a couple of different places. I went out to Wales on a rainy weekend, in a tent, and I took a really high-quality stereo recorder. I was hoping to get thunder, but you can't wait for thunder. It's not something you can program. So I ended up getting a lot of rain. Then I also recorded rain at Ramport on a rainy night. I always had the recorder ready in case we got thunder, but we never did. So I ended up having to use thunder from archival footage."[68]

You can't exactly program sea waves either, and Rod Houison, credited (with Nevison and Townshend) for sound effects on the LP, says some special engineering was required to get what they needed. "I was down with Ron doing the sea stuff," he recalls. "Here we are down in Cornwall on probably the quietest sea day that you've ever imagined, and we're trying to get surf that's going to be breaking not only around us, but behind us, against some kind of imaginary cliff. That was Pete's idea – just find a rocky outcrop, put four mics out there, and get the water to rush by and then crash up the cliff behind.

"We stuck out these enormously expensive mics, and there was this trickle of water. Ron said, 'We're going to be here days!' So he cranked up the mic gain to get the water to sound as if it was actually more than a trickle. But every now and again you'd hear this 'ruff ruff.' There was not a thing in sight; just sea, and that was it. Then we found that three quarters of a mile away was a dog. That's how much we had to crank up the gain in order to get the sea sound. Later, I think it was the next day, all came clear and we got some decent surf. The four Neumann mics were on a rocky outcrop placed so that the waves would pass to the sides of the rock and break on the cliff behind – nice quad effect. When the mics were put in place there was a six-inch depth of calm water between rock and cliff. By the time we came to retrieve them the water was deep enough to be threatening to a non-swimmer, me. Then it was a toss-up: 'Well, who swims? Because somebody's going to have to go out and get four very expensive microphones quickly.' I was elected, so I did it."[69]

Closer to home, Nevison went to Hyde Park's famed Speakers' Corner and was escorted off the property, unaware that taping was not allowed. He wasn't supposed to tape the brass band (used to link 'The Dirty Jobs' with 'Helpless Dancer') in London's Regent's Park either, "but this time I was smart. I hid the microphones in like a bag, and just stuck the heads of the microphones out to pick up the noise."[70]

Townshend himself joined the fun by spending evenings on the Thames at his Goring-on-Thames home recording birds taking off from the water, at one point dropping his tape recorder and mic into the river. "We went out on a dinghy with an outboard motor and recorded lots of little outboard motor sounds and walking, footsteps, just bits and pieces that we used," says Jon Astley, who would later be involved in producing, remastering, and remixing many Who releases, and who at that time was Townshend's brother-in-law. "I was just a student at the time, so it was very exciting. They helped the story along, which is great. When the guy's walking on the beach, you hear the pebbles; you get immediately the picture in your mind of where he is and what he's doing."[71] Pete also walked around London, recording street noises for possible use.

Houison went beyond the line of duty to get the blaring train horn that follows Daltrey's scream on 'I've Had Enough,' by actually stepping onto the tracks himself. "I had a couple of Neumann microphones, and my first attempt was standing by a very fast railway line which wasn't too far from Goring," he remembers. "I was standing about 15-20 feet from the train. The trains would hurtle by, and all they sounded like was a bit like a jet passing. So I thought, OK, we're going to have to get the guy to sound his horn as it passes. Now, trying to actually bribe somebody to do that is completely impossible. So there I was with my headphones, and these things would appear just about 90-100 miles per hour around this bend, and we'd step onto the line. You would then get [mimics an engineer sounding his horn]. So obviously, that became a *train* rather than a jet passing."[72]

The greatest stroke of ingenuity was reserved for the newscast of the Brighton riot, read by an actual BBC radio announcer, John Curle. "He was a very revered and well-loved announcer," Houison recalls. "We bought various ... 'medium-wave simulators,' which didn't work. It never sounded quite right. So in the end, Pete bribed this guy to actually read the actual paragraph on the 6:00 news, or whichever news it was. And he in his very official voice said, 'Down in Brighton,' or whatever. We recorded it off a genuine radio down at Goring-At-Thames and that worked extremely well. As I remember it was recorded live from the AM radio in my XKE Type Jag parked outside the studio. All the AM simulators of the day didn't sound real enough." (Richard Barnes thinks that John Walters, the BBC radio producer who'd commissioned Keith Moon to do the four-episode 1973 summer comedy show *A Touch Of The Moon*, probably helped with clearing the usage of the BBC announcer and other sound effects, accounting for why Walters is thanked in the LP credits.)

Didn't that broadcast sound a bit curious to millions of other listeners, announcing on live radio mod riots that certainly weren't happening in 1973? "Yes, absolutely," says Rod. "Immediately afterward, he gave an explanation. A bit like [when] Orson Welles's *War Of The Worlds* [was broadcast in 1938]. This guy was so well respected that he could do something like that. As far as Pete was concerned, it *had* to be this guy, because of his very recognizable and respected voice." The whistle that rises and descends in the background "was in fact a kettle with the old fashioned removable whistling spout."[73]

Mixing all of this stuff together was not easy with 1973 technology. "The biggest thing I remember about the mixing [is], we had a lot of sound effects," Nevison recalls. "We were on 16 tracks. Can you imagine, with all the synthesizer, all the vocals, all the effects, and everything? We didn't have room to put everything onto the 16-track. So Pete got hold of a couple of these cartridge players that they used in radio stations for commercials. We had two machines – he had one and I had one – and we would load the sound effects. In other words, you'd click a button, and it goes off, and then the next one comes up, and then you hit the button again and the next one goes off, like commercials [which, as a footnote, The Who had actually inserted as links throughout their great 1967 LP *The Who Sell Out*]. So we'd load them in in the order that we had in the mix. He'd have like three or four on one side, and I'd have three or four on the other side. And when we wanted thunder, or we wanted a train whistle, we'd just like hit the button, and sound effects would come out. And that was how we achieved all the sound effects, because we didn't have room for them on the recording."

As an unfortunate side-effect, Nevison points out, subsequent mixes for CD don't "have some of the qualities that we put in there, because we had scattered all that stuff on cartridge machines. The train whistle is gone from '5:15,' even though I think I was very careful to archive all of the sound effects on quarter-inch tape. They probably should have been stored with the mixes and everything else. But because stuff wasn't on the 16-track, they would have lost some.

"Then once the whole thing was mixed, the next thing was cross-fading from one song to another, which was a tricky thing. Each side of [the] four sides of this record had like 100 edits in it. One time I was spooling through one side of the record and the edit came apart, and the whole thing went on the floor. Luckily, nothing was injured. We were freaked out, but a splice had come apart, so we just carefully picked it back up, and certainly it was cool. But the whole Goring thing was just Pete and I, the two of us, mixing. I don't even think there was an assistant there, just the two of us did it. For maybe three weeks we were there."[74] According to Houison, who built the studio, "We had upward of maybe 12, 13, sometimes 15 machines running in the room at the time on the mix. There were endless amounts of effects running. Setting up the room used to take forever."[75]

There would later be complaints that the mix wasn't all it could have been, and particularly criticisms that Daltrey's vocals weren't prominent enough. "The thing that disappointed me about that album was the production," Roger told *Crawdaddy*, "because there's so much on the album, but you can only hear it with the cans on, and that's not what albums are about. An album has to have a sound that makes people leave it on when they're having conversation. We narrowed the market with *Quadrophenia* by making an album you have to sit down and listen to. Most people don't have that kind of time."

In the January 2003 issue of *Uncut*, Daltrey was more explicitly critical. "My main regret on that album is the recording process," he groused. "Ron

Nevison, who was the producer [sic] at the time with Pete, recorded it with echo on the vocal which can never be removed now. It just makes the vocal sound thin. It was the biggest recording mistake we ever made. The echo diminishes the character as far as I'm concerned. It always pissed me off. From day one I just fucking hated the sound of it. He did that voice and I've never forgiven Ron for it."[76]

"I have to say that the mix still holds up for me," Nevison counters. "I did talk to Pete a few years ago, and he still likes the mix that we did. Pete and I did what we thought sounded right. This happens in almost every project I've ever done [and Nevison has done many, including engineering albums by Led Zeppelin and The Rolling Stones, and production for numerous others]. Not everybody's happy with all the mixing you do. In this case, as an engineer, I followed Pete. Pete was the producer. If I thought he was making a mistake, I would speak up. But it wasn't about Roger. It was about The Who."[77]

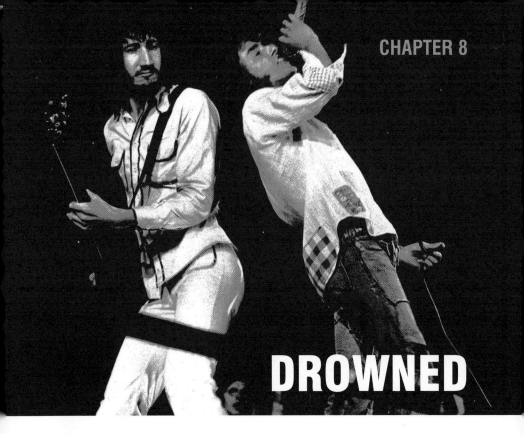

CHAPTER 8

DROWNED

As strong as it was, *Quadrophenia*'s music could not convey the full depth of its driving concept on its own. This would be particularly true outside of the UK, where the mod movement wasn't well known, and especially in the all-important North American market, where mod was a rumor at best. And just as there was no other album where sound effects were as important in fleshing out the music, there was no other album where the physical packaging was as important in making its message understood. Pete Townshend would indicate to *Disc* that this was done primarily for the American audience, probably in the hope of making the very British story more easily comprehensible to Stateside listeners.[1]

The Who were not strangers to elaborate gatefold jackets, *Tommy* having been a six-panel production with a cover design by Mike McInnerney, another acolyte of Meher Baba. *Quadrophenia* would have the four-panel design common to gatefold double LPs, but The Who, and particularly Pete Townshend, realized that more was needed. The left panel of the inner gatefold featured a Townshend narrative of sorts in Jimmy's voice, running to more than a dozen paragraphs. Not only did it explain, more or less, what

Jimmy was up to in the days leading up to his epiphany on the Rock, but it was told in a half-articulate manner, reflecting his scrambled psyche. Nor was it devoid of self-mocking humor, most memorably in the unsentimentally realistic description of The Who as Jimmy saw them on stage, with a guitar player who "was a skinny geezer with a big nose who twirled his arm like a windmill. He wrote some good songs about mods, but he didn't quite look like one."

The gatefold's short story, Townshend fretted in *Rock* magazine, was "a little strained because it's put together around the album itself. It's a little bit of character-building put in to let you know just how uneducated the character was, but also the fact that he was all right besides that. That was really all that was for, but I found it quite hard to write. You can see I went incredibly heavy on a sort of *Catcher In The Rye* thing to get it across."[2]

Better yet was the 44-page LP-sized booklet, which was entirely devoted, aside from a couple of lyric sheets, to black-and-white pictures by *Who's Next* photographer Ethan Russell. No captions, no explanatory text – just shots of Jimmy (played by Terry 'Chad' Kennett, who'd been spotted by Townshend in a pub on Cecily Street near the studio) riding his scooter, hanging out with the mod gang, working as a dustman, walking and sleeping on the beach, taking a boat to the Rock, riding the 5:15 train, and even watching the real-life 1973 Who posing in front of London's Hammersmith Odeon. The very first shot of Jimmy, on page three, shows him riding the scooter in what appears to be an especially dismal neighborhood, smokestacks spewing in the background; this is in fact the very street on which Ramport Studios was situated, as Daltrey told *Rolling Stone*.[3]

More effectively even than the short story, the booklet made the mod experience graspable to those too young or remote from Britain to have lived through it firsthand, almost as though the photos were stills from a film of the opera. Crucially, it also did so without glamorization. Quite the contrary – if the stereotypical image of the Swinging Sixties is in glowing Technicolor, this is the gray, grim, but more realistic flipside, down to the close-up of a disgusting half-finished meal of chips, peas, eggs, toast, and sausage (a particular favorite among US fans unfamiliar with the delights of proletarian British cuisine). "I don't know whose idea [the booklet] was, probably Pete's, but it was fucking brilliant," says Richard Barnes. "It could be questionable that he got an American photographer. Americans don't understand mods.

But on the other hand, it was quite good, because Ethan didn't have any preconceived ideas."[4]

However, as John Atkins rightly speculates in *The Who On Record*, it's difficult to believe Russell or (more likely) Townshend had not seen the obscure 1970 British cult film *Bronco Bullfrog*. For that movie's tale of down-and-out East London teens has a black-and-white bleakness quite similar in tone to the photos in the *Quadrophenia* booklet. This could be dismissed as coincidence, but a couple of scenes from the movie, set at the end of the 60s rather than the mid 60s, strongly foreshadow specific Russell shots. Particularly striking is the similarity between *Bronco Bullfrog*'s shot of its hero's smashed bike and the image of a smashed scooter on page 22 of the booklet. Another *Bronco Bullfrog* sequence shows its hero walking on his own through London's ghostly Greenwich Foot Tunnel, which runs beneath the River Thames; on page six of the booklet, Jimmy strolls alone through the exact same tunnel. Indeed, some elements of *Bronco Bullfrog* are echoed, although not as strongly, in the story of *Quadrophenia* itself. Both feature misunderstanding parents, a gang of directionless working-class youths, and a waterside anti-climax where the protagonist seems to have run out of options. But such is the dead-end mood of *Bronco Bullfrog* – no pills, beachside riots, or rock'n'roll are even on hand to alleviate the boredom – that it makes Jimmy's predicament seem a bit glamorous in comparison, not least because Jimmy's scooter is way more flash than the anemic example put-puttering in the film.

Originally intended to be 18 pages long, according to Russell's memoir *Dear Mr Fantasy*, the booklet took on a life of its own. "Pete rang me up and said, 'I'm having ever so much trouble with this fucking cover because everybody's got their own idea of what mods were,'" Richard Barnes remembers. "'We're getting nowhere, and we've been on it for weeks. We've not shot anything. No one can agree on anything. Why don't you come in and art-direct it?'" So it was that he was tasked with helping to cast the kids and find the appropriate scooter and wardrobe, verifying "clothing details, attitudes, etc" with his unpaid assistant Linden Kirby, a 60s mod thanked simply as "Linden" in the LP credits.

"I thought, 'Why should I know?'" he admits. "But I went and got hold of some mods and asked them. … They all did what I said. If I said 'They wore this' – not in my view, what I was told by my advisors – that's what they

240

wore. So in a way it was good, because Ethan then wouldn't be involved with dressing up the kids and getting them looking right. Because he wouldn't have a clue." Yet as Barnes puts it, "Ethan did a wonderful job, and I thought we got those kids looking just like fucking mods. Not particularly top mods, but just everyday straight kid mods. The main guy we got to do it, this guy Chad, he was brilliant. And we got Paul, Pete's [much younger] brother, because he looked like a young Pete." Most of the kids were recruited from the run-down working-class neighborhood around Thessaly Road, where Ramport was situated.

"We were just left alone to get on it with it, it was brilliant," Barnes continues, although they did have to get permission from the local authorities to pull off the shots of the gang wrecking and overturning a car. "It was quite a long shoot. We went to lots of different places, and sort of did one or two scenes a day. Nobody queried the budget. We ended up buying the clothes. I had a fucking chauffeur-driven car driving around location to location. We spent a lot of time in Brighton, and we broke into the West Pier, which is boarded up – the dangerous one, which is the more beautiful Victorian pier – and took pictures. I think we climbed over the padlocked fence and barbed wire. I spent a whole afternoon in a bookshop looking at porn pictures for that boy's bedroom."

The shooting almost came to a premature end, according to Russell's memoir, when Kennett had to appear in court on charges of stealing a bus. The photographer had to testify that the 20-year-old was essential to the project before they were free to shoot the final sections of the booklet in Cornwall. Russell only learnt that Kennett couldn't swim after taking the picture of Jimmy jumping off a boat.

The Who's management told Russell that a half-dozen trainloads of paper were ordered for the booklet, in what was turning out to be a very expensive release, even aside from the considerable studio and production costs for the music alone. "I think there was a shortage of silver that was used in film in those days at the time he was taking the pictures, because he took so many fucking pictures," Barnes laughs. "He took fucking millions of shots. They had a whole vault of pictures. ... They're all lost, they've all disappeared."[5]

If the hope was for the booklet to illustrate the mod experience to American audiences in particular, The Who probably succeeded to an extent that has yet to be fully acknowledged. Despite subsequent speculation that the LP underperformed in the USA, in part because of Stateside listeners' inability to understand its cultural context, many fans eagerly absorbed the basics from both the music and the packaging. "I was 12 years old when *Quadrophenia* came out and, as a fairly sheltered pre-teen living in Los Angeles, I had no knowledge of the mod scene beyond my already-established love of The Who and The Kinks," says Barry Smolin, now the host of the Sunday night *The Music Never Stops* program on LA radio station KPFK. "Despite this ignorance, I was immediately captivated by the music on *Quadrophenia*, both its power and ambition. The lyrics contained many references I didn't understand at first hearing ('zoot suit, white jacket with side vents,' 'my mother found a box of blues,' 'maybe a touch of seersucker with an open neck,' 'G S scooter,' 'wartime coat,' etc), but through context and inference I was able to make some sense of it on my own.

"The booklet that came with the LP, though, was what brought mod culture alive in my mind and helped me visualize Townshend's imagery more concretely. The booklet created a more evocative experience for a kid so far removed from mod culture and the zeitgeist of that era in Britain – the way it looked and felt and even smelled. I would listen to the album and stare at the booklet for hours on my bed. The black-and-white photography, the foggy gray atmosphere, the wetness of the roads, the dark sea, the fashions worn, the haircuts, the posters on the walls – all of it came alive visually, which, in turn, added to the impact of the music."[6]

While Russell photos of a beach and a half-drowned scooter were backdrops on the back cover and inner gatefold, the front cover (shot on August 24, the same day as The Who posed in front of the Hammersmith Odeon) used a striking rear-view picture of Kennett on a scooter, cloaked in a jacket with The Who's insignia. Taken by Roger Daltrey's cousin, Graham Hughes (also responsible for photography on *Meaty Beaty Big And Bouncy*, as well as the front cover of Townshend standing on a floor of eggs on *Who Came First*), it also featured four rear-view mirrors on the scooter, each showing a reflection of a different member of The Who. Along with the use of the title lettering for *Quadrophenia* on all four sides of the cover, it was the LP's most visual representation of Jimmy and The Who's "quadrophenic" personality, and perhaps more memorable than any such reference in the songs themselves.

"We had to carry ... almost drive this scooter up the stairs to my first floor studio," Hughes recalled in *Anyway Anyhow Anywhere*. "The front cover picture was taken against a special sky-blue canvas. Roger thought of the idea of painting The Who logo on the back of the kid's parka. I still hadn't figured out where the group were going to appear, when the idea of the wing mirrors suddenly dawned on me. I asked Pete, John, and Roger to crouch down and stare into the glass while I shot each image. Keith had disappeared, so I had to go down to Tara and photograph him separately in his greenhouse to get the same effect."[7]

As to why Hughes and not Russell got to do the cover photo, Richard Barnes felt that was "politics. That's because Roger complained that it was all Pete's album, Pete's idea. The thing about *Quadrophenia* was that Pete didn't involve the rest of the band in it like he did with *Tommy*. Really, *Quadrophenia* is Townshend's solo album using The Who. He had involved John a bit in it; John had done some recording of brass, because that's John's bag. But I don't think he involved the others. There was also this thing that, roughly, they took turns in doing the covers. It was kind of Roger's turn. I was outraged, because I thought Ethan had worked so hard and had got such fantastic photographs, [though] I like Graham, I think he's a great photographer. I thought it was a bit much, but Pete just accepted it, 'cause I think he realized that he was doing absolutely everything."[8]

In a sense, *Quadrophenia* ended up being, in a more low-key way, the kind of multimedia work Townshend had hoped to create with *Lifehouse*. There wasn't a film – although it would eventually be adapted into a superb movie – but the booklet was close to being one. And while there wasn't a book (as Pete had reportedly been considering for *Lifehouse*), there was a short story. The booklet, story, and cover art were much enhanced by the 12-by-12-inch format of the vinyl era, which brought with it an impact that's impossible to replicate when the artwork is shrunk down to CD size.

There was one much hoped-for multimedia component that didn't come off, however. Part of the reason that the album had been titled *Quadrophenia* was that The Who hoped to issue it in quadraphonic sound. Only recently introduced for vinyl releases, the format never would take off as stereo had. Few listeners had (or were interested in getting) equipment that could enable them to listen to quadraphonic recordings. The Who's US label, MCA, "had adopted a certain system for this quadraphonic bullshit, which is all it was," says Ron Nevison. "It was supposed to be the next thing after stereo. But it was a bunch of crap. They took the stereo and they folded in out-of-phase tracks. It wasn't any kind of what we call discrete quad, where you have dedicated left-right front, left-right rear [channels].

"We started recording the drums before we found out that we weren't gonna do quad," he continues. "I didn't know what the fuck to do, really. I had no clue. We started on four tracks, so I just put the drums on four tracks, and mixed them out with the drummer seated in the middle, with the snare and the kick in the middle. I figured that at least that way, it would be centered, with the drums out to the right and to the left, and the cymbals in the back maybe. But it worked in stereo, and that's what I made sure of – that the four tracks, when mixed together, worked in stereo. So even though it was in quad, it was really a big stereo.

"When we tried a test mix halfway through with the album – when we finally got the equipment to encode these bullshit quad tracks – we realized that the front-to-back separation was like 5dB [decibels]. It was like a big giant mono." In other words, listeners playing the album would hear far less difference between the channels than could be heard in the four-channel mixes created in the studio. They wouldn't be hearing anything like the mix as The Who intended it to be experienced. Instead, there would be little to distinguish the sound coming out of the two rear speakers from the sound emanating from the two normal stereo front ones. As a point of reference, the left-right separation between speakers on a typical home stereo at the time would have been in the 70-80 dB range; by comparison, the front-to-back quadraphonic separation of 5 dB was puny.

"Pete said, 'You know, I am not going to do a quad mix that's worse than the stereo mix. Period.' And that was it. He sent that memo to MCA. They were furious, I think, because they wanted to launch their whole quad thing with *Quadrophenia*, [on] a Who album, the follow-up to *Tommy*. The whole kind of nine yards. And I was right with him, man. I thought this was a bunch of shit."[9]

Rod Houison was building Townshend's home studio in his house at Goring-on-Thames. "Certainly everything we built was based on quadraphonic sound," he recalls. "We bought four of everything. Putting it on four-channel tape is one thing; that's very easy to do, and you get beautiful effects and everything is nicely separated. But how do you get that onto vinyl? That was where everyone was going, 'Oh my god, this isn't going to work, is it?' But CBS said, 'Oh yes, we've got this thing called an encoder-decoder.' So Pete said, 'OK, well, we'll buy one then,' and plugged it up. Pete and I were doing some tests, and it was about a 3dB difference, [which is] sort of nothing. It was just laughable. Yes, it was very difficult to achieve quadraphonic sound on vinyl. So that never really worked out."[10]

"I think that in the end," Nevison concludes, "the quadraphonic thing that MCA and record companies were trying to do in those days was gimmicky. It would have sold [a] decoder and two more speakers and amplifiers. So you have your normal stereo, and then you put it through a decoder and add another amplifier with two more speakers, and you have quad. But what you have is mono, and we weren't buying it. It would have been nice to have done a quad thing in 1973. Wouldn't that have been fabulous? But it wasn't to be."[11]

At the time of the album's release, Townshend also found that the technology was not up to the task. "We're fairly happy with the quadraphonic mixes we've done, but you know the problem with the transcription down to disc," he told *NME*. "It's all very well on tape, but when you try and get it down onto a record, everything goes completely berserk. We were talking about a January 1st release date for the quadraphonic version, but at the moment it's a bit of a myth. Apart from anything else, I heard The Doobie Brothers' quad album of *The Captain And Me* and it just doesn't come anywhere near the stereo version."[12]

As late as the May 1974 *Hit Parader*, Townshend indicated there would be a quadraphonic version of *Quadrophenia*. "We're going to do a completely new album, practically. Because so much of the album is actually in the mixing, the blending and everything ... For a while we'll see our records as two editions, one in stereo, the other in quad ... one in a stereo mix, one in a quad mix. That has to be the way it has to be because stereo at the moment is so much more mature and advanced than quad is." The paragraph wasn't over, however, before Pete was overcome by skepticism. "Every day they make an improvement in the quad set-up; you know every day I get a piece of mail through from CBS telling me that they've got another dB of separation from front to back and that, you know, if we buy the new modified encoder-decoder we'll get better results. And then the next week there's another modification you can buy for another $40,000 which gives you another dB separation front to back and a positioning encoder which puts all your 16 tracks at various points – guaranteed positional separation, and that's an extra $40,000! It's a load of ..." he trailed off.[13]

With 21st century technology, it would seem that 5.1 surround sound in particular would offer some intriguing possibilities for creating mixes that, if not exactly quadraphonic, could be presented with more multidimensional depth than was possible in 1973. As with *Who's Next*, however, less than ideal preservation of the source materials might make that hard to realize. "He always felt it fell down in the mix when he mixed it with Ron Nevison," says Jon Astley, who would later work on the remastering and remixing of the album for CD. "I think the pressure was on to get it done. It was a bit rushed, and they didn't really check stuff. When we decided to remix it – it was actually my idea – a lot of these quarter-inch masters we couldn't find. We had safety [copies], but Polydor wanted to reissue this and said to me, 'Can't you just use those?' I said, 'Well, they're inferior to the masters, and I can't find the masters anywhere.' I was at MCA in Los Angeles.

"Eventually most of them all did turn up about five years later. Despite being told probably five times, 'No, we haven't got the *Tommy* masters,' five years later – 'Oh, we *have* got the *Tommy* masters.' I was totally convinced they were there, and eventually they came clean. And I said, 'Have you got *Quadrophenia* as well,' and they said, 'Oh, we'll have a look. Oh, there it is. Surprise surprise!' So it was a real pain in the ass.

"That was MCA going through a very, very difficult time with some of their library people. A guy in LA told me one of the guys that worked at the MCA library was taking home tapes and cutting together his own little playback reels. When MCA found out about this, they kind of went, 'Right. Anybody asks for a master, we haven't got it.' They recovered all the tapes and built a little editing room in the library where some bloke would piece them all back together again. So over a period of time, they just denied all knowledge about having masters while this was going on. I was told time and again that the stereo masters were missing, which was the real reason that we started to remix everything. And out of that came this mix of *Quadrophenia* that Pete said, 'Oh, that's the way it should have sounded.' So it was kind of driven because we didn't have the original masters more than anything."

"It would be nice to do a proper 5.1 of it, and actually the one I did with Andy McPherson of 'The Real Me' is just stupendous; it just sounds incredible. We ended up doing two tracks into 5.1, and then Pete decided he didn't want to go down that route anymore. We were going to do a Super Audio release, and Super Audio versus DVD-A was going on, and I don't think anybody quite knew which format was going to win. So he just said, 'No, let's leave it for now and see what happens.'

"But if they do do a remix [and] reissue a 5.1, Pete would like to go back to his eight-track. Because the whole thing about *Quadrophenia*, it was done in eight-track, and then 16-track, and then 24-track. So by the time you get to your stereo masters, some of the elements that were recorded were already four generations old. Pete would like to rethink some of the eight-track stuff that he did, which got bounced down onto one or two tracks when it went to 16. So all those single violin tracks and stuff can be exploded and put into different positions in the 5.1 or the stereo mix. Quality-wise, they'll be a lot better than they were when they got to 24-track. That would be a great project to get involved in, and I think he has tried, and made some inroads into doing that.

"It would have been great if they'd done it to four-track, and then we could just lift out the four-track and hear it in glorious 5.1. I think *Quadrophenia* in 5.1 would be an absolute masterpiece, because of all the sound effects and the stereo panning. Pete always said that the guy who was behind Dolby at the time kept hanging around the studio to see how they were getting on with his matrix quadraphonic four-track recording that they were experimenting with. Pete said he could see the wheels going on in his brain about 5.1 Dolby encoding back then, in 1973."[14]

Back in 1973, according to Ethan Russell's *Dear Mr Fantasy*, there was one final unexpected hurdle to be overcome before the masters for *Quadrophenia* could be delivered. By chance, he took the same flight as Townshend when Pete traveled to Los Angeles to personally deliver the tapes to The Who's US label. "At customs the people from MCA Records meet Pete," Russell recalls. "The customs man reaches for the tapes held under Pete's arm. Townshend jerks them back and starts stamping his boots at the customs man's feet. 'Not leaving my hands, mate. Not for a second.'"[15]

Another multimedia notion that didn't work out would have used film footage as a backdrop at Who concerts featuring *Quadrophenia* material. The group would have played in front of three giant screens, which would have been quite innovative for 1973. It might also have proved useful in bringing to life images from the *Quadrophenia* opera, particularly as much of the audience wouldn't have been familiar with the story when The Who did their first tours, right after the album's release. Filmmaker Peter Neal (soon to direct the 1975 Yes concert movie *Yessongs*) even shot footage of the group in rehearsal for this purpose on August 17.

But the idea didn't come off, in part due to the difficulty of building screens big enough for what was wanted or needed. A report by *Crawdaddy*'s John Swenson at a September rehearsal gives a glimpse of both the potential of the multimedia presentation and the frustrations that led the band to abandon it. "The pre-taped organ part for 'Won't Get Fooled Again' starts, and triple images of each member of the group are juxtaposed slot-machine-style with pictures of cherries, pears, lemons, and bananas," he wrote. "Somebody misses a cue, Townshend winces, shouts 'It's not fucking loud enough!' and gestures exasperation as the tape drones on unaccompanied by the band. The technicians realize their error and wind it back. The break gives everyone time to get more brandy, and after a mild looning session Moon vaults his drum kit, begins to rev up with a solo, Townshend crunching a power lock chord behind as the band jams until the tape comes around again. The screens flash shots of Daltrey flinging the microphone, Entwistle puffing on his French horn, Townshend amid a mighty leap and Moon performing insane facial and bodily contortions, all in time with the music and a visual correlative to what is actually happening onstage. After a few more test runs the audition seems complete, yet nobody is sure, now that they've gone through all the trouble to coordinate the films, whether it's actually a good idea."[16]

"We're not gonna use those films after all," Daltrey told Swenson shortly afterward. "It all seemed like too much of a gimmick to me, and I don't think we need gimmicks to get The Who across anymore. My wife went to see the Stones last week and said they looked like they were trying anything just to get a response. I don't want the group to get caught up in all that stuff."[17]

In hindsight Townshend regretted, if not that exact decision, that the band had not been able to capitalize on multimedia technology in playing *Quadrophenia* in concert. "I think if I'd have had the kind of tours that we have today – computers and computerized instruments, and multimedia computers to develop screened images, and wonderful JumboTron projection equipment to use in concert – that's the way we would have done it back then," he said in the *In The Studio* radio special on *Quadrophenia*. "As it was, we had tape machines. And I had a whole rack of synthesizers, which I'd become expert at, and we tried to incorporate those into our live performances, unsuccessfully."[18]

A big impetus for doing *Quadrophenia* (as with *Tommy* and *Lifehouse/Who's Next*) was to develop material around which a new stage act could be centered, so The Who were taking preparations for touring the album very seriously indeed. The few weeks leading up to the kickoff of the UK leg of the tour were fraught with tension. This was, of course, nothing new for The Who; indeed, in many ways they thrived on it. But looking back, there were signs that for the next few months not all would go as harmoniously as they had hoped.

Firstly, Keith Moon had left his home at the beginning of October, as his marriage fell apart; about a week later, his father died. Moon didn't need much of an excuse to wreak havoc, but he might have been feeling even more wound up than usual when his behavior at the taping of a *Top Of The Pops* performance of '5:15' on October 3 helped get The Who banned from the BBC Club (quickly revoked after the group sent a letter of apology). After the song was inaccurately introduced as their first single in two years, the group sang to a pre-recorded backing track. Pete and Keith indulged in a bit of dispirited-looking guitar-smashing and equipment-hurling at the end, even as the taped music continued onward.

"It augurs well for new Who music, and should usher in a new era in their creative career," *Melody Maker* gushed in its review of '5:15.'[19] "Without a doubt the most dynamic single released by anyone so far this year," *NME* added.[20] Yet when the single was issued a couple of days later, about a month in advance of the LP, it reached only Number 20. In the USA, MCA opted for another track entirely, issuing an edited version of 'Love Reign O'er Me' on 45 at the end of October (rewarded by a measly peak of Number 76) that ended, unlike the LP version, with a sustained synthesizer note instead of a slashing guitar-chord. On the B-side of both singles was the 1970 out-take 'Water,' by now a distant echo of those pre-*Lifehouse* days; maybe it was thought vaguely appropriate, given that several key *Quadrophenia* songs included references to the sea, rain, and the like.

While The Who had been using backing tracks of synthesizers on stage for 'Baba O'Riley' and 'Won't Get Fooled Again,' *Quadrophenia* would require much more in the way of backing tapes to approach replication of the studio arrangements. Four-track backing tapes for that purpose were made in Ronnie Lane's mobile studio on October 11, and perhaps the difficulties in syncing to them helped fray tempers as The Who rehearsed in earnest at Shepperton Studios. Sometime during those rehearsals, things came to a head between Daltrey and Townshend, who hit Roger in the head with a guitar. In the ensuing scuffle, Daltrey – to no one's shock, as he was by far the better man with his fists – knocked Townshend out with a single punch, sending the guitarist to hospital. Although Pete's old filmmaker friend Richard Stanley was filming a promo at the rehearsals, it was never released – unsurprisingly, given the circumstances.

"We played the whole of *Quadrophenia* while the film crew sat on their camera equipment," Daltrey recalled in *MOJO* in 2006. "We'd just finished 'Doctor Jimmy,' and I was really giving it something. I was like, 'Are you going to sit on your fucking equipment? When [are] you going to start fucking filming?' Pete by this time, he'd already drunk at least one bottle of brandy, if not two, and he came over and said, 'Shut the fuck up, they'll film when I tell them to.' He started poking me with his finger, and the roadies jumped on me, because they thought I was going to whack him. But this was my peaceful period, I had no intention of whacking him."[21] In *Q* magazine, Townshend recalled that Daltrey had got his goat by saying "that I'd taken too much control, that I'd done it all single-handedly and that I'd mixed him down in the mix and it didn't sound right and it didn't work and I was so hurt by that that I hit him."[22]

As part of the human comedy that seemed to follow the group around, Who PR man Keith Altham had just picked up a staff member from the group's record label at the airport and driven him to "where they were rehearsing for *Quadrophenia* and actually filming it. As we walked in, we were just in time to see Roger right-hook Pete and knock him out. And the guy turned to me saying, 'Shit, is it always like this?' I said, 'No, today's a good day. We'll now retire to the bar and wait for the judges to count their votes.' The result was that Townshend was taken off in an ambulance to hospital with Roger holding his hand and saying, 'You know I love you, Pete, I didn't mean it.' I don't think it *felt* like he loved him to [Pete]. But Pete provoked it. He lost his temper, swung his guitar at him. And you don't do that kind of thing to Daltrey and expect there not to be retaliation. That was quite funny. First time [the guy from the label] ever met the group – welcome to the wonderful world of The Who! Round one!"[29]

Townshend wasn't seriously hurt, which was fortunate as the album's release was imminent, along with the first show at which *Quadrophenia* material would be featured. There would be no *Quadrophenia* tour, exactly; The Who would play a couple of weeks of shows in the UK starting on October 28, go to North America for about three weeks soon after that, play a few London shows shortly before Christmas, and then some French concerts in February. These were, however, the only shows The Who would play prior to 1996 at which nine or more songs from *Quadrophenia* formed the centerpiece of their set, preceded and followed by more familiar pre-1973 songs.

The Who, and to some extent audiences and the media, felt the shows were mixed and troubled affairs, especially with the buildup *Quadrophenia* was getting as the group's first post-*Tommy* opera. From whatever direction it came, the criticism usually boiled down to two targets: the snafus in coordinating the backing tapes into the arrangements, and the crowds' unfamiliarity with the songs, which required long-winded onstage introductions and explanations that some felt tedious and unnecessary.

In retrospect, the dissatisfaction seems at least a little overblown. The Who had used backing tapes on stage since 1971 for songs in which synthesizers were prominent, albeit in a much more limited fashion. They had rehearsed the material for *Quadrophenia* that would require them. Judging by the Daltrey-Townshend punch-up, those might not have gone so smoothly. But then, what did go smoothly in Wholand? In addition, *Tommy* had been played on stage even a bit prior to its release, and toured in the USA for a few weeks right after it came out. Yet *Tommy* songs seem to have been greeted by universal enthusiasm even by audiences who had yet to hear the record, as were *Who's Next* songs played in advance of that album's release.

Quadrophenia reached the shops some days later than expected, especially in the UK, where it was issued on November 2 (almost a week after its US release date of October 27). The 1973 oil crisis had just started, and the delay has been blamed on a lack of raw material with which to press the vinyl – of which there was a lot, as this was a double LP with big advance orders, especially since it was being ballyhooed as a *Tommy* follow-up of sorts.

A *Melody Maker* report in late October confirmed "the record industry is rapidly reaching a crisis point because the world shortage of raw materials is gravely affecting supplies [of] vinyl."[24] The Who probably didn't help matters by vocally complaining about the delay on stage during the first few shows. Townshend even stated that "the Japanese have bought up all the plastic" at the group's November 1 concert in Manchester.

Just as *Tommy* had not actually been played in its entirety during the 1969-70 shows – a few songs were always left out – *Quadrophenia* was never played from beginning to end in concert while Keith Moon was in the band. The plan had been to play most of it, but that was modified right after the first show at Stoke-on-Trent on October 28. 'The Dirty Jobs,' 'Is It In My Head?' and 'I've Had Enough' – songs forming the bulk of side two, in fact – were eliminated.

By the next evening in Wolverhampton, just 12 of the 17 songs were left. Frustration might have already been catching up with Townshend, who complained from the stage that the album "should have been in the bleedin' shops by now," adding that the band weren't going to play the opera in its entirety since "if we played it all, you'd fucking fall asleep." The omission of the instrumental 'Quadrophenia' might have been understandable, but the absence of 'Cut My Hair' from any 1973-74 performance is less so, as it's perhaps the most important song for setting the opera's plot in motion. Dropping 'The Dirty Jobs,' oddly, didn't keep Daltrey from explaining its place in the opera anyway at their November 12 concert, only adding to the awkwardness.

"There is no way you can determine what will work on stage in the studio," Moon pointed out to Roy Carr, in an interview featured on a CD included with Carr's book *A Talk On The Wild Side*. "Because what works in the studio doesn't work theatrically ... you really do have to approach the studio and the stage with two totally different frames of mind. When we first started doing *Quadrophenia* ... we were just finding ourselves, and what numbers should be in, and what numbers shouldn't. The only way we could ever do that is by being onstage and playing. From *Quadrophenia*, there was a lot of stuff that worked on record, but didn't work [in concert]."[25]

Fortunately for Moon, one song that was often rapturously received, if only for the opportunity to hear him sing, was 'Bell Boy.' His own rapture was probably diminished, however, by the cumbersome setup the song demanded. To keep in time with the backing tapes, he had to wear headphones to play along with a click track, which came complete with his own spoken commentary: "middle eight coming up – 1, 2, 3, 4," for example. When the time came for his vocal, he had to take the mic from Daltrey at more or less precisely the right moment, like a relay runner being handed a baton, simultaneously take off his headphones, so he could hear himself sing, and then hand the mic back to Roger when his bit was finished. As a consequence, he couldn't keep drumming as he sang. In surviving footage of some concerts, he sometimes seems in danger of accidentally strangling himself when he takes his headphones on and off in the midst of the operation.

"The problem was trying to satisfy everyone, and what material to leave out," says Irish Jack Lyons, who would travel with the band for their notorious show in Newcastle on November 5. "After a few more shows Pete discovered he was actually making something like 20 guitar changes, as a lot of the songs required capos. Then the heat from the stage lights began to bend the strings out of tune. Gradually the *Quadrophenia* setlist got honed down to an acceptable set of numbers that sufficiently told the story."[26]

Although The Who were probably thought of as about the most confident band on the planet, especially on stage, they might have been more anxious about their status in the fickle rock world than people realized. "I remember PT was a little nervous, much to do with the time in their career," says Humphrey Ocean, bassist in Kilburn & The High Roads, the pub-rock band (with future star Ian Dury on lead vocals) who supported The Who on the October-November UK shows. "They had been going for a good ten years, so were not the young scene any more. Of course this may seem absurd in hindsight. But The Who in 1973 were at an in-between stage. I remember our drummer David Newton Rohoman saying to Keith Moon early on in the tour, 'Oh, it's easy for you guys, you just go out there and they love you.' Keith said, 'Don't you believe it. The higher you are the further you fall.'"[27]

Partly as a result of their frustration over the album not being in the shops, and partly to fill up the time caused by logistical adjustments (including Townshend switching between guitars), Roger and Pete indulged in some of the most expository introductions heard at any rock concert. For the most part they were merely trying to explain the plot. But at times they verged on the comical, like the contestants in the Monty Python sketch who had to summarize Marcel Proust's *Remembrance Of Things Past* in 15 seconds. In the rock press, Townshend was often given several paragraphs to articulate subtle concepts. That wouldn't do in front of several thousand fans, and for the November 1 show in Manchester, his summary of the opera was reduced to the following: "This is an album called *Quadrophenia*, and it's a story about a kid who goes down to the rock in the middle of the sea and looks back on a couple of weeks when he leaves home and a few backwardly nostalgic glimpses."

The problems with syncing up with synthesizers were especially vexing. "In those days, synthesizers were in their very very early stages," Daltrey later observed. "And the technology was nonexistent to kind of carry that thing around to put it on stage. We experimented working with quadraphonic sound, which was interesting but not very successful. To work with tapes on the *Quadrophenia* sections really did limit the show. Because once the tape had started, you were stuck into playing within that envelope. And previous to that, The Who had always been very very much a freeform band. Almost jazzy, in a way. I mean, things would literally grow block by block. But once you started that tape, you had to play with that tape until it finished. And then you could do what you liked, if you still had any brain left. It was a really big problem. And it was a big problem for me, because from where I stood on the stage, I could never hear the damn tape anyway. Even Keith had to wear earphones. It was a nightmare."[28] Back in 1975, he was more succinct, telling *Rolling Stone*'s Barbara Charone, "We got drowned in synthesizers in *Quadrophenia*. That was my main argument; you'll never get The Who to play like machines. We're not robots."[29]

John Entwistle also found it difficult. "We had to play in time to the prerecorded tapes, and we found that if we couldn't hear them, even though Keith had the backing track on his earphones and could continue drumming in time, the rest of us would be completely lost," he recalled in *Headliners: The Who*. "It turned out that we weren't able to hear the tapes most of the time, and we started to play sloppily and got bored and we noticed the kids were getting bored too. It's one thing to play to the sort of metronomic backing track of 'Won't Get Fooled Again,' but with the complex time changes of *Quadrophenia* we got crossed up too easily. We had to play it perfectly to make it work each time, we had to play it with an incredible amount of energy or it sounded bad, whereas our normal act is set up with songs that even if we play badly will still sound good, so we can afford to have a bad night and still get away with it."[30]

A piano player such as Nicky Hopkins (who had sometimes guested on stage with The Rolling Stones and Jefferson Airplane) or Chris Stainton might have helped fill out the arrangements so that they more closely resembled the studio tracks. In fact, they did consider asking Stainton along, but they decided to stick to their regular foursome, as they'd always done on stage. "Tradition, really," is how Townshend rationalized the decision in *Sounds*, "and also the feeling – a point put by Roger – things do tend to escalate. You get used to having a pianist around, you lean on him a bit and then maybe you get someone else in and you end up like the Stones, with a whole brass band."[31] While neither Stainton nor, possibly, anyone else could have played the synthesizer parts live, his re-creation of the piano parts on the three *Quadrophenia* tracks on which he played, as well as others (such as 'Cut My Hair') on which piano figured prominently, might have been welcome additions.

Townshend would describe the October 28 show as "bloody horrible" from the stage the following night at Wolverhampton. Yet that Wolverhampton show, and indeed most of the concerts over the next few months, would get pretty positive reviews. It could have been a combination of a forgiving press overjoyed to see The Who back on stage doing their new opera, or the shows not actually having been as bad as legend would have it. But *Melody Maker*'s Chris Welch reported that The Who themselves "seemed well pleased with their efforts" at Wolverhampton, and his praise for the *Quadrophenia* songs was enthusiastic if a bit guarded. "Musically, it wasn't as effective as the record, but when it gets worked in it should prove fairly phenomenal. [The concert] could have benefited by trimming it down."[32] In *Disc*, Ray Fox-Cumming thought that "despite odd moments of uncertainty, it was clear that by the end of the tour the *Quadrophenia* 'suite' will really be sizzling," although he also noted "PA problems which swallowed up much of the lyrics," making Moon's vocal cameo on 'Bell Boy' "almost totally inaudible."[33]

Rolling Stone also managed to combine praise with a cautionary note. "The Who put on one of the greatest revivalist shows I've ever seen," Robin Denselow wrote. "They managed to mix the excellent new material from *Quadrophenia* with the nostalgia of old Who hits, and present even the new concept songs as if they were bashing them out in the Marquee Club back in the mid 60s." But "with only a few words of explanation from Townshend to go by, and the hall's acoustics distorting some of the vocals, it was doubtful if many of the audience understood what it was all about."[34]

Another positive review came from *NME*'s Roy Carr. "I witnessed quite a number of shows," he recalls today, "and I can't recall there being any noticeable technical problems. But in the early stages I know that there were recurring hassles with regard to the synchronization of Townshend's pre-recorded tapes and what happened on stage. This greatly annoyed Daltrey on a number of occasions. However, as the public was still somewhat unfamiliar with *Quad*, such problems may have slipped by relatively unnoticed by the majority of observers."[35]

The Who's unhappiness with the backing tapes in particular, and possibly some other things not working out to their expectations, exploded at their show in Newcastle's Odeon Cinema on November 5. Nearly an hour into the show, after the tapes for '5:15' started up 15 seconds too late, Pete Townshend began tearing the soundboard to pieces. The pre-recorded tapes for their stage performances of songs from *Quadrophenia* were destroyed, with Townshend assaulting and berating long-suffering soundman Bobby Pridden for good measure, before smashing his guitar on stage to crown a tantrum that left even the rest of The Who dumbfounded. At that moment, Pete later told *Penthouse*, he felt "that I would never, ever walk on the stage again."[36]

"Machines go wrong, and when they go wrong, it doesn't matter whose fault it is," Pridden said in the *Classic Albums* documentary on *Who's Next*. "Everyone looks at the person that's next to it. Even still to this day, when we do that on the road, my heart goes into my mouth when I hit that button. Like before I'm looking at it thinking, 'Are you going to work?' I don't trust machines. They go wrong."[37]

"It was a ridiculous display of unwarranted violence," Steve Hughes wrote in the *Newcastle Evening Chronicle*. "Stage hands rushed to disconnect electric amplifiers and Townshend's electric guitar after he swiped it into the stage floor. Tempers flared after drummer Keith Moon had trouble with headphones. He let the drumsticks fly as the sound engineers battled to fix them. Then Townshend intervened, yelling at the engineers behind control panels on the side of the stage. He ripped out backing tapes and heaved over equipment into the side curtains. The three other members of the band ... just stared."

After a gap of between 10 and 25 minutes (depending upon which account you read), the group reassembled, abandoning the *Quadrophenia* songs to finish the set with some older tunes. At the end, Hughes wrote, "Townshend hurled his guitar against the upstanding microphone and smashed it into a score of pieces by banging it against the stage floor. He then turned on a row of piled amplifiers at the back of the stage and hurled a top one to the floor. Moon waded through his range of drums, spilling them across the stage and Daltrey took a last kick at his microphone."[38]

According to Keith Altham, "Something went wrong with the sound that night and Pete went into a massive tizzy and wasn't ever gonna talk to anybody again, and was never doing another interview. It was the technology that kind of let it down, and he was so hurt by it, really. Because he felt humiliated. It wasn't that bad to the rest of us. But they were perfectionists in that respect. They wanted everything to be exactly so. They would simply not be prepared to settle for second best. The fights backstage were all about that."[39]

Townshend quickly engaged in damage control, apologizing to Pridden and appearing with Moon on the local television show *Look North* to smooth over the situation. For all its hallowed place in Who lore, the aborted concert hardly ruined the tour, as shows at Newcastle the next two nights passed without incident. Pete's sensitivity to imperfections extended to venues as well as equipment, as he took the exceptional – for rock stars in general, but not for him – step of apologizing in *Melody Maker* to fans whose view was obstructed at three shows at London's Lyceum a few days later.

Those Lyceum shows got a wary assessment by Michael Watts in *Melody Maker*. "What actually transpired was that Pete Townshend's new generation of the 60s mod ethos was less successful than The Who's replay of their old mod hits," he wrote. "To a large extent, of course, our ears have not yet accustomed themselves to the unfamiliarity of it all. Besides, The Who haven't quite worked out their sound logistics on it; a huge fist of sound crashes about one's ears but it's often hard to divine the thread of the story – a factor that Townshend and Daltrey are obviously aware of, since both of them run a commentary on the numbers throughout (a little embarrassedly, I thought, as if worried they were going over the heads of the kids)."[40]

In Watts's estimation, the real highlights were not the songs from *Quadrophenia*, but time-honored crowd-pleasers like 'Won't Get Fooled

Again,' 'Magic Bus,' and the *Tommy* finale. Townshend had written *Quadrophenia* partly to close the door on their past so they could move on to newer horizons. But that past was so glorious that it was getting in the way of appreciation of *Quadrophenia* itself – a problem no doubt on The Who's mind as they prepared, a week after the final Lyceum show, to take the new set to the United States.

Quadrophenia is sometimes regarded as an album that underperformed with both the public and the critics. Chart positions and reviews, however, demonstrate that such a view is unjustified, unless the album is judged solely against the ever-present specter of *Tommy*. The record went to Number Two in both the UK and the USA, which was higher than either *Tommy* or *Who's Next* had managed in the States. This was accomplished without the benefit of a hit single; 'Pinball Wizard' had given *Tommy* at least a bit of a push. The album did lack *Tommy*'s longevity, staying in the American Top 40 for 18 weeks (where *Tommy* had perched for almost a year) and in the British LP charts for 13 weeks. It's likely, too, that most of its sales were guaranteed even before release; it went gold (500,000 copies) just two days after its US release, but didn't break the RIAA-certified million mark until 1993.

Nonetheless, it was quickly apparent that *Quadrophenia* wouldn't be a massive success, at least if you use *Tommy* as the yardstick. "Basically, the album was a failure," says Richard Barnes. "The album was a commercial success, but it was one of those albums where people would say 'Yeah, I've got *Quadrophenia*,' [but] they'd never fucking play it. They'd rather listen to [Fleetwood Mac's] *Rumours* or something like that. *Tommy* was accessible. *Tommy*'s like modern Gilbert & Sullivan. It's got light and shade, and it's got little ditties in it. This is why I used to call [Pete] Tannhäuser" – in mock homage to the Richard Wagner opera of the same name – "because I thought [*Quadrophenia*] was so Wagnerian and heavy. [Even when] he sent me a few demos, I thought, 'Fuck me, it's all very Wagnerian.'"[41]

With critics, however, it was a somewhat different matter, even if they greeted the album with rather more rabid enthusiasm than Joe Public. Two weeks before *Quadrophenia* was even released in the UK, *Melody Maker* stalwart Chris Welch anointed it "better than *Tommy*," hailing it as "more than an LP – a battle cry, and a hammer of heartbeats. For this is a masterpiece –

The Who at their greatest yet, sap flowing from the roots of their creation. In the way that *Tommy* was unreal, an acid trip and finally a monster, *Quadrophenia*, although it deals in aggression, frustration and sorrows, is so real, you can almost taste the HP sauce and smell the fag ash."[42]

Journalists for British music weeklies who'd been in The Who's camp for years could be expected to indulge in a little hyperbole, but they weren't the only ones with high praise for the record. But as John Peel wrote in the less street-level BBC magazine *The Listener* just a few weeks later, "Already all manner of boring people have whipped out pages of deep analytical stuff about the LP in question, *Quadrophenia*, and most of them have used the word 'masterpiece' pretty generously." As a longtime radio show personality, Peel himself was possibly the most beloved figure in the British rock media, and joined the chorus in his nearly full-page review in *The Listener*, finding it "as much an advance over *Tommy* as *Tommy* was over the earlier (and much briefer) 'A Quick One, While He's Away.' It's not just the use of synthesizers and sound effects, although their use is telling and tasteful, nor is it the wider dynamic range of the music: what counts is the wider emotional range. ... There's so much energy thundering out of my speakers as I write that it's difficult for me to keep my seat and plod on to some sort of fitting conclusion."[43]

In the USA, any new album by The Who was guaranteed to receive major coverage in the music press, American rock critics having avidly championed the group since long before they were stars. Add to that a record that examined the history of both The Who and a major youth cultural movement the group reflected and helped spawn, and it's possible more writers were climbing over themselves to review the album than any previous release by anyone. To dig up American reviews of *Quadrophenia* is to be confronted by the names of the most heavyweight rock writers of the era. While they too had good words for the record, they were also inclined to zero in on its imperfections, perhaps in part because of the greater cultural distance between them and the mod phenomenon.

According to *Rolling Stone*'s Lenny Kaye, then a year or two away from rising to prominence as guitarist in the Patti Smith Group, "*Quadrophenia* is The Who at their most symmetrical, their most cinematic, ultimately their most maddening. They have put together a beautifully performed and magnificently recorded essay of a British youth mentality in which they

259

played no little part, lushly endowed with black and white visuals and a heavy sensibility of the wet-suffused air of 1965." Yet Kaye also was a bit dissatisfied with its cumulative impact, viewing the record as a series of "effective moments" that ultimately fell "short of the mark."[44]

Lester Bangs, the most colorful rock journalist of his generation, weighed in with a similarly ambivalent evaluation in *Stereo Review*. He thought *Quadrophenia* was "a far more personal statement" than *Tommy*, "a handy gimmick for Townshend to make another Big Statement and simultaneously cash in on the burgeoning quadraphonic fad/revolution. But his literary ambitions are much more satisfactorily realized here than in the earlier extravaganza. ... It has as much excitement as anyone else in the rock establishment is providing right now, but, as with *Tommy*, you've got to question seriously whether it was an overdose of inspiration or ego that convinced them they needed two whole discs to get it across. All the songs inevitably run together, and there's a cut-to-cut and side-by-side sameness that vitiates the full impact." Still, he praised it as "with minor cavils, a fine, involving, manageably pretentious piece of rock artistry."[45]

As founder of *Bomp!*, the first American magazine to specialize in serious rock history, Greg Shaw was bound to view *Quadrophenia* as an album worthy of investigation. So he did, with a marathon piece in *Phonograph Record Magazine* that was as much a history of The Who as it was a review of *Quadrophenia*. When he did get around to discussing the album, he was not disappointed. "*Quadrophenia* is at once nothing like *Tommy* and everything *Tommy* should have been," he wrote. "Its theme is also a young man's quest for meaning, and it is also a fully developed opera, with movements, themes, and roles assigned to each member." Overoptimistically, given his American readership, Shaw added, "There's nothing abstruse or remotely arcane about it. Everyone will understand it, on some level."

Yet Shaw wasn't blind to picking out deficiencies, especially as "reading the lyrics gives rise to anticipations of an album full of uncompromising mid-60s rock'n'roll. The songs are full of all the right references and attitudes regarding clothes, pills, social relationships, and all they would need to have been right at home on *The Who Sings My Generation*. Musically, however, there's no mistaking that this is the modern Who. They rock hard enough, when required, and there are some nice riffs. But there is also a profusion of symphonic and electronic sound effects, and a lack of really blazing dynamism in even the most driving segments." Presciently, he also expressed hope it would be made into a film, which he felt "couldn't fail to be great."[46]

Canada might have been considered a secondary market compared to the USA and UK, but *Quadrophenia* did well there, too – peaking, in fact, at the exact same Number Two position as it had in the American and British charts. The record also had a lengthy review in the Canadian rock magazine *Beetle* (distributed throughout North America). Had he seen it, Townshend would have been gratified that Bob Dunne grasped how the record "paints an all-too-clear portrait of the hopes and aspirations of an entire generation whose unity has since been dissipated by disillusionment, boring maturity, the evolution of we old codgers' fatalistic attitude. The common dreams and ideals which transcended political and linguistic barriers, which we look upon now with cold, disassociated, jaundiced eyes, are all present on *Quadrophenia*, without ever having to be spelled out. The resurrection of the memory is painful for all who dared to dream that the youth of the 60s could put an end to pollution, stop a war, end racial hatred or replace the profit motive with a higher, more spiritual priority. On this level, *Quadrophenia* succeeds as no other album has."

On another level, Dunne found it a bit wanting. "Though *Quadrophenia* is sketchy in places, though the various conflicting characters within Jimmy's fatigued mind are a bit unclear, and though one has every right to expect something a little more musically gratifying from a band of The Who's caliber after a two-year silence, *Quadrophenia* is a good album," he concluded. "Certainly not 'the best rock album ever recorded,' as MCA has been stating, but a must for all ardent Who followers or anyone else with aspirations of intelligence."[47]

Critiques of *Quadrophenia* weren't confined to the rock press. Hubert Saal's *Newsweek* review opened with the portentous claim that "in the history of rock music, three milestones spring to mind: *Jesus Christ Superstar* [yes, in the early 70s some people did consider that a milestone], The Beatles' *Sgt Pepper*, The Who's *Tommy*. Now there is a fourth. Nothing as ambitious has been attempted as The Who's newest two-record album. ... *Quadrophenia* is a dour look at the world. To use Townshend's phrase, this is a work about spiritual desperation – Jimmy's, Townshend's, The Who's, ours. Post-Beatles rock has tended to avoid the big work. The Who remind us that music can still embrace big themes and produce big excitement."[48]

Despite Saal's huzzahs, *Quadrophenia* would *not* attain the same stature as *Tommy*. As Bob Dunne wrote in *Beetle*, "The arrival of *Quadrophenia* has gone relatively unnoticed. No mass acceptance of a thrillingly new concept. ... No fireworks."[49] In part that was because there was no way any rock opera, no matter how brilliant, could have the same cultural impact as *Tommy*, the first such work to receive wide attention. But in part it was down to a more gauche reality. For all its merits, *Quadrophenia* simply didn't have as many memorable hooks. As rock critic Chris Charlesworth puts it, *Tommy* "was more accessible. It was easier to assimilate. And *Tommy* somehow had repetitive [themes] which came in and out throughout the whole piece, to a greater extent than *Quadrophenia* did."[50]

A couple of prominent American rock critics also picked up on another unavoidable truth: that Jimmy's "quadrophenia," and how his four personalities reflected four different aspects of The Who, was not exactly seamlessly blended into the flow of the opera, or even particularly obvious. "*Quadrophenia* has no plot at all, or one that is hidden well enough to qualify the piece for the appellation 'plotless,'" felt *High Fidelity*'s Mike Jahn, who had been one of the first critics granted space in the *New York Times* to write about rock, and wrote one of the first rock history books, 1973's *Rock*. "Jimmy is professedly an amalgam of the personalities of the four members of The Who, and if you think being four people is tough on Jimmy, think of what it means for the audience. It's impossible to follow, so one is advised to give up trying and enjoy the music ... If it were accompanied by words one could follow, *Quadrophenia* would be a masterpiece like its predecessor. As it is, this newest recording is a fashionably obscure substitute."[51]

In his *Creem* review, Dave Marsh, one of The Who's biggest advocates in the rock press, also found the opera downright hard to follow. "What form of madness is this?" he asked. "It might be a rock opera. If it is, it might be about the mod era, and it might tell you something about how Townshend feels about how he and The Who fit into that. It might be a lot of things. Unfortunately, not very many of them seem to matter. And not very many of those seem to be very well presented. ... Part of the problem, without question, is that Townshend gets so immersed in his projects for so long that you need a libretto, a translation and a full-length, personal interview to understand what he's on about this time. None are here, unless I lost the lyric sheet" (not an easy task, it should be pointed out, since the lyrics were printed in the LP-sized 44-page booklet). Marsh went on to summarize *Quadrophenia* as "four parts in search of a whole. I think they could find the whole, but it might require going through their own record collections to do it."[52]

Marsh articulated his dissatisfaction with the four-sided personality trait of the main character nearly a decade later in his biography, *Before I Get Old: The Story Of The Who*, noting that the assignments of different personalities to different members of the band "become lost in the details of the action, and they are never developed lyrically. At the end, the singer is not an integrated personality – he's the spiritually desperate seeker (Pete). ... Indeed, it isn't at all clear why Jimmy is termed quadrophenic or even schizophrenic. He has one consistent personality, even though he exhibits fury, sorrow and self-pity. ... Townshend not only doesn't pursue these themes, he never really establishes them in the first place."[53]

Back in early 1974, perhaps taking a page out of Townshend's own book, Marsh flip-flopped his original opinion just two months later. "*Quadrophenia* is the least accessible part of [their] stage show, but it is also the most intelligent, and the most important record of last year," he declared in a *Creem* article titled 'The Who: *Quadrophenia* Reconsidered.' "*Quadrophenia* is alive, and it is deep; it grows on you, which is why it takes three months to be able to hear it."[54] That might be one of the most crucial differences between The Who's two completed rock operas: *Tommy* can be absorbed immediately, while *Quadrophenia* needs time to appreciate. But in late 1973, The Who didn't give their audience three months to listen to *Quadrophenia* before they played it live. Instead, they were heading to the United States just three weeks after its release.

Although it would later be said that The Who were presenting *Quadrophenia* to American concert audiences before listeners had a chance to assimilate it, by most standards the visit was very well timed. The record had been out for three weeks and was zooming up the charts by the time the tour started in San Francisco on November 20, with up-and-coming southern rockers Lynyrd Skynyrd as support. Accompanying the band was a 12-man sound and lighting crew, hauling about 20 tons of equipment in three 45-foot vans. The itinerary, while not exhaustive, would take in most of North America's biggest markets (with the conspicuous exception of New York), including Los Angeles,

Dallas, Atlanta, St Louis, Chicago, Detroit, Montreal, Boston, Philadelphia, and Washington DC. Yet it could have hardly gotten off to a worse start.

Accounts differ as to whether he was spiked or not, but somehow Keith Moon had ingested animal tranquilizers before the show at San Francisco's Cow Palace. He made it through most of the concert, including the entire *Quadrophenia* section, without much seeming amiss. Then, around four minutes into 'Won't Get Fooled Again,' he passed out.

What happened next has been reported in several different ways. But the existence of a two-camera, black-and-white videotape of the concert, made for concert promoter Bill Graham's archives, with crude but listenable sound, makes for an objective record of what actually unfolded.

The Moon-less Who gamely soldiered on to the end of 'Won't Get Fooled Again,' with Townshend then asking the audience to bear with the band "for about three weeks" while they revived their drummer by punching him in the stomach and giving him an enema. Keith was out cold, Pete admitted, probably due to having eaten something he shouldn't have. Having made as light of the situation as he could, Townshend then struck an uncommonly serious note: "The horrible truth is that without him, we're not a group."

After some delay, it was back to laughs as Townshend and Daltrey mock-dragged a revived Moon to his drum kit. The levity was shortlived, however, as Keith collapsed for good near the end of 'Magic Bus' and was carried off stage by drum technician Mick Double and Grace Slick's future husband, Skip Johnson, who was working at the concert. Without pause, the remaining trio went into some shapeless hard-rock improvisation, perhaps hoping Moon would magically come to life again, before presenting a drumless 'See Me, Feel Me' that was quite moving under the circumstances.

As The Who had actually gotten through most of their set, they could have been forgiven for calling it a night at this point. Something possessed Townshend, however, to ask if anyone in the audience could play the drums "somebody good." That was the cue for 19-year-old Scott Halpin, who'd paid $20 to scalp a concert ticket, to volunteer his services – or, as he'd later remember it, get pushed forward by a friend to let Bill Graham know he was up for the job. Actually he hadn't played in a band since junior high and hadn't played at all for a year, but he was willing and available. After a run through the Howlin' Wolf blues standards 'Smokestack Lightning' and 'Spoonful,' to find his feet, the show concluded with 'Naked Eye.' Halpin did a pretty good job considering the circumstances, and although 'Naked Eye' hadn't even been issued on record at this point, he'd claim in *Rolling Stone* that he was already familiar with all three tunes.

"He asked me if I was a drummer and if I was any good," Halpin told the magazine. "I said I was good. I didn't have time to think about it and get nervous. Most of the stuff was four-four. There was only one six-eight. But it was easy to follow because Pete signals when to end it by jumping up and down. I really admire their stamina. I only played three numbers, and I was dead." Daltrey, not one to suffer fools, praised Halpin's drumming in *Rolling Stone*, while Townshend explained why the show went on. "When Keith collapsed, it was a shame," he said. "I had just been getting warmed up at that point. I'd felt closed up, like I couldn't let anything out. I didn't want to stop playing. It was also a shame for all the people who'd waited in line for eight hours."[55]

Mostly due to Moon's incapacitation, the Cow Palace show is sometimes seen as a disaster. Certainly, Phil Elwood of the *San Francisco Examiner* thought so. "There wasn't much joy among Whofreaks last night in the Cow Palace," he wrote. "The mighty Who, usually the most consistently impressive and musically overwhelming rock group on the globe, came close to striking out. ... *Quadrophenia*, with synthesizers, pre-taped effects and a complex theme-and-storyline, wasn't going over well and the sound system, alas, was badly unbalanced."

Elwood made it clear, incidentally, that he did know what *Quadrophenia* was about. "The overall effect of *Quadrophenia* is one of murkiness in musical lines and obscurity in lyric theme," he continued. "On record, especially with headphones after repeated playing, it emerges as a towering rock composition. But in truncated concert form it didn't seem worth an hour's time. Especially since we didn't get much of anything else in last night's unfortunate presentation."[56] Looking back from 2009, David Teborek, a fan who was in attendance, tends to agree. "It was boring," he says. "It was an unprofessional show. Townshend didn't really do much in the way of leads, just strummed. I was so disappointed, I swore I was never going to listen to them again. I was about ready to throw every album out."[57]

Rock journalist Jeff Tamarkin, who'd seen The Who numerous times since their first US visit in 1967, has a somewhat different impression. "I think it was a challenge for any band to sound good in that place," he points out. "But they were making the most of it. Maybe somebody that had seen

The Who 100 times or had seen the rest of the tour or something might think they were a little off. But I think to the average fan like myself who'd seen 'em maybe 10 or 12 times, it was just another great Who show."[58] Going by the Graham footage, the band did play reasonably well, with less of the between-song commentary than one would expect, Townshend appearing a bit abashed about the hokiness of introducing the swish of quadraphonic sea noise preceding 'Doctor Jimmy.'

As for Moon, Townshend told *Musician* in 1989, "He was in a wheelchair for two days. I have a Super-8 film of when we brought him off the plane in a wheelchair. The doctor from the Free Clinic [said], 'His heart is only beating once every 30 seconds! He's clinically dead!' And Keith says [mumbles], 'Fuck off.'"[59] Moon recovered in time for the two shows a couple of days later in Los Angeles, although according to MCA publicist Will Yaryan, Keith – perhaps reeling more from his separation with his wife than he was willing to admit – "was mostly in a daze during the tour. He carried around a blow-up porno doll and even, I think, got it a seat on the plane."[60]

Judging by the almost universally laudatory reviews for the tour from this point onward, you wouldn't suspect the group to be suffering from any notable problems or gnawing self-doubt. According to *Billboard*'s review of one of the shows, in front of nearly 20,000 in LA, "Almost everything worked to perfection, from the excellently mixed repertoire to the synchronization of background tapes with live music, for a near flawless performance ... they simply sing and play some of the best rock'n'roll."[61]

In his *Phonograph Record* review of the show (inaccurately labeled by the publication as a review of their November 28 concert in St Louis), future *USA Today* music editor Ken Barnes even singled out the *Quadrophenia* portion for special praise. It was, he wrote, "stunning. The concert rendition supplied all the raucous power seemingly latent in the storyline, and the added dimension invested the monolithic *Quad* with the true rock'n'roll excitement missing in large part from the album. The Who, especially Townshend, seemed genuinely enthusiastic playing the new material ... and it showed in a galvanizing performance. Inevitably the remainder of the concert was a trifle anticlimactic."[62]

Yet to some observers, something seemed not to measure up to the highest standards The Who had set for themselves. Even Barnes today admits that, "keeping in mind that The Who were my favorite live (and often, although not by then, recorded) band, my guess is that I was probably trying to put a good face (no mod pun intended) on the whole experience. I probably hadn't seen them for a while, got caught up in the anticipation, loved the idea of *Quadrophenia* (if not the execution so much), and put a more positive spin on the whole thing than it deserved.

"I can't imagine I would have thought the non-*Quad* material to be 'anticlimactic,' unless they were really going through the motions and most of it was overexposed *Who's Next/Tommy* stuff, instead of what I always considered the true gems, the stuff from the first three albums, approximately. And I probably thought the *Quad* stuff was more exciting live than on record, with the visual element added and the band's (or Townshend's, anyway) enthusiasm for the project. So, no, I wouldn't be confident in bucking the notion that the tour was sub-par. On a Who level, it probably was sub-par."[63]

Chris Charlesworth, who reviewed the LA shows for *Melody Maker*, remembers "thinking to myself that the show wasn't running as fluently as Who shows had done in the *Who's Next* period or the *Tommy* period that preceded it. I think it was quite a lot for the audiences to digest as well. *Quadrophenia* had only just come out, and it was well over 60 minutes' worth of brand-new music all played in one sweep. It was hard going for them to sort of ingest all that new stuff at one go, and they probably far rather [would] have heard the stuff they were familiar with, which The Who weren't prepared to play any more. Roger wanted to try and explain the storyline between numbers, and Americans didn't have a clue what mods were. Pete just wanted to get on with it. So there was an onstage tension between the two of them, which didn't help."[64]

Some differences on this matter were evident when *Rolling Stone*'s Charles Perry and Andrew Bailey interviewed Townshend and Daltrey at different points in the tour. "We've been getting differing audiences – differing like the reviews of *Quadrophenia*," Pete admitted. "Some don't respond to it. It doesn't have a resolved theme, a logical conclusion, and it's tough to expect an audience to go away ... unsatiated."[65] Daltrey, it was reported, had the idea in Los Angeles to have spoken transitions between the songs, although at least some had been used in all of their fall shows. "It helps people follow the new material," he maintained. "In a couple of months when everybody knows the album, we wouldn't have to explain."[66]

"Roger and I have different ideas about *Quadrophenia* ... we get different things out of it," Towshend countered. "I think the storyline isn't so complicated it bears much explaining. A kid sits on a rock and remembers the things that have happened in the last few days. I think if you explain the storyline too much it demeans all the other things in the music, makes it too *Tanglewood Tales*. The story, after all, is just a peg to hang ideas on. When Roger gets too literal about the story, I have to cut in and make it lighter."[67] This didn't stop him from scolding the Detroit audience: "I don't like talking when other people are shouting. I did enough of that in Chicago." Entwistle, as usual, didn't waste words when it came to voicing his opinion; according to *Rolling Stone*, he interrupted a two-minute Daltrey introduction in Chicago by stepping to the mic and uttering, "Fuck it."[68]

Even when Pete made game attempts at between-song explanations, he sometimes left the audience more confused. Take his introduction to 'I'm One' at the second Los Angeles concert: "I don't know if you ever get the feeling that maybe there's always somebody else that's a little bit better looking than you, a little bit better dressed than you, a little bit smarter than you, a little bit more up to the minute than you, a little bit tougher. ... Well, this song's about the feeling that it doesn't matter what shape you are, or small you are, or out of date you are, or how significant one is – only royalty ever say 'one.'" Perhaps sensing he was losing the room, he concluded, "You're still ... all right."

"Roger thought that *Quadrophenia* wouldn't stand up unless you explained the story," Townshend told Dave Schulps of *Trouser Press* in 1978. "It was done sincerely, but I found it embarrassing and I think it showed, so I was glad when we dropped it. I couldn't really work out what must be going on in the audience's mind when they were being told, 'There's this kid and he's just like you and me...' and then the music began; and then, 'Then this kid he...' The whole thing was a disaster. Roger ended up hating *Quadrophenia* – probably because it had bitten back."[69]

The Who were finding it hard not only to escape the shadow of *Tommy*, but also to shake off their image as rock's baddest boys. The tour got its biggest publicity not for an especially thrilling presentation of *Quadrophenia*, but for the trashing of a suite at the Bonaventure Hotel in Montreal on December 2. "I got suites in each hotel and coordinated press passes and a few interviews with writers, and I held receptions after the shows for record retailers and other important people," Will Yaryan recalls. "After the party in Montreal, Moon, Townshend, and [Bill] Curbishley [who had become involved in The Who's management] hung out and the two crazies began telling stories about previous misdeeds, illustrating them by destroying a painting, splashing the wall with ketchup, and throwing a TV and coffee table out the double-paned (it was winter) window. This was in a penthouse suite and the stuff either stuck in the window or only fell on a roof.

"I must admit, I egged their antics on, wanting to see what all the fuss was about. A dope dealer and I retired to the bedroom with a couple of groupies and the next thing we knew, the police were banging on the door. The hotel had been surrounded and everyone in the party (25 or so) was taken to jail. Since it was my room, I was presumed the ringleader and got my own cell. Townshend and Moon were next door and if I recall, seemed to be getting a kick out of the whole thing. Daltrey, I later learned, was not pleased, having gone to bed early. Not sure how long we were in jail, about four-five hours I think, until the promoter paid some outrageous sum for the room and we were taken to limos in the basement."[70]

Townshend hailed the incident as "one of the greatest room-smashings I've ever seen" in an interview with John Swenson for *Modern Hi-Fi & Stereo Guide* a couple of days later (conducted, appropriately enough, in Pete's Philadelphia hotel room). Less convincing was his rationale for the rowdiness. "I know it's kind of hard to justify in terms of higher ideals," he told Swenson. "I feel the same way toward hotels that our audience feels toward us – I'm kind of grateful that they're there, but I hate the prices they charge. We kind of feel that a bit of room-smashing ... it does them some good to know there's still a few bastards left in the world."[71]

Montreal promoter Donald K. Donald had left the party early, only to be woken up in the middle of the night to learn the band and their entourage were in prison. For the bail, he somehow managed at 4am to find local club owner Norman Silver "at a chicken barbeque. He went back into his offices and got me $6,000 in cash." Combined with an additional $2,000 scoured up by Donald, Peter Rudge (another new member of The Who's management team as they made the transition from Kit Lambert and Chris Stamp), and others, that was enough to spring the lot.

"So I organized a fleet of limousines to come by, and then, one by one, they let the guys out of jail," says Donald. "The whole experience had been a bit of a joke and a lot of fun for The Who, because they were singing most of the night; 'Don't Fence Me In,' soccer songs, and whatnot. But by this time, the nerves of the guards, police, and everybody around the cell had been frayed a lot." A Montreal inspector known to both Donald and Rudge "suggested that it would be a good idea if I or Peter would let them know that it was time to shut the fuck up, and when they were being released, step out of the prison cell, go quietly to the cars, and leave Canada. I can remember Peter [Rudge] standing as they were letting the guys out, and every time the guys were singing and yelling and screaming, he would put his hand over their face or quiet them down.

"Eventually we got them into the cars, and they went on to Boston for their show that night. It didn't take Peter too long to send me back the money I'd loaned them, and it was one of those things that will go down in rock and roll folklore. The Who was a walking powder keg, with Keith Moon. It was rock and roll on the cutting edge, getting into shambles every night."[72]

However long The Who hoped to make *Quadrophenia* the pillar of their shows, there were probably expectations that the concerts would improve and evolve as they went along. "Just wait until we really get into *Quadrophenia*," Daltrey had boasted to *Melody Maker* back at the Los Angeles shows.[73] At their Detroit show a week later, Townshend even told the audience, "we're still kind of evolving our stage presentation of this beautiful work, and it kind of changes likes the weather." As the tour had only four gigs to go at that point, one wonders if they realistically expected to complete the evolution by the time it wrapped up.

Fortunately, the last two concerts of the American 1973 tour were recorded by the Record Plant's 16-track mobile studio for use by DIR Radio's nationally syndicated program, *The King Biscuit Flower Hour*. Now officially available for internet listening at wolfgangsvault.com (but not yet on CD, and omitting their December 4 performance of 'Love Reign O'er Me'), these are by far the best live recordings of The Who during those few months when *Quadrophenia* was their in-concert focus. And although the general reputation of these shows has suffered due to numerous accounts of the screw-ups and other problems, they do show the band apparently settling into the material, and playing it well. (Two of the songs from the December 6 show, '5:15' and 'Won't Get Fooled Again,' were issued in 2010 on *Greatest Hits Live*.)

Although there's not universal agreement as to what was actually broadcast, most sources agree that excerpts were selected (but not aired until March 31) from the first of these shows, at Philadelphia's Spectrum on December 4. Gremlins aren't wholly absent. The band crashes in a line too early behind Daltrey's solo vocal on 'The Real Me'; the opening of 'Bell Boy' is similarly uncoordinated; and Bobby Pridden is gently chided by Townshend for not having the wind and crashing waves cued up precisely on time at the start of 'Doctor Jimmy.' Overall, however, the group play with passion, even if they are inclined to go on too long, especially on a ten-minute 'Drowned.' The Who certainly liked playing that tune in concert, as Daltrey would introduce it as "our favorite song of the album" at their Paris concert on February 10 the following year. "It's probably not obvious by the recording of it," he said, "but on stage it's become THE song to us."

There's also some genuine good humor – a quality sometimes lost in *Quadrophenia*-era overviews – especially when Moon snarls a new lyric in 'Bell Boy' that references The Who's very recent past. "Remember the place in Canada that we smashed?" he asks. Listeners to the original broadcast got another bonus in that department, as Keith read off the credits in his best over-the-top imitation British gent voice as 'Cobwebs And Strange' blared in the background, making sure to thank the Montreal Hotel Association. (Unfortunately, no radio show could capture another comic touch when Moon brought out an umbrella during 'Sea And Sand.')

The integration of sound effects from the backing tapes is impressive, including not only sea waves, but even the audience cheer in 'The Punk Meets The Godfather' and the train whistle on '5:15.' The introductions do tend toward the grandstanding and overly literal, especially for 'I Am The Sea' and '5:15,' where Daltrey describes England as "about twice the size of Philly." In contrast, Townshend's explanation of the autobiographical elements of 'I'm One' is genuinely moving, as if to insert a moment of authenticity in the midst of what was a fairly theatrical presentation. Their most famous theatrical trick, one that long predated *Quadrophenia*, was still in force as well, with Pete smashing his guitar at the end of the concert.

A few months later, in *Stereo Review*, Steve Simels went as far as to call it "one of the four or five all-time great rock concerts I've ever attended ...

Much as I like the record, seeing *Quad* [which seems to have been adopted by critics as an abbreviation, but then quickly dropped from common parlance] done live was a revelation – the pruning, I suspect, had something to do with it – Keith Moon bashing away at his drums like a maniac, Daltrey (who ... has really turned into a first-rate singer) twirling the microphone like a yo-yo, and Townshend leaping and windmilling his guitar while making the most majestic noises imaginable. ... Musically, they were several leagues beyond impeccable; all the synthesizer and brass stuff was on tape, and they had it synced perfectly with the symphonic sounds they were producing live."[74]

In contrast, the *Washington Post* found the next and final US concert, at Capital Center in nearby Largo, Maryland, on December 6, "tired and sloppy – almost like a second-rate rock outfit trying to imitate The Who. Daltrey seemed strained, Moon frequently off the beat, and Townshend's leads lacked their electric force and frenzied energy."[75] Perhaps that's why nothing from the recordings made at this show seems to have been broadcast, even though the performances sound pretty similar to those from the Philadelphia concert. Whether because of editing or not, the linking announcements were considerably shorter, and band complaints about unruly audience behavior more vocal. "Unfortunately there were a number of rough spots," John Swenson recalled in *Headliners: The Who*, "and when Moon ended the final show of the tour with a total demolition of his drum set, you knew it was as much an expression of disgust with the way it all had gone as a crowd-pleasing bit of merriment."

The US tour had finished after a mere three weeks, but The Who weren't quite done with their 1973 shows yet. Back in mid November, it had been announced that four shows would take place shortly before Christmas in North London's Sundown Theatre, giving fans who hadn't been able to get tickets to their Lyceum shows a chance to see the group before the year was out. Rough-sounding audience tapes confirm the band were playing well. But it had been a tumultuous year for the group – as every year had been, really, since 1964 – and the strain might have been starting to tell. "The Who, to be honest, seemed to tire rapidly as their two-and-a-half-hour set progressed," Jeff Ward wrote in *Melody Maker*. "Roger Daltrey, believed to be suffering from some throat trouble, was consequently not in best voice. Though there were highspots that only The Who can attain there seemed a definite lack of energy, which was unlike them."[76]

Nonetheless, as The Who headed into 1974, there still seemed a lot of life left in *Quadrophenia* as a stage act. They hadn't done all that many shows featuring the material in either the UK or USA, where they hadn't even played one of their chief strongholds, New York City. They hadn't yet played any *Quadrophenia* shows on the European continent. The first of those would follow in February, with the band doing a half-dozen concerts in France over the course of three weekends. These would also – even though it's likely no one knew for certain at the time – be the *last* such concerts.

"I was mixing their sound live," says Ron Nevison. "It was amazing. We would leave like Friday afternoon in a private plane, fly to like Nancy or Lyon or whatever gig we were gonna do." As the weekends ended, "we'd be home by one o'clock in the morning. Then we'd be back in the studio."[77] But not to work on a new Who album. For the group were now working on, or rather contributing to, the soundtrack to an upcoming *Tommy* movie. Ken Russell had been enlisted to direct the film version that had threatened to erupt for almost five years, and had visited the *Quadrophenia* sessions to talk about the movie; he was there, in fact, for the infamous flooding during the recording of 'Drowned.' In the fall, it had been reported that Daltrey would be playing Tommy, and that Townshend was already writing additional music for the soundtrack. It was one sign that the group's attention, having been absorbed by *Quadrophenia* for so long, was now turning to a new project, especially since *Quadrophenia* showed no signs of becoming a phenomenon like *Tommy*.

Yet as The Who were still playing nine songs from *Quadrophenia* in France, the decision to downplay the opera probably hadn't been set in stone. In the opinion of *Melody Maker*'s Steve Lake, at their February 10 Paris show, "it was the numbers from the new album that sounded the freshest."[78] They remained in place for the final French gig, in Lyon on February 24. But when The Who played their next concert – one of their biggest, in front of almost 100,000 people at London's Charlton Athletic football ground – nearly three months later, just four songs from *Quadrophenia* were played. It was the end of the line not just for the evolution of *Quadrophenia*, but also for The Who's ambitious concept albums and operas as a whole.

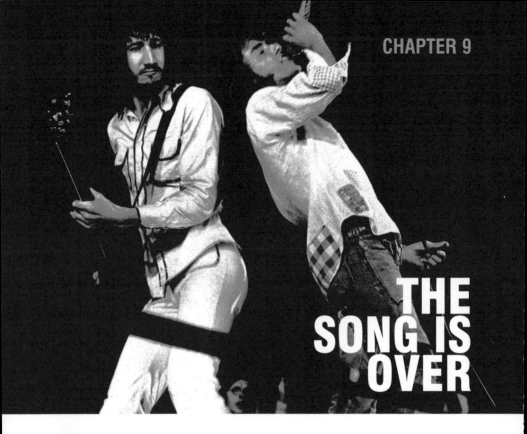

CHAPTER 9

THE SONG IS OVER

There was no announcement that *Quadrophenia* material would no longer form the core of The Who's live act. That wasn't the kind of thing you announced, and anyway, the band didn't have any tours planned. Aside from a few shows in the spring of 1974, they wouldn't play again until October 1975, despite reports that they had intended to tour for a year after *Quadrophenia*'s release. But it was becoming apparent that *Quadrophenia* hadn't lived up to the group's expectations, which might itself have played a part in their decision to take a break from touring.

With characteristic honesty, Pete Townshend admitted it hadn't worked out, at least on the concert stage, in the May 11 1974 edition of *Sounds*. "Obviously I was delighted to read headlines like '*Quadrophenia* Caps *Tommy*,' but I think they were written by critics who were just as relieved as we were to find that we could write and play another sustained 'concept' album," he said. "Obviously, when I was writing it I had in my mind that we could do with something to play on stage that would do the same as *Tommy*, give us the same kind of dynamic range, but it turned out a failure. On stage it didn't do that. I don't think it could have. *Tommy* happened at just the right time, for the audience, and also at a time when our managers were working at their most dynamic brilliance."[1]

In the same day's *NME*, Roger Daltrey shouldered his part of the responsibility. "We tried to make it another *Tommy* – and it was my fault because I especially tried to get that kind of feel into the act again," he said. "It meant we put too much emphasis on it and lost sight of what The Who really is after ten years. We shouldn't be concerned with trying to top *Tommy*, we've now realized. The Who is something more than just trying to be better than we were last year. We shouldn't try and forget our past like that.

"We found *Quadrophenia* eventually became like an endurance test every night. I found it very unenjoyable – and when that happens it gets worrying. By the beginning of the year, when we were touring France, it got very oppressive. We knew we weren't really communicating somehow. Most nights it seemed like there was a barrier between us and the crowd. It was very frustrating but our own fault. I mean, we blew it."

And how refreshing, for once, to hear a rock star admit that good reviews could hurt as well as help. "The publicity angle, for instance, exaggerated it out of proportion, to something bigger than it was," Daltrey said. "It was almost like there was too much good press about it, which, instead of letting people just make what they could of it, was hammered down their throats."[2] To be fair, he had done his own bit to build the hype, calling *Quadrophenia* "ten times more clever than anything we've ever done" in *Crawdaddy*.[3]

Even in concert, *Quadrophenia* couldn't escape the *Tommy* comparisons. "The problem was we didn't think past the record about the stage," Daltrey said. "The Who act of *Tommy* was totally different from the record, which made *Tommy* that much bigger. But *Quadrophenia* didn't do that."[4]

Townshend, typically, had a more cerebral explanation for the failure of *Quadrophenia* to connect. *Quadrophenia* encapsulated how The Who had mirrored its audience – the very same audience that had been crucial to changing the group from just another London R&B band into something much greater. Now, however, that audience was imposing limitations on its heroes. "We allow audiences to dictate a lot to us, subconsciously," he told *ZigZag*. "If you like, we allow ourselves to let audiences make us stay the same. Because when we try to change, audiences are confused and we can't bear that period, however short it might turn out to be."[5]

That might account for how quickly The Who abandoned *Quadrophenia* on stage, after only about four months of irregular touring. At their show at Charlton's football stadium on May 18, the band had reverted back to playing a set that spanned material from their whole career. Just four numbers from *Quadrophenia* were featured – 'Drowned,' 'Bell Boy' (probably retained in the set to give Keith Moon a chance to take a lead vocal, however brief), 'Doctor Jimmy,' and '5:15.' The Who executed these well, but without spotlighting them or trying to explain *Quadrophenia*'s concept. The Charlton gig could have been shrugged off as a one-time exception to The Who's new program, but a similar set was followed at the one-off concert given on May 22 at Portsmouth for 1,500 extras in the *Tommy* film. Here even 'Bell Boy,' possibly the most beloved of the *Quadrophenia* songs, didn't come off as planned, the band stopping mid-tune so the backing tape could be rewound to allow them to start the song again.

If any doubts were lingering, Townshend cleared them when the group did four shows at New York's Madison Square Garden in June, again including just those four *Quadrophenia* songs in the set. "I wrote *Quadrophenia* to replace the old stage act," he told the *New York Times*. "But it didn't work, and we're back to playing our old hits."[6] More self-realization followed in the December 1974 issue of *Penthouse*. "It's incredible how well it works on record and how badly it works on stage," Pete said. "I found it so embarrassing to have to explain the album in between numbers."[7]

At least one member of The Who might have been reluctant to dwell on an album he viewed as unrepresentative of the band as a collective enterprise. "I liked *Quadrophenia* at the time it was released," John Entwistle observed in John Swenson's *Headliners: The Who*, published in 1979. "It was an enjoyable record for me to make as far as my playing went. But looking back on it I think the reason it didn't work was because it was more of a Townshend solo album with The Who as a backup band. ... *Quadrophenia* wasn't as much of a group project as *Tommy* was; it was more or less presented to us in final demo form and all the parts were set. *Tommy* was originally a single album which was enlarged upon in the studio from suggestions by other members of the band and the producer, Kit Lambert."[8]

"With *Quadrophenia* we did tour too soon," Townshend told *Trouser Press* in 1978. "*Quadrophenia* was an extremely slow album. In fact, it still hasn't sold very well in America to this day [although its Number Two chart peak would seem to argue otherwise]. It's a very good seller in [the UK] because I think people are able to identify with it more, but it did very badly in America for a Who album. I think the answer is that we weren't prepared to work to gain our audiences' reactions. We wanted it instant and pat and the way to do that is to go on and play something that they recognize, which whips people up immediately."[9]

If the LP did underperform in the USA, some have speculated that this was due to American incomprehension of the mod movement. But as Ken Barnes (a prominent US rock critic then and now) says, "I don't know that the mods storyline on the album was a big obstacle to its American acceptance. Americans had no problem with the deaf/dumb/blind-boy storyline, which wasn't exactly a model of coherence, and had a lot of Britishisms (holiday camps, for one) in it. If there was an acceptance problem, it was probably more tied into the ponderous nature (relatively speaking) of the songs and the lack of any relatable hits on the level of immediacy that the *Who's Next* stuff had."[10]

In *Trouser Press*, Dave Schulps asked Townshend whether he was disappointed with how *Quadrophenia* was received in concert. "With that album, and with *Who's Next* as well, I was disappointed by the lack of good stage material to come out of it," Pete replied. "When we went to rehearse *Tommy*, we went to some little rehearsal hall in Southall [west of London] and ran through the whole album, everything on it; it all felt great, we couldn't believe it. *Quadrophenia* didn't work that way. Neither did *Who's Next*; just a couple of tracks came out of it. They were recording studio efforts, whereas the amazing thing about *Tommy* was that it was very organic, very simple, very pure, and it did work very well on stage."[11]

The Who's appetite for touring might have diminished in any case. "As a general rule, they were disappointing then," feels Chris Charlesworth, who saw all of the Madison Square Garden concerts. "They were off the boil for those shows. What you tended to find with The Who is that if they played regularly, they were terrific. But if they didn't rehearse, at the beginning of tours they weren't quite as fluent as they usually were. Once they'd done about six shows, and they were into the tour, six or seven shows, they were out of this world, no one could touch them. But sometimes they were a bit rusty. They were like an athlete that hasn't been training, and they hadn't been training before those four shows at the Garden. They'd never played the Garden before. I don't think they got the acoustics right, or the equipment. And Pete was drinking a huge amount as well, which didn't help. I was party to a fearsome row backstage on the opening night. They improved during the course of the week, but they were all pleased the week was over."[12]

Why the loss of momentum, not just for squeezing more life out of *Quadrophenia*, but for working as The Who at all? Certainly some of it can be blamed on disappointment with how *Quadrophenia* had been played and received. But it also had to do with the fact that the individual members of The Who – four personalities who made a whole, as Townshend had tried to reflect in *Quadrophenia* – were growing in different directions, and wanted to do different things on their own.

The Who had been rumored to be on the verge of splitting for so many years that it was almost a normal state of affairs for the band. Now, however, they had more definite individual commitments and projects. Such solo endeavors had done their part to break up The Beatles a few years before, and while The Who managed (barely) to keep them in check, the band would curtail their concert and recording activity drastically over the next year. Recording sessions for their next album wouldn't begin until April 1975; their first concert since the Madison Square Garden shows wouldn't take place until about five months after that.

Maybe, having delivered the ultimate tribute to their past in *Quadrophenia*, The Who and Townshend were reluctant to deal with the tougher task of coming up with something completely different that had nothing to do with their own history. "What worries me in a sense about *Quadrophenia* as an album is that it comes across to me in retrospect as looking incredibly calculated, a kind of winding up of Who affairs in that era, but not really giving any indication of what's going to happen next," Pete admitted to *Modern Hi-Fi & Stereo Guide* when the band's 1973 US tour was ending. "So, thinking I was getting myself off the hook, I was really fooling myself, because now I've got the biggest problem ahead of me as a writer, and I think the band has got the biggest problem ahead of them as a group that they've ever faced in their career."[13]

Whether as a way of putting off this daunting task or not, much of Townshend's time in 1974 was occupied with Ken Russell's film version of *Tommy*, particularly its soundtrack. While in a sense it fulfilled the group's longtime ambition to move into films, it was arguably a waste of Pete's resources when he could have been devoting his efforts to new works. The movie had its moments, but could hardly be considered either a highlight of

The Who's career or a screen realization of the quite serious themes the opera investigated. In June, the *New York Times* reported that Townshend was "talking about trying to make a television version of *Quadrophenia*," but (fortunately, as it turned out, in light of the 1979 movie) nothing came of it.[14]

Townshend might have diverted his energies from the still-fresh *Quadrophenia* to the five-year-old *Tommy* in the belief that *Tommy* had more staying power, at least as a work that could be reshaped for different media, like film and theater. As for *Quadrophenia*, he told Richard Barnes in *The Story Of Tommy*, "The day that tape was delivered to MCA Records it was dead, from an evolutionary point of view. It was a statement made and isolated." He said the difference between *Quadrophenia* and *Tommy* was that "*Tommy* was evolving and sort of living, so you don't mind if it changes a little bit here and there because it still feels like it's working."[15] *Quadrophenia* would prove Pete wrong by being developed for the screen just a few years later, and for stage in the 21st century. But in the mid 70s, *Tommy* looked like by far the surer bet.

On April 14, Townshend did his first solo concert, at a benefit at the Roundhouse in London. This was a true solo concert, in that he played all the instruments (principally guitars), in addition to using backing tapes. Whether by design or not, nothing from *Quadrophenia* was included. Nor, for that matter, was anything from *Lifehouse*, besides 'Behind Blue Eyes' and 'Let's See Action.' There were a few Who hits, but otherwise Townshend opted for unlikely covers of songs by the likes of Jimmy Reed, Bob Dylan, Tim Hardin, and French singer-songwriter (and Stephen Stills's then-wife) Veronique Sanson, as well as 'Join My Gang,' a mid-60s obscurity he'd donated to an artist simply named Oscar. He also made noises about doing a solo work. "Everything that I've written so far has been given to The Who for first refusal," he told the *New York Times*'s John Rockwell in June. "What I'm saying is that that's going to stop, and that I'm going to get first refusal."[16] Bold words, but he wouldn't put out a non-Who album for three years, and even that LP, *Rough Mix*, would be co-billed to Ronnie Lane.

A little surprisingly, it seemed for a while that Roger Daltrey, not Townshend, would have the most to gain from solo activities. Not so much on the recorded music front (although he did put out a mid-1975 solo album, *Ride A Rock Horse*, that charted respectably in both the USA and UK); but as the star of the film version of *Tommy*, Daltrey now had the possibility of a career as an actor. The critical trashing of Ken Russell's 1975 film *Lisztomania*, in which he played classical composer Franz Liszt, slowed his rise in the cinema, however.

Entwistle made a fourth solo album, *Mad Dog*, that sold no better than his previous outings. Less wisely, he took his band, Ox, on a tour of the UK and USA in late 1974 and early 1975 that drew relatively small audiences and lost a lot of money. "The problem with John is, speaking completely honestly, that he hasn't got stage presence," Daltrey bluntly informed *Melody Maker*. "Not in the way that he could ever front a group."[17]

Entwistle's greatest contribution to The Who's legacy during this period was compiling the group's out-takes/rarities album *Odds & Sods*, which among other things aired quite a few rejects from the *Lifehouse* days. Issued in fall 1974, it outsold by a healthy margin any of the solo releases by Who members. Even more than *Quadrophenia*, it solidified The Who's reputation as the band most obsessed with its own history, especially as it came with detailed track-by-track liner notes by Townshend himself. "All of these tracks have been part of bigger ideas," he wrote, alluding to the disappointments of the last few years, "or at least grand dreams that didn't see the light of day."[18]

Keith Moon was the most at sea without regular group activities to keep him occupied, if not wholly out of trouble. His 1975 solo album *Two Sides Of The Moon* was a disaster, in part due to the inexplicable decision to use other drummers for most of the tracks. He didn't have the vocal or songwriting talent to carry a solo musical career, and while he seemed a natural for work as a comic actor, his roles in *That'll Be The Day* and its 1975 follow-up, *Stardust*, didn't lead to more. To record his album, he'd moved to Los Angeles, where proximity to more hedonistic celebrity-gang indulgence than anywhere else on the planet did him no more good than it had John Lennon during the same period.

When The Who did regroup in spring 1975 to record another album, the prospect of another opera or conceptual work doesn't seem to have come up. Maybe Townshend was tired of using troubled youth and adolescence as his inspiration, as he had for *Quadrophenia* and (less prominently) *Tommy*. He'd said as much in the December 1974 *Penthouse*, portraying *Quadrophenia* as "a rejection of that sort of work ever again. Or at least the adolescence obsession, the teenage frustration thing. I've got some lyrical growing up to do."[19] *The Who By Numbers* was hardly a concept album in any accepted sense, but it did have a good number of songs dealing with the melancholy trials of aging and maturity. Pete's most useful sounding board for grand ideas, Kit Lambert, was now even further out of the picture than he had been for *Quadrophenia*, having announced his intentions in mid 1975 to take legal action against other parties in The Who's management. Although some material from the group's 70s albums was included when they toured *The Who By Numbers*, they now seemed resigned to *Tommy*'s overruling status, making consecutive songs from that opera the centerpiece of the set.

While it's too isolated an incident to call it a backlash, some of the cheekier rock critics might have been getting a little fed up with the pomp of Townshend's big ideas, or at least his proclamations. 'Pete Fills A Scripture' read the headline of a spoof review of *Bible One*, The Who's next (fictional) masterpiece in the October 1975 *Creem*. No less than a retelling of the bible from Genesis to Deuteronomy, the ten-record set would come with a limited edition 125-page booklet, weigh nearly nine pounds, and retail for a hefty (by 1975 standards) $24.59. The projected series would run to 15 such ten-LP boxes, climaxing with the New Testament.

"In a recent interview, Townshend was asked if he could ever hope to top *Bible*, when it finally gets released in its entirety," Jeffrey Morgan wrote. "He answered that, no, he probably couldn't, and that it would probably be his final work. Knowing Pete, however, I went over to Townshend's house the other day and asked him about the plans for a marathon live concert presentation of *Bible*, for future release as a live album and feature length (*Bible* runs over 80 hours) film. He looked at me, smiled, and I thought I caught a small gleam in the corner of his eye. 'Well,' he said, 'You never know ...'"[20]

Ridiculous, yes, but *Lifehouse* had been scarcely less ambitious. And there continued to be murmurs of reviving *Lifehouse* somehow, with a few ideas dating back to those days, such as the synthesizer pulse of 'Who Are You,' finding their way into their newer songs. But when their next album finally appeared, in 1978, *Who Are You* was another LP of songs unconnected by a theme or story (although Entwistle would reveal in *Record Collector* that one of his compositions, '905,' was part of "a concept album along the same lines as *Lifehouse*," set in a future where men were eating women).[21] The death of Keith Moon on September 7 1978, shortly after *Who Are You*'s release, seemed to put paid to the idea of reviving the *Lifehouse* script (mentioned by Townshend as a possibility in *NME* just a month prior to Moon's passing), or indeed doing any other major work as a band. Even though *Quadrophenia* might have failed to make the most of its premise of blending The Who's four personalities into one, they really did need each and every member to make a whole entity, whether it was a group or an opera.

After Moon's death, The Who pretty much discontinued working on or performing *Lifehouse* and *Quadrophenia*. But over the next three decades, both projects refused to go away. Both of them have been revived, in different mediums and on numerous occasions, sometimes quite successfully, sometimes not. The best of these, the 1979 film adaptation of *Quadrophenia*, was the first.

Even before Moon's death, casting had started for *Quadrophenia*, to be directed by Franc Roddam. (*Melody Maker* reported days after Keith's passing that filming of *Lifehouse* would begin in 1979, but unsurprisingly this never got off the ground.[22]) "The biggest danger is that it could come out looking like *That'll Be The Day* or *Stardust*, because low-production British pictures have that look about them," Townshend told *Melody Maker*. "I suppose I'm banking on the fact that Franc Roddam is, I think, the only British director who's going to properly make that transition to film. If he does pull it off I don't think there's going to be anything stopping him."[23]

"We talked it through and they had a script that had been written by a fan, but it wasn't really a script," Roddam said in the December 2009 issue of *Clash*. "It was a rambling 220 pages of something, but it wasn't a script. You just couldn't make it into a film. They said the money was there, the record company was willing to pay for the film. This was in June and they wanted to start in September! In film, sometimes you wait seven years for finances and we had a film fully financed, ready to go but with no script. It was quite exciting in a sense.

"I was 18 in 1964, so I just stressed my experiences," Roddam continued. "Things like experimenting with drugs, living in a small house, there's no space, everyone's on your case, the ignorance of your parents, hating your boss, hating going to work. ... I just put all those ideas into the script. I think the film was very authentic because I'd experienced these things myself; I could tell what was fake and what was not fake."[24]

Considering all the things that could have gone wrong with *Quadrophenia* – as had happened with Ken Russell's *Tommy* – it's amazing how well it turned out. Roddam was in most essential respects faithful to the plot as it had been laid out (if minimally) by the songs and Townshend's short story in the gatefold jacket. The film was gritty, naturalistic, and witty. Best of all, it was extremely and unsentimentally conscientious in re-creating the milieu of the mod gang, down to the fashions, scooters, pills, Brighton brawls, and the music.

Some critics took exception to points they felt Roddam hadn't gotten quite right, like the prominence of romance in the storyline (even though some of *Quadrophenia*'s lyrics do make apparent Jimmy's longing for a girl who rejects him). On a more trainspotting level, in the party scene, the sleeve for a 1973 reissue of *A Quick One/The Who Sell Out* is seen – an impossibility for a film set in the mid 60s. Still, the opening scene, with Jimmy scootering through London streets while 'The Real Me' played on the soundtrack, fitted exactly with the picture conjured up by this author just from listening to the album. The scene of Jimmy venomously shouting "bellboy!" at a young Sting is also an especially satisfying visual enactment of the hero's disillusionment.

One decision by Roddam proved especially crucial, and courageous, considering he had to overrule The Who's leader. "At first, Pete wanted to ... do a new soundtrack with an orchestra, like he did with *Tommy*," he revealed in his commentary track to the *Quadrophenia* DVD. "I resisted that and said, 'Look, I want to reflect street life, I want to reflect rock'n'roll. You can't have strings in rock'n'roll. And I want it to be a raw picture, and I want to truly reflect the mod movement.' He'd already made the track with the strings, and he'd brought in the demo. And I said 'Look, it's not going to work for me.' He was very smart and very sweet and immediately said, 'OK, that's fine. You do your thing.' And I stayed very much with the Who music."[25]

As a result, while The Who themselves don't appear in the film (except when they're seen playing 'Anyway Anyhow Anywhere' on TV), many of their tracks from *Quadrophenia* are heard, almost as if to amplify or accentuate the on-screen action and emotions in the Greek chorus tradition. Also incorporated as part of the action are vintage mid-60s rock and soul tracks that mods would have been listening to at dances and parties, including The Who's own 'My Generation.' A combination of those oldies and Who songs from *Quadrophenia* would comprise the double-LP soundtrack album, although as it turned out, the *Quadrophenia* material wasn't exactly the same as that heard on the original 1973 release.

First, there were three new songs, all recorded after Moon's death. All were intended to flesh out the *Quadrophenia* story to some degree, but as so often happens when a quality product is subjected to improvements, none of them were up to the standard of the original. 'Get Out And Stay Out' was a monotonous song literally announcing Jimmy getting thrown out of his family home; 'Four Faces' was an innocuous piano-driven ditty, perhaps written out of pressure to come up with a song that finally spelled out Jimmy's quadrophenic personality. 'Joker James,' written back in the mid 60s, was the kind of novelty-tinged humorous character sketch Townshend had favored in the 1966-67 era, but hardly up to the standards of 'Happy Jack,' and far too upbeat to fit into *Quadrophenia*.

Even more problematic was the decision for Entwistle not only to remix original *Quadrophenia* tracks, but also to subject these to some overdubs. An electric guitar was added to 'The Punk Meets The Godfather,' a piano to 'I'm One,' and a flute to 'Love Reign O'er Me.' John even re-recorded his bass on eight of the songs. Again the result was not to strengthen the material, but to weaken or dilute it, if only slightly.

"He was always unhappy with his bass sound," Roger Daltrey recalled in an interview included with the DVD of *The Kids Are Alright*. "He'd literally go in and redo the bass of something he did 15 years ago, 20 years ago, just to get the sound better. And I'd just think, you shouldn't fuck with it, it doesn't matter. It's like Picasso [taking] a painting off the wall of a museum and saying, 'I think I'm going to do this a bit better.' It's not better, it would just be a little bit different. 'Better' is the moment. Or best is the moment."[26] Elsewhere Daltrey, never happy with how low his vocals were in the *Quadrophenia* mix, expressed his opinion that there was too much bass. At least the soundtrack LP did, for the first time, put the 1964 High Numbers B-side 'Zoot Suit' into wide circulation, sounding like a far more authentic reflection of Jimmy's time and place than the three new songs did.

The *Quadrophenia* movie's chief accomplishment was not its soundtrack; repressings and reissues of the original LP thankfully retained Entwistle's original bass tracks and refrained from adding overdubs. Its true significance was, as it became one of the biggest cult movies of all time, in translating *Quadrophenia* into a bigger cultural milestone than it had ever been as a record. This was particularly true in the USA, where (despite Daltrey's prediction that "I can't see how American kids are going to identify with it") the lively visual representation of the mod movement finally made it tangible and comprehensible to a country that had never directly experienced it.[27]

If the UK mod revival sparked by *Quadrophenia* seems in hindsight tame and silly – in terms of both its retro fashions and the retro bands it spawned, none of them remotely in The Who's league – it too did its part to entrench *Quadrophenia*, both on record and film, as a cornerstone of British popular culture. In Richard Barnes's estimation, Townshend "did more for Meher Baba than anyone else, but he also did more for mods. There's hardly any real plot [in *Quadrophenia*]; it's difficult to know what it's about. It's probably about unrequited love and disillusionment. But at least he's singing about haircuts, side vents, and scooters – all the things that the mods found interesting, and all those things that were important to mods who wanted to show off to other mods. I thought that was great."[28]

While *Quadrophenia* would never attain the fame of *Tommy*, it could be argued that it has finally escaped from its famous predecessor's shadow. "Although *Tommy* is probably more commercial, people in the *Quadrophenia* camp are more attached to it because it articulates a very important moment in their lives," Daltrey said in *Classic Rock* in 2004. "Whether you're today's generation, 20 years ago's generation or our generation, it articulates a specific area of your life that every adolescent goes through. And those people that discover *Quadrophenia*, and identify with it, attach it to themselves more strongly than anyone ever attached *Tommy* to themselves."[29] Even Barnes, so critical of *Quadrophenia*'s flaws in some respects, now says that he thinks "it'll be the thing that probably they're remembered for in 50 years' time. It's probably my favorite Who thing [now]."[30]

So durable was public's fascination with *Quadrophenia* that, nearly 25 years after its initial mixed reception, the unthinkable happened. The Who had staggered on for a few years after Moon's death with replacement Kenney Jones, before splitting at the end of 1982, then engaging in a lukewarm reunion tour in 1989. In 1996, they reunited for the express purpose of performing *Quadrophenia* on stage in its entirety. Not just once, but show after show, throughout North America, Europe, and (if less extensively) the UK, well into the summer of 1997. No, it couldn't be the same without Keith Moon, but Ringo Starr's son, Zak Starkey, was about the best available substitute. There were also a bunch of extra musicians on stage to fill out the sound or take parts here and there, rather than let the core quartet carry the entire load on their shoulders, as they'd attempted to do back in 1973.

Even in the 21st century, *Quadrophenia* continues to have an afterlife, if nothing to challenge the majesty of the original LP. Several theatrical adaptations have been attempted, including one that toured part of the UK in 2009. And on March 30 2010, what was left of The Who – Entwistle having died in 2002 – did a one-off performance of the opera at the Royal Albert Hall, with a guest appearance by Eddie Vedder of Pearl Jam.

Revivals of *Lifehouse*, in contrast to those of *Quadrophenia*, have been quirkier, more fitful, and ultimately less successful. Townshend told *NME* in April 1980 that a treatment had been sent to top science fiction writer Ray Bradbury in the hope that he could help with a script, and that Nicolas Roeg, every bit as iconoclastic a film director as Ken Russell, might direct a *Lifehouse* film.[31] But it never has reached the screen, although advances in various aspects of cinematic technology would probably make some of the logistical obstacles far more surmountable in the 21st century.

With the passage of time, Pete Townshend seemed to have realized that what he envisioned for *Lifehouse* was simply not possible given the limitations of both the era and The Who. "I thought this was a huge technical magnum opus that could have been absolutely extraordinary," he told *Q* in 1996. "It would have been *Fahrenheit 451*, *2001*, *Lawnmower Man* and many other films rolled into one. *Woodstock*, even. I couldn't understand how it hadn't happened. This was an extraordinary moment of visionary imagination from me, and it seemed to have been wasted. Now I understand that not everything you imagine is necessarily at the appropriate time. We were incapable of doing it. We could write songs, make albums, tour. That was about it."[32]

Townshend couldn't quite let it go, however, even after The Who had ceased to be active. In the 90s he made some attempts to revisit the project, albeit in a modified form. The trigger was his 1993 solo album *Psychoderelict*, the third of the solo conceptual records he'd attempted outside of The Who (the previous ones being *White City* and *The Iron Man*). There were obvious parallels between its protagonist, Ray High, and what Townshend had been through with *Lifehouse*; Ray was haunted by a work he'd failed to realize in the 70s, *Gridlife*. Realizing that he continued to be haunted by *Lifehouse*, Pete set about presenting it to the world in some form. That turned out to be a 1999 BBC radio play, a medium apparently not considered when so many larger-scale ideas were bouncing around in 1970 and 1971.

The radio play (issued on discs five and six of the *Lifehouse Chronicles* boxed set, which prints the script in its liner notes) wasn't quite what the script for *Lifehouse* would have been in the early 70s. There was no "Bobby" now, and no obvious villain, whether named "Brick" or "Jumbo." The story very much centered on a couple's struggle to find and reconnect with their daughter Mary, with the father named, in an obvious nod to *Psychoderelict*, "Ray." Exchanges between Ray and a younger, more idealistic version of himself, "Rayboy," were crucial to the narrative, although they weren't part of the deal in *Lifehouse*'s first incarnations. It did still incorporate many songs, but these weren't Who recordings. Instead, early 70s Townshend demos and re-recordings of material he'd written during the era were used, along with one familiar song, 'Who Are You,' which certainly wasn't completed during the period. The radio play did share one thing with *Lifehouse*'s original iterations: its story wasn't easy to follow.

The *Guardian* was savage in its appraisal. "Though Townshend's aphorisms strove to be meaningful, they rarely got beyond art-school precious. ... The only memorable tunes he wrote earlier, specifically for 1971's *Who's Next* album. Neither the echoey, multi-track production nor the first half's slightly fractured narrative managed to give it a modern feel. Townshend may be a rich and once creative musician, but someone should have had a word in his ear."[33] More diplomatically, even old chum Richard Barnes didn't think the radio play had "anything to do with *Lifehouse*" as it was originally planned. "I think he did that with the benefit of hindsight," he adds.[34] Still, Pete wasn't discouraged from pursuing the next part of his plan: the six-CD *Lifehouse Chronicles* boxed set, released in 2000 (although only sold through his website, and as of this writing no longer available).

For the official release of two CDs of *Lifehouse* demos alone, *Lifehouse Chronicles* was an essential historical document – even if, as previously discussed, some of the songs might not have been written for the original project. As for the other four discs, one wonders whether Townshend should have quit while he was ahead. Two were of the radio play; one was devoted largely to late-90s live reworkings of the songs, as well as miscellany like a 1999 demo of 'Can You Help The One You Really Love?' and a piano rag that seemed ever more distant from the original *Lifehouse* concept. Yet more tenuous was disc four, with classical arrangements of pieces by Townshend (including 'Baba O'Riley') and composers such as Purcell and Scarlatti.

Townshend also hoped to bring *Lifehouse* to the concert stage somehow, even without any of the original Who musicians necessary to maximize its potential. This he did in London concerts at Sadler's Wells on February 25 and 26 of 2000, as commemorated on DVD a couple years later as *Music From Lifehouse*. Not even Roger Daltrey was involved in these shows, which used accompaniment from the London Chamber Orchestra in addition to more standard aggregations of rock musicians and singers. The presentation was tasteful and reverent, yet somewhat tepid, especially considering the power The Who would have brought to the material. Also, the specific tracks chosen for the DVD were not the exact songs that would have made a Who *Lifehouse* album, nor were they sequenced in the same way – although, to be fair, such determinations were never finalized back in the early 70s, and will always remain elusive.

Jon Astley, who has worked closely with Townshend on archival projects (including *Lifehouse Chronicles*), found it a worthwhile embodiment of the spirit of *Lifehouse*. "For me, that epitomizes what *Lifehouse* was," he says. "I think he got it right that night. I think that was lovely." Yet he acknowledges what a tall order it would have been to recreate *Lifehouse* as it might have taken shape in the early 70s, as "to a certain extent, most of Pete's records evolve as they go along. It would have been very difficult to say, 'OK, this is the story of *Lifehouse* and this is the running order.' I did an awful lot of work on *Psychoderelict*, and *Psychoderelict* evolved dramatically as the first eight, nine tracks got put down. Then the whole story started to come out. I mean, Pete had the story in the back of his mind, but the way that these things evolve certainly would have happened in the studio a lot, during the recording process."[35]

Even more ambitiously, Townshend entertained hopes of bringing his concert into reality with a gathering at which many people could hear compositions created especially for them, all of them combining for a grand finale. That was essentially what he'd had in mind as *Lifehouse*'s climax all along, and he even wrote a proposal, detailed in *Lifehouse Chronicles*' liner notes, for a computer company to sponsor such an event. A website, the Lifehouse Method, was even put up that would make electronic portraits of sorts from information entered by users. This was an update, of course, of a technologically cruder process Pete had discussed in detail as part of his original *Lifehouse* concept and had even used to create some of the synthesizer tracks on *Lifehouse* songs. In his *Lifehouse Chronicles* notes, he envisioned a limited edition release, also entitled *The Lifehouse Method*, that would include a free ticket to the Lifehouse Concert, should it occur.

The Lifehouse Method, probably to no one's surprise, didn't play out as expected. There would be no Lifehouse Method package with access to software and a signed certificate from Townshend, as he'd detailed in his *Lifehouse Chronicles* notes. The Lifehouse Method website did generate more than 10,000 pieces of music, but as of this writing consists solely of a page with a brief statement, reading in part: "Our wonderful experiment on this site has come to an end. We are no longer accepting new sitters and creating musical portraits."[36] It's tempting to conclude that Pete had once again gone through the cycle of building up hopes beyond what he could deliver, his admirable aspirations scuttled by cold realities.

Such is the mystique that's built up around the work, however, that some younger musicians have been inspired by *Lifehouse* as an entity entirely separate from *Who's Next*. In early 2009, the San Francisco Bay Area band Mushroom went to the unusual extremes of performing *Lifehouse*, or their approximation of it, at two special concerts, as well as on the nationally syndicated radio show *The Grateful Dead Hour*. Faced with the extraordinary challenge of performing an album that didn't actually exist, Mushroom devised a set including every *Who's Next* song save 'My Wife,' as well as four of the most likely additional contenders ('Pure And Easy,' 'Too Much Of Anything,' 'Time Is Passing,' and 'Naked Eye').

Two guitarists, two singers, and about as many keyboards as Matt Cunitz could squeeze onto a small stage were needed to simulate the original article, reinforcing how much of a challenge it would have been for a four-man band to play it, or even most of it, on stage in sequence in 1971. Cunitz literally wore out his vinyl copy of *Who's Next* to write out the 'Won't Get Fooled Again' solo note-for-note, since while "a lot of that animation and motion that happens in the solo and the intro was just done for [Townshend] while he held multiple notes down, I had to play everything."[37]

In one view, Townshend could be said to be fulfilling some visionary aspects of his original *Lifehouse* conception by treating it as a living work, subject to changes, embellishments, and mutations over time and by developing technology. Were he even aware of Mushroom's attempt to translate it to the concert stage, he might have been pleased that other musicians were also treating it as a living piece that could be presented to

21st-century audiences. More objectively, his more recent mutations of the source material weren't measuring up to either the surviving early 70s solo demos and Who recordings of the songs, or to the highest experimental ambitions he'd entertained as part of the concept.

In this respect, the trajectory of *Lifehouse* somewhat resembled that of other unrealized masterworks, such as The Beach Boys' *Smile* or The Beatles' *Get Back*, which also underwent endless tinkering and piecemeal release after their initial abandonment. No matter how elaborately Brian Wilson tried to reconstruct *Smile* for record and stage in the 21st century, or how diligently Paul McCartney de-Spectorized *Let It Be* for the 2003 CD *Let It Be ... Naked*, the results weren't quite what either listeners or creators heard in their heads when imagining how the projects might have sounded had they been completed in line with their creators' original intentions. *Lifehouse* seems doomed to a similar fate, the moment of seeing it through to completion in its purest form having passed sometime in early to mid 1971, when The Who abandoned it.

Yet *Lifehouse*, and The Who's work from the early 70s in general, can hardly be considered a complete failure. It might seem facetious to say that one out of two ain't bad, but in *Quadrophenia* they did complete a rock opera that might be their most artistically successful work of its kind, even including *Tommy*. In the decades it took to find its full audience, it embodied and influenced youth culture more than almost any artistic creation of the 20th century.

Lifehouse, meanwhile, yielded many enduring songs, and remains perhaps the most ambitious multimedia project attempted by any major act in rock music. It stands as a benchmark for future generations, in the hope that they might even take rock music on the evolutionary leap Pete Townshend felt but could not articulate. It also encourages artists of all sorts to dare to dream, even if the goal seems impossible to reach. Townshend has expressed that idea in many interviews, then and since. But he may never have said it as well or as simply as he did in 'Pure And Easy,' the song from which *Lifehouse* sprang:

"We all know success when we all find our own dreams."

Endnotes

INTRODUCTION
1   *Classic Albums: Who's Next* (TV documentary), 1999
2   *Amazing Journey: The Story Of The Who* (DVD documentary), 2007

CHAPTER 1
1   *Melody Maker*, September 19 1970
2   Author's interview, May 21 2010
3   *Rolling Stone*, December 21 1972
4   *Sounds*, July 17 1971
5   Barnes and Townshend, *The Story of Tommy*
6   Barnes and Townshend, *The Story of Tommy*
7   Barnes and Townshend, *The Story of Tommy*
8   *Disc*, October 24 1970
9   *Los Angeles Free Press*, December 24 1971
10 Author's interview, June 4 2010
11 *Melody Maker*, July 19 1969
12 *Melody Maker*, January 10 1970
13 *Rolling Stone*, July 19 1969
14 *Creem*, November 1970
15 Author's interview, May 21 2010
16 *New Musical Express*, July 4 1970
17 *Rolling Stone*, May 14 1970
18 *Disc*, October 24 1970
19 Interview on *Live At The Isle Of Wight Festival 1970* DVD 2006
20 *Rolling Stone*, May 14 1970
21 *Disc*, October 24 1970
22 *New Musical Express*, July 4 1970
23 *Creem*, November 1970
24 Liner notes to The Who *Odds & Sods* (1974) by Pete Townshend
25 *Record Mirror*, May 8 1971
26 *New Musical Express*, July 17 1976
27 *Jazz & Pop*, September 1970
28 *Melody Maker*, January 10 1970
29 *Downbeat*, May 1970
30 Author's interview, March 3 2010
31 Author's interview, March 3 2010
32 Author's interview, March 3 2010
33 Author's interview, June 29 2010
34 Author's interview, June 29 2010
35 Author's interview, June 29 2010
36 Author's interview, December 18 2009
37 Author's interview, March 3 2010
38 Author's interview, February 26 2010
39 Author's interview, March 3 2010
40 *Rollling Stone*, May 14 1970
41 *Rolling Stone*, November 26 1970
42 Khan, *The Mysticism Of Sound And Music: The Sufi Teaching Of Hazrat Inayat Khan*
43 Khan, *The Mysticism Of Sound And Music: The Sufi Teaching Of Hazrat Inayat Khan*
44 *Melody Maker*, September 19 1970
45 Khan, *The Mysticism Of Sound And Music: The Sufi Teaching Of Hazrat Inayat Khan*
46 *Melody Maker*, September 19 1970
47 Khan, *The Mysticism Of Sound And Music: The Sufi Teaching Of Hazrat Inayat Khan*
48 *Penthouse*, August 1983
49 *Lifehouse: The One That Got Away* (BBC Radio One documentary), January 1996
50 Author's interview, June 11 2010
51 Author's interview, June 16 2010
52 Tobler and Grundy, *The Record Producers*
53 Author's interview, June 16 2010
54 Author's interview, June 22 2010
55 Author's interview, October 23 2009
56 Author's interview, March 2 2010
57 *In The Studio: Tommy* (radio documentary), May 24 1993
58 Author's interview, March 2 2010
59 Pollock, *In Their Own Words*
60 *Disc*, October 24 1970
61 *Sounds*, June 24 1972
62 *Disc*, October 24 1970

CHAPTER 2
1   Liner notes to Pete Townshend *Scoop* (1983) by Pete Townshend
2   Author's interview, June 7 2010
3   Herman, *The Who*
4   *Melody Maker*, January 23 1971
5   *New York Times*, February 7 1971
6   *Crawdaddy*, December 5 1971
7   *New York Times*, February 7 1971
8   Liner notes to Pete Townshend *Lifehouse Chronicles* (2000) by Pete Townshend
9   Author's interview, May 21 2010
10 Heylin, *Bootleg: The Secret History Of The Other Recording Industry*
11 *Melody Maker*, July 17 1971
12 Author's interview, October 16 2009
13 Author's interview, February 26 2010
14 *Penthouse*, December 1974
15 *Circus*, November 1971
16 *Lifehouse: The One That Got Away* (BBC Radio One documentary), January 1996
17 *Melody Maker*, July 17 1971
18 *ZigZag*, March 1974
19 Townshend, *A Decade Of The Who: An Authorized History In Music, Paintings, Words And Photographs*
20 Liner notes to Pete Townshend *Scoop* (1983) by Pete Townshend
21 Townshend, *A Decade Of The*

Who: An Authorized History In Music, Paintings, Words And Photographs

[22] Townshend, A Decade Of The Who: An Authorized History In Music, Paintings, Words And Photographs

[23] Liner notes to Pete Townshend Scoop (1983) by Pete Townshend

[24] Melody Maker, July 17 1971

[25] Crawdaddy, December 5 1971

[26] Interview with Roger Scott of BBC Radio One, June 20 1989

[27] Chris Faiers, Eel Pie Dharma eelpie.org/epd.htm

[28] Author's interview, December 29 2009

[29] Rolling Stone, February 4 1971

[30] Author's interview, December 29 2009

[31] Author's interview, December 28 2009

[32] New Musical Express, August 21 1971

[33] Amazing Journey: The Story Of The Who (DVD documentary), 2007

[34] Carr, A Talk On The Wild Side

[35] McKnight and Silver, The Who ... Through The Eyes Of Pete Townshend

[36] Rolling Stone, December 10 1987

[37] Classic Albums: Who's Next (TV documentary), 1999

[38] Sounds, June 24 1972

[39] Classic Albums: Who's Next (TV documentary), 1999

[40] Liner notes to The Who Odds & Sods (1974) by Pete Townshend

[41] Disc, October 24 1970

[42] Liner notes to Pete Townshend Scoop (1983) by Pete Townshend

[43] Sounds, June 24 1972

[44] Liner notes to The Who Odds & Sods (1974) by Pete Townshend

[45] Liner notes to The Who Odds & Sods (1974) by Pete Townshend

[46] Jazz & Pop, September 1970

[47] Billboard, December 19 1970

[48] Author's interview, March 3 2010

[49] Author's interview, December 18 2009

[50] Author's interview, June 11 2010

[51] Author's interview, June 29 2010

[52] Classic Albums: Who's Next (TV documentary), 1999

[53] Barnes and Townshend, The Story Of Tommy

CHAPTER 3

[1] Sounds, January 2 1971

[2] Author's interview, May 21 2010

[3] Sounds, January 2 1971

[4] Classic Albums: Who's Next (TV documentary), 1999

[5] Unpublished interview with Phil Sutcliffe, March 2004

[6] Record Mirror, January 23 1971

[7] Sounds, January 2 1971

[8] Amazing Journey: The Story Of The Who (DVD documentary), 2007

[9] Classic Albums: Who's Next (TV documentary), 1999

[10] In The Studio: The Who Live At Leeds (radio documentary), May 22 1995

[11] Author's interview, March 2 2010

[12] Melody Maker, January 23 1971

[13] Melody Maker, July 17 1971

[14] Melody Maker, January 23 1971

[15] Liner notes to Lifehouse Chronicles (2000) by Pete Townshend

[16] New Musical Express, April 19 1980

[17] New York Times, February 7 1971

[18] Record Mirror, January 23 1971

[19] Unpublished interview with Phil Sutcliffe, March 2004

[20] Lifehouse: The One That Got Away (BBC Radio One documentary), January 1996

[21] Liner notes to Pete Townshend Lifehouse Chronicles (2000) by Pete Townshend

[22] Lifehouse: The One That Got Away (BBC Radio One documentary), January 1996

[23] Unpublished interview with Phil Sutcliffe, March 2004

[24] Author's interview, October 23 2009

[25] Unpublished interview with Phil Sutcliffe, March 2004

[26] Unpublished interview with Phil Sutcliffe, March 2004

[27] Sounds, July 24 1971

[28] Lifehouse: The One That Got Away (BBC Radio One documentary), January 1996

[29] Penthouse, December 1974

[30] Melody Maker, February 13 1971

[31] Hit Parader, May 1974

[32] Liner notes to Pete Townshend Lifehouse Chronicles (2000) by Pete Townshend

[33] McKnight and Silver, The Who ... Through The Eyes Of Pete Townshend

[34] Classic Albums: Who's Next (TV documentary), 1999

[35] Lifehouse: The One That Got Away (BBC Radio One documentary), January 1996

[36] Unpublished interview with Phil Sutcliffe, March 2004

[37] Lifehouse: The One That Got Away (BBC Radio One documentary), January 1996

[38] Author's interview, March 2 2010

[39] Unpublished interview with Phil Sutcliffe, March 2004

[40] Melody Maker, February 13 1971

[41] Author's interview, March 2 2010

[42] Author's interview, June 16 2010

[43] Liner notes to Pete Townshend Lifehouse Chronicles (2000) by Pete Townshend

[44] Unpublished interview with Phil Sutcliffe, March 2004

[45] Sounds, January 2 1971

[46] Liner notes to deluxe CD reissue of The Who Who's Next, 2003

[47] ZigZag, April 1974

[48] ICE, October 1995

[49] Liner notes to deluxe CD reissue of The Who Who's Next, 2003

[50] Author's interview, November 30 2009

51 *Guitar Shop*, June 1995
52 livedaily.com/news/2386.html, December 28 2000
53 *Guitar Shop*, June 1995
54 Interview with Roger Scott of BBC Radio One, June 20 1989
55 *ZigZag*, April 1974
56 Author's interview, December 28 2009
57 *ICE*, October 1995
58 Author's interview, December 28 2009
59 Author's interview, December 18 2009
60 *Guitar Shop*, June 1995
61 Author's interview, December 28 2009
62 Liner notes to Link Wray *The Link Wray Rumble* (1974) by Pete Townshend
63 Author's interview, December 28 2009
64 Liner notes to deluxe CD reissue of The Who *Who's Next*, 2003
65 *Revolver*, Fall 2000
66 Liner notes to deluxe CD reissue of The Who *Who's Next*, 2003
67 *Classic Albums: Who's Next* (TV documentary), 1999

CHAPTER 4
1 *ZigZag*, April 1974
2 *Los Angeles Free Press*, December 24 1971
3 Author's interview, 1985
4 *Amazing Journey: The Story Of the Who* (DVD documentary), 2007
5 Tobler and Grundy, *The Record Producers*
6 *Sounds*, July 17 1971
7 livedaily.com/news/2386.html, December 28 2000
8 *Melody Maker*, March 13 1971
9 Tobler and Grundy, *The Record Producers*
10 *Los Angeles Free Press*, December 24 1971
11 *Los Angeles Free Press*, December 24 1971
12 *Melody Maker*, December 11 1971

13 *Rolling Stone*, December 9 1971
14 *Melody Maker*, December 11 1971
15 *Disc*, October 23 1972
16 Author's interview, June 4 2010
17 Author's interview, December 14 2009
18 Author's interview, December 14 2009
19 *Record Mirror*, May 8 1971
20 *Record Collector*, September 1994
21 *Circus*, November 1971
22 *Crawdaddy*, August 1971
23 *Classic Albums: Who's Next* (TV documentary), 1999
24 *Uncut*, January 2003
25 Author's interview, June 11 2010
26 Author's interview, June 16 2010
27 *Sounds*, July 24 1971
28 *Sounds*, July 24 1971
29 *Rolling Stone*, June 10 1971
30 *Record Mirror*, May 8 1971
31 *Classic Albums: Who's Next* (TV documentary), 1999
32 Interview with Roger Scott of BBC Radio One, June 20 1989
33 *Crawdaddy*, December 5 1971
34 *The Who, The Mods, And The Quadrophenia Connection* (DVD documentary), 2008
35 Author's interview, May 21 2010
36 *Record Collector*, September 1994
37 *Uncut*, January 2003
38 *Rolling Stone*, June 20 1974
39 Author's interview, May 21 2010
40 *Classic Albums: Who's Next* (TV documentary), 1999
41 *Amazing Journey: The Story Of the Who* (DVD documentary), 2007
42 Interview with Roger Scott of BBC Radio One, June 20 1989
43 *Guitar Player*, November 2009
44 Author's interview, June 4 2010
45 *Los Angeles Free Press*, December 24 1971
46 *In The Studio: Who's Next* (radio documentary), January 30 1995
47 Author's interview, October 30 2009

48 Interview with Roger Scott of BBC Radio One, June 20 1989
49 *In The Studio: Who's Next* (radio documentary), January 30 1995
50 *Classic Albums: Who's Next* (TV documentary), 1999
51 Interview with Roger Scott of BBC Radio One, June 20 1989
52 McKnight and Silver, *The Who ... Through The Eyes Of Pete Townshend*
53 Author's interview, June 4 2010
54 *In The Studio: Who's Next* (radio documentary), January 30 1995
55 *Record Collector*, August 1995
56 Marsh and Swenson, *The Rolling Stone Record Guide*
57 *Los Angeles Free Press*, December 24 1971
58 *Los Angeles Free Press*, December 24 1971
59 *Crawdaddy*, December 5 1971
60 Author's interview, October 23 2009
61 *Record Mirror*, May 8 1971
62 *Los Angeles Free Press*, December 24 1971
63 *Rolling Stone*, December 5 1974

CHAPTER 5
1 *Melody Maker*, June 26 1971
2 *International Times*, September 9 1971
3 *International Times*, September 9 1971
4 Author's interview, October 20 2009
5 Author's interview, October 20 2009
6 Russell, *Dear Mr Fantasy*
7 *ZigZag*, March 1974
8 Russell, *Dear Mr Fantasy*
9 *Stereo Review*, November 1971
10 Interview with Roger Scott of BBC Radio One, June 20 1989
11 *In The Studio: Who's Next* (radio documentary), January 30 1995
12 *Melody Maker*, July 17 1971
13 *Crawdaddy*, August 29 1971
14 *Melody Maker*, July 17 1971

15 *Crawdaddy*, August 29 1971
16 Interview with Roger Scott of BBC Radio One, June 20 1989
17 *Rolling Stone*, September 11 1975
18 *Creem*, October 1971
19 *Melody Maker*, August 21 1971
20 Marsh and Swenson, *The Rolling Stone Record Guide*
21 Marsh and Swenson, *The Rolling Stone Record Guide*
22 Author's interview, June 1 2010
23 Interview with Roger Scott of BBC Radio One, June 20 1989
24 Author's interview, June 2 2010
25 *Los Angeles Free Press*, December 24 1971
26 Author's interview, May 21 2010
27 Barnes and Townshend, *The Story Of Tommy*
28 *New Musical Express*, July 17 1971
29 *Melody Maker*, October 23 1971
30 *Rolling Stone*, August 5 1971
31 *Crawdaddy*, December 5 1971
32 *Rolling Stone*, December 9 1971
33 *Melody Maker*, October 16 1971
34 *New Musical Express*, October 16 1971
35 *International Times*, September 9 1971
36 *Los Angeles Free Press*, December 17 1971
37 *Sounds*, June 24 1972
38 *New Musical Express*, August 21 1971
39 *Melody Maker*, October 16 1971
40 *Melody Maker*, October 30 1971
41 *Melody Maker*, November 6 1971
42 *Rolling Stone*, February 3 1972
43 *Melody Maker*, October 23 1971
44 Author's interview, October 23 2009
45 *ZigZag*, April 1974
46 Author's interview, February 26 2010
47 Author's interview, December 15 2009
48 *Night Times*, December 22 1971
49 *Los Angeles Free Press*, December 31 1971

50 *Los Angeles Free Press*, December 31 1971

CHAPTER 6
1 *Disc*, October 24 1970
2 *Creem*, December 1970
3 *Melody Maker*, October 23 1971
4 *New Musical Express*, December 19 1970
5 Author's interview, March 2 2010
6 Quoted in Tremlett, *The Who*
7 *Disc*, October 23 1972
8 *Creem*, February 1973
9 Author's interview, May 21 2010
10 Townshend *A Decade Of The Who: An Authorized History In Music, Paintings, Words And Photographs*
11 Author's interview, July 7 2010
12 *Circus*, April 1972
13 *Classic Albums: Who's Next* (TV documentary), 1999
14 *New Musical Express*, July 17 1976
15 Liner notes to The Who *Odds & Sods* (1974) by Pete Townshend
16 *Guitar Player*, May 1972
17 *Los Angeles Free Press*, December 24 1971
18 *Melody Maker*, August 19 1972
19 *Sounds*, August 12 1972
20 *New Musical Express*, December 16 1972
21 *Circus*, November 1971
22 *Rolling Stone*, October 26 1972
23 *Sounds*, August 12 1972
24 *New Musical Express*, December 16 1972
25 *Sounds*, August 12 1972
26 *New Musical Express*, December 16 1972
27 Author's interview, July 7 2010
28 *Rolling Stone*, October 26 1972
29 *Rolling Stone*, December 21 1972
30 *High Fidelity*, February 1973
31 *Melody Maker*, October 14 1972
32 *Crawdaddy*, January 1973
33 Author's interview, May 21 2010
34 Liner notes to *Two's Missing* (1987) by John Entwistle

35 Quoted in Neill and Kent, *Anyway Anyhow Anywhere: The Complete Chronicle Of The Who 1958-1978*
36 *Sounds*, August 12 1972
37 *Sounds*, December 2 1972
38 *Rock*, January 14 1974
39 *Sounds*, August 12 1972
40 *Clash*, December 2009
41 *Modern Hi-Fi & Stereo Guide*, August 1974
42 *Sounds*, August 12 1972
43 *Melody Maker*, August 19 1972
44 *New Musical Express*, August 19 1972
45 *The Who, The Mods, And The Quadrophenia Connection* (DVD), 2008
46 Author's interview, May 21 2010
47 Barnes and Townshend, *The Story Of Tommy*
48 Author's interview, May 21 2010
49 Author's interview, February 18 2010
50 *Hit Parader*, May 1974
51 *New Musical Express*, May 26 1979
52 Author's interview, February 18 2010
53 Author's interview, May 21 2010
54 Author's interview, May 21 2010
55 *New Musical Express*, November 17 1979
56 *Evening Argus*, May 18 1964
57 *Quadrophenia* (DVD), 2001
58 Author's interview, February 18 2010
59 Author's interview, May 21 2010
60 *Melody Maker*, June 22 1974
61 *Penthouse*, December 1974
62 *In The Studio: Quadrophenia* (radio documentary), October 14 1996
63 *Sounds*, August 12 1972
64 *Rolling Stone*, September 9 1972
65 *Record Mirror*, September 23 1972
66 Author's interview, June 7 2010
67 *Sounds*, December 2 1972
68 *Record Mirror*, December 23 1972
69 *Disc*, January 26 1974

[70] Author's interview, May 21 2010
[71] Sounds, December 2 1972

CHAPTER 7
[1] Melody Maker, February 10 1973
[2] Melody Maker, April 7 1973
[3] Sounds, October 27 1973
[4] Author's interview, November 30 2009
[5] Liner notes to Pete Townshend Scoop (1983) by Pete Townshend
[6] Author's interview, June 7 2010
[7] Sounds, August 12 1972
[8] Record Mirror, December 23 1972
[9] ZigZag, March 1974
[10] Melody Maker, October 27 1973
[11] Melody Maker, April 7 1973
[12] Author's interview, November 9 2009
[13] Tobler and Grundy, The Record Producers
[14] Author's interview, May 21 2010
[15] Author's interview, November 30 2009
[16] Author's interview, November 9 2009
[17] Author's interview, November 9 2009
[18] Author's interview, June 7 2010
[19] Author's interview, November 9 2009
[20] Author's interview, November 9 2009
[21] Author's interview, June 7 2010
[22] Author's interview, December 17 2009
[23] Sounds, October 27 1973
[24] Author's interview, November 9 2009
[25] The Who, The Mods, And The Quadrophenia Connection (DVD), 2008
[26] Author's interview, May 21 2010
[27] Author's interview, October 26 2009
[28] Author's interview, March 2 2010
[29] Rolling Stone, September 14 1968
[30] Circus, June 1973
[31] Rolling Stone, January 3 1974

[32] Melody Maker, October 27 1973
[33] In The Studio: Quadrophenia (radio documentary), Octobor 14 1996
[34] Modern Hi-Fi & Stereo Guide, August 1974
[35] Author's interview, February 18 2010
[36] In The Studio: Quadrophenia (radio documentary), October 14 1996
[37] Q, September 1994
[38] New Musical Express, November 3 1973
[39] Author's interview, December 17 2009
[40] Author's interview, November 9 2009
[41] Townshend A Decade Of The Who: An Authorized History In Music, Paintings, Words And Photographs
[42] Rock, January 14 1974
[43] Live At The Isle Of Wight Festival 1970 (DVD), 2004
[44] Zoo World, December 20 1973
[45] Zoo World, December 20 1973
[46] Rolling Stone, January 3 1974
[47] Townshend A Decade Of The Who: An Authorized History In Music, Paintings, Words And Photographs
[48] Hit Parader, June 1975
[49] Pollock, In Their Own Words
[50] Penthouse, December 1974
[51] Zoo World, December 20 1973
[52] The Who, The Mods, And The Quadrophenia Connection (DVD), 2008
[53] Author's interview, November 9 2009
[54] Townshend A Decade Of The Who: An Authorized History In Music, Paintings, Words And Photographs
[55] Zoo World, December 20 1973
[56] In The Studio: Quadrophenia (radio documentary), October 14 1996
[57] New Musical Express, November 3 1973

[58] In The Studio: Quadrophenia (radio documentary), October 14 1996
[59] Pollock, In Their Own Words
[60] Modern Hi-Fi & Stereo Guide, August 1974
[61] New Musical Express, August 19 1972
[62] In The Studio: Quadrophenia (radio documentary), October 14 1996
[63] Creem, April 1975
[64] BBC TV interview, September 26 1974
[65] Zoo World, December 20 1973
[66] Amazing Journey: The Story Of The Who (DVD documentary), 2007
[67] New Musical Express, November 3 1973
[68] Author's interview, November 9 2009
[69] Author's interview, November 30 2009
[70] Author's interview, November 9 2009
[71] Author's interview, June 4 2010
[72] Author's interview, November 30 2009
[73] Author's interview, November 30 2009
[74] Author's interview, November 9 2009
[75] Author's interview, November 30 2009
[76] Uncut, January 2003
[77] Author's interview, November 9 2009

CHAPTER 8
[1] Disc, January 26 1974
[2] Rock, January 14 1974
[3] Rolling Stone, January 3 1974
[4] Author's interview, May 21 2010
[5] Author's interview, May 21 2010
[6] Author's interview, May 21 2010
[7] Neill and Kent, Anyway Anyhow Anywhere: The Complete Chronicle Of The Who 1958-1978
[8] Author's interview, May 21 2010
[9] Author's interview, November 9 2009

10 Author's interview, November 30 2009
11 Author's interview, November 9 2009
12 *New Musical Express*, October 27 2003
13 *Hit Parader*, May 1974
14 Author's interview, June 4 2010
15 Russell, *Dear Mr Fantasy*
16 *Crawdaddy*, January 1974
17 *Crawdaddy*, January 1974
18 *In The Studio: Quadrophenia* (radio documentary), October 14 1996
19 *Melody Maker*, October 6 1973
20 *New Musical Express*, October 6 1973
21 *Mojo*, February 2006
22 *Q*, September 1994
23 Author's interview, March 2 2010
24 *Melody Maker*, October 20 1973
25 Carr, *A Talk On The Wild Side*
26 Author's interview, February 18 2010
27 Author's interview, December 1 2009
28 *In The Studio: Quadrophenia* (radio documentary), October 14 1996
29 *Rolling Stone*, September 11 1975
30 Swenson, *Headliners: The Who*
31 *Sounds*, October 27 1973
32 *Melody Maker*, November 3 1973
33 *Disc*, November 10 1973
34 *Rolling Stone*, December 6 1973
35 Author's interview, March 7 2010
36 *Penthouse*, December 1974
37 *Classic Albums: Who's Next* (TV Documentary), 1999
38 *Newcastle Evening Chronicle*, November 6 1973
39 Author's interview, March 2 2010
40 *Melody Maker*, November 17 1973
41 Author's interview, May 21 2010
42 *Melody Maker*, October 20 1973
43 *The Listener*, November 8 1973

44 *Rolling Stone*, December 26 1973
45 *Stereo Review*, February 1974
46 *Phonographic Record Magazine*, December 1973
47 *Beetle*, December 1973
48 *Newsweek*, November 12 1973
49 *Beetle*, December 1973
50 Author's interview, October 23 2009
51 *High Fidelity*, February 1974
52 *Creem*, January 1974
53 Marsh, *Before I Get Old: The Story Of The Who*
54 *Creem*, March 1974
55 *Rolling Stone*, December 20 1973
56 *San Francisco Examiner*, November 21 1973
57 Author's interview, December 15 2009
58 Author's interview, December 14 2009
59 *Musician*, July 1989
60 Author's interview, December 8 2009
61 *Billboard*, December 8 1973
62 *Phonograph Record Magazine*, January 1974
63 Author's interview, June 2 2010
64 Author's interview, October 23 2009
65 *Rolling Stone*, January 3 1974
66 *Rolling Stone*, January 3 1974
67 *Rolling Stone*, January 3 1974
68 *Rolling Stone*, January 3 1974
69 *Trouser Press*, April 1978
70 Author's interview, December 8 2009
71 *Modern Hi-Fi & Stereo Guide*, August 1974
72 Author's interview, October 26 2009
73 *Melody Maker*, December 8 1973
74 *Stereo Review*, April 1974
75 *Washington Post*, December 7 1973
76 *Melody Maker*, January 5 1974
77 Author's interview, November 9 2009
78 *Melody Maker*, February 16 1974

CHAPTER 9
1 *Sounds*, May 11 1974
2 *New Musical Express*, May 11 1974
3 *Crawdaddy*, January 1974
4 *Crawdaddy*, April 1975
5 *ZigZag*, April 1974
6 *New York Times*, June 13 1974
7 *Penthouse*, December 1974
8 Swenson, *Headliners: The Who*
9 *Trouser Press*, April 1978
10 Author's interview, June 2 2010
11 *Trouser Press*, April 1978
12 Author's interview, October 23 2009
13 *Modern Hi-Fi & Stereo Guide*, August 1974
14 *New York Times*, June 13 1974
15 Barnes and Townshend, *The Story Of Tommy*
16 *New York Times*, June 13 1974
17 *Melody Maker*, February 9 1974
18 Liner notes to The Who *Odds & Sods* (1974) by Pete Townshend
19 *Penthouse*, December 1974
20 *Creem*, October 1975
21 *Record Collector*, August 1995
22 *Melody Maker*, September 16 1978
23 *Melody Maker*, October 14 1978
24 *Clash*, December 2009
25 Interview on *Quadrophenia* DVD, 2001
26 Interview on *The Kids Are Alright* DVD, 2003
27 *New York Times*, November 13 1979
28 Author's interview, July 7 2010
29 *Classic Rock*, June 2004
30 Author's interview, May 21 2010
31 *New Musical Express*, April 19 1980
32 *Q*, June 1996
33 *Guardian*, December 6 1999
34 Author's interview, May 21 2010
35 Author's interview, June 4 2010
36 lifehouse-method.com
37 Author's interview, June 11 2010

Bibliography

Atkins, John *The Who On Record: A Critical History, 1963-1998* (McFarland 2000)

Barnes, Richard *The Who: Maximum R&B* (St Martin's 1982)

Barnes, Richard and Pete Townshend *The Story Of Tommy* (Eel Pie 1977)

Black, Johnny *Eyewitness: The Who* (Carlton 2001)

Carr, Roy *A Talk On The Wild Side* (EarBooks 2009)

Catterall, Ali and Simon Wells *Your Face Here: British Cult Movies Since The Sixties* (Fourth Estate 2002)

Cawthorne, Nigel *The Who And The Making Of Tommy* (Unanimous 2005)

Charlesworth, Chris and Ed Hanel *The Who: The Complete Guide To Their Music* (Omnibus 2004)

Fletcher, Tony *Dear Boy: The Life Of Keith Moon* (Omnibus 1998)

Forrest, Peter *The A-Z Of Analogue Synthesizers* (Susurreal 1998)

Frame, Pete (ed) *The Road To Rock* (Charisma 1974)

Herman, Gary *The Who* (November 1971)

Heylin, Clinton *Bootleg: The Secret History Of The Other Recording Industry* (St Martin's 1994)

Khan, Hazrat Inayat *The Mysticism Of Sound And Music* (Shambala 1996)

Kooper, Al *Backstage Passes & Backstabbing Bastards* (Billboard 1998)

Marsh, Dave *Before I Get Old: The Story Of The Who* (Plexus 1983)

Marsh, Dave & John Swenson (eds) *The Rolling Stone Record Guide* (Rolling Stone 1979)

McKnight, Connor and Caroline Silver *The Who ... Through The Eyes Of Pete Townshend* (Scholastic 1974)

McMichael, Joe and 'Irish' Jack Lyons *The Who Concert File* (Omnibus 2004)

Motion, Andrew *The Lamberts: George, Constant & Kit* (FSG 1987)

Neill, Andy and Matt Kent *Anyway Anyhow Anywhere: The Complete Chronicle Of The Who 1958-1978* (Virgin 2002)

Pollock, Bruce *In Their Own Words* (Macmillan 1975)

Russell, Ethan *Dear Mr Fantasy* (Houghton Mifflin 1985)

Schaffner, Nicholas *The British Invasion* (McGraw-Hill 1982)

Swenson, John *Headliners: The Who* (Tempo Star 1979)

Tobler, John and Stuart Grundy *The Record Producers* (St Martin's 1982)

Townshend, Pete *A Decade Of The Who: An Authorized History In Music, Paintings, Words And Photographs* (Music Sales 1977)

Townshend, Pete with Jeff Young *Lifehouse* (Pocket Books 1999)

Tremlett, George *The Who* (Futura 1975)

Wilkerson, Mark *Amazing Journey: The Life Of Pete Townshend* (Bad News 2006)

Wolter, Stephen and Karen Kimber *The Who In Print: An Annotated Bibliography, 1965 Through 1990* (McFarland 1992)

Index

Words *In Italics* indicate album titles unless otherwise stated. Words 'In Quotes' indicate song titles. Page numbers in **bold** indicate illustrations.

A
'Accidents' 168
Adams, Jack 103, 104, 208
Alcock, John 59–60, 196, 205, 206, 210, 222
Altham, Keith 51–2, 92, 99, 100, 169, 214, 250, 257
Altman, Robert 83
Amazing Journey (DVD documentary) 75, 92, 114, 130, 232
Amazing Journey 40
'Ambition' 174
Another Scoop 175
'Anyway, Anyhow, Anywhere' 114, 117
Arbus, Dave 65, 133, 162
As He Stands 66
Ascher, Kenny 109
Astley, Jon 110, 118, 131, 288
'Atom Heart Mother' 41
Aubrey Jr, James T. 84
Awopbopaloobop Alopbambamboom (book) 61

B
'Baba O'Riley' 36, 37, 39, 45–7, 49, 64, 65–7, 68, 70, 71, 72, 77, 107, 120, 132–3, 135, 136, 153, 157, 161, 162, 164, 250, 288
Baba, Meher 40, 41, 42–3, 49, 50, 56–7, 64, 65–7, 69–71, 77–8, 79, 141, 144, 151, 159, 169–71, 178–83, 224, 226, 228, 238, 285
'Baby Don't You Do It' 105–6, 107, 121, 150, 164, 177
backing tapes 94, 123, 162, 250, 251, 253, 254, 256, 279

'Bargain' 63, 70, 71, 117, 120, 121, 131, 134, 135, 153, 164
Barker, J. Edward 144, 146
Barnes, Richard 23, 28–9, 63, 89, 128, 155, 170, 171, 180, 182, 187, 198, 208, 213, 227, 235, 239, 240, 243, 258, 279, 285, 287
Barrel One, Barrel Two (movie) 83
BBC Radiophonic Workshop 45
Beach Boys, The 18, 60, 290
Beatles, The 18, 27, 29, 33, 34, 36, 48, 51, 89, 90, 93, 115, 117, 125, 129, 139, 140, 144, 147, 152, 155, 157, 172, 177, 261, 278, 290
'Begin The Beguine' 57–8, 170, 179, 183
'Behind Blue Eyes' 63, 68–9, 70, 75, 107, 108, 109, 121, 135, 153, 159, 161, 164, 279
'Bell Boy' 203, 212, 225–6, 229, 230, 252, 255, 271, 276
Bell, Maggie 197
Bent Frame 168
'Bony Maronie' 121
Bonzo Dog Band, The 55, 71, 169
Bootleg (book) 63
Boy Friend, The (movie) 40
Bradbury, Ray 286
Brewster McCloud (movie) 83
Bronco Bullfrog (movie) 240
Bronfman Sr, Edgar 84
Brown, Arthur 24
Brown, Derek 96
Butler, Anya 110

C
'Can You Help The One You Really Love?' 82, 287
Cavaliere, Felix 108
'Celebration Of The Lizard' 18
Clapton, Eric 199
Clark, Petula 71
'Classified' 183

Clayton, Merry 196
'Cobwebs And Strange' 271
Cohen, Allan 56
Cohn, Nic 61, 165, 172
'Content' 57, 58, 179
Cort, Bud 84
'Cousin Kevin' 138
Cunitz, Matt 46, 124, 289
Curbishley, Bill 83, 214, 269
Curle, John 235
'Cut My Hair' 186, 203, 204, 220, 223, 252, 255

D
Da Costa, Mike 56, 171
Daltrey, Roger
  As actor 279;
  announces *Guitar Farm* film 156; on backing tapes 123, 254, 256; dabbles in record production 168; dissatisfaction with *Quadrophenia*'s production 236; on Entwistle 280, 284; finds *Quadrophenia* "unenjoyable" 275; first solo album, *Daltrey* 197, 200; fist-fight with Townshend 250; as harmonica player 162, 164; on Glyn Johns 207; on Kit Lambert 111; on *Lifehouse* 92, 126, 128; praise for *Quadrophenia* 285; and the Press 50; *Quadrophenia* 'theme' 222, 230; second solo album, *Ride A Rock Horse* 279; as singer 64, 65, 90; as songwriter 91; on Townshend 60; on *Who's Next* 151
Daltrey 200
'Day Of Silence' 57, 58, 183
Dear Mr Fantasy (book) 147, 240, 247
Decca 35, 86, 114, 148, 159, 172, 178, 180
Denny, Sandy 196
Direct Hits 157
'Dirty Jobs, The' 203, 213, 222, 232, 234, 252
'Do The Albert' 169
'Doctor Jimmy' 201, 216, 226, 250, 266, 271, 276

Donald, Donald K. 269
Doors, The 18, 34, 162
Double Pisces (movie) 36
Double, Mick 264
Douglas, Jack 104, 115
'Drowned' 203, 204, 213, 224–5, 228, 271, 273, 276
Dunlop, Frank 87, 89, 94–95, 97, 101
Dury, Ian 253
Dylan, Bob 183, 279

E
Earhart, Amelia 38
East Of Eden 133
Eel Pie Hotel 73
Eel Pie Studios 29
Ellis Group, The 168
Ellis, Steve 168
Empty Glass 174
Entwistle, John
  On backing tapes 254; as bass player 90, 212, 219; compiles *Odds & Sods* 280; death 286; first solo album, *Smash Your Head Against The Wall* 91, 141; fourth solo album, *Mad Dog* 196, 280; frustrations as songwriter 141; and 'Heaven And Hell' 31; horn playing 212; and 'My Wife' 63, 138–9, 141; on *Lifehouse* 92; and '905' 281; overdubs *Quadrophenia* tracks 284; 'Ox' persona 90; and 'Postcard' 30, 31, 129; and the Press 50; *Quadrophenia* 'theme' 226, 230; reflects on *Quadrophenia* 276; second solo album, *Whistle Rymes* 177, 196; third solo album, *Rigor Mortis Sets In* 196; and 'When I Was A Boy' 136, 141; on Young Vic concerts 98, 125
Evans, Cliff 99
'Eyesight To The Blind' 106

F
Faces, The 56, 209
Faiers, Chris 73–5
Farren, Mick 144, 146

Feast Of Friends (movie) 34
Ferrante, Dennis 109
'Fiddle About' 130
'Finale' 229
'5:15' 201, 204, 211, 212, 213, 220, 223, 232, 249, 256, 271, 276
Fontaine, Dick 35–37
'Four Faces' 229, 284
Friend, David 49

G
Geesin, Ron 40–2, 56, 66, 162–3
Genius Of Pete Townshend, The 63, 78
Gershwin, Jerry 83
Get Back 18, 290
Get Carter (movie) 40
'Get Inside' 174
'Get Out And Stay Out' 229, 284
'Getting In Tune' 68, 77, 109, 117, 122, 131, 134, 162
'Giving It All Away' 200
Glastonbury Fayre 183
'Goin' Down' 164
'Going Mobile' 54, 58, 63, 67, 116, 120, 132, 134, 147, 153, 162, 224
Gorden, Helmut 190
Got Live If You Want It! 114
Greatest Hits Live 164
'Greyhound Girl' 81
Guitar Farm (story and movie) 37–41, 67, 83–6, 156–7

H
Halpin, Scott 264–5
Hanel, Ed 26
Happy Birthday 56–7, 141, 151, 170, 171, 178, 179, 182
'Happy Jack' 25, 202, 284
Hardin, Tim 279
Harris, Richard 197
Harrison, George 36
Hastilow, Dave 171
Havens, Richie 196
'Heaven And Hell' 31, 32, 53, 138, 141
'Helpless Dancer' 201, 222, 226, 232, 234
Hendrix, Jimi 18, 36, 102, 104, 148, 153, 195
Heylin, Clinton 63

'Hitchcock Railway' 213
Hitler, Adolf 41
Hodges, Mike 40
Hoffman, Abbie 160
Hopkins, Nicky 72, 117–8, 122, 134, 137, 213, 255
Houison, Rod **11**, 202, 203, 233, 236, 244
Hughes, Graham 242

I
'I Always Say' 183
I Am 64, 171–2
'I Am The Sea' 201, 219, 220, 229, 271
'I Can See For Miles' 146
'I Can't Explain' 114, 187
'I Don't Even Know Myself' 30, 31, 32, 33, 36, 53, 80, 121, 129, 144, 150
'I'm A Boy' 23, 25–6, 187, 195, 212
'I'm One' 189, 192, 193, 203, 221–2, 268, 271
'I'm The Face' 158, 190, 204
'I've Had Enough' 203, 204, 210, 212, 222, 223, 232, 234, 252
In C 65
'In Love With Meher Baba' (magazine article) 43, 56
Innes, Neil 169
International Times (magazine) 42, 144, 159,
Into '71 (TV show) 33
Iron Man, The 286
'Is It In My Head?' 175, 176, 201, 222, 226, 252
'Is It Me?' 226

J
Jagger, Mick 34, 115, 169, 206
Jansch, Bert 171
'Jig-A-Jig' 133
Johns, Andy 119
Johns, Glyn 49, 113–7, 119, 127, 129–30, 133, 136, 143, 147, 149, 153, 172, 176, 184, 206–8, 222, 227
Johnson, Skip 264
'Join My Gang' 279
'Join Together' 81, 173, 174, 175, 177, 184
'Joker James' 187, 195, 229–30, 284

Jones, Brian 31
Jones, Kenney 285

K
Kameron, Peter 83, 213
Keane, Speedy 36
Kennedy, Maud 57
Kennett, Terry 'Chad' 239, 241, 242
Kerkorian, Kirk 84
Khan, Hazrat Inayat 43–6, 54, 61, 68, 77
Kids Are Alright, The (TV documentary) 200, 284
'Kids Are Alright, The' 22, 25, 232
Kilburn & The High Roads 253
Kilty, Gavin 73–4
King Biscuit Flower Hour, The (radio show) 270
King, Allan 35
King, Dave 148
Kinks, The 36, 114, 117
Kirby, Linden 240
Knowland, Nic 35
Kooper, Al 108

L
Lambert, Constant 22
Lambert, Kit **7**, 22–5, 30, 34, 35, 53, 70, 83, 91, 95, 101–4, 106–111, 114–5, 119–120, 128, 155, 166, 184, 190, 206, 207–8, 213–4, 227, 269, 276, 281
Lane, Ronnie 56, 172, 179, 206, 209, 279
Law, Roger 148
Lennon, John 35, 36, 102, 104, 109, 218, 280
Lerner, Murray 37
Let It Be (movie) 34, 89, 93, 125, 157, 177
Let It Be 115, 147, 290
Let It Be ... Naked 290
'Let My Love Open The Door' 81, 183
'Let's See Action' 79, 129, 137, 158, 159, 160, 173, 179, 180, 279
Lifehouse (radio play) 69, 286–7
Lifehouse 17–20, 22–30, 35, 37–46, 58–73, 76–103, 105, 108, 110-3, 117–130, 134–5,

137–140, 144, 147, 149–151, 154–7, 162, 165, 167, 172–4, 177, 179, 186, 188, 194, 199, 201, 207, 215, 216, 219, 227, 243, 279-282, 286-290
Lifehouse Chronicles (boxed set) 60, 62, 63, 69, 70, 79, 81, 82, 86, 94, 95, 98, 101, 105, 111, 119, 174, 287–9
Lindsay-Hogg, Michael 177
Lisztomania (movie) 280
Live At Leeds, 28–9, 31, 32, 80, 119, 121, 133, 163
Lone Ranger (movie) 36
'Lone Ranger Street Reduction' 36
'Long Live Rock' 175, 176, 184, 189, 195, 200
'Love Ain't For Keeping' 63, 70, 108, 109, 121, 132, 134, 138, 153, 162, 183
'Love Man' 57, 183
'Love Reign O'er Me' 175, 176, 197, 201, 204, 223, 227, 214, 249, 270, 284
Lyons, Irish Jack 188–9, 191, 218, 253

M
Mad Dog 196, 280
'Magic Bus' 80, 258, 264
Mahoney's Last Stand 172
Mangan, Richard 96, 97, 100
Manzarek, Ray 34
'Mary' 63, 79, 81, 129
'Mary Jane' 57, 183
MCA 86
McCartney, Paul 290
McInnerney, Mike 42, 144, 238
Meaden, Pete 190
Meaty Beaty Big And Bouncy 157–8, 163
MGM (film studio) 35, 37, 40, 41, 54, 83, 84, 86
Miller, Glenn 38, 39
mods 215–6
Monterey Pop (movie) 34
Moon, Keith
As actor 169, 195; and 'Bell Boy' 225; banned from BBC Club 249;

comedy show, *A Touch Of The Moon* 235; death 281; and drugs 103, 116; as drummer 90, 212, 219, 227; housewarming party 144, 147; marriage break-up 249; passes out onstage 264–6; and the Press 50, 169; *Quadrophenia* 'theme' 225, 230; solo album, *Two Sides Of The Moon* 280; and Viv Stanshall 55, 169; studio antics 110; on Townshend's demos 23; and 'Wasp Man' 183
Morrison, Jim 34
Mountain 106
Mushroom 46, 124, 289
Music From Lifehouse (concert DVD) 60, 70, 79, 81, 82, 288
Music From The Body 41
'Music Must Change' 82
'My Generation' 25, 97, 114, 121, 152, 203, 204, 217, 218, 221, 283
'My Wife' 63, 138–9, 141, 153, 159, 289
Myers, Mike 35, 37–9, 41–2, 84–5, 157
Mysticism Of Sound And Music, The (book) 43–5, 54, 61, 68, 77

N
'Naked Eye' 30, 32, 33, 53, 80, 94, 121, 129, 137, 150, 264, 265, 289
Neal, Peter 248
Nevison, Ron 208, 209, 233, 234, 237
'905' 281
Nicholls, Billy 171
'Normal Day For Brian, A Man Who Died Everyday, A' 31
'Note, The' 54
'Now I'm A Farmer' 30, 32, 53

O
'O Parvardigar' 171, 172, 179, 181, 182
Ocean, Humphrey 253
Odds & Sods 32, 77, 80,

81, 105, 110, 117, 136, 137, 150, 174, 175, 200, 229, 280
'Odorono' 187
Oh Dear, What Can The Matter Be? (movie) 37
Olympic Sound Studios 116–7, 130, 172
Ono, Yoko 35, 36, 104
'Overture' 212
Ox 280

P
Pappalardi, Felix 107
'Parvardigar' *see* 'O Parvardigar'
Peel, John 259
Pentangle 83, 171
Pete Townshend Meher Baba 178
'Pictures Of Lily' 25, 212
'Piledriver' 36
'Pinball Wizard' 61, 96, 121, 182, 258
Pink Floyd 40, 73, 99, 146, 160, 167–8, 232
'Postcard' 30, 31, 32, 53, 129
Postle, Denis 35, 37, 39, 40, 42, 67, 83, 84, 85, 157
Powell, Roger 47– 9, 101, 124
Presley, Elvis 40
Pridden, Bob 28, 122
Prior, Barry 191–2
Psychoderelict 286
'Punk Meets The Godfather, The' 202, 203, 204, 221, 232, 271, 284
Purcell, Henry 23
'Pure And Easy' 22, 39, 54, 58, 63, 72, 76, 77, 79, 92, 108, 122, 129, 136, 137, 150, 179, 289, 290
'Put The Money Down' 81, 174, 176

Q
quadraphonic sound 89, 93, 96, 97, 99, 103, 168, 194, 206, 233, 243–7, 254, 266
Quadrophenia 17, 19, 22, 24–6, 43, 53, 124, 158, 175–7, 185–199, 201–6, 208–237, 238–271, 273–290
'Quadrophenia' 201, 220

Quadrophenia (movie) 191–2, 282–5
Quads 23–4
Quick One, A 174, 186, 283
'Quick One, While He's Away, A' 24, 259

R
'Rael' 24–5
Rainbow In Curved Air, A 65
Ramport Studio 59, 199, 204–6, 209–10, 212, 214, 227, 239, 241
'Real Me, The' 201, 202, 219–220, 246, 271, 283
Record Plant 102–3, 119
Reed, Jimmy 279
Reizner, Lou 196–7
'Relay' 81, 173–4, 184, 200
Renbourn, John 171
Ride A Rock Horse 279
Riding On The Crest Of A Slump 168
Rigor Mortis Sets In 196
Riley, Terry 65–6
Ring Cycle, The 41
'Riot In A Female Jail' 174
'Road Runner' 121
Rock From The Beginning (book) 61
'Rock, The' 201, 220, 226, 227
Roddam, Franc 191, 282
Roeg, Nicolas 286
Rohoman, David Newton 253
Rolling Stones Rock And Roll Circus, The 34, 42, 177
Rolling Stones, The 27, 29, 34, 51, 64, 73, 80, 113, 115, 117, 118, 119, 124, 131, 147, 158, 237, 255
'Rough Boys' 174
Rough Mix 279
Rowley, Chris 144, 146
Rudd, John 160
Rudge, Peter 214, 269–70
Russell, Ethan 147, 149, 239, 240, 247
Russell, Ken 40, 273, 278, 279, 282, 286

S
Sanson, Veronique 279
Scaffold, The 169
Scoop 59, 63, 69, 71, 78, 176, 201, 204, 228

'Sea And Sand' 186, 201, 203, 204, 223, 271
Sebastian, John 162
'See Me, Feel Me' 121
'Seeker, The' 29–30, 37, 56–7, 58, 182, 183
Self-Portrait 183
'Sheraton Gibson' 179, 183
Silver, Norman 269
Sinatra, Frank 40
'Sister Disco' 82
'Slip Kid' 82
Smash Your Head Against The Wall 141, 196
Smile 18, 60, 290
Smith, Richard 37, 39
'Smokestack Lightning' 264
Smolin, Barry 242
Solow, Herb 37, 39–42, 83, 84
'Song Is Over, The' 63, 67, 71, 77, 117, 120, 132, 134, 135, 136, 138, 162
Sound And Picture City (TV series) 34
Souster, Tim 45
'Sparks' 30, 35
'Spoonful' 264
Stainton, Chris 213, 224
Stamp, Chris 22, 24, 34, 83, 95, 99, 114, 139, 181, 190, 213, 214, 269
Stanley, Richard 35–7, 40–42, 83, 156–7, 250
Stanshall, Viv 55, 169
Stardust (movie) 280
Stargroves 115–6, 119, 06
Stark, Ray 54
Starkey, Zak 285
Starr, Ringo 36, 196
Stewart, Ian 'Stu' 119
Stewart, Rod 196
Stills, Stephen 279
Sting 40
Stockhausen, Karlheinz 45
Strick, Joe 155
'Summertime Blues' 31, 98
'Suspicion' 169
synthesizers 46–9, 97, 124, 162, 212, 218, 249, 254

T
Talmy, Shel 114–5, 157
Tam Lin 83
Tanen, Ned 86
Tattoist International 35–42, 53, 83–6, 156–7
'Tattoo' 25, 187, 230

Tearson, Michael 153–4, 155
That'll Be The Day (movie) 195, 280–1
The Who By Numbers 200
'There's A Fortune In Those Hills' 31
'There's A Heartache Following Me' 179
Thunderclap Newman 37
'Time Is Passing' 63, 78, 79, 110, 120, 121, 129, 137, 150, 179, 289
Tommy 19, 22, 23, 25–37, 40, 42, 43, 49, 52–4, 55, 56, 65, 88, 89, 91–2, 98, 102, 106, 114, 121, 126, 136, 138, 144, 151–2, 161, 166, 187, 188, 193, 196–7, 201, 204, 207–8, 214, 216, 224, 238, 243, 244, 246, 251–2, 258–263, 273–277, 279, 281, 285, 290
Tommy (movie) 28, 34, 82, 83, 95, 155–6, 273, 278, 279, 282
'Too Much Of Anything' 79, 81, 117, 120, 121, 129, 150, 289
Townshend, Pete
  Announces Lifehouse idea 21; and Meher Baba 42–3, 56–7, 169, 171–2, 178, 180; confrontation with Kit Lambert 110; defends 'Won't Get Fooled Again' 145; early 'operas' 23–5; and Eel Pie Hotel commune 73–5; and Lifehouse/Who's Next demos 63–82; explains

Lifehouse 54, 61–3, 67, 69, 70, 73, 88; explains Quadrophenia storyline 216–7; first solo concert 279; and Guitar Farm 37–42, 84–6, 157; and home recording 23, 59, 102; and Hazrat Inayat Khan 43–5, 68, 77; knocked out by Daltrey 250; and Lifehouse (radio play) 287; and Lifehouse (solo live show) 288; and Live At Leeds 28–9; "nervous breakdown" 129; onstage tantrum 256; and the Press 50–2; and Psychoderelict 286; and Quadrophenia demos 201–4; Quadrophenia ideas 167, 185, 187–8, 194, 231; reflects on Quadrophenia 274–7; scraps Lifehouse 128; and synthesizers 45–9, 211; and Tattooist International 35–42, 83, 156; and Tommy 24–6; and Tommy movie 28, 34, 54, 82, 155; and Who Came First 179–82; and Young Vic shows 87, 89, 93–102, 118, 123, 125
Track Records 83, 106, 147, 180
Trackplan 60
Truffaut, François 62
'Two Fills' 229
200 Motels 169
'Two Of Us, The' 54
Two Sides Of The Moon 280

Two's Missing 164, 183

U
Ummagumma 167
'Underture' 35
Universal (film studio) 28, 35, 83–6, 90, 101, 112, 126, 155–6
'Unused Piano: Quadrophenia' 204

V
Vedder, Eddie 286
Velvet Underground, The 102
View From A Backstage Pass 164

W
Wagner, Richard 24, 41, 258
'Walking The Dog' 121
Walsh, Joe 71, 135
Walters, John 235
Warner Brothers (film studio) 54
'Wasp Man' 110, 183
'Water' 30, 32, 53, 80, 121, 122, 129, 150, 249
Waters, Roger 41
'Wayfaring Stranger, The' 70
'We Close Tonight' 229
'We're Moving' 54, 58
West, Leslie 106–7, 109
'When I Was A Boy' 136, 141, 158
Whistle Rymes 177, 196
White City 286
Who Are You 82, 281
'Who Are You' 82, 281, 287
Who Came First 77, 78, 79, 177–83, 242
Who Is Richard Smith? (movie) 37

Who Sell Out, The 24, 102–3, 108, 148, 174, 236, 283
Who Sing My Generation, The 114
Who's Next 19, 22, 36, 47, 49, 63–5, 67–73, 76–7, 79, 91, 103, 105, 108–9, 116–123, 127, 129–139, 143, 147–155, 158–163, 165, 172, 173, 184, 194, 197, 199, 206–7, 211, 246, 249, 251, 258, 267, 277, 289
Wilson, Brian 290
Winwood, Stevie 196
With Love 183
'Wizardry' 229
Wolff, John 'Wiggy' 205
'Won't Get Fooled Again' 20, 36, 46, 50, 72–6, 107, 109, 116, 135–6, 143–7, 153, 159, 160, 248, 250, 254, 257, 264
Woodstock (movie) 34
Wray, Link 110, 183

Y
Yardbirds, The 73
Yaryan, Will 266
'Young Man Blues' 121
Young Vic Theatre 22, 58, 77, 78, 79, 80–81, 87, 89, 93, 94, 96–102, 112, 118–9, 123, 125–6, 134–6, 137, 144, 150, 151, 162, 168
Your Turn In The Barrel (movie) 83

Z
Zappa, Frank 169
'Zoot Suit' 186, 190, 284

Picture credits

Jacket front Chris Morphet/Redferns/Getty; spine Gijsbert Hanekroot/Redferns/Getty; back Ron Howard/ Redferns/Getty; 2–3 Graham Wiltshire/Rex Features; 6–7 Chris Morphet/Redferns/Getty; ARP manual courtesy of Matt Cunitz; 8 Ron Howard/Redferns/Getty; 9 Gijsbert Hanekroot/Redferns/Getty (2); 10 Michael Putland/ Retna; 11 Chris Morphet/Redferns/Getty; Rex Features; 12–13 David Redfern/Redferns/Getty; 14 Marc Sharratt/ Rex Features; Chris Morphet/Redferns/Getty; Ian Dickson/Rex Features; 15 Michael Putland/Retna; 16 Chris Morphet/Redferns/Getty.

About the author

RICHIE UNTERBERGER is the author of numerous rock history books. The first of these, *Unknown Legends Of Rock'n'Roll* (Backbeat 1998), profiles underappreciated cult rock artists of all styles and eras; the next, *Urban Spacemen & Wayfaring Strangers: Overlooked Innovators & Eccentric Visionaries Of '60s Rock* (Backbeat 2000), features in-depth surveys of 20 underrated greats of the era. He's also author of a two-part history of 60s folk-rock, *Turn! Turn! Turn!: The '60s Folk-Rock Revolution* (Backbeat 2002) and *Eight Miles High: Folk-Rock's Flight From Haight-Ashbury To Woodstock* (Backbeat 2003). His Backbeat book *The Unreleased Beatles: Music And Film* won a 2007 Association for Recorded Sound Collections award. He is also the author of *White Light/White Heat: The Velvet Underground Day-By-Day* (Jawbone 2009).

Unterberger is also author of *The Rough Guide To Music USA*, a guidebook to the evolution of regional popular music styles throughout America in the 20th century, and *The Rough Guide To Jimi Hendrix*. He is a frequent contributor to the All Music Guide and *MOJO*, and has written hundreds of liner notes for CD reissues. He lives in San Francisco.

More information about Richie Unterberger, his books, and the music he documents can be found on his Web site at richieunterberger.com. Email can be sent to him at richie@richieunterberger.com.

Acknowledgements

The Who have generated a more devoted fanbase than almost any other band, and this book would not have been nearly as comprehensive without the help of many of their ardent supporters. Especially helpful in tracking down rare material, and providing useful contacts, was Pat Thomas, who has done this on behalf of my books for more than a decade. Richard Morton Jack retrieved countless UK clippings that would have been otherwise unobtainable. Jon Arnold and Tom McQuown helped find numerous rarities vital to my research; Sam Hammond chipped in with a few, as well as supplying vital technical assistance.

Thanks to Phil Sutcliffe for permission to quote from his unpublished interviews with staff at the Young Vic Theatre, and to Redbeard, producer/host of the *In The Studio* radio series (inthestudio.net), which has broadcast specials on several Who albums. Also thanks to Larry Crane, editor of *Tape/Op* magazine, and Matt Cunitz for advice and clarification on technical and production matters related to The Who's recordings.

Thanks also to Brian Cady, Howie Edelson, Sean Egan, Dorothy Moskowitz Falarski, Ken Fallon, Ed Hanel, Doug Hinman, Bruce Kawakami, Alec Lindsell, Gavin Martin, Al Marx, Joe McMichael, Laura Moody, Paul Myers, Chuck Prophet, Kelli Richards, Lynne Sims, Mat Snow, Tony Thompson, Mark Turrell, Michele Whitby, Richard Williams, Todd Wolfe, and Todd Zimmer.

At Jawbone Press/Backbeat Books in London, thanks to Mark Brend, Tony Bacon, and Nigel Osborne for commissioning this book and editorial guidance; Kevin Becketti, Sales and Marketing Manager for Jawbone's US branch, for his advice and support; John Morrish for his meticulous and sympathetic editorial work on the volume; and Jawbone/Backbeat publicist Jon Mills.

The biggest thanks go to the musicians, producers, promoters, filmmakers, journalists, and fans who graciously gave so much of their time to be interviewed about The Who for this book.